INTERPRETING THE WORLD TO CHANGE IT

ESSAYS FOR PRABHAT PATNAIK

INTERPRETING THE WORLD TO CHANGE IT

ESSAYS FOR PRABHAT PATNAIK

Edited by
C.P. CHANDRASEKHAR and JAYATI GHOSH

Tulika Books

Published by
Tulika Books
35 A/1 (ground floor), Shahpur Jat, New Delhi 110 049, India
tulikabooks.wordpress.com

First edition (hardback) 2017

ISBN: 978-93-82381-93-8

Printed at Chaman Offset, Delhi 110 002

Contents

Introduction

Prabhat Patnaik, whose life and work this volume celebrates, is exceptional in many ways. While he is widely recognized as a brilliant economist with mastery over contending theoretical traditions in the subject, he made quite clear his predilection for and commitment to applying, developing and extending the Marxist approach. Known primarily as an economist of the finest calibre, he has also forayed with much effect into a range of allied disciplines in search of an understanding of contemporary reality. He is a much-celebrated teacher and academic whose contributions to scholarly debate have been profound and outstanding – but he also manages to be among the most active of public intellectuals: writing prolifically, travelling and speaking at all manner of venues with unmatched energy and commitment. He stands firm on issues that matter, never hedging or prevaricating; but in personal relations he is unfailingly polite, gracious and generous. His seriousness of purpose is combined with a gentle humanity and appreciation of humour, bringing out the essence of what it means to be truly civilized.

This extraordinary combination of attributes has already left a wide footprint, and a deep and hopefully abiding imprint – not only in terms of his outstanding scholarly publications and impressive body of more approachable writing for the general public, but also in terms of generations of colleagues, students, readers, listeners and others who have been touched and influenced by him in a multitude of ways. A festschrift, therefore, is clearly too small a gesture to recognize his past and ongoing contributions to building India's progressive intellectual tradition. This volume is not intended to be a book that adds to the literature on subjects and topics that he has been interested in. It is an attempt to bring together a group of people who, other than being personally close to him in various ways, have been influenced by Prabhat Patnaik in their own work to different degrees – both through his writings and their direct interaction with his work. Needless to say, the list of those who are close to and have been influenced by him is much longer and would include many multiples of the number of contributors to this volume. Our only claim is that this set is representative of that group.

Given the nature of this group, the choice of the topic they would like to address in their contribution to the volume was left to the authors and their own judgement of an issue worth engaging with, given the objective of the exercise. The extremely diverse topics covered in the contributions point to Patnaik's own wide-ranging interests and never-failing curiosity to seek answers to questions he considers relevant, even in disciplines and domains outside his core concerns.

The volume starts with two pieces of personal appreciation and reminiscence, by Ashok Mitra and Rajendra Prasad. As their evocative pieces show, separating the personal from the intellectual and political in their relationship with such a person is impossible, especially for those with intellectual curiosity and progressive inclination. These pieces set the stage for contributions in a range of areas that have engaged Prabhat Patnaik over the years.

Three of the pieces that follow explore the notions of nation, nationalism and secularism that came out of the freedom struggle. Irfan Habib argues that while India as a country had been envisaged earlier, nationalism and the idea of India as a nation came out of the struggle against British imperialism. At first this affected only the educated middle classes. But the idea began gripping the minds of the poor and downtrodden, the people of India, in the aftermath of the analyses of the early 'economic nationalists' such as Dadabhai Naoroji, Romesh Chunder Dutt, Subramania Iyer and Justice Ranade, who explored how British rule was resulting in extensive impoverishment because of tribute levied on India, and how free trade was causing deindustrialization and unemployment. The truly Indian nation was therefore visualized as a regime that would do away with the causes for this impoverishment and deprivation. Gandhi's great contribution was that along with Nehru and others, he carried this idea to the poor. The two elements that Nehru correctly identified as necessary for delivering on this promise of true freedom were adherence to secularism, defined as the rejection of the relevance of religion to life, and commitment to creating a society and nation that delivered the promises made in the Fundamental Rights Resolution of the Karachi Congress (1931).

Akeel Bilgrami, in his contribution titled 'Is there an *Indian* Secularism?', begins with the argument that secularism as a doctrine was not central to the intellectual positions of Nehru and Gandhi. In fact, it was not present in the Constitution until 1976 and in intellectual discussions in

India until well after Independence, and became the subject of 'obsessive focus' only from the late 1980s. This is surprising, given the importance of the concept in modern Europe, where the need (after the Westphalian peace) was to find an alternative to theology (the divine right of the state as it was personified in the monarch) to legitimize state power. That alternative was found in a concept that fused territorial boundaries with a centralized state, which was supported by the feeling of belonging to a nation generated by positing an '*us*' relative to a '*them*', which was an internal other to be despised and supressed. In early forms of such efforts at legitimizing the state, religion (normally of the majority) was central, leading to civil strife and the mistaken impression that religion was the problem. The idea of secularism in Europe emerged as 'a counter to the process that starts with a nationalism founded on religious majoritarianism'.

Bilgrami's argument is that since India never went through a nation-building strategy of the European kind, 'Indian society for centuries was characterized by a completely *un*selfconscious pluralism'. This explains why secularism was not a concern of Gandhi and Nehru. Indian nationalism really sought to replay 'the genuine and lived pluralism of ordinary Indian social life in the political arena of anti-imperialism'. But the inadequacy of those efforts led to religious acrimonies that precipitated partition and the trauma that surrounded it. This led to the rhetoric of secularism emerging more conspicuously in the public arena. But even then it was largely a commitment to freedom of religion, subject to the realization of fundamental constitutional rights that *mention neither religion nor opposition to religion*. Since the 1980s, however, there is evidence that this notion of secularism is competing for space in India with one that is presented as a corrective to a damaging majoritarian nationalism as emerged in Europe after the seventeenth century. This is because of the rise of majoritarian nationalism (and a minoritarian backlash), which, while having antecedents in the pre- and immediate post-Independence periods, cannot be seen to have causal roots in the tactics and strategies adopted by nationalist leaders like Nehru.

Sitaram Yechury in his piece makes the role of the organic intellectual in the current Indian conjuncture one of defending the 'idea of India' – an idea that allows a diverse and divided people to transcend those differences and establish an inclusive unity. Crucial to that unity is the combination of secularism, democracy and the pursuit of the socio-economic freedom of each citizen. Yechury argues that this idea of India is under challenge, inasmuch as the Rashtriya Swayamsevak Sangh (RSS) and the Bharatiya Janata Party (BJP) are pushing to replace the notion with one that equates Indian nationalism with Hindu nationalism, in a throwback to a Westphalian notion of nationhood centred on a non-inclusive unity against the enemy within. The Left, Yechury emphasizes, was crucial to the forging of the 'idea of India' – with its three pillars of secularism, democracy and socio-economic freedom. This, in his view, makes the role of organic intellectuals of the Left central to defending that idea.

C.P. Chandrasekhar suggests that Indian economic nationalism had features that were distinctive when compared with the strategies adopted by governments in many other newly independent, developing countries of the time. All these countries opted for some version of an import substitution strategy to partially insulate themselves from the debilitating effects of exposure to predatory international capital. This was needed not only to encourage indigenous capital, but also to give governments the space to pursue domestic policies that furthered national interests. However, the 'Nehruvian strategy' was distinctive, inasmuch as it declared its intention to adopt policies that would help to pursue a 'socialistic pattern' within the framework of a mixed economy with substantial private ownership. Commitment to this path was reflected in the Second Five Year Plan based on the Mahalanobis model, which sought to use a range of interventionist measures (varying from licensing and price control to tax and subsidy measures) to ensure that investment allocation would proceed according to an *a priori* plan in keeping with 'socialist' ambitions. However, given the character of the Congress Party that brought together sections with very different interests and ideological inclinations, united by a common desire for Independence from British rule, it was to be expected that Nehru and his government had to accommodate and make compromises with different sections when developing policies. Such compromises meant that the institutional changes needed to grow the home market to support a strategy of this kind were not implemented, ultimately resulting in the failure of that strategy.

Continuing with the focus on imperialism, an abiding concern of Prabhat Patnaik's, Aijaz Ahmad is concerned with tracing the rise of the Far Right since the 1980s in the United States and elsewhere in the world, often within the framework of liberal democracy, which it reduces to democracy of the 1 per cent. In that process, the formal structures of liberal democracy have been retained, but they have been combined with neoliberal economic policies on the one hand, and divisive, extremist ideologies such as xenophobic nationalism, racism or communalism imbued with the rhetoric of 'us' and 'them', on the other. While these are signs of fascism coming to liberal democracies, it does not mean that fascism will come to prevail, because this occurs in a context in which the challenge to capitalism from the working class and socialism is either weak or has collapsed. That allows the Right to achieve its objectives within the liberal democratic framework and using the liberal democratic state apparatus.

For Ahmad, a crucial feature of the period of 'globalization', or the universalization of capitalist production, relates to the extensive freedoms that US imperialism won to pursue its agenda without a challenge from an adversarial state system in the form of the many socialisms that had bloomed in the years since 1917. The process began not in 1991 when the Soviet Union collapsed, but when reforms began in China in the late 1970s. The process blunted the edge of the nationalism of the national bourgeoisie in Asia and Africa, and hugely increased the 'reserve army' of cheap labour available to global capitalism generally, which weakened the working class and its organizations in the core countries. The collapse of the Soviet Union, needless to say, further shrunk the challenge to imperialism, allowing for a transition from a period when coercive force was needed to achieve its ends, even partially and often unsuccessfully, to one in which the institutions of liberal democracy and the façade of 'market fairness' were adequate to the task. The upshot is that even periodic and often intense crises do not challenge the hegemony of US imperialism.

The new institutional architecture that enables this continuing imperialist hegemony is explored by Jayati Ghosh. She argues that the volatility and risks involved in globalized capitalism require new superstructures through which transfers of value from the periphery to the metropolis can be ensured, and investment risks can be moderated and contained. These goals are achieved through multilateral and regional trade and economic partnership agreements, as well as other legal measures that protect the cross-border rights of financial investors. These effectively act as controls on governments so that they are forced to put the interests of large capital over the interests (and human rights) of their own citizens. Capitalism also remains 'dynamic' by creating new forms of economic territory, such as control over knowledge that is designated as 'intellectual property', and the privatization of amenities and basic services, which also require institutional changes.

The ways in which international trading regimes are evolving against interests of developing countries are further considered by Biswajit Dhar. He examines three mega-regional trade and economic partnership agreements that have recently been in the process of negotiation: the Trans-Pacific Partnership Agreement of the US with a number of other countries in Asia and Latin America (which was recently signed); the Trans-Atlantic Trade and Investment Partnership between the US and the European Union; and the Regional Comprehensive Economic Partnership bringing together the Association of South East Asian Nations (ASEAN) countries and their Free Trade Area (FTA) partners. He notes that while the multilateral trading regime embodied in the General Agreement on Tariffs and Trade (GATT) and the World Trade Organization (WTO) had many adverse implications for the developing countries, these new agreements are considerably worse in that they do not even recognize the specific requirements of a development agenda. By their very existence, they will also create a challenge for the multilateral system, and could even force all countries into a template dictated by advanced countries, in a way that is reminiscent of the imposition of trading rules upon colonies by colonizing powers in the nineteenth century.

Prakash Karat's article engages with Patnaik's concern with the constraints being imposed on bourgeois democracy as capitalism develops in societies like India, and the accentuation of this tendency in the neoliberal era. While disagreeing with Patnaik's characterization that there is a 'creeping fascism' developing in India and preferring to describe it as 'creeping authoritarianism', Karat discusses how the axis between neoliberalism and communalism stimulates authoritarianism, and highlights the different forms the tendency has taken. The critical question, therefore, is how to link the struggle for democracy and against authoritarianism with the struggle against neoliberal capitalism.

Teesta Setalvad in her essay sticks to the idea that fascist forces are indeed in power in India today, and raises the question as to where the resistance to this rise of communal and authoritarian politics would come from. The obvious relevance of the question is sharpened by pointing to the transformation of the political landscape in Mumbai and Maharashtra, associated with the rise of the Shiv Sena and the establishment of a Sena–RSS–BJP alliance. Setalvad argues that it was the failure to sustain a progressive working class movement that allowed for the political take-over by a corporate–politician–criminal nexus, which found its base in the same depoliticized working class. The implications this has for the task of politically engaging and retrieving support for democracy from the now more fragmented working class are analysed as an important, even if partial, answer to the question on the potential sources of resistance.

Zoya Hasan examines the implications of a watershed moment – the 2014 general elections – which, she argues, have the potential to lead to a fundamental change in the trajectory of Indian democracy. The greater strength of the conservative and religious politics of the BJP and its allied movements in the Sangh Parivar have implications that go well beyond their control of state power, because they are increasingly able to generate and strengthen a new public discourse of Hindu nationalism, which can even reshape the contours of secularism and democracy as they have evolved in the decades since Independence. The idea of the nation based on civic rather than ethnic/religious identity is under threat. Hasan notes that the 'secular constitutional dispensation has been under immense pressure from various quarters' even before the BJP rose to national power, because of 'the ambivalence and contradictions in secular political practice', including of the Congress Party. However, with the Modi government, the very meaning of democracy has shifted from a consensual and accommodative to a majoritarian one.

The rise of revanchist politics has as its counterpart the erosion of the movement to instil a scientific temper that began with independence. Amiya Bagchi's article explores the nature of the scientific temper, starting with an example which establishes that it is not formal education but 'intense curiosity and a determination to test your beginning hypothesis against the cold steel of facts' that matters. But the nature of the scientific pursuit is influenced by capitalism, inasmuch as the incentive for research can be either a desire to make money by finding new products or processes, or the pursuit of new knowledge for its own sake. If the former becomes the primary motive, as it has with the advent of neoliberalism, the diffusion of a scientific temper is likely to suffer badly. Matters only get worse if corporate capital begins to influence the direction of research, as has happened in the pharmaceutical industry, for example, or if the state chooses to misuse science, as happens in times of war.

The resulting challenge to scientific reasoning is visible in the social sciences in a convoluted way: specializations were created by converting idiographic disciplines into monothetic ones, leading to a kind of scientism. But, Bagchi argues, the cure for these and other tendencies is not less science, as argued by the postmodernists, but more of a science rooted in facts of nature, of lived human lives.

The paper by Jha *et al.* on 'Capitalism and 'Labour Reserves' focuses on the understanding deriving from Marx that such reserves or the 'relative surplus population' are a permanent feature that is intrinsic to the spontaneous evolution of capitalism. It argues that there is a difference in the manner in which these reserves were generated in the original capitalist industrializers (of which many turned into imperialist masters), which constitute the metropolitan countries of today, and are being generated in the underdeveloped countries of the periphery. One consequence this has is that the process of accumulation, and the prospects thereof in the peripheral countries, cannot ensure even that degree of absorption of this surplus that was possible in the core countries. In the event, the relative surplus population in the peripheral countries disproportionately suffers the worst nature and conditions of work in the hierarchy of workers within labour reserves, based on Marx's categories of the 'floating', 'latent' and 'stagnant' among them.

The thorny questions of how to develop a revolutionary aesthetic, and of the relations between artists/intellectuals and a revolutionary party, are taken up by Anil Bhatti. He uses the playful metaphor developed in a novel by Peter Weiss, of a particular street in Zurich, the Spiegelgasse or Mirror Street, that in the spring of 1916 was home to Lenin and Krupskaya in a rented flat at one end, and the Café Voltaire that was the meeting place of the Dadaists, the revolutionary group of artists and poets at the other end. The two did not meet, but if they had, the street would really have 'accommodated the whole revolution'. Bhatti points out that 'the complementarity of the two revolutionary intensities lay in their shared neighbourhood. But neither recognized the other yet. The two lines remained rigidly separate, offering the possibility of an asymptotic convergence only in an infinitely remote dimension.' So the street becomes the symbol of a utopian order that does not have the separation of politics and art.

Bhatti brings the discussion to the Indian context by examining the praxis of the group Sahmat, a broad front of artists and intellectuals, which is also based on the combination of aesthetic and political resistance, of 'singing in and of the dark times', that is now evident across the world and particularly in India. He argues that 'Sahmat constitutes not a mechanical but a dialectical continuity of the freedom struggle. And this is based on its 'aesthetics of resistance'. Central to this aesthetics must be the recognition and celebration of plurality: of polycentric and pluricultural, but shared histories.

Finally, Mihir Bhattacharya contrasts the 'public sphere' of knowledge and understanding that is created and evolved through formal institutions including the media, and the 'common world' or universe of voices that has been and remains an inherent part of human existence. The latter – essentially 'talk' in all its forms – constitutes 'an immense world of utterance that cannot be officially controlled'. He describes such acts of oral transmission as the collective work of creativity that is carried on in a matter-of-fact way among ordinary labouring people, which is not confined to folk tales, but spreads across religious and political ideas and much else. This is also true of intellectual creativity within the Left, for example, in India – there are many types of intellectual and cultural activity of people in different walks of life across the country that contribute to it in different ways. The significance of the performing arts, as exemplified by the Indian People's Theatre Association (IPTA) during the struggle for independence, is a case in point. Bhattacharya also takes on the complex issues of the relationship of artists and intellectuals to power, especially when that power emanates from those who profess to change the world in a manner that they are in sympathy with.

These essays touch on only some of the many themes that Prabhat Patnaik has explored in his profound and multifaceted work. But they continue conversations that the authors – and many others – have had with him over the years, and we hope that readers of this book will gain at least some of the intellectual pleasure and excitement that such conversations have evoked in us.

New Delhi
January 2017

C.P. CHANDRASEKHAR AND JAYATI GHOSH

On Prabhat Patnaik

Ashok Mitra

A physical wreck, as I approach the nineties, the thought that overwhelms me concerns the worthlessness of the life I have lived. Suddenly, a cheer lights up the mind. I have actually been the luckiest among the luckiest: Prabhat Patnaik has been, and continues to be, my dearest brother, political comrade and teacher.

He has been teaching me all the while. The collapse of the Soviet Union and the enigma of seeming ideological indifference of a China likely soon to emerge as the world's leading power under the stewardship of an ever-vigilant communist party have little relevance; Prabhat has taught me the rigorous precision of the Marxian prognosis concerning capitalist growth and its inevitable withering away. The obsession of capitalists to maximize profit-making will ensure the steady decline of the rate of profits until it reaches zero, and this would happen irrespective of the scale and state of mobilization of the organized working class. Prabhat also convinced me of the non-contradiction between the tenets of the Marxist testament and Mao's independent formulation in regard to the strategy of rural mobilization of the deprived, exploited peasantry. This in fact can be beautifully integrated with the grand Marxian formulation of social dynamics: the lucidity with which Prabhat, one evening, explained the relationship between the thoughts of Marx and Mao enthralled me. Predictions emerging from analytical premises can well end up in failure or disappoint for a number of reasons; the failure of a particular experiment cannot, and must not, be attributed to flaws or shortcomings in Marx's magnificent dynamics.

It is in this context that another arena of Prabhat's mind-boggling intellectual universe is revealed. He is not prepared to waver an inch from his conviction that Marx is the torchbearer of the classical political economy, the goal of which was spelt out by Adam Smith and elaborated by Ricardo, who actually held a grim, pessimistic view of the future of capitalism. At the same time Prabhat continues to be the most liberal amongst liberals and is open-minded enough to acknowledge the discovery of wisdom in supposedly alien territory. On completion of his academic stint at Oxford, Prabhat moved to Cambridge with a teaching assignment. It was still the era of Keynes, whose thoughts and ideas reigned supreme. Prabhat was impressed enough but not overwhelmed; the firm base of his Marxist ideology could help him to appreciate that Keynesianism was capitalism's last-ditch battle – the public domain cannot be brushed aside in any scheme to save the existing order from the morass into which it was already falling or is about to fall. Keynes, the Bloomsbury sophisticate, was derisive about 'the vile way of writing' of Marxists. Nonetheless, the concept of two 'departments' when characterizing the productive process, he obliquely admitted, had originated with the Marxists. Michal Kalecki would later be more explicit and identify with much greater clarity the significance of the Marxian mode of analysis. In any event, it was Marx who perceived ahead of any others the phenomenon of chronic crisis arising from the lack of 'effective' or 'effectual' demand afflicting the capitalist system, which would turn out to be its nemesis. Class interests of the set Keynes belonged to demanded that capitalism must be saved even as the world economic slump set in, in the early 1930s. Keynes had no hesitation in stealing ideas from the camp of the 'class enemies': the state must step in, indulge in budgetary deficits and float public works to rescue the established order. Perhaps the pervasive influence of Keynesian thought in Cambridge was partly responsible, Prabhat was for a long while almost obsessed with finding traces of other Marxist influences on Keynes's thoughts; Prabhat's concern with what he calls 'the value of money' appears to be a by-product of such endeavours.

I would however still maintain that all this is merely *divertissement* for Prabhat. He has not for one moment forgotten the central fact that economics is political economy and its *quasitum* is, and remains, determining the distribution of the national dividend among the classes constituting society; you may call it by whatever other fancy name, but economics continues to be distilled politics. Ever since the publication of his seminal paper in the *Economic Journal* on an issue concerning the roots of retarded growth, Prabhat has had no other abiding goal in his academic existence.

A considerable number of famous savants, who have contributed in major ways towards the extension and deepening of the mysteries of the universe, or the process and problems of societal behaviour in the spheres of arts, science and technology, are brilliant in the repose of their study or workroom or laboratory, but are pitiably poor communicators. They fumble all the while with words, are unsure of the drawing or mathematics they love scribbled on the blackboard, and are not infrequently on the verge of breakdown while trying to put across ideas they have themselves originated to the eagerly waiting audience. Prabhat is quite the contrary. Every lecture he delivers – whether before a young crop of graduates or undergraduates, or to his academic colleagues at home or overseas, or to a crowd of innocent underprivileged peasantry or members of the working class, all cruel victims of neo-liberal economic tyranny – is sculpted poetry. His talks clarify your understanding even as you keep wondering over his uncanny ability to adjust the process of connecting to the level appropriate to the seekers of knowledge or assurance.

This is where Prabhat stands far apart from the tribe to which he is by convention attributed to belong. With his magnetic attraction as an outstanding teacher, his personal charm and his organizational acumen, he has proved to be a great academic builder; the Centre for Economic Studies and Planning at the Jawaharlal Nehru University in Delhi is now one of the most prestigious sanctuaries where scholars assemble from all over the world. Quite apart from that, though, the Centre is actually a pivotal arena for social activism. The faculty members not only teach and research, they are in the forefront in organizing and leading movements to protest against any instance of inequity, whether within the precincts of the campus or in this conflict-ridden country of ours or the big, wide world. Prabhat is their helmsman, firm but pleasant, hard in bargaining but invariably soft-spoken and polite. I can take a wager that while he has many ideological adversaries, there is hardly anybody who will consider him to be an enemy.

That provides the clue to what Prabhat considers to be his major obligation to the nation and humanity at large. This is much more than the fact that as a front-rank economist his latest creative work immediately becomes the cynosure of excited discussion in countries across the five continents. To Prabhat, much more relevant is his identity as a political activist. He is proud of being a card-carrying member of the country's leading Left formation. All his 'reserve time' is dedicated to the cause of his party, which involves constant writing, in the simplest possible lingo, in party periodicals; constant travelling across the country over the weekends, and sometimes in the course of working days as well, meeting, advising and talking to teachers, students, men and women thrown out of employment, flocks of famished landless farm workers, often a hostile crowd of disbelievers. Prabhat is available to each of them, patiently listening, taking notes, providing courage and assurance, sometimes playing a key role in resolving issues – then rushing back to New Delhi on schedule for classroom assignments or research guidance. This duality is his true identity, making him a 'compleat man': at least so is his credo and belief. Who will dare to debate the issue with him? His sovereignty is his prerogative, and society, even as it is today, has to grant him that.

Finally, though, a confession on my part. I have wasted a few hundred words or so about Prabhat Patnaik, but have kept from referring to what has made him what he is. Put aside all his other traits and attributes, he is a wonderful human being, extraordinarily kind to others, extraordinarily concerned with the problems of others, full of concern for others, loyal to his friends as far as loyalty could stretch, yet squeezing the time to fulfil the domestic obligations that are complex and many. When you meet Prabhat Patnaik, you of course meet a towering economist, but at the same time you have the privilege of meeting someone whose selflessness and determination to do good and instinctive urge to put at the very top of priorities service to others, particularly to the downtrodden, are qualities that are to be found only rarely, if at all, in others.

Allow me to present here a daring afterthought. Prabhat has become what he is, I am convinced, because he had the strange and almost unique opportunity to be reared in his early childhood in a Communist Party commune. Both his parents were dedicated communists who were closely associated with the beginnings of the party in Orissa. In those embryonic days, being a member of the Communist Party was akin to being the embodiment of honesty, integrity, consideration for others, and the deepest attachment to the credo that the sole mission in life is to give and never to ask for anything in return for oneself. Brought up in this milieu, Prabhat knows how to serve the cause of others, never for a moment taking into account the complications that could involve awkward difficulties faced at the personal level.

I am approaching the end of an insignificant life. I am happy and proud, though, that I had the privilege of knowing, loving and learning from Prabhat Patnaik.

Prabhat Patnaik

Friend, Comrade, Marxist Intellectual

Rajendra Prasad

I think I first heard of Prabhat Patnaik in the early 1970s, though in effect I met him and Utsa Patnaik when they joined the Jawaharlal Nehru University (JNU) as members of the faculty of the Centre for Economic Studies and Planning (CESP) in 1973. M.J.K. Thavaraj was on the visiting faculty of the CESP and I met Prabhat in his room. Those were heady days for student politics in JNU. After the first Delhi unit of the Students' Federation of India (SFI) was set up in Delhi University in 1970, the organization emerged in JNU and soon acquired a hegemonic position in the student politics of JNU. The JNU Students' Union (JNUSU) proposed an admission policy that would give weightage to social and economic backwardness alongside reservation for the Scheduled Castes and Scheduled Tribes. Students were to be a part of the admission procedure. A section of the faculty was opposed to such a course of action and the JNUSU had to *gherao* the Vice-Chancellor as well as some faculty members to get this policy implemented. The *gherao* was withdrawn after the intervention of another section of the faculty. The Left teachers acted as a block in a JNU Teachers' Association (JNUTA) meeting, where around thirty-two teachers, a minority, backed the Students' Union. G.P. Deshpande, Anil Bhatti and Imrana Qadeer, along with Prabhat Patnaik and Utsa Patnaik, played a big role in that general body meeting of the JNUTA in support of the demands of the JNUSU.

The first half of the 1970s was a turbulent period: internationally, the protest against the US war in Vietnam was at its peak; within India, semi-fascist terror was being unleashed in West Bengal and a large section of youth was being attracted to ultra-left politics. During those years, Prabhat Patnaik and Utsa Patnaik were steadfast in remaining ideologically with the organized Left. That was also the time when Utsa Patnaik initiated a major debate on the mode of production in Indian agriculture in the pages of *Social Scientist*, which then spilt over to the *Economic and Political Weekly*.

The defeat of US imperialism in Vietnam was a great morale-boosting victory for communists, pacifists and democratic people the world over. In India, the movement initiated by Jayaprakash Narayan had spread to various parts of the country. Railway unions had given a call for, and successfully conducted, an all-India strike – and soon thereafter, the Emergency was imposed by Indira Gandhi, curtailing civil liberties and putting thousands of political opponents in jail. The Communist Party of India (Marxist) (CPI[M]), though not completely underground, was functioning with caution. Prabhat and Utsa remained actively engaged with the party. Utsa wrote a note on P. Sundarayya's survey of agriculture in the villages of Andhra. Comrade Sundarayya, despite being underground, came to discuss Utsa's note, bringing with him a handwritten rejoinder. That period in the history of the CPI(M) is memorable for the kind of attention the party leadership paid to inputs from intellectuals.

After the lifting of the Emergency, the CPI(M)'s centre moved from Calcutta to Delhi, at No. 4, Ashoka Road. The publication of the party organ, *People's Democracy* (*PD*), started from Delhi in May 1977 with Comrade Ramdas as in-charge, and I joined him. Soon Prabhat Patnaik started writing a weekly column titled 'Economic Notes' for *PD*; the first of these appeared in December 1977. Prabhat has continuously written these 'Economic Notes' for *PD*, first under the pseudonym Kartik Rai and later in his own name, for more than half his life – with only a brief break when he was in the US on a teaching stint. He has written on a great variety of political and social subjects, from day-to-day policy decisions to theoretical issues. Although Prabhat writes in very simple language, always explaining his argument logically and with illustrations, a party leader once complained to me that his writing is not accessible to all comrades. When I reported this to Comrade B.T. Ranadive, BTR, he laughed and said that we do not write for the last man on the street. In the early days, Prabhat would not deliver his weekly notes at the *PD* office; he would bring them to our Gitanjali Enclave residence every week, week after week: 1600–1700 closely written words on one side of a single blue notebook page from his office. How I wish had kept those for their archival value!

Another noteworthy event that occurred in the late 1970s was the seminar on 'Marxism and Aesthetics' held at Kasauli in October 1979, in which Prabhat and Utsa, along with around twenty other participants from all over India, took part. The participants included P. Govinda Pillai, Chandralekha, Sadanand Menon, Saeed Mirza, Malini Bhattacharya, Mihir Bhattacharya, Romi Khosla, Kalpana Sahni, Anil Bhatti, G.P. Deshpande, and, of course, Vivan Sundaram and Geeta Kapur who were also the hosts at Ivy Lodge in Kasauli. Papers presented at the seminar were published in the December 1979–January 1980 issue of *Social Scientist*, which was guest-edited by G.P. Deshpande.

In the late 1970s, *Social Scientist*, being published from Trivandrum, ran into problems; the editorial responsibility was shifted to Delhi and Prabhat Patnaik became the editor of the journal. The editorial office moved to Delhi in 1981 and was set up at Kitty Menon's residence at Vithalbhai Patel House on Rafi Marg. (Kitty Menon had played an important role in educating several generations of CPI[M] members in Marxist theory and in building the teachers' movement in Delhi University, particularly among women teachers. After retirement she joined the editorial staff of *PD*.) Prabhat has been editing *Social Scientist* for the last thirty-five years. His interest, reach and contribution have made it the only significant Left journal that has had a continuous run over all these years. Prabhat has also played a prominent role in organizing *Social Scientist* seminars, the proceedings of which have been published in special issues of the journal.

The late 1970s and early 1980s were a time that saw a significant trend of moving away from Marxism among Left and radical circles, both internationally and nationally. *Social Scientist* made an effort to underline the abiding relevance of Marxism and its imaginative application. In October 1981, the journal organized a seminar on 'Lenin and Imperialism' in Delhi. Comrades E.M.S. Namboodiripad and BTR were among those who participated in the seminar, at which sixteen presentations were made by scholars from different disciplines. The seminar was an effort to understand and apply Lenin's theory to contemporary times. In October 1983, a Marx centenary seminar titled 'Marxism and the Analysis of Indian Society' was organized in Delhi, in which twenty-six presentations were made applying Marx's method to understand contemporary Indian reality.

Through these efforts, a conscious attempt was made to innovatively apply Marxist–Leninist theories to the contemporary conjuncture. Comrade BTR, while presenting his views on 'Dictatorship of the Proletariat', discussed the nature of the proletarian state and the dictatorship of the proletariat with reference to the role of the Communist Party, and made the following very incisive points. First, he noted the neglect of the relationship between individual members of the liberated class and the dictatorship of the class as a whole. Second, he referred to the incorrect understanding of the difference between the dictatorship of the working class and the dictatorship of the party. He maintained that 'it was necessary to have, firstly, total guarantees against violation of individual liberties; and secondly, the Party had to devote greater attention to safeguard its own purity'. In the context of the ongoing crisis in the communist parties of the socialist countries, Comrade BTR concluded that it was necessary to have built-in constitutional guarantees to safeguard the individual, and 'the Party has to tell the people that they had not only a right but a duty to criticize the Party and help it to correct its mistakes'.

In a lengthy critique of Carrillo's *Eurocommunism and the State* (1978) in the pages of *Social Scientist*, BTR had pointed to the kind of mistakes committed by the party in socialist societies:

> Resolutions on research on science, on literary criticism, on acceptance or rejection of literary or artistic tendencies of the current period were passed and Party members were asked to conform to them. Based on an immature and wrong understanding of the problems, these decisions led to bureaucratic interference in the development of knowledge, besides ending in unfair, persecutive treatment of those who pointed out their erroneous content. All this shows that the Party has to be extremely cautious before it decides to intervene in such issues by giving a concrete line for immediate guidance. (Ranadive 1978: 14)

Prabhat, as was to be expected, engaged keenly in these discussions. In the period after the collapse of the Soviet Union he emphasized the far-reaching implications of converting the dictatorship of the proletariat into a dictatorship of the party, as had happened in that country:

> . . . the collapse of the Soviet Union underscores the fact that the state of one-party dictatorship, no matter how successful it may appear to be in the immediate defence of socialism against imperialism, ultimately capitulates before *it because it depoliticizes the proletariat and eventually the party itself*. A state where the people (i.e. the proletariat and its allies) wield political power, a state that is not detached from them, not standing above them while speaking in their name, but one that actually sustains their political praxis, is essential for the success of the struggle against imperialism. Second, even as socialism brings into being such a state, its subsequent evolution must be in the direction not of depoliticization of the people but of their enhanced politicization, which alone can prevent the 'substitution' for the people of 'closed' coteries and 'hardened' interest groups, and which alone can be the route towards the 'withering away' of the state. Third, while the process of the 'withering away' of the state may be a protracted one, its centrality to the socialist project must never be underplayed, for then the essentially self-emancipatory nature of this project also gets obscured. (Patnaik 2011: 24)

On 27–29 January 1986, a seminar was organized in Delhi on the

'Indian National Movement': its political, social and ideological dimensions. Both E.M.S. Namboodiripad and B.T. Ranadive participated in the seminar. Prabhat noted, editorially commenting on BTR's presentation (in the issue of *Social Scientist* that carried the papers presented at the seminar):

> The crucial question, as emphasized in the paper by B.T. Ranadive, relates to the role of the agrarian revolution. The National Liberation Struggle can lead on to a struggle for socialism via the agrarian revolution. Working class hegemony over the National Liberation Struggle serves precisely to link this struggle with the agrarian revolution. Bourgeois hegemony over the National Liberation Struggle, by contrast, delinks this struggle from the agrarian revolution. In the process, however, it does not even carry through the democratic revolution to its completion; the result, as in free India, is a superimposition of capitalist development upon pre-capitalist structures, which not only arrests the vigour of capitalist development, but greatly enhances the burden upon the people and preserves the soil upon which casteist, communalist and localist ideologies thrive. Indeed, in the context of capitalist development of this kind, which brings in its train the familiar quota of aggrandisement, impoverishment, frustrations and disappointments, there is a danger of these ideological perceptions which are disruptive of the unity of the working people getting strengthened over time, as has happened in our country. (Patnaik 1986: 2)

And on EMS's paper he wrote:

> The politics of compromise and bargaining with the British, which the bourgeois leadership of the National Movement adopted as a necessary counterpart to its efforts to keep a tight leash upon mass struggles, lest they develop into a torrent leading to an agrarian revolution, had a tragic consequence according to E.M.S. Namboodiripad, namely the partition of the country. Gandhi alone of the entire leadership saw in partition the tragedy of the freedom that had been won. The very incompleteness of the democratic revolution, however, imposes, according to the author, a certain continuity, though in changed circumstances, on the task of the Left. The Left cannot just forget about the completion of the democratic revolution now that the country is free of foreign rule; on the contrary, it has to struggle now, as it sought to struggle earlier, for completing the basic tasks of the democratic revolution, at the centre of which is the agrarian question. (Ibid.: 1)

Prabhat very rightly sees the national movement as a process or 'long revolution', underlying which is 'a remarkable revolution in thought that has rejected the inegalitarianism of tradition and the irrationalism of inherited orthodoxy' (Patnaik 2001: 7).

He draws a far-reaching conclusion for the struggle today: 'the anti-imperialist struggle is not just a struggle over economic policy, crucial through that is, but encompasses the struggle against communalism and indeed the struggle for the democratization of our society and polity' (Patnaik 1998: 10).

There were several other seminars that explored Marxist perspectives on different issues and areas, in organizing which Prabhat played an important role. Among them was the *Social Scientist* seminar organized in 1987 on 'Four Decades of Economic Development', to critically assess different aspects of the path of development pursued in India since independence from a Marxist perspective. In 2007 (22–24 February), *Social Scientist* in association with the Safdar Hashmi Memorial Trust (Sahmat) organized a seminar, 'India Independent: Economics, Politics, Culture', to discuss the developments of sixty years since independence. Prakash Karat and Sitaram Yechury of the CPI(M) participated in this seminar. In 2010 (6–8 December), a symposium was organized (in association with Sahmat and *Communalism Combat*) to critically examine the Ayodhya verdict of the Lucknow Bench of Allahabad High Court. A symposium on 'Marxism Today' was held on 12 August 2011 to mark the eightieth birthday of Professor Irfan Habib. All these seminars and symposia, in which a large number of historians, economists, social scientists, cultural and political activists participated, underlined the abiding relevance of a Marxist analysis.

On 1 January 1989, while returning from the CPI(M)'s Party Congress in Trivandrum, we learnt of the fatal attack on Safdar Hashmi, Marxist intellectual and theatre activist, in Sahibabad near Delhi. The spontaneous protest that followed led to the formation of Sahmat, which has ever since provided a platform for the defence of secular cultural traditions and freedom of expression. From its very inception Prabhat has been extremely active in Sahmat – writing statements, giving lectures and participating in public actions. Based on this involvement, he has theorized the relationship between the party and sympathetic Left intellectuals in an incisive article, 'An Experiment with Political Theory', in the book titled *The SAHMAT Collective: Art and Activism in India since 1989*. Discussing the Sahmat–party dialectics, Prabhat wrote:

> SAHMAT demonstrates a degree of innovativeness all around, the scope for which was created in the post-Soviet world when all the rigidities stemming from earlier certainties of the Communist position

> disappeared; but the fact that this scope was realized is significant and testifies to the robust nature of the Indian Left. (Patnaik 2013)

Prabhat has worked shoulder to shoulder with Sahmat in combating communalism. Theorizing the issue of communalization of education, society and polity, he characterized it as 'nothing less than an assault on reason':

> What we are concerned about is not ideological differences in the sets of beliefs we hold, where each person holds beliefs in a necessarily provisional manner at every moment and is constantly testing these beliefs through the use of reason applied to experience. Such differences permit rational discourse; our concern precisely is that an ideology is being promoted that denies rational discourse. (Patnaik 2001: 5)

He underlined the importance of rational discourse as a necessary condition for the people's march towards freedom. He concluded:

> But while the propagation of the communal outlook is the concentrated expression of the assault on rational discourse, it does not constitute the entirety of this assault. Or, looking at it differently, in terms of the real counterpart of these ideas, the attack on the secular foundations of the State is not merely a phenomenon in itself, but it is an integral part of the social counter-revolution. . . . Combating communalism, preserving the secular foundations of the State, are urgent tasks that have to be undertaken not merely in the interests of the minorities; they are not even tasks whose urgency arises merely because one cannot be free as long as someone else is oppressed; their urgency lies in the fact that communalism is integral to counter-revolution. (Ibid.)

When, in June 1989, incidents at the Tiananmen Square in Beijing disturbed communists all over the world, India was no exception. The CPI(M) was in full support of the stand of the Chinese Communist Party, which had characterized the protests as counter-revolutionary. Prabhat along with other intellectuals signed a statement in support of the students' protests. As was to be expected, a number of CPI(M) members approached the party leadership complaining against Prabhat. Typically, the leadership sent a note to Prabhat. Meanwhile rumours were afloat that Prabhat was going to be replaced as editor of *Social Scientist*. Comrade BTR, however, scotched all such rumours by calling Prabhat and giving him a benign reprimand.

These have not been easy times for the communist movement internationally and Marxist philosophy has faced some of its biggest challenges in this period. The coupling of political power (with or without state power) with the development and elaboration of Marxist philosophy is wrought with great perils. To start with, the political leadership becomes the theoretical leadership as well by virtue of its control over the power apparatus. Secondly, no contestation of ideas is allowed since even theoretical and scientific differences of opinion are treated as subversive and quelled with force. And finally, the party leadership prescribes a position in all areas. That raises questions such as whether in a shared ideological framework two members having differing opinions about, let us say, Premchand as a writer, can exist in the same party; or whether the debate with Lysenko over genetics can be allowed to play itself out without invoking authority.

On these issues, Prabhat takes forward BTR's idea and asserts:

> The stifling of praxis in any form – through a ban on political activity, through a one-party state, through the imposition of a theoretical closure in the name of science – is the source of conflict between the individual and the collective, the hardening of the interests of some members of the collective which become differentiated from those of the collective itself. (Patnaik 2011: 39)

And, he concludes: 'the Party [as a sub-set] itself must not have any interest other than those of the collective' (ibid.).

Of significance here is the question as to how Marxism relates to ideas/knowledge developed in the non-Marxist realm? In the post-revolutionary Soviet Union a tendency grew which was suspicious of all ideas and knowledge that did not emerge from within. In this context, the British Marxist Maurice Cornforth, discussing the role of ideas/knowledge generated outside the Marxist framework and Communist Party organization, observed:

> But there is no irrevocable law of political intellectual activity which concentrates all the political cadres and intellectual forces of the worldwide movement for emancipation into a disciplined collective within the one party of the working class. And as for the communist parties, their capacities to develop revolutionary theory are stultified if they insulate their intellectual life by barriers impermeable to ideas from outside. (Cornforth 1980)

Prabhat Patnaik, in the face of a theoretical crisis, has made a robust and eloquent case for Marxism 'continuously reconstructing itself'. He derives three propositions from Lenin's use of Keynes' ideas in *Imperialism the Highest Stage of Capitalism*:

> First, important elements of 'truth' may be found in the writings of 'philistines' and 'petty bourgeois pacifists' who have nothing to do with Marxism. Second, Marxists can fruitfully use these elements in their theoretical constructions to develop their own theory. Third, for doing so, Marxism has to be 'open-ended' in a dual sense: of being open to new ideas, even those propagated by 'Philistines' and liberal pacifists', and of appropriating them for use in its own fashion. (Patnaik 2008: 20–21)

Further, lack of serious theoretical engagement with the realm of ideas, often camouflaged by debunking all ideas other than those in the classic Marxist 'texts' as bourgeois or counter-revolutionary, produces not only stagnation in the name of 'purity', but also a subterranean hegemonization by the very bourgeois ideas so debunked.

Prabhat Patnaik elaborates this argument as follows:

> Marxist theory is an open system that is continuously reconstructing itself anew by engaging with the world of ideas in general and appropriating, and hence also going beyond, what is scientific in any tradition, no matter what the attitude of that tradition to Marxism. Marxist theory, on this view, while building on certain basic tenets of Marx, also goes beyond Marx and explores the 'continent' that he opened up. (Patnaik 2008: 32)

Prabhat Patnaik's life has been an exploration of that 'continent'. His formidable academic scholarship (on which I am not competent to comment), his popularity as a teacher and his effectiveness as a public intellectual do not cast a shadow on his relationship with his fellow-comrades. On the other hand, his passionate conviction that the tyranny of capitalism can only be overcome by transcending the system is infectious.

References

Cornforth, Maurice (1980), *Communism and Philosophy: Contemporary Dogmas and Revisions of Marxism*, London: Lawrence and Wishart.

Patnaik, P. (1986), 'Editorial', *Social Scientist*, Vol. 14, Nos 8–9.

Patnaik, P. (1998), 'Indian People in the Struggle for Freedom', in *Indian People in the Struggle for Freedom: Five Essays*, New Delhi: Sahmat.

Patnaik, P. (2001), 'Against Communalization of Education', in *Against Communalization of Education: Essays, Press Commentary, Reportage*, New Delhi: Sahmat.

Patnaik, P. (2008), 'The Terrain of Marxist Theory', *Social Scientist*, Vol. 36, No. 11, November–December.

Patnaik, P. (2011), *Re-Envisioning Socialism*, New Delhi: Tulika Books.

Patnaik, P. (2013), 'An Experiment with Political Theory', in Jessica Moss and Ram Rahman, eds, *The Sahmat Collective: Art and Activism in India since 1989*, Chicago: Smart Museum of Art, University of Chicago.

Ranadive, B.T. (1978), 'Carrillo's "Eurocommunism and the State"', *Social Scientist*, Vol. 7, No. 3, October.

Jawaharlal Nehru and the National Movement

Irfan Habib

I should like to begin by making the assertion that the Indian National Movement is the greatest creation so far of the Indian people. This assertion may be debated, but that the Indian National Movement is a unique phenomenon in our history can hardly be questioned. These days, it is true, it is becoming part of post-modernist fashion to belittle it and run down the concept of 'nation'. The Cambridge school tells us that in India, family and caste have been the basic units to be considered, all other things being illusory. To this premise for India, support has come from Benedict Anderson who, in his *Imagined Communities* (1983), argued that the nation was just an illusion created by print media. And Perry Anderson, his elder brother, in his recent tract, *The Indian Ideology* (2012), which in a review I suggested should have been rather titled 'Indian Illusion', says that the Indian National Movement was not necessary at all, since the Government of India Act of 1935 and Japanese military successes in 1941–42 were sufficient in themselves to make India free. Our own 'Subaltern' colleagues, ever since Ranajit Guha's essay of 1982 (in *Subaltern Studies I)*, have been bestowing scorn on the role of the 'nationalist elites'. It is therefore important, first, to see what the National Movement was about, and then, to understand why Jawaharlal Nehru's intervention and leadership were so crucially important for its further development. What the Cambridge School and the Andersons forget is that one of the major factors behind the creation of nations all over the world has been the phenomenon of colonial and imperialist exploitation. India was long regarded as a country, but whether it was a nation before the nineteenth century may well be doubted. As Ram Mohan Roy noted in 1828, Indians were still not patriotic, their basic affiliations being to their castes. It was opposition and resistance to British rule, on the one hand, and modern education and social reform, on the other, that laid the seeds of allegiance to India as a nation. But it created this sentiment first only in a small part of the population, the educated middle classes. The groundwork for the concept of a nation that embraced all the poor and the downtrodden of India was, as Pandit Jawaharlal Nehru himself realized and indeed celebrated in his *Autobiography* (1936), carried out by the early 'economic nationalists', such as Dadabhai Naoroji, 'the grand old man of Indian nationalism', Romesh Chunder Dutt, Subramania lyer, and Justice Ranade. They explored in ways that the Indian poor could never have done for themselves, how Britain was creating extensive impoverishment by levying tribute on India, and how free trade was causing deindustrialization and unemployment. Whatever the 'Subaltern' historians may say, these discoveries could not have come out of 'subaltern' efforts. By 1905, as Professor Bipan Chandra in his seminal work, *The Rise and Growth of Economic Nationalism in India* (1966), points out, the picture of England's exploitation of India in the writings of these Moderates was complete in practically every respect. Here one might mention that if you take Sivasubramaniam's 'National Income of India' statistics, the major statistical effort in the field so far, then the per capita income of India between 1900 and 1947 rose only by 0.2 per cent or less per annum, a minuscule amount. Between 1946–47 and 1990–91, under free India, the growth was not very spectacular, yet it was sensational compared to what happened under British rule in its last forty-seven years. It now amounted to 1.1 per cent, over five times the per capita growth attained during the British Raj under unbridled conditions of free trade, which now all the good newspapers in India and Lord Meghnad Desai want us to go over to as fully as possible.

What happened in the next stage of our National Movement, a stage arriving after 1905, i.e. particularly after the partition of Bengal and notably after the arrival of Mahatma Gandhi in 1915 (he had left South Africa for England in 1914), was that the nationalists' message increasingly got across to the Indian poor, one of the channels through which it got across being Gandhi and his followers. In *Hind Swaraj* in 1909, Gandhi argued that religion has nothing to do with a nation and that in India, therefore, people of all religions should live in amity. He also reproduced the narrative that the economic nationalists had drawn of British exploitation of India, offering a fairly accurate summary of it.

The second thing that Gandhi initiated, for which his experience of South Africa counted so much, was to link the National Movement to the agitations for the rectification of precise grievances of the poor: not mere pamphlets, or mere articles in journals and books, but actual agitation. To that extent, the Champaran Satyagraha of 1917, and the Ahmedabad textile workers' strike and the Kheda Satyagraha of Gujarat peasants, both in 1918, were outstanding events. What followed these agitations was the spread of the National Movement across the country, notably through the April satyagraha against the Rowlatt Acts, 1919, and then the Khilafat and Non-Cooperation Movements of 1920–22. These were unprecedented in the number from among the masses brought into the movement.

Here, however, a point of crisis was reached whose nature must be understood. Gandhiji had indeed brought about a revolution: there is an Urdu verse which, I am afraid, I am often prone to quote: Akbar Allahabadi's couplet of 1921 runs, '*Buddhu miyan bhi hazrat e Gandhi ke saath hain, ek musht e khaak hain magar aandhi ke saath hain*' ('Mr Ordinary Man, who has now joined the great Mr Gandhi, may himself be just a fistful of dust, but is now part of a storm'). But if the lowly and the poor had joined the movement to give it such force, what future did it lay in store for them? If we now turn to *Hind Swaraj* (Gandhi 1909), we see a problem there. Gandhi was against British rule. He knew how India was being exploited by the English. He had derived it all from Dadabhai Naoroji and Romesh Dutt and Gokhale. But when he came to the solution, he had little to offer – not even social reform. No denunciation of the caste system or a declaration of women's rights is to be found in *Hind Swaraj*, and the solution of all problems seems to be just a minimal state, and self-help and moral appeal.

Indians were thus to overthrow British rule in order, after their liberation, to live in honest poverty. Gandhi suggested that there was a model for the future state in the way the rajas and badshahs had ruled with the advice of pundits and maulvis. To many of us this would look like an awful idea, but he thought as late as 1909 that this was an ideal that India should look forward to. In other words, Gandhiji was all the time appealing to people for self-correction. His appeal to the landlords was for them to be good custodians of their tenants, establishing schools and hospitals for their peasants. Similarly, capitalists were to be good custodians of their workers. The state was apparently to have nothing to do with the economy, perhaps beyond maintaining a minimum state of law and order. Could such a prospect make an appeal to the masses? Gandhiji had moved the middle classes like never before on the Rowlatt Acts; he had moved a larger mass on the issue of the Khilafat and Punjab wrongs. Yet all this time one sees hesitation in Gandhiji in even demanding independence. In practice he could be very much of a constitutionalist, like the Moderates. In December 1919, even at the Congress session at Amritsar, he was counselling that Indians should work the 1919 reforms without any carping criticism. In these moderate visions there was hardly any substantive ideal set for the poor.

The sudden withdrawal of the Khilafat Movement in early 1922 brought to a critical point the situation created by the lack of an adequate political programme. At least C.R. Das said that he wanted an Indian state working for the welfare of 'the 98 per cent'. But Gandhi did not want a state to liberate the poor, for he wanted, in effect, only a minimal state. And so, in the cloud of the controversy over individual non-cooperation *versus* limited cooperation conducted between the Swarajists and Gandhians, the question as to what kind of future Indians should aspire to escaped attention. Gandhi's own Constructive Programme was all about voluntary effort to educate and uplift the poor, which simply set the state on one side. The second difficulty with Gandhiji was what Nehru called his 'metaphysics', his lack of rational approach, his declarations being in the nature of arbitrary diktat rather than the results of reasoned arguments. Throughout *Hind Swaraj* there is no celebration of reason and rationalism; there is only celebration of faith and austerity ('perfect chastity').

It is possible that here was the reason why Jawaharlal Nehru underwent, at this point, that mental crisis of which his major biographer, Sarvepalli Gopal, speaks – although Gopal does not relate this to the issues I have raised and locates its source in Jawaharlal's personal relations with Motilal Nehru, the Swarajist leader and his own father, on the one hand, and Gandhiji, on the other. On the issue of individual non-cooperation after 1922, Jawaharlal Nehru supported Gandhiji against his own father, which naturally caused a rift in a hitherto close relationship. Obviously, there is some substance in Gopal's conjectures. But behind this individual problem was surely the larger question of the shape of India's future, which greatly troubled Nehru – something one can perhaps see only now by way of hindsight. And so greatly troubled was he in the mind that in 1926 he went to Europe. That visit, as Gopal recognizes, brought about a total change in his outlook. He came into association with people resisting colonialism throughout the world, the Brussels Congress against Imperialism (1927) being particularly important. He went to Soviet Russia and had his first brief glimpse of Socialism, which made a great impression on him because he could see there in practice 'the Soviet and collectivist ideas' of which previously he had only read. In both his *Glimpses of World History* (1934) and *Autobiography*, Nehru makes statements praising Lenin along with Gandhi as the greatest leaders of the poor of his time.

After he came back there began to be felt a sudden shift in the National Movement, not at all realized perhaps by Nehru himself. Everyone thought that the Madras Congress Resolution for total independence in 1928 was an aberration. But did it get passed simply at Nehru's and Subhas Bose's insistence? There was a more profound factor at work: the general sense of dissatisfaction at the seeming drift in the National

Movement owing to the lack of radicalism in Congress demands. There was undoubted anxiety that the Congress should say something that would make an appeal to the mass of the population, especially to the youth, and surely here Nehru's greatest contributions came. He wrote, as we all know, two major works in the period of Civil Disobedience and its aftermath. Civil Disobedience lasted from early 1930 to 1931 in the first phase, and Jawaharlal was put in prison twice. During his imprisonment he wrote *Glimpses of World History,* comprising letters written to his daughter, Indira Gandhi, which was published in 1934. Then he wrote his *Autobiography*, again while in prison in the second phase of Civil Disobedience, and this was published two years later (1936). In both these works Nehru makes certain points which are extremely important and which demarcate his ideas from Mahatma Gandhi's positions very strikingly.

The first is his celebration of reason. In *Glimpses of World History* what is remarkable is that although religions are described, they occupy a secondary place. Nehru was not prepared to accept at that time that religion contributed anything positive to humanity, sufficiently at least to counterbalance its hostility to reason. Incidentally, another colleague of his of whom one would not think that he would have asked such an embarrassing question, Abul Kalam Azad, had indeed asked it in print some time before 1909: Nehru's major complaint against religion was that it not only deadens the intellect, it makes the human being servile to the illusion of an afterlife. In both of his works he proclaimed his indifference to Hinduism and Hindu practices, and also to the concept of God.

In *Glimpses of World History* he picked a very important statement of the Jesuit fathers about Akbar. The statement was, '*Thus we see in this prince Akbar the common fault of an atheist who refuses to make reason subservient to faith.*' Now Nehru not only picked this quotation out of several Jesuit statements about Akbar in order to commend him, but also added that 'if this is the definition of an atheist, the more we have of them, the better'. One can wonder at the curious shift in the feelings of our people. When in the 1930s Jawaharlal said all this, they yet gave him all their affection and idolized him. What has changed in these two or three generations that the contrary seems to be the case today?

Surely, in such an outspoken proclamation in support of pure reason, Nehru was in total conflict with Gandhiji whom nevertheless he regarded with genuine affection. In his *Autobiography* he spoke of Gandhiji's dangerous addiction to metaphysics and his arbitrary declarations of policies that contradicted agreed decisions, thereby causing much confusion in the movement. He described Gandhiji's immediate followers as people who had been reduced to 'mental pulp' through blindly agreeing to whatever Gandhiji said. That brings me to another wonderful fact, viz., that Nehru should publicly say all this and Gandhi should still declare him to be his heir. One sometimes feels that these two persons were out of this world at the time.

We now return to the answers to national questions that Jawaharlal Nehru did so much to provide in the late 1920s and 30s. If India was to attain independence, what kind of state should it have? Nehru now openly espoused socialism as an objective to strive for. He was, I think, in communist terminology, still somewhat a 'sectarian' when he declared that the communists were wrong in thinking that the National Movement could be converted into a proletarian and pro-peasant movement, since by the very fact of its being 'national', it was bourgeois. The very idea of nation, he said, is bourgeois, a statement that even Stalin in his well-known tract on the 'National Question' did not make, calling it essentially a 'peasant question'. This was not necessarily itself a correct judgment, but it was still a better judgement perhaps than Nehru's dismissive description of the concept of nation and the conclusion he drew from it: since the Congress was a national organization, by its own name, it could not but be a bourgeois party. It must, however, be remembered that the possibility that the Congress could be a multi-class organization had not yet developed even within the communist movement. It was largely left to the Dutt–Bradley thesis of 1936 to conceive of the Congress (even then mostly implicitly) in that light. Nehru in fact said in his *Autobiography* that on many matters what the communists had said had proved correct. This did not mean, however, that he agreed with them on other matters. The main issue was that the Congress should present, even if in a 'bourgeois frame', a picture of what India would be when it became independent. This, to Nehru, was a picture that would be totally different from what Gandhiji had presented in *Hind Swaraj*. Even if Socialism could not be on the nationalist agenda, it was clear to Nehru that people would look forward to an independent India only if they were promised a strong, democratic state committed to obtaining for them certain political and economic rights, with equality, general welfare and industrial development as the main objectives.

In 1945 Gandhiji wrote to Nehru, 'I still stand by the system of government envisaged in Hind Swaraj, the village of my dreams is still in my mind.' Nehru in his reply expressed his astonishment that Gandhiji should think of a state in India in such a way and still believe in what he had said almost thirty-six years earlier in *Hind Swaraj*. Gandhiji, in fact, was soon to encourage Mashruwala to write against food rationing and promoted this article in *Harijan* just because he hated state intervention in these matters. And yet the fact is that the National Movement largely espoused not the glorification of the past in *Hind Swaraj* but Nehru's vision of the future in his *Autobiography*.

Unfortunately, because of Nehru's innate modesty, he did not underline the significance of the Fundamental Rights Resolution of the Karachi Congress (1931), drafted by him. He wrote that what this resolution promised could be provided by any capitalist state. But till then no capitalist state had in practice followed such a programme. This resolution, approved after the discontinuance of the Civil Disobedience Movement in 1931 as modified and in fact strengthened by the All India Congress Committee in August 1931, lays down many fundamental things about the future of free India, including the secular state, about which I shall have soon something to say. It for the first time proclaimed the equality of men and women, which Gandhiji had not even recognized in *Hind Swaraj*. Later on, indeed, he did so, and then he could say, women are superior to men!

It is here necessary to remind ourselves of what the Karachi Resolution promised: no disability would attach to any citizen by reason of his or her religion, caste, creed or sex in regard to public employment, office of power or honour, and in the exercise of any trade or calling. There would then be secured a number of rights to workers, with special protection extended to women. There was partial acknowledgement of the principle of 'land to the tiller' which Gandhiji had until then opposed (and was to oppose even later): 'The system of land tenure and revenue and rent shall be reformed and an equitable adjustment made of the burden on agricultural land immediately giving relief to the smaller peasantry by substantial reduction of agricultural rent and revenue now paid by them.'

Then comes clause 15: 'the state shall own or control key industries and services, mineral resources, railways, waterways, shipping and other means of public transport'. Surely this was not in conformity with Gandhiji's vision of a factory-less rural regime. According to the Karachi Resolution, the state would provide for military training of citizens, though such care for military skill again went against Gandhiji's philosophy. This is a picture that Nehru's draft presented to the Indian people. While accepting the resolution, Gandhiji too realized, I think, in his heart of hearts, that the *Hind Swaraj*-type vision could make no comparable appeal to India's peasants and labouring poor. Indeed Gandhiji, as was surprisingly his wont, not only agreed to move the resolution, but also added one particular paragraph to strengthen it: the words 'Relief of agricultural indebtedness and control of usury, direct and indirect' were his contribution.

The Karachi Resolution was to be made the basis of the election manifesto of the Congress in 1937 and the party had astonishing success at the polls. It was again made the basis of the election manifesto for the 1946 elections.

Wedded as Nehru was to the supremacy of reason, the concept of an unalloyed secularism naturally followed. His ideas about secularism derived from the worldwide view of secularism and not the view of it that India's Supreme Court has now adopted. The worldwide view of secularism is that the state's actions must be based on the concept of human welfare or happiness in this world. Anything done merely because that would bring reward to the doer in afterlife is anathema to secularism. In fact Holyoake, who first used the term secularism in 1851, was looking for a definition of a philosophy of morality in which any desire for afterlife, or just fulfilling a duty set by religion for its own sake, would not count. It is no business of the state to ensure that Muslims should pray five times a day although they might believe that it may lead them to heaven. Or that Hindus should perform pilgrimages for a better status in afterlife – that too should be no business of a secular state.

This was Nehru's own position throughout. He is perhaps one of the few Indian leaders who consistently used the word 'secular' in the 1930s and 1940s. Incidentally, the word 'secular' for the nature of the Indian state did not appear in the original Constitution at all; it was added as late as 1976 through an amendment to the Preamble. The ground has been infinitely muddied by the dictum of that knight-philosopher of ours, Sir Sarvepalli Radhakrishnan. In his book *Recovery of Faith* (1955), he says that when India is said to be a secular state (not France or USA, but India), it does not mean that we reject 'the reality of an unseen spirit'. (If the spirit is unseen, how do you know it is real?) Or that we reject 'the relevance of religion to life', an assertion that is totally against the philosophy of secularism as held by Holyoake, the creator of the term 'secularism'.

'We hold that not one religion should be given preferential status', concludes Sir Sarvepalli. And on the basis of this kind of dicta, a bench of the Supreme Court went further and made a statement of absolute fantasy: that the great values in this world have come from 'sants and saints', implying that it is they who gave us democracy, equality of women and men, and, why not then, socialist values. This is an absurdity, but this is how the law of the land is interpreted today. Where the Constitution specifically prohibits 'religious instruction', the Supreme Court has admitted it in the garb of 'Instruction in religion'. This amounts to a total negation of Nehru's legacy.

Now clearly, it was Nehru's rigorous secular position and not the position of others who believed in a kind of religiously tolerant state that strengthened the National Movement, and gave it an argument against the

Muslim League and other communal parties. Nehru, in fact, perceptively argued in his *Autobiography* that whereas Muslim separatism can be identified as such because Muslims are in a minority, Hindu communalism could masquerade as Indian nationalism. Indeed, it only 'masqueraded': the Hindu Mahasabha or Rashtriya Swayamsevak Sangh (RSS) has no record of any agitation against British rule.

Here, if I am not seen to be too irrelevant, I shall bring to your notice a joke from Pakistan. An article appeared in *Dawn*, which was republished in the *Journal of Pakistani Historical Society*, to the effect that there is a psychological problem in Pakistan, created by the fact that its whole 'national' movement was not directed against the ruling power but against fellow-subjects. There was no quarrel with the British who governed the areas that form Pakistan; the only quarrel was with Hindus. The same applies to the RSS and the Hindu Mahasabha; they had no quarrel with the British, they had only a quarrel with their Muslim fellow-subjects. So, before we laugh at the joke in Pakistan, we should give a thought to the fact that we have just elected a government whose entire nationalist credentials consist only of hostility to fellow-citizens.

Coming back to the importance of secularism, it has been a very great misfortune that the case of secularism could not be put openly and clearly to oppose the idea of a partition of the country. Part of the reason lay in the Quit India Movement, whereafter for three years, all Congress publications were closed and its workers put in jail, thereby giving the Muslim League and the Hindu Mahasabha propaganda an open field.

This brings me to the 1940s, and here I am afraid I must take issue with some of the things Pandit Nehru did in that period. When World War II broke out in 1939 between two sets of colonial or aspiring colonial powers, the Congress took the position that the Nazis were the worse side and they should therefore be opposed, but an agitation against the British government was still sanctioned. The agitation took the form of individual satyagraha so that the government might not be embarrassed. When in 1941 the pendulum had swung in favour of the fascist powers and Germany attacked the Soviet Union, and early in 1942 a very powerful Japanese offensive in Southeast Asia resulted in the occupation of Burma, Gandhiji's position changed. For a man of moral authority this was an astonishing change. He believed, as Pandit Nehru himself recognized and as Sarvepalli Gopal considers to be the case in his biography of Nehru, that Russia and China would be defeated. He did not apparently pay much attention to the German defeat before Moscow, in the winter of 1941, for indeed it seemed in late summer of 1942 that the Germans were again advancing and were about to cross the Volga near Stalingrad. Similarly, he thought, and he wrote in fact, that Japan had no hostile intentions against India. How did he know? It is clear that Gandhiji believed that this was the time to agitate when the Allies were in a weak position, for then the British could be made to yield what they had not yielded through the Cripps Mission. And therefore Gandhiji began, even before anything was decided by the Congress, to develop a movement towards civil disobedience. Nehru wrote in his *Discovery of India* (1946) of the continuous increase in popular excitement upon Gandhiji's statements, made in the course of 1942, warning of an agitation.

Here, for what it is worth, is a small incident I witnessed in 1942. After his rejection of the Cripps Mission, Pandit Jawharlal Nehru began touring, as was his wont. He was a man of action and he did not tour only for elections. He came to Aligarh. Characteristically, his hosts forgot to give him lunch – or what they gave him, he didn't like. He got annoyed and told the volunteers he knew Professor Habib (my father), and asked them to take him to our house. And so around 3.30 pm, when my elder brother and I were playing in the garden, we found Nehru arriving by tonga, getting down, breaking into the house, practically shouting 'Habib, Habib, get me an omelette!' As we hid behind the door and he consumed the omelette, my father told him, 'Panditji, why did you reject the Cripps proposals? We would have had at least hopes of becoming a dominion.' Nehru, looking scornfully at my father, said, 'Habib, you are just a professor. Within five years this country will be free.' And indeed it took five and a half years. This perhaps tells us something of the indomitable optimism of the man. I don't know whether he did in fact want to reject the Cripps proposals, but he certainly was publicly very loyal to that decision.

But was he loyal to his views subsequently? How could anyone agitate for the immediate expulsion of the British government at such a critical point in World War II, a move that could only benefit the Axis powers? And not only that, but adopting a stance that ran down the entire world outside India. Nehru gave pride of place in his *Discovery of India* to a quotation from Gandhiji's statements of 8 August 1942: 'We must look at the world in the face with calm and clear eyes though the eyes of the world are bloodshot today.' What was this world? Russians and Chinese defending their homeland, or Nazis and Japanese generals strutting over subject-countries? The people of the world had done us no harm, so why should we confront the world struggling for freedom? And why should Jawaharlal Nehru have quoted this statement when he himself, in his *Discovery of India*, went on to concede that nationalism had triumphed over internationalism in the Quit India Resolution of August 1942? Indeed, why then did he support that resolution, as also did Abul Kalam Azad?

It was perhaps because if they did not do so, they would be condemned as people who were not brave enough to face British rule – but was this enough of a reason? It may not still be popular to say so, but surely, not only was it an opportunistic step, but it was also an ideologically very wrong step. And one of the results was that the British were given a good reason to suppress the Congress and ban its activities. The Congress was wiped out in many Muslim localities, since all its own official papers or publications were banned, its offices closed, its ordinary workers put in prison, and there was no confrontation offered to Muslim League propaganda.

This brings me to the apologia that is provided in *The Discovery of India* for Pandit Jawaharlal Nehru's own position. One has to agree with Nehru's principal biographer, Professor S. Gopal, that *Discovery of India* is inferior in quality to his two earlier books. But more than the fall in quality, it is some of the statements he made in it that take one by surprise. He spoke of pride in '*the past achievements of our race*'. Race? Are we Nazis? Nehru had said earlier that nation is a bourgeois idea; now even race is sanctioned. So India comes into focus – let other countries suffer, India is to be our sole concern. History too, in *The Discovery of India*, despite its numerous insights, is very dangerously tilted. Sir Sarvepalli Radhakrishnan, after obtaining knighthood from the British government, the most obviously foreign of 'foreign' rulers, could still tell us that Indian philosophical thought languished because we passed under the rule of foreign rulers ranging from Greeks, Shakas and Kushanas to Muslims. On Radhakrishnan's word, Nehru accepted the 'great fall' for a fact. He only caviled at the cause, saying in effect: yes, we were great thinkers in the past but then lost that wisdom, as if he had never heard of Sankaracharya in the ninth century or Abul Fazl in the sixteenth. Nehru held that the fictitious fall came not because of foreign rulers, but that foreign rule came because of that fall, which itself had come because we became imitative and so lost our creativity. If we look at history, however, a country which does not imitate never creates. Europe progressed, as Nehru in his *Glimpses of World History* had himself pointed out, because it imitated Chinese inventions and built on Arab science.

Discovery plays up Indian nationalism in an irrational manner. I would still say that there are great merits in the book, and those merits of course must be recognized. There is a very good treatment of Muslim political movements. There is an honest treatment even of the events that led to the Quit India Movement. Nevertheless, we now hear Nehru saying, 'Religions have helped greatly in the development of humanity.' The ideas of *Autobiography* are surely forgotten when even religion is thus exalted. So should we think that if Nehru did much to resolve the ideological crisis of nationalism in the late 1920s and early 1930s, he himself became a victim of Gandhiji's irrationalism in the 1940s – and that *The Discovery of India* is an attempt to justify, at least partly, this partial surrender? I will end, however, with a final tribute.

In 1947 both Gandhiji and Nehru were united in one matter as never before. Both wanted that communal slaughter should stop; both wanted that even if the partition came, Muslims should continue to live in India, and Hindus and Sikhs in Pakistan. They both felt that their primary duty in this regard lay in India. Frankly, very few top leaders of the Congress felt the same. That could be seen in the Meerut session of the All India Congress Committee where Patel made his speech calling for sword to be met with sword. When Gandhiji, soon to be martyred, went on his fast on 13 January 1948, that was the testing hour. What he was demanding was that refugees in Delhi should desist from occupying Muslims' houses. They had been thrown out of their own houses in west Punjab, their kin had been massacred there, and now that they found refuge here, were they to vacate the houses they had occupied and let in the Muslim owners? The second demand was that India should pay Rs 55 crore to Pakistan as it had pledged, for the Pakistan government was unable, by this violation of India's pledge, to pay salaries to its own public servants.

On the first day of the hunger strike, stones were thrown at Gandhiji and the slogan 'Gandhi Murdabad!' resounded in Delhi's lanes and by-lanes. Yet on the 15th of January Nehru faced and addressed a crowd of 10,000 in front of the Red Fort, asking people to achieve fulfilment of the demands set by Gandhiji. On the 17th a rally of over 1,00,000 marched through Delhi – comprising tongawallas, sweepers, refugees and Gandhi-capped peasants – acclaiming Gandhi and denouncing the rioters. Gandhiji only ended his fast when Muslims began to return to their houses and Government of India agreed to pay the pledged amount to Pakistan. Violence practically stopped in both India and Pakistan. Whenever one disagrees with Nehru or with Gandhiji, one has to do it with the greatest respect and ask the question: could anyone else have done what both of them did in January 1948? Surely, by standing up against a seemingly overwhelming flood, these two men saved for ever the honour and dignity of India.

This is the text of a lecture delivered at the 125th Birth Anniversary celebration of Jawaharlal Nehru, organized by Sahmat, at India International Centre, New Delhi, on 22 November 2014.

Is There an *Indian* Secularism?

Akeel Bilgrami

1

Societies and polities, for all their material underpinnings, are understood, described and navigated by concepts. Concepts are expressed in words. And words are supposed to have definitions. But words which do have definitions in any strict sense tend to express only trivial concepts. As Socrates said at the end of his life, the only concept he had succeeded in *defining* in all those menacing, browbeating conversations he had had with other Athenian citizens, was the one expressed by the Greek word for what, in English, we call 'mud' (which, in case it is of interest, he defined as the mixture of soil and water). Beyond that, he said, he had not succeeded in defining anything. This was not just a flamboyant form of modesty on his part. I reckon what he really meant was that concepts have a history; and when the concepts in question are *non*-trivial, that history is fraught with conflicting claimants with diverse interests and diverse inferential links to other concepts, which themselves turn on a differential field of beliefs and doctrines. So, just to take a relatively simple example, the Greek term 'demokratiya' is related to our concept of democracy via differential relations of inference to the notion of citizenship, because that notion in turn is determined by whether or not slaves exist in the society and whether or not women are considered to be citizens. The term 'secularism' is no exception to this sort of messy conceptual genealogy that frustrates the task of defining it. Our own intense, recent discussions of secularism in India are very much a product of the history of internal developments within the long and fantastically creative period of the freedom movement, and since the history of that movement was itself braided with the history of the colonial masters from whom freedom was being sought, the conceptual history of 'secularism' derives in part from British history and more generally from the history of the rise of nations in the European continent.

I will return to some of those details in a moment, but I state all this at the outset by way of saying that we cannot just stipulate that the term 'secularism' means this or that thing. We must expend a lot of effort to show that any such stipulation is *not arbitrary*. And to do that, we have to follow the demands both of theoretical analysis as well as history and conceptual history, which may require a delicate form of balance and adjudication since these may pull in different directions. It would be to make oneself arcane to produce a philosophical analysis that departed radically from the conceptual history of the term. Thus, philosophy must keep faith with history and philology if its deliverances are to be non-arbitrary. And this is not just an academic exercise but a way of understanding our past as well as our political future.

It is a commonplace of our understanding of the Indian modern that Jawaharlal Nehru was its chief architect, if not also its builder and mason. To underline this commonplace, Nehru is often contrasted by many of his admirers as well as his detractors to stand in contrast with Gandhi, who is said to have aspired to hold Indian modernity in abeyance. It is undoubtedly true that some of the constantly cited rhetoric in some of their writing lends itself to this contrast. But in this essay I want to assemble some equally familiar points from other parts of their writing and thought, and from a sober understanding of the period in which they lived and struggled together and about which they wrote, which suggest that the contrast – *when it comes to the subject of secularism*[1] – is both limited and misleading, and that it focuses on the more marginal rather than the fundamental issues they confronted. Indeed I want to argue, from these points that I will assemble, not only that there is far greater affinity in their thought and the ideals that motivated their actions than these stark contrasts propose, but moreover that secularism as a doctrine, if it is properly understood in its non-arbitrary and historically situated terms, was not a very central ideal for either of them in the period in which they lived and worked together – *not even for Nehru*. And once this argument is in place, it may become easier to understand the significance of their appeal to secularism on the occasions when it did sometimes surface in their thought and writing from the late 1930s onwards, and how that relates to the fierce focus on secularism in our own more recent times.

Let me begin with a salient fact which, though much observed, has not been sufficiently explained by the voluminous writing on the concept of secularism in India. It ought to be made much more of an explanandum than it has, since it is a fact crying out for an explanation: the fact that the term 'secularism', for all the close scrutiny of it in the last thirty years or so, is a very late comer in the official rhetoric of the Indian polity and Constitution. As is well known, the Constitution itself did not introduce the word till 1976, when it was first mentioned in the 42nd Amendment,

Article 25 (2) (b). And formal occurrences apart, it was not even much present in intellectual discussions until some years *after* Indian independence. Why should this be so, and why should it have then burst on to centre-stage and remained there with almost obsessive focus since the late 1980s?

Before these questions can be addressed, we need to give a conceptual genealogy of secularism – a genealogy with which any effort to define or characterize it must accord. It is an utterly familiar point that secularism had its roots in European history of the modern period. (The idea that one sometimes hears, that secularism may be found in various parts of the world in much earlier times, such as during Asoka's reign or in medieval Andalusia or Mughal India, conflates various distinct ideals under the term 'secularism' for reasons that are theoretically very badly motivated. Not all good things are the same good thing. And though there may be rhetorical and strategic reasons to make these unconvincing equations, they bring no conceptual illumination.) Much of the debate in our time in India has been over three positions regarding this originary source of the concept in the modern west, with some saying that India must, in order to emerge as a modern nation, follow the west in its secularism; others rejecting this response as slavish mimicry; and yet others taking the view that secularism is certainly highly relevant for India but it means something entirely different in the Indian context, in particular that secularism in the Indian context is the idea of a state's *neutrality between religions*.[2] This disputation is confusing and could do with some sorting out, and I have some hope that such analysis as I shall try to provide by the end of this essay will cause some at least of this tide of confusing controversy to subside.

To get some clarity on the issue, we must at the outset make an elementary distinction between secularism and secularization. Secularization, a topic first fully explored by Max Weber, unlike secularism, is not a doctrine so much as a name for a process of transformation in society. It has been described in the sociological and historical literature by two quite different rhetorics: the death of God, and the quite different rhetoric of the decline of magic and ritual, thus addressing religion as both belief and cultural practice. Loss of belief in God or in the myths of creation, on the one hand, and the decrease in church-going or habits of pious dress and dietary restrictions, on the other, were two distinct symptoms of the process of secularization in the European modern, speaking respectively to secularization of religious doctrine and practice.

The concept of secularism, by contrast, is concerned less with general historical processes of social and cultural transformation, and is more concerned instead with describing specific institutions and laws that form a polity, i.e. a polity that seeks to shield the formulation and functioning of its laws and institutions from the control and direct[3] influence of religious practices and belief. This distinctness of secularization from secularism has its proof, first of all, in the obvious fact that someone can be deeply religious in both belief and practice (thus not secularized), but be deeply committed to secularism (that is, to a secular polity);[4] and second, in the equally ubiquitous fact that the same place can be secularist in this sense and yet not much secularized, such as, for instance, the United States (especially in its heartland), or it may be highly secularized and yet not secularist (as for instance in a city like Tel Aviv). Western Europe and Australia and China are perhaps the regions of the world where there is most coincidence of both secularization and secularism, while Saudi Arabia and the city of Jerusalem are examples of places where there is least presence of either.

It is of course often possible to try and undermine this distinction by dragging cultural matters, say, for instance, habits of dress, into the realm of policy and polity. Thus, France erected some of its cultural prejudices about the *hijab* into the political realm by actually passing policies and laws about dress in public places. But I will assume, for the sake of simplicity, that for the most part we can maintain a relatively lucid distinction in the study of religion between its significance, on the one hand, for cultural matters such as, say, those of dress or diet, and, on the other, for political matters such as, say, free speech or gender justice. As with all distinctions, one can strain to dissolve this one too, but there is conceptual clarity and illumination to be gained in insisting on it, while noticing and allowing that in many specific contexts (such as Kemalist Turkey and the case of France just cited) it can get muddied.

This essay's interest is entirely focused on secularism and not on secularization.[5] Indeed, I think a great deal of the contrast that has been drawn between Gandhi and Nehru on this terrain has run together the more obvious contrast in their thinking about the issues of secularization with the much less obviously contrastable attitudes they had towards the concept of secularism.

The emergence of secularism as an ideal and doctrine owes to the political fall-out of a certain trajectory in the justification of state power in Europe, from within which the ideal then emerged. The seventeenth century in Europe brought remarkable changes in outlook owing, among other things, to the links that grew between new ideas and emerging worldly forces. With the rise of the new sciences and their increasing elevation to centrality in European culture, starting with England and then moving all across Europe, older forms of justification of state power that focused on the divine right of the state as it was personified in its monarch came to be seen as unsustainable. At the very same time, a new form of entity was emerging after the Westphalian peace. Both these developments converged to produce a radically new political outlook. State power now came to seek its legitimacy in a quite different and far more mundane source, no longer in theology but, for want of a better word, in political *psychology*. It must be made to rest on a *feeling*, a feeling present in the people over whom it exercised power. The feeling that they were to cultivate was not to be directly a feeling for the state itself. Rather, it was to be toward the new form of entity that was spawned by the Westphalian peace, the nation. This entity was of course partly defined in terms of territorial boundaries. But that did not by any means suffice to characterize it. The characterization was not complete until it was fused with a new form of increasingly centralized state, which integrated the more scattered locations of power of a previous time. Thus it was that the nation and the state were existentially fused in their status, undecouplable from each other, an inseparability identified by a hyphen. And so, a feeling among the populace for the first half of the hyphenated conjunction (nation) bestowed upon its second half (the state) a new form of legitimacy for the exercise of its power. Later, this kind of feeling came to be called 'nationalism', and the justification it provided for state power was both fundamental and peculiar to the European modern until it began to spread via colonial conquest to other lands.

However, what is more immediately relevant to understanding Nehru and Gandhi is to look closer at the strategy by which this political psychology, this feeling for the nation and thereby legitimacy for the state, was generated all over Europe. It was done by a method which had its apotheosis in Germany in the thirties and forties of the last century, though its work was done well before that. It was the method of generating a feeling for the nation as *ours* by finding an external enemy within the territory and describing it as '*them*', the outsider within, to be despised and suppressed as 'the Other'. Of course, by the time it came to that hideous culmination in Germany, religion played little, if any, role in the ideology by which the strategy was wielded. Race loomed far larger in the rhetoric. But in earlier exercises of such nation-building and state-legitimating exercises in Europe, religion was often a central factor. When numerical and statistical forms of discourse came to be applied to the study of society and governance, notions of majority and minority were constructed and this method would come to be described as majoritarianism. Often religious majoritarianism would generate a religious minoritarian backlash; and the violence of civil strife that this, in turn, generated made it seem as if religious majoritarian nationalism was not the fundamental source of the problem any more even if it was where the fault-line started, but it was religion itself that contaminated the polity – and until it was steered to sites distant from the orbit of the state, in places of personal life and civil society, the strife could not be quelled. *And so it was that the doctrine of secularism emerged as a large and corrective measure, essentially, as this narrative shows, to be a counter to a process that starts with a nationalism founded on religious majoritarianism.*

If we now turn our gaze to India in the long period of historical developments by which Nehru came to a position of leadership in Indian politics during the freedom struggle, we find that this concept of secularism constructed and intended to counter the effects of such a form of damage was never really a concept that Nehru made central. In this he was quite at one with Gandhi. The reason for this is perfectly obvious, and it partly explains why there is no seriously extensive and detailed talk of secularism till after independence was achieved. To put it explicitly, since India never did go through that form of nation-building strategy, there was nothing in India's traditions that created the kind of political and social damage that fell out of the European form of nationalism that I have just expounded. In short, what secularism was there to correct did not have, for either Nehru or Gandhi, any very audible echo in the socio-political life of India in the first place. There was nothing to be corrected. As Nehru frequently says in *The Discovery of India*, Indian society for centuries was characterized by a completely *un*selfconscious pluralism; this was one of the things he most admired about India's past (Nehru 2004). And so, my elementary argument is that it is not surprising that it never seemed imperative to him that India needed a *selfconscious* adoption of secularism, a doctrine very deliberately constructed to address the loss of pluralism through forms of majoritarian religious domination and defensive minoritarian reactiveness to it. That work of Nehru's, just like a range of writings by Gandhi from *Hind Swaraj* (2009) onwards, for all their many differences of attitude towards religion and science and superstition and so on (all matters that I have said are relevant to secularization but not secularism), constantly applauded India's lived pluralist traditions, their common cultures developed out of a diverse people's mutual influence upon each other, their shared sites of worship, and all the other familiar elements of a civilization that came later to be captured in such tired phrases and clichés as 'composite culture', 'unity in diversity', and so on.

Now, of course, it is very widely recorded that Nehru expressed grief and dismay at the political conflicts between Muslims and Hindus as they developed from the mid-1920s (and I will say more about that by the end of this essay), and no doubt from even earlier due to the communal divisions that the colonial masters are often said to have manipulatively constructed to pursue their own interests of 'rule'. However, it is also very clear from his writing that he did not wish to think of these as so entrenched that they were *defining* of Indian society. In fact he repeatedly denied that they were so, and described them as *anomalous* recent developments that would be undermined by a loftier politics that drew on the more long-standing pluralism. To sum up, then, Indian society for him (and, for that matter, even more explicitly for Gandhi) was not defined either by the sort of problem that secularism was designed to repair or by the specifically European nationalism which created that problem. And so, secularism did not have a centrality in his thinking despite all the rhetoric against superstition and in favour of the scientific method and a rational temper, clichés of their own kind even for those who subscribe to them but irrelevant, as I insist, to the question of secularism, even if relevant to secularization.

What this, then, allows one to propose is: Nehru in the first three or four decades of his political thought and activism was constructing a political philosophy that had no centrally articulated place for the ideal of secularism, for the reasons I have just given, but which, tapping what he took to be the unselfconsciously *pluralist* traditions of India's social past and present, was instead *re*-constructing and *re*-presenting that pluralism in the political arena as a form of *nationalism* – above all, a nationalism that was not only intended to be unlike the European nationalism whose strategies I expounded earlier, but also to prevent the emergence of that form of nationalism in India. If European nationalism was intended to gain its effects through a political psychology generated by excluding minorities within as 'the other' so as to produce a nation that was 'ours' for the majority, then, Indian nationalism for Nehru (and for Gandhi), by deliberate contrast, would seek to be an *inclusive* nationalism that would mobilize the minorities as well, in a common cause of resisting their colonial masters.[6] This strategy was claimed to be, as I said, a *re*-presentation of the lived and unselfconscious pluralist traditions of India (rather than a destruction of pluralism, as in the European nationalist strategy). And so, unlike Europe, there would be no particular focus on secularism to recover from the damage done to pluralism by a form of nationalism that Nehru wanted no place for in India. If you wanted a slogan to summarize this interpretative proposal about Nehru's thinking, it is simply this: Indian nationalism would make unnecessary a secularism that was made necessary by the damaging effects of European nationalism, and it would do this by *replaying* the genuine and lived pluralism of ordinary Indian social life in the political arena of anti-imperialism.

Now, if this is to be plausible as a bit of analysis and argument about Nehru's (and Gandhi's) *thinking* on secularism, it will only be so because it has some empirical grounding in his political *activism*. Without that, the above slogan would be empty. And so, the crucial additional point is that both Nehru and Gandhi, at some peaks of their mobilizational efforts in the freedom struggle, tried to do their bit as leaders to ensure that this slogan was not an empty one. In a sense, the fact of the partition of the Indian subcontinent is a reflection of the ultimate *failure* of those efforts, but that in itself cannot be a sign that their efforts were not genuine – only that in the end they were not efficacious. The reasons for that failure were many – including, no doubt, the fact that those efforts were not strenuous enough at crucial moments – but this essay does not have the scope and the space to explore them. The argument of the essay, therefore, is very modest. It is restricted entirely to the point that secularism should be understood as a notion that has its conceptual genealogy in a historical context of a specific form of nationalism and nation-building in Europe, and since, for Nehru and Gandhi, that context did not loom large (or large enough) in the period prior to independence, secularism played no serious role in the major political formulations of the freedom movement owing to Nehru and Gandhi. What they both assumed (an assumption that I think it would be cynical for us to dismiss, misinterpreting hindsight, as either naïve or dishonest at the time they made it) was that a historically relatively entrenched pluralism in the subcontinent would be the basis of an alternative conception of nationalism, and it is to give that assumption some empirical support in what Nehru and Gandhi *did* that I now turn.

Since so much has been written on the freedom movement, let me just very briefly select and comment on two such efforts that illustrate the slogan's claim to inclusiveness in the nationalist ideal. The first of these – the Khilafat movement – is widely studied, though Nehru's feeling for it is less frequently recorded than Gandhi's, who was its originator. The second – the Muslim Mass Contact Programme – was conceived primarily by Nehru though its leadership was, for obvious reasons, given to figures like K.M. Ashraf; and Nehru supported it to the last even as some of his colleagues in the Congress high command eventually pulled the plug on it.

The Khilafat movement was a typical and early manifestation of Gandhi's political genius, not only of his revolutionary practice but of his philosophical commitment to the form of inclusive nationalism that, I am claiming, pre-empted the need for making secularism central. I choose it rather than the Congress–League pact of a few years earlier, which also marked such an inclusiveness via the compromise of the Congress allowing separate electorates for Muslims and the League reciprocating by embracing Home Rule. That choice is for two reasons. First, because I want to make things difficult for myself by choosing something that is contested by many as having the character of inclusiveness that I am saying it illustrates. (A case, after all, is made stronger if one can work with examples that *prima facie* seem to suggest that one's case is wrong, and show that what seems *prima facie* so is not so.) And second, because the dynamic effects of the Khilafat agitation on the nationalist movement were far greater, showing possibilities that went well beyond the electoral and constitutional effects of the earlier *entente*.

Nehru's excitement over what was opened up by the Khilafat movement is palpable in his *Autobiography*. 'Nineteen twenty-one was an extraordinary year for us', opens his chapter on the movement. 'It was *Hindu–Musullman ki jai* everywhere'; 'this nationalism was a composite force and behind it could be distinguished a Hindu nationalism, a Muslim nationalism, partly looking beyond the frontiers of India, and, what was more in consonance with the spirit of the times, an Indian nationalism'; 'a disciplined, *joint* action on a countrywide scale'. It is not as if Nehru had no qualms about the appeal to religion in the movement, but he saw that factor as, in the end, marginal. He is explicit in saying that it was 'an eddy and backwater' in the 'main direction' of flow of the struggle, which was anti-imperialism (*Autobiography*, p. 72),[7] a platform and a nationalist strategy for much more than a Muslim cause, indeed far more than an anti-imperialist cause because it brought to consciousness how the welfare of the *peasantry* was essential to any future ideal of the nation, and he devotes a chapter to 'Wandering among the Kisans' and their mobilization in the context of the Khilafat agitation. He writes touchingly about how surprised he was by the innocent and yet true instincts of a widespread confusion among the masses who confusedly thought that 'khilafat' came from the term 'khilaf' and assumed that what it therefore expressed was opposition to the British government, taking that to be the main point of the agitation – just the form of subordination of the religious to the national that the movement aimed for, even as it included Muslims *qua Muslims* (Nehru describes in some detail the role of the 'Maulvis and the Maulanas') into this anti-colonial idealism. This last italicized point of involving Muslims *qua* Muslims is of central significance to his ideal of an inclusive nationalism, and I will return to it.

The movement had a tremendously generative effect in many parts of the country. To take just one example, in the immediate aftermath of Khilafat, Bengali politics experienced one of its most dynamic periods with C.R. Das and Motilal Nehru devising the Council Entry plan to carry out sustained and obstructive interventions in the Legislative Council, and, as is well known, when this was thwarted by the Gaya session of the Congress in December 1922, C.R. Das resigned and formed the Swarajya Party within the Congress, which gained immediate successes in the elections to the legislature. He sought active participation by the Muslims and soon thereafter the Bengal Pact with them was formulated, a highlight of Hindu–Muslim amity that would not have happened were it not for the specific possibilities opened by the Khilafat movement. The dividends for such a form of inclusive nationalism in progressive Muslim politics were measurable, even though they were local.

Consider the following very specific case. A close look at the details which surrounded the women's suffrage bill which was passed in 1925 in the provincial legislative council, after having been defeated four years earlier, suggests very strongly that it was the effects of the Khilafat agitation and the ensuing developments in Bengal, including the C.R. Das Pact (adopted in 1923), that were central to this progressive legislative reversal. Muslim members of the legislative assembly had voted predominantly against the bill in 1921, but by 1925 it was the Muslim members, especially the Swarajist Muslims behind C.R. Das, who had been emboldened to vote for it in large enough numbers to make the difference and get the bill passed. And they did so despite the fact that the party exercised no whip and in fact made an explicit decision not to put pressure on them to do so. The entire catalyst provided by Khilafat gave them the confidence to allow the arguments appealing to their own nationalist and pluralist values (which were pressed upon them by their nationalist colleagues) to internally trump their own other values by which they themselves had argued for the opposite conclusion four years earlier, viz., that stricter observance of *purdah* among their women would inhibit them from voting and put the community at a disadvantage. Even on economic issues the effects were progressive, as could be seen in the sizable support given by Muslims – *jotedars*, small peasants, as well as the radical element among the professional salaried classes – who supported the 1923 bill seeking reforms in land tenancy, though the bill went down due to the Hindu leaders of the Congress Swarajya Party backing the large zamindars. I said these were provincial gains in radicalizing Muslims, but they reflected what a strategy of *overtly* including Muslims in a mass nationalist mobilization could produce by way of confidence in them to go well beyond their religious communal interests for progressive causes.[8] And Bengal was by no means the only province to be affected. Uttar Pradesh and Assam were significantly transformed by the movement as well.

The second effort at inclusive mobilization I have chosen is the Muslim Mass Contact Programme, launched some fifteen years after the

Khilafat agitation. Gyanendra Pandey has shown in his study of regional politics in Uttar Pradesh that, for a variety of reasons which he carefully presents, the Muslims there had felt alienated from the anti-imperialist movement ever since the late 1920s (Pandey 1984). If the overall analysis I am giving in this essay is correct, an additional reason for this alienation was that by then the momentum and the mobilizing effects of the Khilafat movement had completely subsided; and one may conjecture that this alienation, which Pandey describes and analyses, was precisely why Nehru felt the urgent need in the first place to start something like the Muslim Mass Contact campaign a decade later. The campaign was far less sustained than the earlier movement. It was aborted early, lasting only a year or so in 1937–38. But it is revealing, despite its brief and limited success because of what motivated it, what exactly was intended by it and the form it took. The Khilafat movement was a more effective form of inclusiveness in nationalist causes than the Congress–League pact of 1916. But it is interesting to compare that pact with the post-Khilafat, Bengal Pact mentioned above, which was entirely different in its significance because it emerged in the catalytic wake of a movement rather than via negotiations among leaders of communities. Nehru, in motivating and devising the Muslim Mass Contact Programme of the late 1930s, made this point explicitly. In his words: 'We have too long thought in terms of pacts and compromises with communal leaders, and neglected the people behind them. That is a discredited policy. There must be direct contact with the Muslim Masses.' K.M. Ashraf was enlisted to organize such contacts over all the regions of the country to draw Muslims inclusively into the nationalist movement. This echoed the Khilafat goal, though, because the precedent had already been set by that movement in explicit terms a decade and a half earlier, it did not this time need any appeal to a symbolic Muslim cause in a foreign land.

The short-term effects of the programme were highly successful, ranging from the activism of the Khudai Khidmatgars in the north-west to the academic community of Aligarh, and lawyers and journalists and the professional classes quite generally all over Uttar Pradesh and Bihar. Even many sections of the *Ulama*, most prominently those under Madani's leadership, and the Deoband seminary and Jamiyat-ul-Ulama (itself founded in the wake of the Khilafat movement) were staunchly supportive of the Mass Contact campaign's non-sectarian nationalism, openly declaring that they fully expected freedom of religion from the Congress leadership of Nehru and Gandhi and Azad; and they were even entirely tolerant of K.M. Ashraf's Marxist rhetoric by which the mass campaign was often articulated.

The short-lived campaign's failure to sustain itself was partly due to the inability to gain full reach to the peasantry, and also due to the unstinting opposition both of Jinnah and the Muslim League and of the Mahasabhaite elements in the Congress, especially at the regional and district levels. Gandhi was supportive throughout the campaign but he did register disagreement with Nehru, saying that it would be better if Hindus and Muslims worked together with the Muslim masses, which would have been a slightly different conception of the campaign than one which left it to the leadership of K.M. Ashraf and a variety of local Muslim leaders in the regions to make the contact with the masses. Nehru was far less inhibited in allowing this autonomy so as to give the community a sense of confidence that they could, *as Muslims*, be fully participatory in causes that had no communal goals in particular.[9]

More than the other, often remarkable, moments in the long freedom struggle, the especial relevance of the Khilafat agitation and the Muslim Mass Contact campaign for the inclusive nature of the nationalism that Nehru was striving for, is that they gave justificatory substance to a well-known stance that Nehru took: the stance of often refusing to recognize Jinnah and the Muslim League as representative of a people that the Congress itself was, as he put it, 'proud to represent'. We stand for everyone, was Nehru's view, and will speak with commitment on behalf of Muslims as much as Hindus. Now, the point is that without efforts of this kind to mobilize under a banner that was unafraid to assert a Muslim cause such as the Khilafat or to assert the name 'Muslim' in pursuing a programme to contact the masses, there was no reason to believe that the Congress *did* in fact represent the Muslims. Simply the presence of Muslim leaders in the Congress was not enough to make it a genuinely representative party of the Muslims, nor were the more politically procedural ploys such as the granting of separate electorates. So, the point really is that nationalism integrates and includes diverse communities only if it finds mobilizing causes in which those communities are given *distinctive* voice, even as the causes are, in the end, not sectarian. It is only movements of this kind that make for the inclusiveness of nationalism, because it is now a nationalism *negotiated* by different participatory voices.

I have used the word 'negotiated' here with careful deliberation, despite it seeming as if movements are the very opposite of negotiation, as is stated in Nehru's remarks (that I quoted) when he started the Muslim Mass Contact Programme. Let me explain. The term 'negotiation' is ambiguous. Nehru, as I cited him, said the Congress must get past negotiated outcomes such as pacts. That is one notion of negotiation. But the movements I have been commenting upon – that Nehru, like Gandhi, made central to nationalism – provide sites of public education for large numbers of ordinary people, and in doing so provide a quite different negotiation into common causes. It is not hard to see what they had in mind by this. There is the sort of negotiation that occurs around tables with representatives. But one also uses the term in expressions such as 'They negotiated the traffic.' It is this latter use of the word that better suits what Nehru and Gandhi meant by the power of movements like Khilafat and the Muslim Mass Contact Programme to include minorities into a negotiating inclusiveness in a national cause. Movements carry a people in a cause through public education and debate into an understanding of the full rationale and purpose of the cause. Nehru was explicit on this, declaring that a particular community, through the various practices of mass participation of this kind, learns to navigate *as a community* a cause that is larger than its immediate communal interest.

Thus there are two notions of negotiation. And the refusal to *formally* negotiate with leaders and representatives of sectarian parties such as the Muslim League would have been a crippling defect in the matter of inclusiveness if these alternative, more *substantially and dynamically* negotiative popular mobilizations were not also a commitment of Nehru and Gandhi. These latter gave substance to the Congress claim to be representing Muslims – and neither Jinnah nor his recent scholarly defenders[10] really understood or acknowledged this. Or, perhaps it is better to say that Jinnah himself understood it very well, was alarmed by it, and worked very hard to undermine its dynamically inclusive effects by his own politics of bargaining for the interests of educated metropolitan Muslims in an India with considerable provincial autonomy for the Muslim-majority regions. I want to be careful not to give any impression here of a Congress-nationalistic, anti-Jinnah bias in what I am saying. My point is merely to record that Jinnah's politics, representing a much narrower class of Muslims throughout this period between the 1920s and 30s, was deeply at odds with the mass politics of Muslim inclusion which these two movements that Gandhi and Nehru had respectively devised. I have no wish to tarnish Jinnah with a separatist brush, but only to say that even if we acknowledge that his rhetoric of separatism was a 'bargaining weapon' for greater *autonomy* for Muslim-majority regions in a *united* India (something that his defenders have plausibly insisted on), the inclusiveness of nationalism meant something entirely different to him than it did to Gandhi and Nehru in these specific mobilizational efforts on their part. Indeed, it is not very clear whether Jinnah and the Muslim League's nationalism had any anti-imperialist force at all in the last two decades of imperial rule. But again, just so as to be clear, my criticism of his supporters for failing to record his blind spot about the inclusive nature of Gandhi and Nehru's nationalism does not require me to deny at all what these scholars have argued and established, viz., that in the few years before independence the Congress party repeatedly resisted the granting of the ideal of confederation and provincial autonomy that Jinnah was demanding. (And it should be pointed out that on this last issue Nehru and Gandhi took very different views, with Nehru resisting that ideal because of a zeal for a centralized state that would *plan* towards a new industrialized political economy, a zeal that Gandhi did not share.) These issues, interesting though they are, are not the concern of this essay; it is only concerned with the concept of secularism and its pre-emption in Nehru's political philosophy prior to independence by a very specific form of inclusive nationalism that he recurringly strived for, a form of nationalism that sat ill with Jinnah's politics and its representational base.

In making the distinction between two notions of 'negotiation' and drawing implications from this, my argument accounting for the peripheral place of secularism in India in the pre-independence period succeeds only to the extent that one stresses, as I have been doing, these dynamic efforts of mobilization by Nehru and Gandhi with the substantial forms of negotiated inclusiveness they carry with them. The claim of the argument, therefore, is *conditional*. Had Congress politics instead been focused exclusively on the more formal sort of negotiative ideal that Jinnah (and no doubt some in the Congress party too) understood by nationalist politics, there would be no grounds to think of Nehru and Gandhi's nationalism as inclusive in the sense that accounts for the pre-emption of secularist notions. When it came to that form of politics, as I said, Nehru's stance was that the Congress stood for Muslims just as much as it did for other religious populations, so negotiating with a sectarian representation of Muslims by the League was not compulsory for the Congress. Hence the conditional is: *only because and only to the extent* that the Congress did not have that exclusive focus can we say with some right that its nationalism was inclusive and constituted such a pre-emption of the secularist ideal. And this suggests that there is a counter-conditional too. Only because and only when – at key moments – it *failed* to sustain the momentum of its own contrasting political methods of substantial negotiation did a more corrosive communal politics have the opportunity to take centre-stage; and those indeed are the counter-conditions that led to partition. (Pandey's book on Uttar Pradesh politics that I have mentioned above gives a regional account of these counter-conditions that I have in mind.)

Once independence was close to being achieved in the way and form that it eventually was, with all the trauma around partition and the political and religious acrimonies that led to it, the assumption of an inclusive nationalism of the kind that would pre-empt secularism as a central notion began to falter, and the rhetoric of secularism, just for that reason, began to emerge more conspicuously in the public arena, even in the speeches and writings of Nehru and Gandhi.

Returning to the distinction between the two notions of negotiation, one cannot help noticing when reading Jinnah's supporters among historians and commentators that there is an assumption in their discussions that nationalism was played out primarily in the arena of formal negotiation, and so they show little appreciation for the honourable aspirations pursued in the other forms of mobilizational negotiation in which Muslims were included, and which I have formulated as a contrasting ideal, despite their eventual failure. As I said, Jinnah himself understood these aspirations very well, and because he was by temperament always uncomfortable with the livelier negotiation that came with the force of movements and mass politics, he did not find that form of inclusive nationalism honourable, and dedicated much of his political will and effort from the late 1920s to resisting and undermining them.

There is no denying, of course, what has often been said in recent years, that a good bit of Indian nationalist 'History', especially at the hands of scholars who were close to the Congress party, went too far in stressing both the sincerity and efficacy of the Congress commitment to pursuing these aspirations through the long freedom movement. Be that as it may, I have no doubt either that Perry Anderson's recent polemic against Gandhi and Nehru, which contains a wholesale denial that there was any sincerity to that commitment, is so carelessly argued and so brazenly ignores the evidence for the genuine efforts that manifested the commitment, that it cannot be taken seriously as a work of responsible criticism.

I have been focusing so far on Nehru in the period before India gained independence, and I have been arguing that secularism was never a very important notion for him in this entire period because secularism (properly understood in its non-arbitrary, historically accurate sense) is necessitated by the effects of a form of majoritarian nationalism that it is intended to combat, a form of nationalism owing initially to Europe and which Nehru precisely wished to avoid in India in the first place, by inclusive nationalist mobilizations such as those that I have been describing. So, at least in this aspect of nationalism (though not the other aspects that I have mentioned in endnote 1), as against what Partha Chatterjee has argued, Nehru and Gandhi were precisely trying to *avoid* a derivative form of nationalism – derivative, that is, of the nationalism that had emerged in Europe since the Westphalian peace.

It is almost tempting to say that the nationalism that Nehru and Gandhi were trying to construct *was* India's version of secularism. But I think we must resist this temptation. All such forms of redefinition of secularism to claim an indigenous form of something that was entirely different from what originated elsewhere (a sort of obsessive and pointless exercise in the Indian academy in recent years), make for no clarity, and in fact confound the conceptual field with confusion and clutter and ambiguity.[11]

2

I want to turn now to the period after independence and explore briefly what secularism, conceived in these historically motivated terms of a European pedigree that I have presented so far, came to really mean in India. In Europe, once religion in the realm of the polity became a target of secularist policy for the historically motivated reasons I have presented, the familiar and celebrated formulation of a range of rights and constitutional principles became the natural and obvious *source* from which that policy sought to target and constrain religious practices. These were precisely the sources which became relevant in the Indian context after independence, and talk of secularism was inevitable in the constitutional issues that came to be debated and resolved through the legal process.

The British Crown had enacted codes of civil and criminal law as far back as 1858, but this left substantial matters having to do with religious law and practice still unattended by codes of this kind: matters such as temple entry, administration of religious establishments and endowments, but most particularly, as is well known, personal or family law which remained uncodified due to sensitivities in broaching matters where religion was most intensely felt and lived by religious people. Many of these matters were addressed with reformist purpose in the construction of the Constitution, but the matter of personal law was addressed later in the Hindu Code Bill of 1955 – and that too only as a result of the force of Nehru's personal influence and weight, which overcame opposition from conservative Hindu voices even within his own party to make it happen.

The subject of secularism is obviously relevant to these developments in reform in India. How could it fail to be? But it seemed entirely unclear to many what secularism was said to mean, given how these reforms were enacted. A standard understanding of the meaning of secularism is found in long-standing slogans of western societies such as 'separation of church and state'. But the manner in which these reforms were conducted in Hindu law found the state brazenly violating the wall of separation and intervening with religious interpretations of Hindu law to justify many of the reforms. Thus, if that slogan of separation defines secularism, then these developments violated secularism in the name of achieving reform that purported to be secularist. This paradox and other such conundrums have led political commentators, such as Amartya Sen,[12] to simply draw back and claim that secularism in the Indian context must really mean something entirely distinct from what it is taken to mean in the west, and some others, such as Partha Chatterjee (1994), have even claimed that secularism is not even the right ground on which to address the matter of religious personal law. What, then, was Nehru's secularism and how does it square with either of these responses to the paradoxical situation that the reform of Hindu law posed for the meaning of the term?

Ex hypothesi, it does not and cannot square with Chatterjee's proposal since Chatterjee's view abandons secularism for another strategy of reform. But what about Sen's proposal? Sen has claimed that Indian secularism comes to religion not by way of any form of opposition to it but rather as a form of neutrality between the different religions in India. This idea of neutrality between religions was very much part of the rhetoric of many Indian leaders who spoke about secularism since independence, and it even occurs in some of Nehru's writings and speeches, *not* as a definition of secularism but as a general bit of wisdom. (How exactly that wisdom relates to what Nehru *did* understand by secularism is an interesting question, and I will try and give a more or less exact answer to it further below.) As a matter of well-known historical fact, ironic though this may be for a proposal trying to define a peculiarly Indian secularism, neutrality of this sort really goes back to a British colonial ideal in India when the colonial government announced that in matters of religion, it would be even-handed among the different religious communities it governed. But Nehruvian secularism, despite the occasional rhetoric regarding such neutrality, was defined in quite other terms, terms familiar from a great deal of reformist constitutional practice in the west and terms that he put forward most clearly when he was advocating the reform of Hindu law.

Secularism in the Indian context since independence was entirely in keeping with western ideas about it, shorn of the misleading sloganizing about a wall of separation. The articulation of secularism for Nehru and in the Indian Constitution begins with two background commitments: (1) a commitment to freedom of religion; (2) a commitment to certain fundamental constitutional rights that *neither mention religion nor mention opposition to religion*. These latter are the basic ideals that a society, in its polity, seeks to live up to, and will bring the resources of the state, including its conceptual resources, to do so. (In liberal polities, free speech and gender equality, conceived as rights, are familiar examples of such ideals that do not make any mention of either religion or opposition to religion.) The articulation then proceeds crucially to declare a *lexicographical ordering* between these two background commitments (1) and (2). The ordering is as follows: were there to be a clash between the deliverances of the commitment to freedom of religion (commitment 1 above) and the basic ideals enshrined in rights that neither mention religion nor mention opposition to religion (commitment 2 above), then the latter must be placed first. In other words, if there turned out to be religious practices (which, given the first commitment to freedom of religion, were being 'freely' exercised) that ran afoul of the rights that were mentioned in the second commitment, then the latter should be placed first and those religious practices should accordingly be disallowed. That disallowance directly follows from the lexicographical priority of the second commitment over the first.

The idea of a lexicographical ordering, which originally comes from dictionaries as conceived alphabetically, is elaborated differently in different disciplines – from mathematics to economics. Perhaps the one in economics has some relevance for our purposes. There it is conceived in terms of comparative preferences, where an economic agent prefers an amount of one good (A) to any amount of another (B). More generally, if offered several bundles of goods, the agent will choose the bundle that offers the most A, no matter how much B there is. This approximates to some extent the familiar thing we want from secularism without any obscure and implausible metaphors of separation of church and state, which are so constantly violated in the practice of reform. That is, it captures the idea that unlike secularization, even perhaps defying secularization, we will allow great latitude in religious practice as a freedom that is articulated in commitment 1, so long as those practices do not clash with the basic ideals of a society, ideals that are elaborated *without* mention of religion or the opposition to religion in commitment 2. This was the underlying notion of secularism that Nehru appealed to in promoting the cause of reform of Hindu law. And it is a notion of secularism that keeps faith with the conceptual history of the term in its European genealogy (a history that was very misleadingly characterized by the slogan of a 'wall of separation' between religion and the state.)

Unlike the idea of neutrality between religions, this version of secularism is resolutely prepared to be non-neutral. Should some religion have commitments, say, to blasphemy laws, and should the society in question have basic commitments to freedom of speech, then that religion would feel the weight of secularism far more than religions which have no such laws. This elaboration of secularism, even though it is faithful to its conceptual origins in emerging western liberal societies, is general enough to accommodate all sorts of societies other than liberal societies that may not start with the ideal of free speech but some other ideals instead. Thus, the Soviet Union might have articulated its secularism by declaring that ideals of economic equality would stand in lexicographical priority over religious practices, suppressing those practices should one have to choose between them and economic equality. And they could make this lexicographical ordering without giving free speech a similar priority. The definition of secularism is therefore general enough to include both the liberal societies and the communist societies that we have known in the past, and no doubt other forms of society yet. That is how it should be. Secularism is not identical with liberalism.

If this lexicographical priority ideal is what secularism should be understood to be, how does it relate to the rhetoric of even-handedness or neutrality between religions that was often deployed, even sometimes by Nehru himself? I think the right way to think of that sort of even-handedness is to see it as a *side-constraint*. That is to say, one could demand that the *application* of the lexicographical ordering must be done even-handedly between all religions and not favour some religions over others. (So, for instance, it is precisely this side-constraint that is missing in British secularism because the British government banned Kazantzakis's book, *The Last Temptation of Christ*, for blaspheming against Christianity, but upheld freedom of speech and refused to ban Rushdie's *The Satanic Verses* a few years later for blaspheming against Islam. And it is this side-constraint that was also put aside when the Indian government allowed Muslims to have their own personal laws while pushing through on the reform of Hindu law, a matter I will briefly take up below.)

Viewed as such, neutrality between religions would not be an alternative conception or definition of secularism, as Radhakrishnan and Sen (and, in the non-Indian context, Charles Taylor) have suggested. It would rather only be a side-constraint on a quite different (lexicographic ordering) conception of secularism, the one I say Nehru adopted after Indian independence to push forward reform. Neutrality would *nest within* this conception (*constraining its application*) rather than seek to rival it as an alternative.

Thus secularism in India was neither to be elaborated in terms of metaphors of a wall of separation, nor in terms of neutrality between religions. We have seen that 'separation' was never preserved in the reforms that were carried out in Hindu law. And secularism *qua* neutrality between religions, in any case, would not serve very well to capture the intuitive liberal ideas that India came to have of secularism, because presumably neutrality would be perfectly well served if a state impartially and even-handedly allowed blasphemy laws of a variety of religions to curtail free speech.

There is one point remaining, however, which has been a constant subject of controversy since independence, and though it is a much-mined subject, I could not conclude without saying at least something briefly about it to accommodate it within the conceptual distinctions regarding secularism that I have discussed so far. This is the question of the *exception* that the Indian state has allowed Muslims in allowing them to live by unreformed personal laws. Some have written about this in terms of a prerogative that comes with provisos in the Constitution for *minority rights*. Certainly many Muslim leaders have declared this to be the basis on which the exception has been allowed and political commentators have generalized this to an even broader form of right, the 'right to culture'. Others, such as Partha Chatterjee, have theoretically re-frameworked the entire question of personal law essentially as a protection against secular majoritarianism, and have therefore concluded that the right concept that should be deployed to address such exceptions is not secularism but democracy, the idea being that if one introduced internal democratic representative institutions within communities, one would allow Muslims to come to their own reforms from within their own intra-community democratic institutions. Both these positions would have abandoned the lexicographical conception that I have attributed to Nehru's idea of a secular state.

Chatterjee's position, interesting though it certainly is, has pitfalls of its own, not least of which is the virtual impossibility of actually constructing representative institutions within communities of any size. We have such institutions at the federal, state, district and even municipal level, but the mind boggles at the idea of devising them for something so dispersed as a religious community. In any case, whether this is feasible or not, it is certainly not intended by him as a way of understanding secularism, but rather as one of abandoning secularism at least for the purposes of such reforms. He argues that secularism is now beside the point as a resource with which to contest Hindu nationalism, because, first, as the frequent comparisons with fascism show, such a nationalism is a modern ideology without any invocation of traditional Hindu doctrinal elements; and second, since Hindutva ideologues charge Nehruvians with 'pseudo-secularism', this implies they have implicitly embraced secularism, and so they must be contested by another idea or ideal than secularism. I am not sure I quite understand either of these points. On the first point, there is no reason why religious majoritarianism is not religious just because it surfaces in a modernist nationalist ideology rather than traditional religious forms – as if every other social phenomenon can change, but religion must remain in some unbudging stasis, if it is to be religion. Those who make the analogy with fascism are not, after all, saying that it is race rather than religion which is the ideological source for Muslims being vilified and oppressed as a minority in India, in the way that Jews were in Germany in the 1930s and 40s. It is a transformed, modern, *religious* ideology that is the source. And on the second point, I don't see why someone who wields the term 'pseudo-secularist' against others must have committed himself implicitly to secularism – no more than I see someone who calls something a fake unicorn has committed himself implicitly to there being unicorns. And besides, if X charges Y with pseudo-secularism, he may well be suggesting that Y is failing to live up to something defined by Y's lights. If so, there is no reason to think that Y's lights must also be X's lights.

What, then, about the claim that Nehru's conception of secularism, as I have expounded it, suffers a partial cancellation by the concession – via minority rights – to *sharia* personal laws? Did the Indian state *put aside* the lexicographical conception of secularism in the name of such rights when it granted an exception to Muslims? I think it would be a mistake to think that Nehru must concede that it did. But in order to avoid thinking so, some more distinctions need to be introduced.

If one thought that minority rights could claim a *reversal* of the lexicographic ordering that defines secularism, then we would have indeed given up the notion of secularism in the terms that I have attributed to Nehru. For now, the idea would have to be that minorities have a right to their own conception of what to give priority to, and if their personal laws give a lexicographical priority to their personal laws over the state's laws, demanding, say, gender justice, then there are no resources left by which one can give them reasons to reverse their priorities. Chatterjee seems to suggest this when he argues that if the secularist claims rationality for her side, then there is nothing wrong with the Muslim community declaring, in turn, that it is happy to be deemed irrational. This makes it sound as if the deeper conflict is not about rationality but a *nomic* conflict – law versus law – and if liberal law simply assumes that it has rationality on its side, well, then Muslims can embrace 'the irrational', so long as they hold fast to the deeper claims of the truth that underlies their (*sharia*) law. So, on the question of the lexicographical ordering, this leaves us with a frustrating impasse: there are no ulterior principles by which a lexicographical ordering may be constructed *on either side*. This is a form of a relativist dead-end owing, in Chatterjee's specific argument in that essay, to a certain reading of Foucault. If that is the only framework for understanding the issues, the lexicographical ordering ideal of secularism would indeed have been put aside when Muslims were granted their own personal laws. But this way of configuring the dispute between the secularist state and the minorities decidedly impoverishes the theoretical framework of discussion. I believe the Nehruvian secularist ideal can be – and was in fact – retained, despite the decision to allow Muslims their own personal laws, by a crucial subtlety that is not so much as visible in the cramped theoretical possibilities of a framework that sees it as a relativist impasse between two systems of laws (liberal and *sharia*).

What we need to bring to visibility is that in the matter of implementing secularism (understood in terms of the lexicographical ordering ideal), the human subject who reasons and deliberates to political conclusions about what exactly should and should not be implemented cannot be seen, as a relativist understanding of the issues would, in just *synchronic* terms. If there are no reasons the state can offer Muslims to reform their personal laws, that does not rule out that at a future time, history may have introduced enough internal conflict within Muslim attitudes on the subject of personal law that allows them to be open to state-sponsored reforms. The point is essentially Hegelian. The citizen-subject is always and necessarily in history. And history may inject internal conflict within a minority's values which the state can then seize to give reasons that hitherto were not persuasive. Examples of this happening are pervasive. So, for instance, it is now fairly well documented that the state's arguments for a pro-choice stance on abortion persuaded large numbers of long-standing conservative women in America in the third quarter of the last century, as a result of conflicts injected into their commitments – in particular a conflict that *emerged fully only in that period of history* when, as a result of the rise of service industries and the relative decline of heavy manufacturing-goods industries, the possibility of a more gender-distributed work force was created. A historical change, which provided for greater prospects for employment for women, introduced conflict into the values of even hitherto conservative women, and they became far more open to the pro-choice policies that were promoted by the state. The point, then, is that even if, at a given time, a group's psychological economy[13] seems relatively unreachable by reasons because it is relatively coherent and unconflicted, so long as we think of human subjectivity as diachronically constituted – necessarily being *in history* – internal conflicts may be injected by historical developments to generate internal deliberation in the group that leads it to commitments that held no attraction till then. This is exactly how the Nehruvian state conceived of the concession to Muslim personal laws. The temporal qualifier to this concession was explicitly formulated when the concession itself was formulated.

The general idea and its particular specification here is quite straightforward. One would *put aside* the lexicographical ordering ideal in the name of minority rights only if one thought that there was truth on the side of the relevant *sharia* laws, equal to the truth of ideals of gender equality. But one would *put the ideal merely in abeyance* on quite different grounds – because it would be coercive to implement it until the necessary internal deliberation takes place among Muslims (in the way I just expounded as happening in America with conservative women on the question of abortion). Without being too misleading, this could be thought of as a kind of affirmative action policy rather than a minority right granted to Indian Muslims, a policy of bias in favour of them in the cultural sphere – personal law, in particular – given the deprivations they suffered in other spheres of their lives as a result of partition (such as loss of numbers due to massive migration of their brethren, loss of zamindari, loss of their language Urdu due to the nationalistic pique of conservative figures in the Congress such as Tandon, Sampurnanand, Pant and so on). And like many affirmative action efforts, it was conceived as a temporary measure with the explicit goal of eventually giving them the confidence to stand as equals, and, via their own internal reasoning, embrace the commitments of the rest of the polity in the matter of law and, therefore in turn, in the matter of secularism in the lexicographically prior sense that this essay is presenting as the right understanding of secularism. On this reading, Indian secularism is a very clear example of this understanding, as it sits within the Hegelian framework which I have constructed for its application.

Perhaps those who are given to Chatterjee and Foucault's relativist impulse will insist here that all this still concedes that while the concessive exception to Muslim personal law exists, there is a relativist impasse now between the state's and the minority's legal commitments, which in the future may be overcome – so for now at least, the lexicographical secularist ideal has lapsed. But this deflationary description misses the real theoretical status of the appeal to the subject as diachronically *constituted*. That appeal is precisely intended to repudiate the idea that we should think of subjects as being contained in slabs of time, with relativism about their values holding in one slab and possibly passing away in the next. Despite the talk of different times, that would *still* be to conceive the subject essentially synchronically at each slab of time. A genuinely diachronically conceived subject (hardly ever the subject that is considered by political theorists), a subject conceived neither synchronically nor in discreetly periodized times but rather a subject conceived of as essentially historically open-ended, is exactly intended to replace the subject relativized to a time, when his values may have a 'relative' truth or his reasons a relative closure. Hence the inclination to say, 'Relativism *for now*, but not perhaps *later*!' is to not yet quite be on board with the depth of Hegel's point that lays stress on the importance of history for our conception of human subjectivity. To be fully on board is to see that *no* sort of relativism is sanctioned for subjects conceived essentially diachronically and therefore open to the internal conflicts that history may provide.

If the Indian Constitution is read in this Hegelian way, there is no need to think that it has forsaken the lexicographical ordering that defined the Nehruvian ideal of the secular state, for some minoritarian right to culture. (And, given the fact that the lexicographical ordering allows full freedom of worship and culture until the ordering kicks in – the very idea of an *ordering* presupposes that this is allowed – there is no reason to think, either, that this is some wholesale rejection of the minoritarian right to culture.) I just said, 'If the Indian Constitution is read this . . . way', but really there ought to be no 'if' about it. As I have pointed out and as is very well known to all without my having to point it out, there was a temporal qualifier explicitly stated when the concession to Muslims was made. They were to be granted their own personal laws *until* such time as they were ready for the state's reforms towards a more liberal codification.[14] All I am saying is that this temporal qualifier reflects a theoretical understanding of the issues that is Hegelian (in the way I have just tried to elaborate), an understanding which by strict implication simply cancels (also in the way I have just tried to elaborate) any relativistic reading of what was at stake in the concession, thereby retaining the lexicographical ideal of secularism even despite making the concession.

I have argued that the constant effort to redefine secularism in a peculiarly Indian version is both unnecessary and confusing, and any characterization of secularism can be satisfyingly non-arbitrary by simply keeping faith with (a) the historical motivations for it, and (b) the form of lexicographical priority that it asserted in the west when it emerged to fulfil that historical motivation. In doing so, I have said that this understanding of secularism accounts for why there was no great centrality given to secularism in Nehru's thinking till Indian independence was achieved; and thereafter, it came to be deployed by him and the state that was inaugurated in the context of certain reforms that it undertook. And finally, I have argued that if we construct a roughly Hegelian notion of collective human subjects in politics, the exceptions to such reform that were allowed cannot be seen as an occasion or argument for either revising this notion of secularism in the name of minority rights, nor for abandoning it and replacing it with an intra-community ideal of democracy. And since what is clear, what nobody can deny, is that from the 1980s onward Indian society seems to have sunk into precisely that damaging and deforming majoritarian nationalism which can be traced to a European past, the only notion of secularism there is (the one that was initially formulated to correct that damage in Europe and to which I have tried to give some exact analytic elaboration in this essay) has in the past three decades been summoned for its relevance with an urgency which, I have claimed, had no precedent in the times in which Nehru and Gandhi lived and worked and wrote.

It would be foolish to deny that what gives the concept of secularism this charge in the last few decades did certainly have premonitional antecedents that go back as far back as the 1920s. The Mahasabhaite element in the Congress and the Savarkar ideology, which explicitly *sought* just the form of European majoritarian nationalism that Nehru and Gandhi opposed, did surface, as we know, again and again in the long freedom struggle. But what they sought did not take serious root. That is why I have used the term 'antecedents' with deliberate intent. Political historians (perhaps historians, generally) ought, in their analyses, to observe a distinction that I would describe as the distinction between *antecedents* and *roots*. Something can be an antecedent of something else without being the root from which the latter flowers by any organic, causal stages or path. These earlier Hindu communal elements were *not* the roots, they were merely the antecedents, of what we have seen emerging in India since the late 1980s. So one need not deny that there were these antecedents to current Hindu nationalism in order to deny that there existed in India the sort of European-style majoritarian nationalism which would make it seem that secularism was relevant in the 1920s in the way it is now, and Gandhi and Nehru were wrong not to stress it as early as then.

Nor does one need to deny that there were minoritarian backlashes against these early antecedents to majoritarian Hindu nationalist elements. Indeed, one may even say that they were eventually responsible for the partition of India. But many, both on the Right and the Left, have said something much *stronger* than these undeniable things, claiming that the very sorts of inclusive moments in Indian nationalism that I have fastened on to make my argument in the first half of this essay were the causal *roots* of such religious majoritarianism, and then minoritarian responses to that. How many times has it been argued that if you focus on Muslims in the way Gandhi and Nehru did in these mobilizations, you have communalized the very idea of nationalism?

I believe, on balance, that this stronger reaction (which again comes, paradoxically, both from purist secularists and from Hindutva ideologues) is very wide of the mark. I have tried to convey the ways in which remarkably progressive things came out of these mobilizations and Indian nationalism was indeed made genuinely inclusive by them. The argument that they nevertheless gave the forces of majoritarian nationalism and minoritarian backlashes to it an excuse of precedent to go forward with their agendas is unconvincing – if only because these forces needed no excuse of precedent of this kind. Their leaders were quite capable of generating precedents and energies of their own to combat the dynamic effects of these inclusive movements. A very wide range of reasons account for the communal politics that emerged prior to independence, and there is a good deal of thoroughly instructive scholarship that elaborates those reasons. But the most plausible scholarship on the subject does not locate the fault-line in these efforts to mobilize the Muslim masses that I have invoked in my argument regarding the place (or lack of place) of secularism prior to independence. As I have been selfconsciously careful to say, the fault-line and the failures are by no means all to be laid at the door of Jinnah and the Muslim League. Far from it. Much of the best scholarly work lays it equally at the door of the Congress party, and, as I myself said earlier, it is precisely the failure of the Congress at key moments to keep up the momentum of these inclusive mobilizing nationalist strategies that I have commented on, which partly account for the failures. But that is not any kind of proof that these strategies were not actively pursued in the anti-imperialist campaigns I have described, or that they did not have the effects which I have also presented in some detail. And that is sufficient for the arguments and conclusions regarding secularism that this essay has sought to make.

I repeat that the eventual failure of these strategies are explained by reasons that are various and complex, and that some of them have been presented with care and fair-minded scruple in the available scholarship, some of which, when it was relevant to my specific claims, I have cited. I particularly regret that I do not have the space to explore at the tail-end of an essay that is already too long, a striking strand of explanation given by some scholars – Irfan Habib, for instance – who have pointed out that it was the propertied elements, especially the landlords, that shifted to communal positions to oppose what Nehru and Gandhi had started. It is also well known from criticisms that a wide range of Left commentators and historians have made that Gandhi himself pulled the reins in when what he started got politically radicalized in directions that alarmed him, and that Nehru also back-pedalled from his political radicalism of a three- or four-year period in the 1930s. And, continuing with this general direction of diagnosis, Hamza Alavi had also observed that even as late as the mid-1940s, someone like Sikandar Hayat for a very extended period had widely trans-communal support for his party – it was only when Nehru declared that there would be land reforms in a post-independence India that the Unionist Party, which represented the feudal interests of his region, went over to the separatist cause of Pakistan.[15] All these points suggest further trajectories within which the communalization of nationalist politics prior to independence must be explained, rather than attributed glibly to the precedent set by explicitly Muslim mobilizations of an inclusive anti-imperialistic nationalism.

These further explanations will of course have to appeal not to the older form of propertied interests but to the increasingly neo-liberal political economy of the last few decades to account (at least partially) for the increasingly deep-set majoritarian nationalism of our own contemporary times. Prabhat Patnaik, to whose remarkable work over the last four decades this essay is intended as a tribute, has in a number of writings over recent years provided such explanations with peerless intellectual power and moral fire.[16]

Notes

1 On other issues – such as, for instance, those of industrialization and of centralization of political governance – there are indeed very deep differences. I will not be addressing those issues at all in this essay.

2 This idea of neutrality between religions was explicitly mentioned in the Congress party's Karachi Resolution of 1931, though there *it was not an idea that was declared to be 'secularism'*. Sarvepalli Radhakrishnan was perhaps the first to so declare it, though Amartya Sen has also been saying it more recently. (In a draft of this essay, which I presented to the Indian History Congress in December 2014, I mentioned Sen as a prominent proponent of this view, and Irfan Habib alerted me during the discussion to the fact that Radhakrishnan was in fact the first to assert it as a characterization of secularism.)

3 Assuming there is a distinction between direct and indirect forms of influence, the *in*direct influence of religion can hardly be avoided in a polity when a society is not highly secularized. And it is not the business of a secularist polity to address indirect influences, in any case. One would have to go well beyond secularism to a state-enforced *secularization* to get rid of indirect sorts of influence of religion, as was said to be done in Kemalist Turkey.

4 In the tiresome hectoring of Richard Dawkins, Christopher Hitchens, Sam Harris and others, there is a detectably sophomoric denial of the possibility of secularism of polity without a comprehensive secularization of society.

5 Much confusion has resulted from political theorists conflating secularization with secularism, but one philosopher who has, implicitly at least, been careful in seeing the point of the distinction in his work is Charles Taylor. His massive study, *A Secular Age* (Taylor 2008), is focused on secularization. Some subsequent articles of his are strictly on secularism and do not run together his claims in the book with the claims they make. See, for instance, Taylor (2011). My essay 'Secularism: Its Content and Context' (Bilgrami 2014), is critical of his writing on secularism, while my essay 'What is Enchantment' (Bilgrami 2010) is appreciative of his book, which is primarily, as I said, on the theme of secu-

larization. See my 'Reply to Justin Neuman' in the Symposium on my essay, 'Secularism: Its Content and Context', on the website *Immanent Frame*, for more on the confusions that come from conflating the distinction – in particular conflating Taylor's distinct work on each.

[6] My focus in this essay is entirely on the inclusiveness of different religions in nationalism. The whole question of *caste* completely transforms the very idea of such an inclusive nationalism (indeed puts into question the very idea of pluralism that the inclusive nationalism was tapping) and must remain the focus of a quite separate essay that I hope to write in the future. The charged stimulus provided by highly polemical recent writings on the subject by Arundhati Roy and Perry Anderson has made this subject so fraught in the current intellectual context in India that it is hard to undertake that task just at this moment with a sufficiently detached intellectual distance.

[7] All quotations above are from Nehru (1953).

[8] On the legislative issues discussed above, see *Bengal Legislative Council Proceedings*, September 1921 and August 1925. For worthwhile and instructive scholarship on Bengal in the 1920s, see Ray (1985), Broomfield (1968), Southard (1995) and Engels (1996).

[9] There is very little scholarship on the Muslim Mass Contact Programme, a serious gap in a much-mined era of Indian history. See Mushir-ul Hasan (1986).

[10] Jinnah has been well served by recent scholarship that has corrected some of the Congress-nationalist caricatures of him. See, primarily, Wolpert (1984), Jalal (1985), Seervai (1989) and Khair (1995).

[11] It might be said that I too am *redefining* 'nationalism' of an Indian sort that is distinct from nationalism as it emerged first in Europe, so why shouldn't we do the same for 'secularism'? But the term 'nationalism' was not at all uncommon in the period of the freedom struggle (not only in India but in many colonized countries) to describe an inclusive form of anti-imperialism, mobilizing different groups within colonized countries. It is not a new coinage or redefinition on my part. By contrast, 'secularism' was never another term for (what I described above as 'unselfconscious') pluralism, nor for the inclusive forms of nationalism that were based on those pluralisms. It is certainly wilful coinage to call these 'secularism'.

[12] *The Argumentative Indian* (Sen 2005) gathers the essays written earlier in which Sen discusses secularism, identity and other related issues.

[13] I am assuming that groups have a psychological economy. If one were a methodological individualist and wanted to deny this, the point I am making can be accordingly reformulated without any loss of philosophical force.

[14] One way of their coming to be ready for these reforms, one assumes, could be by a process of internal deliberation of the sort that is exemplified in the case I mentioned above, of women in the United States internally deliberating their way to a different view of abortion. One should be careful, however, not to confuse this idea of *internal deliberation* towards the acceptance of state-sponsored reforms with the idea of *internal reform* via intra-community representative institutions that Chatterjee has proposed. Of course, if Muslims were in the future to carry out internal reforms, as he proposes, someone committed to secularism could do nothing but applaud. But the point is that the Hegelian understanding of the Constitution's commitment towards secularism in the matter of Muslim personal law does not require that the reforms *must* come that way. In his paper 'The Anti-Secularist Critique of Hindutva: Problems of a Shared Discursive Space' (Sarkar 1994), Sumit Sarkar mistakenly equates my view with Chatterjee's, because he simply fails to see this basic distinction between inter-

nal deliberation by which someone or some group may acquiesce to a state's demand for reform (the Hegelian reading of the Constitution) with the idea of internal reform of a community (Chatterjee's proposal).

[15] For Irfan Habib, see his contribution to Habib, ed. (2005). For Hamza Alavi, see Alavi (2009).

[16] Most recently in Patnaik (2014), but see also his essays in *Re-Envisioning Socialism* (Patnaik 2011).

References

Alavi, Hamza (2009), 'Misreading Partition Signs', *Economic and Political Weekly,* 2 November.

Bilgrami, Akeel (2010), 'What is Enchantment', in Michael Warner, Craig Calhoun and Jonathan Van Antwerpen, eds, *Varieties of Secularism*, Cambridge, Mass.: Harvard University Press.

Bilgrami, Akeel (2014), 'Secularism: Its Content and Context', in *Secularism, Identity, and Enchantment*, Cambridge, Mass.: Harvard University Press.

Broomfield, J.H. (1968), *Elite Conflict in a Plural Society*, Berkeley: University of California Press.

Chatterjee, Partha (1994), 'Secularism and Toleration', *Economic and Political Weekly*, Vol. XXIX, No. 28, 9 July.

Engels, Dagmar (1996), *Beyond Purdah: Women in Bengal 1890–1939*, Delhi: Oxford University Press.

Gandhi, M.K. (2009), *Hind Swaraj*, Cambridge: Cambridge University Press.

Habib, Irfan, ed. (2005), *India: Studies in the History of an Idea*, Delhi: Munshiram Manoharlal.

Hasan, Mushir-ul (1986), 'The Muslim Mass Contact Campaign: An Attempt at Political Mobilization', *Economic and Political Weekly*, Vol. XXI, No. 52, 27 December.

Jalal, Ayesha (1985), *The Sole Spokesman: Jinnah, The Muslim League, and the Demand for Pakistan*, Cambridge: Cambridge University Press.

Khair, Saad R. (1995), *Jinnah Reinterpreted: The Journey from Indian Nationalism to Muslim Statehood*, Karachi: Oxford University Press.

Nehru, Jawaharlal (1953), *An Autobiography*, Lndon: The Bodley Head.

Nehru, Jawaharlal (2004), *Discovery of India*, fourth edition, New Delhi: Penguin Books.

Pandey, Gyanendra (1984), *The Ascendancy of the Congress in Uttar Pradesh 1926–1934: A Study in Imperfect Mobilization*, Delhi: Oxford University Press.

Patnaik, Prabhat (2011), *Re-Envisioning Socialism*, New Delhi: Tulika Books.

Patnaik, Prabhat (2014), 'Neo-Liberalism and Democracy', *Economic and Political Weekly*, Vol. XLIX, No. 15, 12 April. Ray, Rajat Kanta (1985), *Social Conflict and Political Unrest in Bengal 1875–1927*, Delhi: Oxford University Press.

Sarkar, Sumit (1994), 'The Anti-Secularist Critique of Hindutva: Problems of a Shared Discursive Space', *Germinal*, Vol. I.

Seervai, H.M. (1994), *Partition of India: Legend and Reality*, Bombay: N.M. Tripathi Pvt. Ltd.

Sen, Amartya (2005), *The Argumentative Indian*, New Yok: Farrar, Strauss, and Giroux.

Southard, Barbara (1995), *The Women's Movement and Colonial Politics in Bengal*, Delhi: Manohar.

Taylor, Charles (2008), *A Secular Age*, Cambridge, Mass.: Harvard University Press.

Taylor, Charles (2011), 'Why We Need a Radical Redefinition of Secularism', in Jonathan Van Antwerpen and Eduardo Mendieta, eds, *The Power of Religion in the Public Sphere*, New York: Columbia University Press.

Wolpert, Stanley (1984), *Jinnah of Pakistan*, New York: Oxford University Press.

The Organic Intellectual and the 'Idea of India'

Sitaram Yechury

The present conjuncture in which the international balance of class forces favours imperialism is dominated by newer onslaughts against class struggles seeking the transcendence of capitalism. Imperialism, in its quest to tighten its hegemonic grip, has unleashed an offensive on all fronts. Under its leadership global finance is imposing neo-liberal prescriptions across the world. Through the consequent profit maximization and associated intensification of exploitation of the working people, it is seeking to bypass the current continuing global capitalist economic crisis. The Indian ruling class, earning the sanction of international finance by implementing such dictates, is reducing its role to that of a junior partner of imperialism in all major aspects. This has unleashed a new wave of 'primitive accumulation' both globally and domestically. Of course, popular people's resistance is growing. But it is mainly defensive in nature, i.e. safeguarding existing rights and livelihood levels from further erosion. This is manifesting itself in electoral outcomes, mainly in the countries of Latin America. However, nowhere in the capitalist world has such resistance reached levels that permit mounting a class offensive capable of overthrowing the rule of capital.

The Indian state, under the current RSS–BJP (Rashtriya Swayamsevak Sangh – Bharatiya Janata Party) leadership, is institutionalizing a pronounced rightward shift in Indian politics. Thus, neo-liberal economic policies and an energized communal polarization combine to mount an all-round offensive. Ideologically, the objective is to replace India's rich syncretic civilizational history with Hindu mythology, and Indian philosophical traditions with Hindu theology. This, in the main, seeks to negate the very 'idea of India' as it evolved and manifested in the epic struggle of the Indian people for independence. These processes seek to undermine the modern Indian Republic, on the foundations of which the class struggles in India advance towards achieving the goal of a revolutionary transformation. A larger army of 'organic intellectuals' to hasten the realization of the 'idea of India' is thus integral for advancing class struggles in India in the 'concrete conditions' of our times. The need, in the final analysis, is to sharpen and strengthen the revolutionary weapon of social change. 'Is it not a fact', Lenin had asked, 'that the task of theory, the aim of science, is here defined as assistance for the oppressed class in its actual struggle' (Lenin 1977: 327–28).

I

Antonio Gramsci once remarked, 'all men are intellectuals, one could therefore say: but not all men have in society the function of intellectuals'. He elaborated 'this function of intellectuals' in the context of the revolutionary advance as developing an intimate relationship between the revolutionary working class movement and progressive intellectuals. The rise of intellectuals who are organic to the working class and those thrown up by other classes, but having internalized the Marxist world view, are an integral part of the revolutionary working class movement. Such organic intellectuals can never be 'made to order' but are created on the 'original terrain of an essential function in the world of economic production'. Gramsci was, of course, systematizing the observations of Marx and Engels, advanced later by Lenin and Mao Zedong, that the working class in the discharge of its historic task of overthrowing the bourgeoisie and transcending capitalism can do this only by combining its struggles on the economic, political and theoretical fronts. Without the creation of such an all-encompassing counter-hegemony to replace the ruling-class hegemony, the transcendence of capitalism cannot succeed.

Marx and Engels had said:

> The ideas of the ruling class are in every epoch, the ruling ideas: i.e., the class which is the ruling material force of society is at the same time its ruling intellectual force. The class which has the means of material production at its disposal, consequently also controls the means of mental production so that the ideas of those who lack the means of mental production are on the whole subject to it. The individuals composing the ruling class possess among other things, consciousness and therefore think. In so far therefore, as they rule as a class and determine the extent and compass of an historical epoch, it is self-evident that they do this in its whole range, hence among other things rule also as thinkers, as producers of ideas, and *regulate the production and distribution of the ideas of their age*; thus their ideas are the ruling ideas of the epoch. (Marx and Engels 1976: 67; emphasis added)

This hegemony of the 'ideas' of the ruling classes, Gramsci explains, is not enforced merely by the state. The state is only the 'outer ditch' behind which stands a powerful system of 'fortresses and earth works', a network of cultural institutions and values which buttress the domination of the ruling classes.

This hegemony is mediated and transmitted through a complex web of social relations and the consequent social structures. The family, the community, caste, religion, its places of worship like temples, churches, mosques, gurudwaras, etc., are the institutions that constantly provide the fodder to shape values and opinions bolstering the hegemony of 'ideas' of the ruling class. In the process, they create the 'myth' of a 'common culture'. This 'common culture' is nothing but the selective transmission of class-dominated values passed off as 'common sense'.

Organic intellectuals catalyse the revolutionary movement through the language of culture of the times, the feelings and experiences of which the revolutionary classes themselves may not and often cannot muster. The creation of such a counter-hegemony over society, through the creation of a 'new culture' embracing not only the relations of production but also the state (political society) and civil society, is essential for successful revolutionary transformation. Such organic intellectuals in our times, while actively participating in practical life, create precisely such a counter-hegemony to undermine existing social relations. They are thus the essential components of generating ideas which, as Marx once said, 'become a material force as soon as it has gripped the masses' (Marx and Engels 1975: 182).

Such is the role of the 'modern Prince', as Gramsci calls the organic intellectual of our times, drawing upon the symbolism of Machiavelli's classic work. It is by embracing the philosophy of praxis that the 'modern Prince' plays this crucial role in the process of social transformation. There has been much debate on why Gramsci should have described Marxist philosophy as the philosophy of praxis. Often it is suggested that this was done to bypass the censorship of those times. However, Gramsci titled the next section of his *Notes* as 'Problems of Marxism'! He was, of course, making an important point. Adopting a term used by Antonio Labriola (in nineteenth-century Italy) to describe Marxism as the philosophy of praxis, Gramsci underlined that Marxism is a synthesis of theory and practice, without presuming the primacy of either.

For sure, Gramsci was only extending what Marx had said in his *Theses on Feuerbach* (1845): 'Philosophers have only interpreted the world in various ways; the point is to change it.' And what Lenin wrote in *What is to be Done?* (1901–02): 'Without revolutionary theory, there can be no revolutionary movement.' Mao Zedong had similarly elaborated – in his work, *On Practice* (1937) – the unending process of refining theory through practice and then taking it back to the people. This is the only manner in which application of the inviolable Leninist principle, that 'concrete analysis of concrete conditions is the living essence of dialectics', can take place.

Gramsci locates the role of the intellectual in the first section of his *Notes*, while discussing the problems of history and culture. This location is significant. Culture, as a manifestation of the overall hegemony of the ruling classes, is the terrain for the growth of organic intellectuals and the counter-hegemony that they generate encompassing the totality of human existence – the human essence.

Marx, again:

> If man's *feelings*, passions, etc., are not merely anthropological phenomena in the [narrower or limited] sense, but truly *ontological* affirmations of essential being (of nature), and if they are only really affirmed because their *object* exists for them as an object of *sense*, then it is clear: That they have by no means merely one mode of affirmation, but rather that the distinctive character of their existence, of their life, is constituted by the distinctive mode of their affirmation. In what manner the object exists for them, is the characteristic mode of their *gratification*. (Marx [1959] 1993: 127, 128)

Multiple modes of such gratification find expression in sensuous affirmation, feelings, behaviour, enjoyment, etc. Such modes of gratification also include the negation of the intellectual 'objects' produced by ruling-class hegemony by positing the elements of 'counter-culture'. By doing so, organic intellectuals erect the structures of counter-hegemony. The totality of such affirmations, i.e. the totality of the multiple modes of human gratification, finds expression in all forms of creative activity – the totality of which, in turn, constitutes what we can call the counter-'culture' of the revolutionary movement.

Such culture is always based on the material conditions of existence. Production not only provides the material to satisfy a need, but it also provides the need for the material. Marx, writing on production and consumption, stated:

> Production not only supplies a material for the need, but it also supplies a need for the material. As soon as consumption emerges from its initial state of natural crudity and immediacy – and, if it remained at that stage, this would be because production itself had been arrested there – it becomes itself mediated as a drive by the object. The need which consumption feels for the object is created by the perception of

> it. The object of art – like every other product – creates a public which is sensitive to art and enjoys beauty. *Production thus not only creates an object for the subject, but also a subject for the object.* Thus production produces consumption (1) by creating the material for it; (2) by determining the manner of consumption; and (3) by creating the products, initially posited by it as objects, in the form of a need felt by the consumer. It thus produces the object of consumption, the manner of consumption and the motive of consumption. (Marx 1987: 92)

This is as true for intellectual products as it is for material products. Capitalism inevitably produces its own 'grave diggers'.

II

Seen in the current Indian conjuncture, the intellectual products thrown up in response to this very conjuncture generate the organic intellectuals of our times. In our current context, the creation of a counter-hegemony is integrally connected with the defence and further realization of the 'idea of India'.

This 'idea of India' emerged during the epic people's struggle for India's freedom from British colonialism. *What is this 'idea of India'?* To put it in simple terms, though conscious of its complex multiple dimensions (all of which together contribute to the creation of the counter-hegemony), this concept represents the idea that India as a country moves towards transcending its diversities and divisions in favour of a substantially inclusive unity of its people.

Akeel Bilgrami, in his introduction to a volume of essays containing revised versions of lectures on the relations between politics and political economy in India, given at a seminar in 2010 (at the Heyman Centre for the Humanities at Columbia University, New York, a centre that he chaired then), says the following about my observations on the idea of India:

> [This] might be viewed as an ideal of a nation that rejects the entire trajectory in Europe that emerged after the Westphalian peace [negotiated between 1644–48 between major European powers. These treaties laid the basis for the emergence of nation-states; the concept of sovereignty and a host of international laws many of which remain in force today]. What emerged then (and there) was a compulsion to seek legitimacy for a new kind of state, one that could no longer appeal to older notions of the 'divine right' of states personified in their monarchs. It sought this legitimacy in a new form of political psychology of a new kind of subject, the 'citizen', a psychology based on a *feeling* for a new form of entity that had emerged, the 'nation'. This feeling, which came to be

> called 'nationalism', had to be generated in the populace of citizens, and the standard process that was adopted in Europe for generating it was to find an *external* enemy *within*, the outsider, the 'other' in one's midst (the Irish, the Jews, to name just two), to be despised and subjugated. In a somewhat later time, with the addition of a more numerical and statistical form of discourse, these came to be called 'minorities' and the method by which this feeling for the nation was created came to be called 'majoritarianism'. (Bilgrami 2011: 1–2)

The RSS–BJP objective of replacing the secular democratic modern Indian Republic with their concept of a 'Hindu *rashtra*' is, in a sense, a *throwback* to the Westphalian model where the Hindu majority subjugates other religious minorities (mainly Muslim: the *external* enemy *within*) to foster 'Hindu nationalism' as against 'Indian nationhood'. This, in fact, represents a *throwback* to notions of nationalism that dominated the intellectual discourse prior to the sweep of the Indian people's struggle for freedom. Such a state, based on 'majoritarianism' – their version of a rabidly intolerant, fascistic 'Hindu *rashtra*' – negates the core around which emerged the consciousness of Indian nationhood contained in the 'idea of India' as a reflection of the emergence of 'a political psychology of a new kind'.

The RSS–BJP ideologues dismiss the 'idea of India' as a mere idea, a metaphysical concept. The RSS–BJP today are spearheading the most reactionary 'throwback' to Indian (Hindu) nationalism as against the idea of Indian nationhood (the 'idea of India') that emerged from the epic people's struggle for freedom from British colonial rule. Bilgrami captures this as follows: 'The prodigious and sustained mobilization of its masses that India witnessed over the last three crucial decades of the freedom struggle could not have been possible without an alternative and *inclusionary* ideal of this kind to inspire it' (Bilgrami 2011: 2).

India's diversity – linguistic, religious, ethnic, cultural, etc. – is incomparably vaster than that of any other country the world knows of. Officially, it has been recorded that there are at least 1,618 languages in India, 6,400 castes; six major religions (four of which originated in this land), six anthropologically defined ethnic groups – all put together to be politically administered. A measure of this diversity is that India celebrates twenty-nine major religio-cultural festivals and probably has the largest number of religious holidays amongst all the countries of the world.

Those who argue that it was the British that united this vast diversity ignore the fact that it was the British that engineered the partition of the subcontinent, leading to over a million deaths and communal transmigration of a colossal order. British colonialism has the ignominious history of leaving behind legacies that continued to fester as wounds through the partition of the countries they had colonized – Palestine, Cyprus, in Africa, etc., apart from the Indian subcontinent. It was the pan-Indian people's struggle for freedom that united this diversity and integrated more than 660 feudal princely states into modern India, giving shape to a pan-Indian consciousness. The Indian Left played an important role in the evolution of this 'idea of India'. Indeed, for this very reason, given its visionary commitments to the long struggle for freedom, the Left's role is absolutely central to the realization of the 'idea of India' in today's conditions.

Let me illustrate this with reference to three issues that continue to constitute the core of the idea of India. The struggles on the land question unleashed by the communists in various parts of the country in the last century – Punnapra Vayalar in Kerala, the Tebagha movement in Bengal, the Surma Valley struggle in Assam, the Warli uprising in Maharashtra, and the most important among them, the armed uprising in Telengana – brought the issue of land reform to centre-stage. The consequent abolition of the zamindari system and landed estates drew the vast mass of India's peasantry into the project of building the 'idea of India'. In fact, such struggles contributed the most in liberating crores of people from feudal bondage. This also contributed substantially towards creating the 'Indian middle class'.

Secondly, the Indian Left spearheaded massive popular struggles for the linguistic reorganization of the states in independent India. It is thus chiefly responsible for creating the political 'map' of today's India on reasonably scientific and democratic lines. The struggles for Vishalandhra, Aikya Keralam and Samyukta Maharashtra were led, amongst others, by individuals who later emerged as communist stalwarts in the country. This paved the way for the integration of many linguistic nationalities that inhabit India, on the basis of equality, into the process of realizing the 'idea of India'.

Thirdly, the Left's steadfast commitment to secularism was based on a recognition of India's reality. The unity of India with its immense diversity can be maintained only by strengthening the bonds of commonality in this diversity, and not by imposing any uniformity upon this diversity as the communal forces currently seek to do. While this is true for all attributes of India's social life, it is of critical importance in relation to religion. Following the partition of India and the horrendous communal aftermath, secularism became crucial for the realization of the idea of India. The Indian ruling classes, however, went only half-way in meeting the Left's objective of defining secularism as the separation of religion from politics. This means that while the state protects the individual's choice of faith, it shall not profess or prefer any one religion. In practice, the Indian ruling classes have reduced this to define secularism as equality of all religions. Inherent in this is an in-built bias towards the religious faith of the majority. This, in fact, contributes to providing sustenance to the communal and fundamentalist forces today.

These are illustrative of some of the constituents of the 'idea of India'. The drawing-in of the exploited majority of rural India; the drawing-in of the numerous linguistic nationalities; the drawing-in of the multi-religious Indian population; and, above all, the drawing-in of all Indians on an inclusive path of economic and social justice, constituting the core of the inclusionary 'idea of India', remains an unfulfilled agenda. The struggles for realizing these incomplete tasks constitute the essential ingredients for the creation of the 'counter-hegemony' of the working class-led movement.

Battle of Visions

The concept of the idea of India arose from a continuous battle between three visions that emerged during the course of India's struggle for freedom in the 1920s, on the conception of the character of independent India. The mainstream Congress vision had articulated that independent India should be a secular, democratic Republic. The Left, while agreeing with this objective, went further to envision that the political freedom of the country must be extended to achieve the socio-economic freedom of every individual, which would be possible only under socialism.

Antagonistic to both these was a third vision, which argued that the character of independent India should be defined by the religious affiliations of its people. This vision had a twin expression: the Muslim League championing an 'Islamic state' and the RSS championing a 'Hindu *rashtra*'. The former succeeded in ensuring the unfortunate partition of the country, admirably engineered, aided and abetted by the British colonial rulers, with all its consequences that continue to foster tensions till date. The latter, having failed to achieve their objective at the time of independence, continue with their efforts to transform modern India into their project of a rabidly intolerant, fascistic 'Hindu *rashtra*'. In a sense, the ideological battles and political conflicts in contemporary India are a continuation of the battle between these three visions. Needless to add, the contours of this battle will continue to define the direction and content of the process of realization of the 'idea of India'.

Further, the Indian Left argued then, and maintains today, that the mainstream Congress vision of consolidating the secular, democratic foundations of our republic can never be sustainable unless independent India frees itself from its bondage to imperialism and breaks the stranglehold of feudal vestiges. The Congress party's inability to take the freedom struggle to this logical culmination became clear from its serving the interests of the post-independence ruling classes – the bourgeoisie in alliance with the landlords, led by the big bourgeoisie. This, by itself, weakens the foundations of a secular, democratic republic. First, it relegates the anti-imperialist social consciousness that forged the unity of the people during the freedom struggle to the background. Secondly, instead of strengthening an *inclusive* India, it progressively *excludes* the growing majority of the exploited classes. This has been convincingly vindicated by our experience during the last six decades of independence. That experience provides 'grist to the mill' of the communal forces, or the third vision, to strengthen itself by exploiting the growing popular discontent against the policies pursued by the ruling classes.

Mere declaration of the creation of a secular, democratic republic and its reassertion by the Congress today, by definition, are inadequate to realize in full the inclusive 'idea of India'. There is another equally important factor that prevents the realization of the 'idea of India'. The inability to eliminate the vestiges of feudalism results, at the level of the superstructure, in the perpetuation of the social consciousness associated with feudalism and other pre-capitalist formations. The domination of religion and caste, integral to the social consciousness of pre-capitalist formations, continue to be powerful in today's social order. The efforts at superimposing capitalism only create a situation where the backwardness of consciousness associated with feudal vestiges is combined with the degenerative 'consumerism' of today's globalized capitalist consciousness.

The Caste Factor

The process of class formation in India, as a consequence of such circumscribed capitalist development, is taking place within the parameters of historically inherited structures of a caste-divided society. It is taking place not by overthrowing pre-capitalist social relations but in compromise with these. This results in an overlapping commonality between the exploited classes and the oppressed castes in contemporary India. Class struggle in India, therefore, can advance only through simultaneous struggles against both economic exploitation and social oppression.

Thus, at the level of the superstructure, feudal decadence is combined with capitalist degeneration to produce a situation where growing criminalization of the society coexists and grows in tandem with such social consciousness dominated by caste and communal feelings. Instead of overcoming such consciousness for the realization of the 'idea of India', it is exploited by the ruling classes for their political-electoral benefits.

Such a reality provides the fertile ground that engenders the current rightward shift in Indian politics, buttressing the efforts for negation of the 'idea of India' and the erection of a 'Hindu *rashtra*' in its place.

III

There are some not-so-obvious aspects of the culture of 'Hindutva', products of this rightward shift in Indian politics, that are emerging in the terrain of ruling-class cultural hegemony in the present Indian context, that merit attention.

Modernity vs. Modernoxity

Modern society is often defined as a society 'characterized by an attitude of equality with, and respect for, others'. It is not as if in a modern society all are actually equal. Yet, in spite of the many differences that exist among people, modernity demands a baseline equality so that people can live with dignity and can realistically avail of opportunities to better their conditions of existence. It is on this bedrock of equality that other differences and inequalities are superimposed. But such foundational equality cannot be compromised, for it is on this that claims of citizenship are made in modern societies. In feudal orders, there were rulers and subjects, but no citizens.

An Iranian intellectual, Jalal-e-Ahmad, coined the term 'westoxication', as opposed to 'westernization', in the context of the Ayatollah Khomeini-led Iranian revolution, when the Iranian elite returned from exile in Western Europe flashing branded fashion wear and advanced gadgets. With due apologies, I wish to extend this, in the Indian context, as *modernity vs. modernoxity*. Intoxication with modern consumerist displays of the latest commodities and gadgets is equated with modernity. This has become India's symbol of an 'emerging economy' rubbing shoulders with the developed countries at the G-20 high table. A mere glance through the matrimonial columns of our newspapers will show us how the most modern sections of our society, including NRIs (non-resident Indians) who have never stepped on Indian soil, seek marital alliances in their sub-castes. Those who scrupulously respect the law in western countries are the most eager to violate the law in India. Such is the culture of modernoxity, not modernity. This admirably buttresses the rightward political shift.

India's march towards modernity is being subverted not merely by the tenacity of past institutions – caste-based social oppression, the patriarchical order, *khap panchayats*, unequal treatment of religious minorities, etc. These are kept alive and buttressed by the values of neo-liberal consumerism (modernoxity), which include treating women as objects of display and not as human beings. These are also strengthened by the widespread opportunism inherent in our electoral system whereby all the unjust and unequal features of our social order are reinvigorated for electoral gains. Thus, there appears to be no contradiction when people wearing the most 'modern', fashionable branded clothes and brandishing 'modern' technological gadgets indulge in these practices that ought to be consigned as anachronistic in a modern democracy.

'Modernity' defined as the equality of all citizens, irrespective of 'caste, creed or sex', as the Indian Constitution guarantees, is thus an inalienable component of the culture that is essential for establishing the counter-hegemony of the revolutionary movement.

Cultural Industry

Alongside the tremendous concentration of wealth and assets, this trajectory of neo-liberal reforms engenders the growth of a cultural industry. Globally, institutions formed through the merger of Information, Communications and Entertainment corporations (ICE) control the bulk of the world's production and distribution of goods and services, seeking to convert the world into a single, global cultural market.

The cultural hegemony that such a process seeks is expressed in the need to create a homogenization of public taste. The more homogenous the taste, the easier it is to develop technologies for the mechanical reproduction of 'cultural products' for the masses at large. In many third world countries (confirmed by surveys in Sub Saharan Africa), illiteracy may be rampant but images of Walt Disney cartoon characters are familiar to children!

Viewed in terms of class hegemony, the culture of neo-liberalism seeks to divorce people from the actual realities of their day-to-day life. Culture here acts not as an appeal to the aesthetic but as a distraction, a diversion, from the pressing problems of poverty and misery. Consequently, it seeks to disrupt the energy of the people and their struggles to change their miserable existence. Michael Parenti says:

> A far greater part of our culture is now aptly designated as 'mass culture', 'popular culture', and even 'media culture', owned and operated mostly by giant corporations whose major objective is to accumulate wealth and make the world safe for their owners, the goal being exchange value rather than use value, social control rather than social creativity. Much of mass culture is organized to distract us from thinking too much about

> larger realities. The fluff and puffery of entertainment culture crowds out more urgent and nourishing things. By constantly appealing to the lowest common denominator, a sensationalist popular culture lowers the common denominator still further. Public tastes become still more attuned to cultural junk food, big hype, and trashy, flashy, wildly violent, instantly stimulating, and desperately superficial offerings.
>
> Such fare often has real ideological content. Even if supposedly apolitical in its intent, entertainment culture (which is really the entertainment *industry*) is political in its impact, propagating images and values that are often downright sexist, racist, consumerist, authoritarian, militaristic, and imperialist. (Parenti 1999: 13)

Thus both neo-liberalism and communalism, domestically, seek the homogenization of public tastes: the former to strengthen its cultural hegemony and to reap superprofits; the latter, in addition to this, to pave the way for the establishment of a rabidly intolerant theocratic state – the RSS vision of a 'Hindu *rashtra*'. Its slogan of 'one country, one people, one culture' can acquire a real status and meaning only through such homogenization negating the very fundamental foundations of India's rich cultural diversity. Further, both neo-liberalism and communalism seek to divert the attention of the people away from day-to-day problems and, importantly, weaken their struggle against the existing exploitative order.

The struggles for establishing the 'counter-hegemony' of the working class thus need to bring back on to the cultural agenda people's issues, the obfuscation and erasure of which is the *raison d'être* of the culture of neo-liberalism and communalism.

Objective conditions for the overthrow of capitalism are periodically created. Major capitalist crises, however, need to be converted into revolutionary situations. This requires, as Lenin described, the 'subjective factor' – the revolutionary movement led by the party of the working class – ripening to mount the political offensive for the overthrow of the bourgeoisie; in other words, the force that can utilize the very 'objects' created by capitalism to mount the revolutionary offensive. Organic intellectuals, by creating the culture of counter-hegemony as a component of this revolutionary movement, motivate the 'subject' to acquire capabilities for utilizing these 'objects' to overthrow the bourgeoisie.

IV

Fascism?

Does all this point to the emergence of fascism in India? The most authoritative and to date scientific analysis of the nature and emergence of fascism was made by Georgi Dimitrov in his penetrating address to the Seventh Communist International in 1935. He defined fascism as the 'open terroristic dictatorship of the most reactionary, most chauvinistic and most imperialistic elements of finance capital'. The capturing of state power by fascism is not an ordinary succession of one bourgeois government by another but the substitution of one form of the ruling-class state by another – bourgeois parliamentary democracy by an openly terroristic dictatorship.

This came as a response, in Europe, of the ruling classes to the actual crisis that threatened its class domination. This was the case with German monopoly capital in the period preceding Hitlerite fascism. This threat emerged as a consequence of the crisis generated by the ruling classes' own rule, both from within its own camp as well as, and often simultaneously, with the challenge to its class rule by the toiling sections of the working people – the proletariat.

The situation obtaining in India today is not similar to the period leading to the emergence of fascism in Germany. The threat of immediate seizure of power by the proletariat is not yet on the agenda, on such a scale. Further, the crisis of the bourgeois–landlord class rule has not reached a stage where the jettisoning of parliamentary democracy by the ruling classes is on the immediate agenda.

Hence, the assumption of power by the RSS-led BJP does not mean the establishment of fascism in its classical sense. Undoubtedly, the RSS vision of a 'Hindu *rashtra*' is a fascistic vision. If the RSS *does succeed* in realizing this vision, then it would be a qualitatively different situation. That, however, is a *situation* that the revolutionary forces work towards rendering unrealizable. The present situation, therefore, can be more appropriately described by the fact that the crisis of the bourgeois–landlord class rule has reached a stage where one section of the ruling classes, the most reactionary section, represented by the RSS–BJP and the 'Saffron Brigade', has succeeded in capturing state power for the moment.

However, there are striking similarities in the propaganda methods employed by European fascism and the RSS. The RSS–BJP today adopt fascistic methods of appropriation of popular symbols, create a false consciousness of deprivation amongst the majority community and appeal to extreme jingoism as their methods to advance. Dimitrov had said, 'Fascism acts in the interests of extreme imperialists but presents itself to the masses in the guise of a wronged nation and appeals to outraged "national" sentiments.' In order to present the RSS as such a champion, a false consciousness is created that the Hindus had been and continue to be deprived, while, at the same time, generating hate against the Muslims (taking a cue from Hitler's rabid anti-Semitism) to the effect that they are responsible for such 'deprivation' of the Hindus. To achieve its goal of a 'Hindu *rashtra*', the RSS has perfected the Goebbelsian technique of 'telling big enough lies frequently enough to make them appear as the truth'.

Dimitrov could well have been talking about the RSS–BJP's current campaigns and the people's experiences with its control of the state since the 2014 general elections in India. This shows a chilling convergence with the fascist methodology. Importantly, this strengthens the grip of ruling-class hegemony, which requires to be urgently confronted.

V

Finally, a word of caution. Concluding a discussion on these issues is, in any case, not possible. Such discussion is, and should be, a continuum, at least until the decisive emergence of the 'counter-hegemony'.

The effectiveness of the organic intellectual crucially depends on not falling prey to 'subjectivism'. This, I believe, is of critical importance. Lenin, while discussing Kant's philosophical positions in his writing, 'Conspectus of Hegel's Science of Logic', notes the need to struggle against subjectivism, i.e. of taking 'up the data of experience one-sidedly'. Lenin says:

> . . . by proposing and taking as valid experience not in its concrete totality but as example, and only in that direction which is serviceable for the hypotheses and the theory. Concrete experience being thus subordinated to the presupposed determinations, the foundation of the theory is obscured, and is exhibited only from that side which is in conformity with the theory. (Lenin 1965: 210)

The need to combat subjectivism in revolutionary praxis is an important element in Lenin's struggles against all sorts of deviations in the working class movement. In fact, the very concept of the stages of the revolution that Lenin theoretically postulated arose from an objective study of the concrete situation. In his 'Letters on Tactics', on combating class deviations within the Russian revolutionary movement, he says: 'But are we not in danger of falling into subjectivism, of wanting to arrive at the socialist revolution by "skipping" the bourgeois-democratic revolution – which is not yet completed and has not yet exhausted the peasant movement?' (Lenin 1964: 48)

In his work on 'Objective Data on the Strength of the Various Trends in the Working Class Movement', combating both Plekhanov and Trotsky's subjectivism, he says: 'At every step they try to pass off their desires, their views, their appraisals of the situation and their plans as the will of the workers, the needs of the working class movement' (Lenin 1972: 382).

During the course of the Chinese revolution, Mao Zedong had initiated a big campaign to combat subjectivism inside the Communist Party of China and all its organs. He characterized subjectivism as a method of thinking in all party bodies which 'questions our attitude towards Marxism–Leninism, of the attitude of all party comrades in their work. As such, it is the question of extraordinary, indeed of primary importance.'

A 'concrete analysis of concrete conditions' can only be possible if the concrete situation is properly comprehended. Incorrect estimations of the concrete situation – underestimations or overestimations – will render all consequent 'concrete analysis' useless. Similarly, an incorrect 'concrete analysis' renders even a correct estimation of the 'concrete conditions' redundant.

Lenin needs to be invoked once again.

> The irresistible attraction of this theory (Marxism), which draws to itself the socialists of all countries lies precisely in the fact that it combines the quality of being strictly and supremely scientific (being the last word in social sciences) with that of being revolutionary, it does not combine them accidentally and not only because the founder of the doctrine combined in his own person the qualities of a scientist and a revolutionary, but does so intrinsically and inseparably. (Lenin 1960: 327)

Organic intellectuals, who catalyse and galvanize the revolutionary struggles led by the working class, are practitioners of the philosophy of praxis – politics as philosophy, philosophy as politics – in erecting the counter-hegemony to challenge the hegemony of the ruling classes. In the current Indian conjuncture, the struggle to comprehensively realize the 'idea of India' is an important contribution towards effectively building such a counter-hegemony.

The working class, along with all other exploited classes and strata of the Indian people, looks forward to the emergence of a larger army of organic intellectuals, which is so very essential for transcending capitalism. Marx once described 'modern society' (capitalism) simply in the following words: 'There must be something rotten in the very core of a social system which increases its wealth without diminishing its misery.'

Postscript: This discussion, if it has not become obvious by now, is a recognition, with gratitude, by the Indian communist movement, of the continuing work and contribution of Prabhat Patnaik in this direction.

References

Bilgrami, Akeel (2011), 'Introduction', *Social Scientist*, Vol. 39, Nos. 1–2, January–February.
Lenin, V.I. (1960), *Collected Works*, Vol. 1, Moscow: Progress Publishers.
Lenin, V.I. (1964), 'Letters on Tactics', in *Collected Works*, Vol. 24, Moscow: Progress Publishers.
Lenin, V.I. (1965), *Philosophical Notebooks*, in *Collected Works*, Vol. 38, Moscow: Progress Publishers.
Lenin, V.I. (1972), 'Objective Data on the Strength of the Various Trends in the Working Class Movement', in *Collected Works,* Vol. 20, Moscow: Progress Publishers.
Lenin, V.I. (1977), *Collected Works*, Vol. 1, Moscow: Progress Publishers.
Marx, Karl and Frederick Engels (1975), *Collected Works*, Vol. 3, Moscow: Progress Publishers.
Marx, Karl and Friedrich Engels (1976), *The German Ideology*, Moscow: Progress Publishers.
Marx, Karl (1987), *Grundrisse: Outlines of the Critique of Political Economy*, in Karl Marx and Friedrich Engels, *Collected Works*, Vol. 29, Moscow: Progress Publishers, 1987.
Marx, Karl ([1959] 1993), *Economic and Philosophic Manuscripts, 1844*, Moscow: Progress Publishers; reprint, Calcutta: National Book Agency.
Parenti, Michael (1999), 'Reflections on the Politics of Culture', *Monthly Review*, Vol. 50, No. 9, February.

Nehru, Planning and India's 'Socialistic Pattern'

C.P. Chandrasekhar

For reasons right or wrong, the strategy of economic development that the Indian government espoused in the immediate aftermath of independence and till the late 1960s has been attributed to Jawaharlal Nehru. In fact, the economic policy framework that was put in place during the 1950s and 1960s is often referred to as the 'Nehruvian strategy'. While many of the ideas that were incorporated into post-independence policy documents had been discussed within and outside the Congress well before independence, Nehru is seen to have played a central role in those discussions and taken forward the conclusions he derived from them once he was given control of the reins of the post-independence government.

Given the character of the Congress that brought together sections with very different interests and ideological inclinations, united by a common desire for independence from British rule, it was to be expected that when Nehru helped formulate positions or the government under him its policies, he had to accommodate the views of and make compromises with the different sections. Nehru was quite conscious of this pressure to compromise. Justifying such compromise, he argued that he 'felt that, bourgeois as the outlook of the Indian National Congress was, it did represent the only effective revolutionary force in the country. As such, Labour ought to help it and cooperate with it and influence it, keeping, however, its own identity and ideology distinct and intact.' And, he 'hoped that the course of events and the participation in direct action would inevitably drive the Congress to a more radical ideology and to face social and economic issues' (Nehru 1982: 198).

But judged by the rhetoric of the Congress, Nehru seems to have often had his way, even before independence. So, the attribution of the post-independence strategy specifically to Nehru is also partly the result of knowledge that many senior leaders in the Congress, including Gandhi, neither espoused such views to the extent that they laid out an economic strategy, nor were fully persuaded by Nehru that this was the best way to go. This is significant because, though broadly similar to the import substitution strategies of development adopted by many other underdeveloped countries of that period, the Indian strategy was seen as distinctive. The reference to a Nehruvian strategy was also a recognition of that distinctiveness.

Unlike what is implicitly suggested or explicitly stated by some, this distinctiveness did not stem from the role it gave the state as a leading player in development, both as an agent influencing private decisions and regulating private activity, and as a direct participant in economic activity. The framework of a mixed economy in which the private sector had an important role to play, but state presence was crucial, was a characteristic of most late developers, including many that are now listed among the developed market economies.

The crux of the issue here is the interpretation of the rhetorical commitment to a 'socialistic pattern', on the one hand, and 'planned development', on the other. If the defining features of the post-independence strategy were only a commitment to an important role for the state as a regulator and a facilitator of development, and to a more egalitarian path of development than what an unregulated market economy would deliver, it would imply that the Congress and Nehru were using the terms 'planning' and 'socialism' in ways stripped of substance. Socialism was not seen as a system characterized by full or overwhelmingly dominant public ownership, but as a welfare regime that places emphasis on minimizing asset and income inequalities and takes account of long-run social costs and benefits, rather than just private profit, when allocating investments. Within that framework, the role of 'planning' would be to identify the volume of investments and the appropriate investments to be made, and to find ways of nudging private investments into or ensuring public investment in areas that ensured realization of the government's welfare objectives.

If this is the way in which India's post-independence development agenda is read, it is by no means all that distinctive. Governments have to intervene in some fashion in all capitalist economies, and different governments have some, even if widely varying, degrees of commitment to redressing income inequalities and addressing the worst forms of deprivation. That is required not just to ensure social stability and political legitimacy, but also to facilitate capitalist development. It was not surprising, therefore, that when India's leading industrialists, who had some influence on the Congress and the national movement, came together in 1944 to formulate the 'Bombay Plan', delineating the strategy that must be adopted by a post-independence government, they argued in favour of a substantial role for the state.

But there was more to the Nehruvian strategy. To start with, on more than one occasion, the impression conveyed was that the post-independence government would ensure gradual encroachment of the state, through ownership, into newer domains and to those providing control over the 'commanding heights' of the Indian economy. The *Report of the Economic Programme Committee* of the All India Congress Committee (AICC), chaired by Nehru, which was released in 1948, argued that new undertakings in 'defence, key and public utility industries', and in units that 'are in the nature of monopolies' or 'which serve the country as a whole or cover more than one province', should be started under public ownership. Moreover wherever large-scale industries competed with cottage or small-scale industries (which were 'for the most part to be responsible for production of food articles, clothing and consumer goods'), they were to be brought under state control. In addition, existing undertakings in areas reserved for the state were to be brought under public ownership after five years. This amounted to widening the area of operation of the public sector hugely, including into consumption goods production. The *Report* was immediately and strongly opposed by Indian business, and by the time of the Industrial Policy Resolution of 1948, the Congress's position was considerably diluted. But there was a case being made for public ownership in areas other than those that were typically state-owned among the late industrializers: those characterized by lumpy investments and long gestation lags, which the private sector would avoid; or those that were prone to 'natural monopolies', which the private sector should be kept out of.

Secondly, starting well before independence, this case for wide public ownership was combined with an emphasis on 'planning' for successful economic development, along lines being pursued at that time in the Soviet Union. Among other things, this view led to: (i) the creation of a powerful Planning Commission that functioned directly under the Prime Minister; (ii) the adoption of a policy of putting in the public domain a series of 'prior' five year plans, which underlined the emphasis, defined the targets and discussed the means to be adopted to achieve those targets over a definite time-period; and, above all, (iii) the adoption of the Mahalanobis model as the conceptual underpinning for deciding the pattern of investment allocation during and after the Second Five Year Plan.

The Mahalanobis model suggested that despite India's low level of aggregate and per capita consumption, the government must not only seek to raise the rate of investment in the economy, which for any given level of the incremental output–capital ratio is a prerequisite for raising the rate of growth, but also (to achieve this) hike the share of investment allocated to the investment goods sector. A sacrifice in terms of the consumption goods made available in the short run, in order to produce machines that can enlarge the volume of consumption goods production in the future, was seen as yielding more benefit in the medium or long term. Given India's low level of consumption and production of consumption goods, this argument seemed counter-intuitive to some. The result was based on an assessment that India's potential for exporting goods to finance imports of machines was limited, so that any attempt at accelerating growth without creating more machine-producing capacity would result in balance of payments difficulties that undermine growth. That made the inadequate domestic production and availability of capital goods the basic constraint on India's development.

Pursuing a strategy informed by this insight was not an easy task in an economy where incomes accrued in substantial measure to agents in the private sector. These private agents would make decisions with regard to how much to consume and save. So, measures had to be devised to restrict consumption (through taxes or rationing) to levels that released adequate resources for the investment plan. And instruments had to be devised that would direct the resulting savings to the chosen areas of production, especially in investment and basic goods. Left to themselves, private investors would be more interested in investing in more lucrative consumption goods industries, especially those catering to the upper-income groups. The state had to find ways of influencing the allocation of income between consumption and savings, and the allocation of investment across sectors.

The similarity of the Mahalanobis model to the Feldman model from the Soviet Union of the late 1920s, depicting how growth can be accelerated in an economy with very different institutional conditions, especially with respect to public ownership, but subject to 'capitalist encirclement', gave India's effort at planning the reputation that it was more than the 'indicative planning' prevalent in some market economies.

Thus, there are two ways in which the so-called Nehruvian strategy can be seen as distinctive. The first is that its idea of a 'socialistic pattern' went beyond measures aimed at redressing income inequality, improving welfare and delivering social justice, to a consideration of the need for enhanced public ownership. This commitment was accompanied by an unwillingness to resort to disruptive asset expropriation, if that was feasible at all. Rather, the notion of a 'socialistic pattern of society' was seen as accepting an element of gradualism in the transition to a system with substantial social ownership. To quote one effort at such an interpretation:

> Now, while this (i.e. social ownership of the means of production) is the character of an overall socialized economy, there is nothing to prevent

> us from seeking to realize it by stages. A socialized industry is surely compatible with an otherwise capitalist economy. Indeed there are few countries today where they do not have a socialized sector, even though the general structure of the economy is capitalistic. Pure capitalism is as much a figment of the imagination as pure socialism. Bearing this in mind, one can perhaps give concreteness to the concept of a 'socialist pattern of society' by interpreting it as a pattern that aims at a gradual incorporation into the economic system (of) the basic ingredients of socialism. (Dasgupta 1957: 91)

It was perhaps based on such a reading that the terms socialism and socialistic society lingered on in the discourse of the Congress, and by the time of the Avadi Congress session of January 1955, the achievement of a 'socialistic pattern of society' became an objective.

The second way in which the Nehruvian strategy can be seen as distinctive is its emphasis on a relatively strict notion of planning. 'Planning' in its technical sense refers to the centralization and coordination of investment decision-making in an economy, to determine the volume of investment, decide on its allocation across sectors and choose the technologies in which it is embedded, so as to realize a growth trajectory that is in keeping with an *a priori* plan or conspectus. Such investment coordination, which defines the 'planning principle' and distinguishes it from the 'market mechanism', is expected to better serve society in two ways when compared with the operation of the market.

First, investment coordination overcomes the 'secondary uncertainty' inherent in a regime where individual, atomistic decision-makers take decisions without much knowledge of what other similarly placed investors are likely to do. This results in the 'anarchy' characteristic of a capitalist market. In such a market, the level and allocation of investment get determined by the 'guesses or expectations of a large number of independent decision-takers (entrepreneurs), in the long run "revised" by *ex post* movements of market prices' (Dobb 1960: 5). What are these guesstimates based on? Prices in the recent past or historical prices, it is sometimes argued. But existing prices cannot be a guide to future prices, because the atomistic, individual investment decisions made on the basis of prevailing prices together influence future demands and supplies, and, therefore, subsequent movements in prices. So, those movements cannot be predicted based on past trends. Without an anchor on which to base expectations, there is no reason to expect that those expectations would actually be realized. This in turn would lead to decision errors that then result in unutilized capacity, closure and unemployment. Since investment in durable fixed capital cannot be reversed by definition, such decision errors are costly in individual and social terms.

The second benefit of investment coordination is that it permits a process of maximizing growth subject to restrictions, such as the minimum consumption requirements set by social and political conditions. It can do this by incorporating appropriate inter-temporal judgements that affect the quantity of investment (and therefore the ratio of investment to national income), the allocation of investment, and technology choice or the technical form in which investment is embodied. Without such coordination, the allocation of investment may not be what would be required to ensure the pattern of production needed to raise the rate of saving and investment, and maximize the rate of growth. Models such as the Mahalanobis model serve as guides for such efforts at coordination.

So, Indian planning was an effort at approximating central planning – but within a mixed economy framework. That was no easy task, as noted earlier. Realizing investment coordination in a hypothetical (though not necessarily actual) economy with a substantial degree of state ownership of productive assets is easy to envisage. In such an economy, surpluses largely accrue to agencies of the state, and the volume of such surpluses relative to total output can be determined by a combination of turnover taxes and an appropriate prices-and-incomes policy. Once in the hands of the state, those surpluses can be allocated as per plan.

This, however, is not possible in a mixed economy, where much of the income accrues to private agents, and the state is not in direct control of savings and investment decisions. In such environments, if investment levels and allocation are to correspond to what has been laid out in an *a priori* plan, the state must curb private consumption through a combination of measures such as taxation, import controls (on non-essentials) and restrictions on production (licensing, for example). It must also guide investment in directions recommended by the *a priori* plan, through licensing, provision of appropriate incentives to private investors, or public investment financed with taxes on surplus incomes. In fact, the large number of physical and price control measures adopted by the Indian government after independence were justified by reference to the need to align consumption, savings and investment decisions with the requirements of the plan. Such intervention was expected to work on both the demand and supply sides. Appropriate taxes would, for example, influence the structure of demand and influence investment. Measures such as licensing would restrict production of non-essential commodities while encouraging production of others that were prioritized.

While this does involve a departure from pure central planning as theorized, it also adheres to the basic planning principle. In hindsight, it does appear to have been a plausible experiment to pursue. Experience shows that centralized planning could result in bureaucratization and associated incentives that defeat the purpose of planning itself. But the success of the experiment with investment coordination in an economy with substantial private ownership of the means of production presumes a large area of control and influence for the state. If the pattern of asset distribution and the correlation of social forces it gives rise to limit the ability of the state to successfully pursue its interventionist strategy, aimed at approximating the trajectory defined in an *a priori* plan, failure is inevitable.[1]

There are reasons to believe that Nehru was inclined towards a strategy that sought to derive a significant part of the benefits expected from central planning, without 'disruptive' acquisition of private assets, but based on the use of a range of fiscal, trade, industrial and monetary policy instruments. This belief was, in turn, driven by the conviction he had that while Marxism provided a set of broad principles for a socialist economy and the Soviet Union provided an example of it, each country would have to find a version of 'socialism' according to its specific context and the consequent possibilities. An early indication of this position was evident in the 'Confidential Report' submitted by Nehru to the Congress Working Committee after the International Congress against Colonial Oppression and Imperialism, which he attended in February 1927, in the course of his transformative trip to Europe. His biographer S. Gopal quotes Nehru's report as saying that:

> A victory for the Chinese means the creation of a great Soviet republic in the East closely allied with Russia and together with it gradually dominating Asia and Europe. This does not mean that the Chinese Republic will be fashioned wholly on the lines laid down by Marx. Even Soviet Russia, owing to the pressure of the peasantry, has had to give up part of its communism, and in China where the small peasant is the deciding factor, the departure from pure communism will be greater. (Gopal 1975: 103)

Following this, Nehru advocated his case for a socialist path in the 1929 Lahore session of the Congress as follows:

> The philosophy of socialism has gradually permeated the entire structure of society the world over and the only point of dispute is the pace and methods of advance to its full realization. India will have to go that way too if she seeks to end her poverty and inequality. Though she may

> evolve her own methods and adopt the ideals to the genius of her race. (Nehru 1929)

Subsequently – in 1936, in Lucknow – he concluded with an oft-quoted statement:

> I see no way of ending poverty, unemployment, the degradation and the subjection of our people, except through socialism. That involves vast and revolutionary changes in our political and social structure, the ending of the vested interest in land and industry as well as the feudal and autocratic Indian state system. That means the ending of private property except in a restricted sense and the replacement of the present profit system by higher ideals of the cooperative services. (Nehru 1936).

As is well known, this was the area in which the compromise within the Congress and by Nehru was the greatest after independence. Nehru's later tendency to compromise may have been influenced by the willingness of the moderates and the conservatives within the Congress to allow him the space he seems to have had in influencing the pre-independence rhetoric of the Congress and the declared post-independence economic strategy. He was not only repeatedly elected to important positions in the Congress, but was also allowed to draft resolutions and reports that gradually pushed the 'socialistic' agenda as the ideology of the Congress. It is not enough to say that he benefited from Gandhi's backing, since that does not explain why Gandhi backed him despite major disagreements between them on economic issues.

One argument used to explain the accommodation of Nehru in high positions in the Congress is that this was the way in which conservative sections within the Congress could keep the radicals and communists at bay – in the belief that Nehru could be persuaded not to damage well-entrenched vested interests that had built close links with the Congress. It should not be forgotten that at the time when the Congress-led national movement was gaining in strength in the 1920s and 1930s, there was increasing evidence of rebellion among the 'passive' Indian peasantry, and unrest among the increasingly assertive and radicalized working class. The radical Left was gaining ground and had control over the Congress Socialist Party and influence within the Congress as well. The Soviet Union was an existing example of a non-capitalist order, and communists had found a base in India. It would be foolish not to expect feudal interests and big capital to rally together, to try and limit the Left.

The conservatives possibly thought that fronting Nehru would help in two ways. One, by keeping the more radical elements within the Congress out of power, by presenting Nehru as a suitable compromise. Two, by 'stealing' the rhetoric of the radicals outside the Congress, since Nehru was veering round to their point of view and had the ability to present those arguments.

In fact, Nehru himself was often surprised by his own ability to push through more radical formulations in what were Congress documents and resolutions. Two incidents reported by him in his *Autobiography* illustrate this. While recognizing that the importance he possessed as a socialist worker lay in the fact that he 'happened to be a prominent Congressman holding important Congress offices', Nehru felt he had discovered that there were many other Congressmen who were beginning to think likewise:

> This was most marked in the UP Provincial Congress Committee, and in this Committee we even tried, as early as 1926, to draw up a mild socialist programme. We are a zamindari and taluqdari province, and the first question we had to face was that of land. We declared that the existing land system must go and that there should be no intermediaries between the State and the cultivator. We had to proceed cautiously, as we were moving in an atmosphere which was, till then, unused to such ideas.

But, to his surprise, in 1929,

> the U.P. Provincial Congress Committee went a step further and made a recommendation, definitely along socialist lines, to the All India Congress Committee. This latter Committee, meeting in Bombay in the summer of 1929, adopted the preamble of the U.P. resolution and thus accepted the principle of socialism underlying the whole resolution. (Nehru 1982: 183)

This support from the moderates was also signalled by what occurred in the Trade Union Congress of 1928 in Jharia, which was the first Nehru attended. Without his knowledge, in the elections that were held after he had left the venue, he was elected president of the congress. In his own words:

> I had been put forward by the moderate group, probably because they felt that I stood the best chance of defeating the other candidate who was an actual worker (on the railways) and who had been put forth by the radical group. If I had been present at Jharia on the day of the election I am sure I would have withdrawn in favour of the worker

> candidate. It seemed to me positively indecent that a newcomer and a non-worker should be suddenly thrust into the presidentship. (Nehru 1929: 186–87)

But Nehru did accept, although his sympathies were with the radicals.

Perhaps influenced by this willingness of the moderates and conservatives to give him much space, Nehru was ambivalent on the larger issue of private property, especially in the means of production. He possibly hoped that he could persuade the Congress leadership in time, despite indications to the contrary. In 1928, when the All Parties Conference met in Lucknow to discuss the Motilal Nehru Committee report on the contours of the future constitution, it was decided 'to add to the Fundamental Rights in the proposed constitution, at the instance of the Oudh taluqadars, a clause guaranteeing their vested rights in their taluqas'. Nehru had this to say: 'The whole constitution was, of course, based on the idea of private property, but it did seem to me to be an outrage to make the property rights in the huge semi-feudal estates one of the irremovable foundations of the constitution' (Nehru 1982: 173). This reflected the ambivalence implicit in the idea of a 'socialistic pattern'. It, like Nehru, saw the need to do away with certain forms of private property, while not calling for social ownership as the norm.

All this suggests that Nehru believed in the possibility of a gradual transition to substantial social ownership within a framework in which not all means of production had to be socialized. But, the extent of socialization notwithstanding, the system must follow a growth path that was planned, have a strong and growing state-owned sector, privilege social over private returns, and emphasize addressing of the problems of unemployment, poverty and social deprivation. If there had been no commitment to such a strategy, there would have been no need to fashion such an elaborately interventionist regime, and to combine it with a macro-frame of the Mahalanobis kind, which was more suited to a centrally planned system. The compromise was in the pace and extent of socialization of property.

The problem with compromise is that deciding where the boundary between essential or non-negotiable and less essential principles should be drawn is not always a matter of choice. This comes through, for example, from the description of what Nehru went through when, in 1929, a 'Leaders' Conference', hastily convened in response to Viceroy Irwin's announcement of a forthcoming Round Table Conference, arrived at a joint resolution in the form of a manifesto offering to cooperate subject to conditions. Nehru was opposed to pitching for anything other than full independence, and saw the resolution as a comedown for the Congress. He reported as follows: 'I hesitated and refused to sign the manifesto (Subhas Bose had definitely refused to sign it), but, as was not unusual with me, I allowed myself to be talked into signing' (Nehru 1982: 197).

For a person prone to compromise in order to ensure unity within the party, the open-endedness with respect to private property perhaps led to an acceptance that the most that could be done was to address the worst kind of asset inequality in the rural and urban areas. And whatever was done had to be done without upsetting the compromise on the issue of protecting private property. In time, even on the ambit of public ownership, while the emphasis on the state owning assets in strategic areas continued, Nehru increasingly emphasized the view that nationalizing existing private property was meaningless: 'to take over the private industries already created is an infantile idea', because 'the state should not block resources, scarce capital in old industries for acquiring junk in the private sector' (quoted in Singh 1993: 97). The compromises made within the Congress, which Nehru saw as the only 'effective revolutionary force' during the freedom struggle, spilt over into the post-independence period. This could have had a lot to do with the limited success of the post-independence development strategy.

It could be argued, counter-factually, that despite the choice of a mixed economy framework with some private ownership, the 'Nehruvian strategy' could have been more successful than it actually was if the compromise on asset ownership in practice had not gone as far as it did after independence under Nehru's prime ministership. The strategy, while delivering high industrial growth between 1951 and the mid-1960s, a substantial public sector, and a diversified industrial base, failed in two senses. First, the high growth of the first fifteen years of planned development could not be sustained, leading to a long period of deceleration of industrial growth till the end of the 1970s, often referred to as the period of 'secular stagnation'. Second, the state could not ensure the level of savings and investment, and the pattern of allocation of investment provided for in the Mahalanobis model-inspired Second Five Year Plan. This resulted in bottlenecks in the supply of certain products and services crucial for industrialization, excess capacities in many non-essential areas, and the diversion of essential inputs and scarce foreign exchange to the production or import of non-essential goods.

The first failure, which has been much discussed in the literature, was related to another feature of the 'Nehruvian strategy', which, though not distinctive, was noteworthy. This was the belief that accelerated development could be achieved through industrialization that catered to a domestic market. Given the still underdeveloped character of the domestic capitalist class, this required import protection to moderate or eliminate competition from stronger international firms. But it also required efforts to grow the domestic market. In what was then an overwhelmingly agrarian economy, home demand had to come in some measure from demand for manufactured mass consumption goods in the rural areas. This required an increase in rural incomes, with a greater share of incremental incomes accruing to the relatively poor, who would spend it on manufactured mass consumption goods. A similar effort to 'expand the lower middle' was required in urban areas as well, as total urban incomes rose over time.

Thus, the need to expand the home market made land reform, involving asset expropriation and land redistribution, imperative. Asset expropriation that breaks down land monopoly was also needed to ease the constraints on productive investment and income growth. If that had been done, not only would it have undermined the barriers to investment and productivity increase resulting from land monopoly and high rents, but the actual cultivator (rescued from being subjected to rack-renting) would have had both the means and the incentive to invest. It could be argued that doing away with landlordism would also have changed the social conditions that subsequently operated to segment labour markets in India and generate other barriers to economic expansion.

It is true that in practice, by making land reforms a state subject, the Constitution took the decision-making and implementation of this element of the strategy out of the hands of the central government and Prime Minister Nehru. We can only speculate as to how different the experience with land reforms would have been if the central government had had a greater role in the matter. In effect, other than for a couple of states, there was little advance on this front across the country. All that was achieved was that the worst forms of absentee landlordism were reduced, if not eliminated.

This had implications that went beyond the pace of agricultural growth and the size of the home market. Radical land reforms of the kind that were envisaged would have galvanized the peasantry and won for Nehru's government the social sanction needed to discipline capital, and advance towards a planned economy and a socialistic pattern of society. Having failed to curb landlord power, Nehru and his government were hard put to discipline Indian big business in order to enhance tax revenues, raise the rate of investment and ensure investment allocation as per plan. The government found itself unable to use the instruments it had at hand, varying from taxes and subsidies to licensing and price controls, to ensure the realization of the planned rate of investment or the allocation of investment according to plan. It also strengthened Indian business, especially big business, and led to a situation where its influence over policy was far greater than the power exercised by the rural aristocracy in the colonial and immediate post-colonial periods.

One consequence was that, not only was the effort to tax the surpluses in the hands of the rich far from adequate, but even taxes that were due were not paid by adoption of means of evasion and avoidance. This meant that the state was not mobilizing through direct taxation the resources needed to finance its ostensible leadership role. That mattered in more ways than one. Since the land reform effort had failed to take off, the mass market for manufactures that it could have helped to create remained constricted. But since the whole strategy was based on generating growth based on an expanding home market, an alternative stimulus was needed. That stimulus partly came from public expenditures, particularly the public investment being undertaken to support industrialization in the mixed economy and the move towards greater public ownership for a socialistic pattern of society.

This in itself would not have been a problem if the public expenditures were financed in a non-inflationary manner. But, given the feeble direct taxation effort, government expenditures had to be financed with revenues from indirect taxation and by borrowing. Indirect taxation disproportionately burdened the poor, while supply-side constraints, especially in agriculture, made debt-financed spending inflationary. In India, as in many other developing countries, the supply of wage goods from the agricultural sector was supply-constrained, for many reasons. One reason, already noted, was the failure to implement land reforms and distribute surplus land to the actual cultivators. This institutional constraint, together with the continued dependence on the monsoon, resulted in slow growth and high volatility of agricultural production. To compound the problem, the view that agriculture was a 'bargain sector' from which much could be garnered at little cost resulted in a neglect of investment in agriculture. The slow growth resulting from these factors meant that the demand generated by debt-financed public expenditure could trigger price increases. The result was a built-in tendency towards agricultural price inflation whenever industrial growth accelerated.

Food price inflation had two consequences that had important implications for industrial performance. First, it put pressure on the government to adopt measures to control inflation and thereby forced a contraction in government expenditure. Second, by pushing poorer households to allocate a larger share of their income for food, it reduced the demand for manufactured mass consumption goods and, through the decisions of firms producing them, the demand for a wider range of manufactures.

In sum, food price inflation tended to slow the pace of industrial growth or even precipitate an industrial recession. That brought to an end the period during which the Nehru–Mahalanobis strategy was seen as at least a partial success.

To summarize, the compromise on the land front, whether arrived at consciously or otherwise (i.e. by agreeing to a particular division of powers in a federal polity), proved to be a crucial factor in determining the degree of success (or lack of it) of the economic strategy. It shifted the boundary between non-essential and essential principles so far that the full potential of the Nehru–Mahalanobis strategy was never tested. That having been said, there was nevertheless much that the pursuit of the strategy did give India. These gains varied from the emergence of a strong public sector that set the benchmarks and raised the bar for wages and labour relations in industry, to the creation of a significant and diversified industrial and technological base. Further, the Congress government under Nehru during the first decade and a half after independence managed to put in place a framework that did limit the power of not just foreign but also big domestic capital, to a substantial degree. It is another matter that big capital managed to evade or circumvent many regulations, and that the constraints imposed on it were often not the most appropriate. But, in all likelihood, the extent of asset and income inequality increase during the Nehru years would have been far greater if the interventionist strategy it adopted had not been in place.

Not surprisingly, there was widespread belief in the feasibility of the Nehruvian strategy even after the mid-1960s. By then a host of official committees had found that the state's licensing policy had been subverted, the power of domestic monopoly had increased and inequality was probably on the rise. But the search for remedies recognized that structural constraints resulting from policy failure, rather than an erroneous strategy, were responsible for the impasse. This led to interventions like the Monopolies and Restrictive Trade Practices (MRTP) Act, the Foreign Exchange Regulation Act (FERA) and, above all, bank nationalization. While the acceptability of the Nehruvian strategy waned over time, the Congress reverted to versions of it, to different degrees and for various reasons, at different points in time till at least the 1990s.

Unfortunately, all that proved insufficient and perhaps came a bit too late. What followed was an attack on the Nehruvian strategy (even from within the Congress) and the adoption of neo-liberal reform (facilitated by a tenuous embrace of foreign financial capital), which amounted to a declaration that structural issues like asset ownership and the inequalities therein are not matters to be discussed any more. The market power that asset concentration provides a few is now seen as a social good. The closure of the (much weakened) Planning Commission is symbolic of this transition. The transition also implies that, all talk of India's aspirational middle class notwithstanding, growth will now depend on exports rather than on the domestic market. That is what 'Come, Make in India' is all about. Besides the fact that this is a strategy which hopes growth will ride on the backs of underpaid and exploited workers, it does not seem all too feasible in the current global environment. Failure may force a rethink. But the cost to be paid to learn a lesson that the Nehru years have already taught us is too high for all but the super-rich. That lesson is that there are institutional prerequisites for the successful pursuit of any economic strategy. And, the more ambitious the strategy, the more demanding the institutional prerequisites can be. Nehru recognized this, but perhaps hoped that 'the course of events' would deliver the needed transformation. It did not, instead delivering the simple lesson: 'Structure matters.'

Note

[1] Patnaik (1995) argues that the false assumption that the area of control of the state was large enough to make private financial decisions correspond to the state's physical plan was an important factor explaining the failure of the Mahalanobis strategy.

References

Dasgupta, A.K. (1957), 'Socialistic Pattern of Society and the Second Five Year Plan', *Economic Weekly*, Annual Number, January: 91–92.

Dobb, Maurice (1960), *An Essay on Economic Growth and Planning*, London: Routledge and Kegan Paul.

Gopal, Sarvepalli (1975), *Jawaharlal Nehru: A Biography, Vol. 1*, New Delhi: Oxford University Press.

Nehru, Jawaharlal (1929), 'Presidential Address at the Lahore Congress Session', available under *Select Speeches and Writings of Nehru*, at http://celebratingnehru.org/english/nehru_speech2.aspx, accessed 10 January 2015.

Nehru, Jawaharlal (1936), 'Nehru's Presidential Address 1936 Lucknow', available under *Select Speeches and Writings of Nehru*, at http://celebratingnehru.org/english/nehru_speech34.aspx, accessed 10 January 2015.

Nehru, Jawaharlal (1982), *Jawaharlal Nehru: An Autobiography*, New Delhi: Jawaharlal Nehru Memorial Fund and Oxford University Press.

Patnaik, Prabhat (1995), 'P.C. Mahalanobis and the theory of development planning', in *Whatever Happened to Imperialism and Other Essays*, New Delhi: Tulika Books.

Singh, A.K. (1993), 'Nehru: Socialism and mixed economy', in N.B. Das Gupta *et al.*, eds, *Nehru and Planning in India: Proceedings of the National Seminar on Pandit Jawaharlal Nehru, Planning Commission and Planned Development in India*, New Delhi: Concept Publishing Company: 93–100.

Fallouts of 1989

Aijaz Ahmad

Preamble

I wrote an essay, 'The Imperialism of our time', a few months after the US invasion of Iraq (Ahmad 2004). The title was chosen as homage to Kalecki's seminal essay, 'Fascism of Our Time', that he had written at the time of Barry Goldwater's bid for US Presidency in 1964 (Kalecki 1972). What would fascism look like, he had wondered, if it ever came to a country of advanced capitalism where liberal democratic institutions were entrenched but with no powerful working class movement to stem the fascist tide. Recalling Kalecki's essay seemed pertinent because the kind of forces he had so feared some decades ago were beginning to take hold of state power in the United States during the Bush Presidency. Ideological premises as well as policy projections for the Bush regimes were getting formulated already by a cabal-like combination of Wall Street luminaries, Christian fundamentalists, Zionists, neo-conservatives and militarists; Bush Jr himself was a 'born-again' Christian. It seemed likely even then that political culture in the US would keep moving further to the right, with the possibility of even more extremist regimes rising there in a not-too distant future, and that imperialist aggressions would become more widespread and even more brutal.

If Bush, the right-wing Republican, had given us invasions of Afghanistan and Iraq, Obama – Nobel Peace laureate, liberal Democrat, first Black President of the US – has given us the destruction of Lybia, Syria and Yemen. Formerly a part-time Professor of Constitutional Law at Chicago University, he is the first head of a modern liberal democracy to personally select individuals who are to be assassinated in one country or another, mostly through blind drone attacks. The next US presidential elections are likely to be fought between two candidates, Hillary Clinton and Donald Trump, who are both very much more to the Right than Goldwater who had frightened Kalecki so very much. Trump is in the habit of tweeting Mussolini's lines to his six million followers, has all the clinical traits of an authoritarian personality which he combines with right-wing populism of a fascist type that appeals to those whose lives have been broken by Reaganite/Clintonian economics; Ms. Clinton is decidedly more dangerous than him on issues of imperialist aggressions. By now, this rise of the Far Right is a global trend, in varying degrees, and in ways that are also novel and specific to our time. Socialist state systems and social democratic projects have come to grief already. Now liberal democracy, reduced by neo-liberalism to becoming a democracy of the 1 per cent, is also under increasing stress in most of the countries where it exists. The tendency among analysts is to use the term 'fascism' too quickly.

It may well be the case that we are at the threshold of a profound transformation in the nature of the capitalist state in these neo-liberal times whereby the formal structures of liberal governance are kept intact, but neo-liberal economic policies are combined with a high degree of xenophobic nationalism, racism and/or religious zealotry, and arbitrary authoritarian rule laced with rhetorics of 'Us' and 'Them'. This is neither the fascism familiar to us from the inter-war period nor a liberal order based on the idea of equal rights of citizenship, even though this hybrid form does take elements from fascism as well as liberalism which have previously served as alternative and antithetical forms for the political superstructure of the capitalist state. The provisional term I use for this evolving state form is simply 'post-democratic'. This is easier to witness in the case of Modi's India or Erdogan's Turkey. However, the same tendencies are rampant in numerous countries in Europe, West and East, and across the political spectrum in the Republican party which serves as one of two ruling parties in the US; some sectors of the desperately poor in the voter base of the Democratic party are also likely to move over to Trump. Thus, we are again faced with the question Kalecki posed half a century ago: what happens if fascism comes to a liberal democratic country that has no powerful working class movement to counter its ascendancy? The answer is not: fascism will prevail. The question itself is in fact transformed by the very conditions within which it is arising today: with no truly powerful challenge from the working class in sight, why would forces of the Far Right need to abrogate the liberal democratic form to take hold of the state? In other words: if the Left is not even a party in the real struggle for state power, can the Far Right not achieve its core objectives through apparatuses of the liberal democratic state itself? I have examined this question specifically in relation to India in a separate text (Ahmad 2016).[1]

A General Framework

As the socialist state system approached its final unravelling in 1989–91, we began to hear more and more of 'globalization', a relatively new and theoretically rather vacuous term at the time. Gradually, a new consciousness began to dawn among Marxist scholars that globalization of capitalism, in industry as well as finance, was now adopting methods that were structurally different, which then got discussed as a 'new Imperialism' (or variants thereof). Nevertheless, the tale of global capitalist reproduction during this entire period is told as a story of the unfolding of globalization thanks to new advances in a range of technological fields, from automation to aerial transport, and an increasingly deregulated freedom for financial and speculative capital; a crisis of *general* profitability in the leading capitalist economies and consequent long-term stagnation; the success of neo-liberal economic policies in maintaining high rates of profit-making for the *core* corporate capital despite stagnation in the real economy of advanced capitalism, and regardless of declining incomes and purchasing power for the general populace; general depression of primary commodity prices because all countries producing such commodities are trying to out-sell each other in the world's deregulated markets; and so on. All of this is of course true and essential. However, virtually all interpretations available in western Marxism tend not to offer any structural account to explain what the disappearance of an adversarial state system meant for the extensive new freedoms for the operations of imperialism, post-1989 and, more broadly, after the so-called 'Deng reforms' in China. In my view, by contrast, US imperialism was now able to pursue far more aggressive and unfettered operations despite economic stagnation within its own domain precisely because of the unravelling of the socialist state system, on the one hand, and, on the other, the defeat/demise of the nationalism of the national bourgeoisie across Asia and Africa. It was already so dominant within the capitalist world that there was no prospect of it facing the kind of inter-imperialist rivalry that Lenin had written about and which indeed was a key factor in the first half of the twentieth century, helping to ignite two world wars. The unravelling of the socialist state system now meant that there was no longer any inter-systemic rivalry either, in which the Soviet Union had been a credible rival. And, the defeat/demise of the nationalism of the national bourgeoisie in Asia and Africa, much of which had emerged out of colonialism at various points after World War II, meant also that the kind of resistance that was widespread even as late as the late 1970s would now be quite disorganized and comparatively much weaker, hence easier to either isolate or incorporate. Combined with the accumulating ravages caused by the success of neo-liberalist policies across the global capitalist system, these factors have served to produce arguably the worst balance of class forces that the working classes have had to face in over a century, as well as a generalized catastrophe for a majority of humankind.

The United States had been the leading capitalist power since at least World War I. With the dissolution of the European colonialisms after World War II, which had also vanquished all the other capitalist powers – the colony-possessing (e.g., Britain, France) as well the colony-seeking (e.g., Germany, Italy) – the US had acquired a global (non-colonial and post-colonial) empire and a very different kind of superiority over the other advanced capitalist countries. It had entered World War I not for acquiring colonies but as an arbiter of European disputes, as Woodrow Wilson's dominating role at Versailles demonstrated. After World War II, the US emerged as the inheritor of European empires, as the chief architect of the new post-war capitalist order, and not only as the world leader in the anti-communist crusade in which Europe was assigned forward positions in the geographical sense but far inferior positions in the formulation of policy and strategy. The US was also acknowledged as the superior power to which Western Europe was indebted for liberation from fascism and indebted also for post-war reconstruction: the Marshall Plan, the restructuring of European firms on the US model, formation of the US-led NATO (North Atlantic Treaty Organization), etc. US forces, military bases and weapon systems (including nuclear weapons) were dispersed all over Western Europe but none of those countries were allowed a real national defence policy or, as de Gaulle found out, an autonomous military force. This paramountcy within the capitalist world got extended on the global scale after the collapse of the socialist state system. Starting with the transitional Clinton Presidency and fully blossoming under Bush Jr, the US began to enunciate, sometimes directly but mostly by innuendo, what in that article of more than a decade ago I had already described as twin doctrines of imperial constitutionalism for itself and of limited sovereignty for all others. By now, that faltering attempt at imperial constitutionalism (the assertion that US domestic law trumps the laws of other nations) has grown into a fully-fledged assertion of an imperial sovereignty, in which such niceties as the Geneva Conventions, the UN General Assembly and the whole Westphalian tradition of national sovereignties can be ignored in the name of whatever the US defines as its own national security. The Twin Tower attacks (the infamous 9/11) were utilized for declaring what amounts to a permanent State of the Exception (an open-ended 'War on Terror') by which, then, the US permits itself to intervene militarily within the territory of other states whenever and in whatever way, overt or covert, or at whatever scale it wishes, owing no explanation of its actions to any authority other than its own. Jurists on the German Far Right have been the only ones in the whole history of modernity to expound with great rigour so absolute a notion of sovereignty and of the State of Exception, but even they had theorized it on the scale of the nation-state and not as imperial/global prerogative.[2]

That earlier reflection on imperialism had laid out my basic argument in broad outline. However, the broader argument was in some respects overshadowed by the fact that it was drafted under the shadow of the then recent invasion of Iraq and the argument itself was therefore framed within the requirement of that conjuncture – i.e. the need to explain the nature of the regime led by Bush Jr and that regime's domestic and international ambitions for the near future. The current article proceeds from that argument, but is now focused narrowly on what the unravelling of the socialist state system has meant for imperialism and its adversaries. Many other issues related to imperialism and to resistance against it remain outside the scope of this essay as well, and shall be taken up elsewhere. A particularly fascinating fact, which is taken up in a separate section, is that the two countries that played the central role in the history of socialist revolutions and where the ensuing state system was dissolved, namely China and Russia (the latter comprising the territorial bulk of the Soviet Union), have now re-emerged as the two powers on whom the US is concentrating as potential threats to its unchallenged supremacy in the long term. Japan and (West) Germany were second and third most powerful economies for some decades (and have so far been displaced only by China), but neither was ever seen as a threat, nor was the European Union (EU) as a whole, which had as large an economy and a domestic market as the US; they were and still are partners – junior partners, of course – in the overall architecture of global capitalism. Only Russia and China – communist adversaries of yore, capitalist upstarts of today – are wholly indigestible. Why? Are we at the threshold of yet another sort of inter-imperialist rivalry? Does China alone, or the Sino–Russian alliance combined with a set of auxiliaries, have the potential to become a rival imperialist centre?

At least three factors make the current conjuncture especially dangerous and volatile. First, the economic fallout of World War I followed by the Great Depression had led to the widespread desperation and social disintegration that fed into the rise of the Far Right to power across much of Europe through varieties of fascism and military dictatorships. More than three decades of neo-liberalism has created an analogous situation for a great majority of today's humanity, as the system lurches from one crisis to the next. We may yet witness the rise of regimes even more prone to war than the last several US administrations have been, as well as a collapse of the familiar kind of political order in much of the capitalist world. Second, the US is of course still the world's most powerful economy, but its productive economy is in irreversible comparative decline while its debts and deficits are spiralling on to unsustainable levels, and there is now a very slow but perceptible decline in the status of the dollar as the primary currency for the storage of the world's wealth and by far the most indispensable currency for world trade. Meanwhile, its military power is in aggregate terms greater than all other states combined. This disproportion between levels of economic power and military power results in seeking military solutions for economic problems and ambitions. Third, the greatest weakness of the Chinese economy is that even under the best of conditions, China is simply a very resource-poor country and must import the strategic resources that its economy needs from diverse sources spread out across the planet. Today, the two economies, the American and the Chinese, have become highly inter-dependent, but the logic of rivalry is that each must over time try to reduce its dependence on the other as much as possible; for example, China's attempts to diversify its export destinations have meant that the European Union (EU) has already emerged as a larger market than the US for Chinese exports. In case of a real rivalry, the US will very likely use its military might, indirectly and directly, to deny to China the resources the latter needs so desperately; the great expansion of US military might in all corners of Africa, for instance, undoubtedly has that edge. This becomes all the more likely in this age of dwindling natural resources and rising potential for resource wars, cold as well as hot.

How did we get here? The inter-systemic rivalry between the capitalist order and the socialist state system had served to impose severe restrictions on imperialism's ambitions to reject the Westphalian presuppositions of the system of sovereign nation-states, or to altogether ignore the intricate web of international law and institutions of collective security that arose after 1945, at imperialism's own behest in fact. It had to eventually recognize the limits of its own power even in Indochina where it used all its military might and violated every legal boundary or moral principle and yet lost the war, thanks largely to the valour and tenacity of its victims, but also to the extent of material support those victims received from the socialist states. Moreover, and partly because of the space opened up by the existence of the socialist states and allied parties, this was also a period of powerful working class mobilizations and revolutionary movements in countless parts of the world. Even within the US, this was the period of full employment and rising wages, hence a certain space for hard bargaining by the trade unions; a widespread militancy in various registers (from

Malcom X to Martin Luther King Jr to the Black Panthers among the African-Americans); and the rise of a New Left that was critical of the old communist movement but was also inspired by the Cuban Revolution, the Vietnamese resistance and the wars of liberation in Indochina. Nor was it possible to dismantle reform structures of the New Deal at that time, as has been choreographed in slow motion since the Clinton administration. In core countries of European capital the liberal state was transformed in the social democratic direction in varying degrees, to absorb the working class pressure from below and the pressure of the socialist state system next door, whether or not social democrats were in power. This was true even of the European late-comers to the liberal order: Greece, Portugal and Spain, which all had powerful working class movements. This was in addition to powerful communist parties and movements (in Italy, France, Portugal, Greece), and a variety of movements and groupings further to the Left, cumulatively far more powerful than their American counterparts. Considerable parts of the tricontinent were in the grip of wars of national liberation. In various other countries where revolutionary movements were strong and/or anti-imperialist economic nationalists were in power, agendas of the Far Right simply could not be implemented through politically liberal governmental structures and outright dictatorships had to be imposed for various lengths of time, as was frequently the case in Latin America. In Indonesia, communists and economic nationalists had to be suppressed through a historic bloodbath that might have taken as many as half a million lives. In Egypt, Nasser's anti-imperialist nationalism could only be broken through external invasion by Israel in 1967.

The ending of that period has meant that global restraints on imperialist prerogatives have been greatly weakened and the leading imperialist country, the United States, is acting unilaterally under a set of political and legal prerogatives that it has reserved for itself in its global conduct, and which I define as an 'imperial sovereignty' that is historically quite unprecedented. Secondly, the comprehensive defeat and disorientation of the forces of the historic Left, combined with abandonment of economic nationalism by a majority of the national-bourgeois states of the tricontinent, gives to imperialism the confidence that the essential properties of the social state in the Euro-American core can be dismantled gradually and safely, and that the implementation of neo-liberal agendas can be intensified in states of peripheral capital in the tricontinent within the existing structures of governance, without fear of unmanageable social upheavals either at the core or in the peripheral zones; the few exceptions – Venezuela, Bolivia and the like – can be isolated and corroded from within, as is currently being done openly in Greece and somewhat more covertly in Venezuela. This runs parallel to what we argued above: liberal capitalism's extraordinary accommodation with – and in many cases outright patronage of – right-wing nationalisms, religious zealots and neo-fascisms across the board; today's post-coup Ukraine and Erdogan's Turkey (NATO's own Islamists) are cases in point.[3]

It should be obvious that when we speak of contemporary imperialism, we speak primarily of the US which has had extraordinary success in subordinating all the other countries of the imperialist core to its own purposes as it functions both as a nation-state protecting its own national corporate capital through all means necessary, and, simultaneously, as the internationalized state that protects the interests of the integrated global finance capital in all corners of the world. In this latter role, the US commands three overlapping sources of power. First, the sheer size and depth of its economy means that all components of the world capitalist system are invested in the stability and growth of that economy, which gives to the US extraordinary decision-making and coercive powers. Second, the status of its currency as the primary means for storage of wealth in the world and the dominant currency in global trade, notably oil trade, gives to the US treasury a unique power over all other central banks in the world as well as the freedom to run up debts without fear of repercussions of the kind that other, lesser states would have to face. Third, its military power is cumulatively greater than that of all the rest of the world's armies combined, with the unique privilege of having military bases in all corners of the earth; its Special Operations units alone are active in 135 countries. Beyond that, it also plays the key role in the functioning of an order of power that substitutes for a formal world government, and consists of such things as multilateral institutions of various kinds, alliances and expeditionary forces for global interventionism, and networks of overlapping media houses across the world for ideological management. Not only do the nine Unified Combatant Commands of the US military cover literally every inch of the earth's surface,[4] they are then supplemented by a US-dominated NATO whose mission has been expanding so very exponentially that its interventionist brief already covers much of the globe. In all this, the US addresses a structural contradiction in global political economy: while finance capital itself has been thoroughly internationalized and globally integrated in its economic operations, the political system prevailing in the global theatre of its operations consists of a system of nation-states with very real historical depth and entrenchment within their own national territories. The widely propagated idea that the processes of neo-liberal globalization have rendered obsolete the nation-state form is erroneous. Transnational capital needs nation-states to guarantee favourable labour regimes and legal protections within their own respective jurisdictions, as much as it needs supra-national authorities and agencies of various kinds. The US state plays the double role of representing the capital of its own country, as well as that of defending and promoting the collective interest of all other units of the integrated global finance capital as a whole. The economic side of the political economy of contemporary imperialism has been closely analysed and extensively documented in debates within international Marxism. I deal with these matters cursorily, taking those analyses and data for granted, and offer a different kind of narrative for this very period.

Post-Soviet Imperialism: A Mapping

Precisely because the centrality of the Soviet collapse in the history of the present is so systematically ignored in so many accounts of imperialism since that collapse, it is necessary to summarize at some length the meaning of that event, and of the unravelling of the socialist state system, at various levels: for the working classes of the world in general; for the remaining socialist states, national liberation movements and communist parties generally; for fundamental reorientations in the ideological sphere. These other shifts are the necessary preconditions for the emergence of an era of imperial sovereignty, post-democratic states, and the permanence of overt and covert unilateral war across the planet. Before delving into a more detailed discussion of these consequences it is best to clarify that the intent here is not to present the Soviet Union or Maoist China in some idyllic terms, either as vibrant socialist homelands marching unproblematically toward a communist future or as (competing) paragons of internationalist virtue. Whatever reservations one may have regarding the actual nature of those bygone states, it is imperative to carefully take stock of the consequences of their dissolution. Those consequences are a very large part of the structural basis for such great power of imperialism in our time; a capitalism so very stagnant and crisis-ridden in its central formations could not have otherwise adopted such aggressive imperialist offensives with such impunity. Charting out those consequences is to explain some of the concrete material conditions in which imperialism now operates.

Let us begin, then, with what can reasonably be conceived as the founding moment of globalization itself, i.e. the unravelling of the socialist state system ('collapse of communism', in common parlance). For, it is only with the unravelling of that state system that the capitalist mode of production (CMP) is universalized, for the first time in human history. This globalization of the CMP is now so naturalized in accounts of the present that there appears to be a willed amnesia about how very recent and dramatic this event actually is – and amnesia also about the fact that in one place or another on the planet, at one time or another in the course of the twentieth century, roughly a third of humanity passed through the experience of trying to build, however exhilarating or flawed those attempts might have been, some sort of socialism in defiance of the power of capital and empire. That much is probably uncontroversial even though this fact hardly ever receives, in at least the western Marxist circles, the kind of central attention it deserves. My next proposition is likely to be controversial, however, even among perhaps a majority of my own comrades, namely that in my view, the socialist state system begins to unravel not in 1989 in the COMECON (Council for Mutual Economic Assistance) countries, but about a decade earlier, 1976–78, in the People's Republic of China (the slogan attributed to Deng, 'It is glorious to be rich', is paradigmatic). Which also means that the final disappearance of the Soviet system was indeed rather sudden, unpredicted by even the Central Intelligence Agency of the US, but also that the overall process of unravelling actually took well over a decade. It is quite clear from the writings of Gorbachev's close advisors that Deng's restorationist reforms in China had provoked much thinking about the perceived need for similar changes in the USSR as well. In this sense, Lenin and Deng are the two most decisive figures in the making and unmaking of communism in the twentieth century, albeit for opposite reasons. It is chastening to recall some of the primary consequences of that unravelling.

In 1980, the global working class at the disposal of capital was estimated to be around 1 billion; twenty-five years later, it was estimated at about 3 billion. The primary difference was the collapse of the socialist state system, since China and the formerly COMECON bloc of countries accounted for roughly half of that increase. Workers in those countries were of course devastated, having made a transition from the highly protected conditions of employment and social entitlement to being thrown to the mercies of the world market in extremely unstable national conditions. Their availability at miserable levels of remuneration served to depress the global wage rate and contributed vast numbers to the army of the unemployed. In the capitalist core, the US working class was hit particularly hard, since the US became the largest market for the cheap goods produced with Chinese labour while so many US corporations kept shifting operations to China. However, all the analysts and ideologues who never tire of complaining that US jobs have been shifted to China never linger to clarify that this shifting ('off-shoring') would not have been possible if Chinese socialism had not been disbanded; the irony, of course, is that much of the US working class can keep up some semblance of its customary consumption by buying precisely those same cheap China-made goods. It is unlikely that the global wage rate will improve substantially in the near future. Further wage depression in this era was of course far more devastating all across what is now called 'the global South', formerly known as 'the third world' (my preferred term is 'tricontinent'; or we could simply say 'imperialized countries').

Thanks to this very dynamic, imperialist capital gained workers who were not only paid low wages now (lower money wage, vanishing social wage), but who also came with generally higher skill levels and productive capacities than elsewhere in Asia or Africa, relatively more sound general education as well as generally healthier bodies – strengths inherited from the now abandoned socialist systems of mass provision. In time, of course, the 'Shock Therapy' of capitalism that was applied in the formerly COMECON countries devastated those health standards, job security and work conditions for the majority of the population there, leading to all manner of social and psychic disorientation including criminality and neo-fascist political tendencies. In China, the withdrawal of social provision was more gradual and less extreme (in Chinese terms), but even in zones of the country where imperialist capital was to get concentrated and wealth produced at prodigious scales, the working class often lived and laboured in a work environment bordering on slave-labour conditions. Throughout the former socialist countries, imperialist capital found working classes that were disorganized, disheartened and often just supine.

Imperialism also gained extensive fertile grounds for investment of a fair amount of its excess capital in enterprises that relied on that cheap but reasonably competent labour, with guaranteed profit rates of a kind unimaginable in the Euro-American capitalist core. Much is to be learned from any analysis of how much of the value added in an iPhone goes back to the Chinese worker, how much of it goes to the intermediate Taiwanese companies that manufacture the parts, how much to sale intermediaries in the international trade chains, and how much, finally, into the pockets of the top brass at Apple. All this was in addition to the immense amount of property stock that was picked up at fire-sale prices; not only East Germany, for instance, but also such neighbouring countries as Slovenia or Hungary became playgrounds for not just the capitalists but even the middle classes from what was then West Germany.

Furthermore, there were decisive shifts in the balance of political forces across the globe. The weaker socialist countries (Yugoslavia, Cuba, Vietnam, Nicaragua) suffered enormous setbacks, though each in its own way. An internal crisis had been undoubtedly brewing inside Yugoslavia for some time, but not of a sort that would have led to an implosion of the kind that in fact occurred. Nor was Yugoslavia part of the Soviet system of states – indeed, there was hostility between them. And yet it was the unravelling of socialism in the Soviet bloc and the collapse of the Soviet Union itself, not only as a socialist state but also as a unified territorial entity, that gave impetus to the various separatist tendencies in the constituent units of the Yugoslav state to go the same way, starting with Slovenia which was openly egged on by West Germany. The newly contrived aversion to live in multinational federal states, combined with the explosion of regional nationalisms and primordial identities of religion and ethnicity, led to the territorial collapse of Yugoslavia and the rise of sundry ultra-right forces, including full-fledged militias, that were headed by those whose immediate ancestors had fought on the fascist side during World War II and then against the Partisans during the ensuing civil war. The fraternal ethnic cleansings that were encouraged, and often financed and armed, by western imperialist powers gave the latter a chance to then supervise the rearrangement of territory and power relations in the former Yugoslavia through massive bombings of cities and principalities – Belgrade, Kosovo – in a kind of devastation not seen on European soil since World War II. This was a horrific, historic irony. The great *raison d'être* of NATO during the whole of the Cold War period was the defence of Europe against Soviet hordes – the invading hordes that never materialized. Instead, as soon as the Soviet Union collapsed, NATO found itself bombing a corner of that same Europe itself, with no one left to stop them.

We will not go into the complexities of the Nicaraguan Revolution, first triumphant in 1978–79 and its subsequent defeat a decade later (1989–90). Suffice it to say that it could have been as decisive a moment in Latin American history as the Cuban Revolution of 1959 had once been, except that it occurred at the wrong historical moment and coincided almost exactly with the decade when the socialist state system was coming unstuck (China 1978, USSR 1989–90). When the US unleashed the counter-revolutionary armies of the Contras, the army of the FSLN (Sandinista National Liberation Front) needed and simply did not get the kind of backing that Fidel's forces had received during the period of revolutionary incubation after seizing power in Havana. The Sandanistas eventually had no choice but to retreat, sign off the Tela Accords, disband the FSLN army, and agree to elections that were to be held on US-dictated terms with the predictable outcome that the US-sponsored candidate would win.

Cuba and Vietnam survived, but with a much diminished socialist possibility. Cuba went through a period of intense economic crisis after Soviet support disappeared, and it was only Fidel's own noble tenacity and the support he received from a very substantial part of the party which saved what remains of Cuba's socialism from total dissolution, as a considerable part of the party was then advocating. For sheer survival, though, it was forced to introduce into its socialist system many elements alien to it and which may well prove to be much too corrosive. About Vietnam, the least that can be said is that at the end of the war of liberation in 1975 it inherited the consequences of such massive human carnage and destruction of even land, livestock and other basic resources of human survival, that it was left with very little that could be used for building anything resembling socialism; even bare survival was going to be miraculous. This is what Chomsky tried to capture when he proposed that the real victors of the war had actually been the Americans, whose aim was not to occupy Vietnam for all eternity but simply to destroy all possibility that Vietnam might be able to build a socialist society and set an example for other, weaker, agrarian countries. Moreover, four years after the liberation, Vietnam had to suffer a military attack from the new, post-Maoist, Dengist China that was emerging not only as a capitalist but also a deeply national-chauvinist state, and that was resentful of the fact that this new, independent Vietnam had once been a dependency of the Chinese imperial court. The pretext for the attack, namely that Vietnam had sent its forces to emancipate the Cambodian population from Pol Pot's genocidal regime, an ally of the Chinese, was particularly grotesque. The disappearance of the Soviet Union and the COMECON system was a further blow. The capitalist turn in Vietnamese politics and economy is inseparable from these facts, with the monumental historical paradox that the successor generation in the Vietnamese party that had once fought the legendary war against the US is now among supplicants for US technology and finance; in the bargain, the US may even obtain military bases on Vietnamese territory as part of the encirclement of China. National chauvinism can be a two-way street and imperialism can benefit from both sides of a political process that has turned China and Vietnam, revolutionary allies of yesteryears, into regional antagonists.

Alongside the defeat and disarray of the weaker socialist countries is the plight of the national liberation movements. South Africa's African National Congress (ANC) and Arafat's Palestine Liberation Organization (PLO) are cases in point. Neither, of course, had any commitment to building a socialist society or to decisively curtail the privileges of capital. Some of the processes of degeneration in both cases have older roots. In the case of the ANC, it is undoubtedly true that throughout the late 1980s, its elite leadership and particularly the exiled section of its leadership (though not the closely allied Communist Party and not so much the ANC of the interior) had been preparing an accommodation with White South African capitalists and, through them, with global capital in general. It is also arguable that in his vision of the political economy of the post-apartheid South Africa, Mandela himself was not much more than a radical representative of the Black middle class. It is also the case, however, that the Left within the ANC was exceptionally strong, especially the working class elements and the revolutionary youth, and that the South African Communist Party (SACP) had played a decisive role in politics and, even more so, the armed struggle. A leftward consolidation in post-apartheid South Africa was eminently possible. However, the negotiations that began in 1990 and eventually culminated in the formation of Mandela's first post-apartheid government in 1994 covered a span of time that witnessed the dissolution of the Soviet system, and the onset of 'Shock Therapy' and social decomposition throughout the former Soviet territories. It is very doubtful that even the left-wing of the ANC and much of the SACP itself were not mindful of the fact that the balance of forces in the world had changed radically. They had fought their war of liberation with weapons provided by the socialist bloc, but that bloc was no longer there to help the Black South Africans against White capital in post-apartheid reconstruction. The end of apartheid was a historic victory; the rise of the first post-apartheid government, headed by the legendary Nelson Mandela, was also, however, the moment of the beginning of the restoration. The tendency in the ANC to compromise and collude with the power of capital was older, as I said earlier, but the disappearance of the Soviet alternative must have greatly strengthened that tendency.

On the question of Palestine I shall be brief. As in the South African ANC, the process of corruption in the dominant force in the PLO, namely Arafat's Fatah, was much older, thanks in part to the relations of dependence, especially money dependence, on the wealthy monarchies. However, Arafat was a man of deep nationalist commitment, as were many lesser people in the Fatah, particularly in its left-wing and among its armed cadres; and then there was the Palestinian Left, also a part of the PLO. In any case, it is also eminently arguable that the surrender that was formalized at Oslo was in considerable measure a product of its bleak historical moment. The Iran–Iraq War (1980–88), which took half a million lives, and then the Gulf War (1990–91; but one that has, in a sense, yet not ended) had already begun the process of the region's descent into what may yet turn out to be Middle Eastern history's worst nightmare. Reliable, substantial outside support from the socialist countries during those difficult years would have been a major element in sustaining a sense of security and independent initiative on the part of the PLO, as it had been in the past; yet, it was precisely at this critical juncture that the socialist state system finally disappeared altogether. The whole process that led up to the Oslo Accords of 1993 and 1995 chronologically coincided with the process that led to the dissolution of the Soviet bloc and the aftermath of that dissolution, almost exactly the same way as in the case of the ANC.[5] These developments on the regional and national levels must have been very unnerving for leaders of the PLO, many of whom were already far too close to the Americans. The Gulf War must have demonstrated to them how completely the US was now going to dominate the region for the foreseeable future. They too fell more fully in line.

More broadly, one could say that the Soviet bloc had played a many-faceted role in the tricontinent. First, it provided crucial support to the weaker socialist countries (e.g., Cuba, Vietnam) and to the anti-imperialist national liberation movements; as Amilcar Cabral was to put it, every bullet that was fired for national liberation in Africa had come from the socialist countries. Second, even though the Bandung project of non-alignment and independent (national-bourgeois) development was formally equidistant from the US and USSR, in practice it relied heavily on the Soviet bloc in its efforts to resist undue imperialist pressure. The USSR thus helped substantially in protecting tricontinental economic nationalism from imperialist pressure, and remained a pole of attraction even for anti-communist nation-builders as an alternative that was useful in driving harder bargains with the imperialist countries as well; Nasserite Egypt here is a significant example. Indian economic nationalism had weakened very significantly during the 1980s, leading up to the Rao–Manmohan reforms, but one wonders whether or not it would have succumbed so very completely had the Soviet pole of attraction still been available. And not only economic nationalism; even in countries like India, Soviet technology played a crucial role in building military capacities, from training military personnel and providing advanced aircraft and weapons systems to actual transfer of high-level technology. India's dramatic turn to a military alliance so exclusively with the United States, and then with Israel, is certainly influenced by the perception that there really is no alternative.

Third, the Soviet Union served to somewhat restrain imperialism's larger military ambitions. Even in Indochina, where imperialism fought such a tenacious war and wreaked so much havoc, Soviet support was the largest external factor, aside from the fundamental role of the indigenous revolutionaries, in determining the final outcome. It is very doubtful that the kind of devastation the US has visited so unremittingly and over so vast an area over the past decade and a half – from Afghanistan to Libya, Iraq and Syria included – could have been undertaken with such impunity if the US had to calculate, as it used to previously calculate in its moves in the Arab world, what the Soviet response might be. It is undoubtedly true that the Cold War was cold only for the major combatants and the Euro-American zones; hot wars were fought in many a corner of the tri-continent. However, for the most part and with singular exceptions like the Iraq–Iran war, offensives came from both sides; there were imperialist offensives, and there were offensives initiated by forces of revolution and national liberation. That symmetry disappeared with the disappearance of the Soviet Union. Aside from some local, senseless, ethnic convulsions here and there, all wars in the post-Soviet period have been initiated by imperialism – nothing else. There are no more phalanxes of revolutionaries initiating anti-imperialist wars of liberation. Those have been replaced by the *jehadis*, who first emerged as a fighting force in the service of imperialism and have since then had ambivalent relations with their Frankensteinian creator. Many of them now speak the language of revenge and retribution against that creator itself; Mr Baghdadi, the founder of the 'Islamic State of Iraq and the Levant' (ISIL), is a veteran of American torture chambers.

Finally, communism collapsed not only in south-eastern Europe, but also in Western and south-western Europe, even though much of communism in those zones had already broken with the Soviet Union under the sign of Eurocommunism. As communism and revolutionary socialism soon ceased to be a significant political force in Europe, for the first time in the twentieth century, political culture there was deeply transformed. It is quite unclear why an old, deeply rooted mass party like the Italian Communist Party (PCI), which had transformed Italian political culture and given to Europe such an array of brilliant communist thinkers, should have collapsed so completely in consequence of the collapse of the Soviet Union; those unwilling to forego the party's historic mission and who thought that it was the right moment to re-found communism on a new basis did carry on energetically, but also lost out in the end. Other parties (e.g., France, Spain) were smaller, and suffered further decline and internal decay. All in all, even Eurocommunism disappeared as a significant force as did the left-wing of social democracies in most of Europe. It was as if the existence of the Soviet system somehow legitimized their own existence as dissidents within the communist tradition; and that they somehow lost their very reason for existence with the disappearance of that which they opposed. At the other end were many (though not all) Trotskyist groupings which already held, through their own forms of reasoning, a view of the Soviet Union that more or less coincided with that of Ronald Reagan: 'evil empire'. Disappearance of that 'evil' was logically greeted with much jubilation. In no Trotskyist writing of the time does one encounter any understanding of how much imperialism on the global plane would get strengthened as a result of the dissolution of that system, and what it would mean for the working classes and anti-imperialist forces of the world.

Leaving the Scandinavian countries somewhat to the side, we could say that European social democracy – German, French, Italian and even the British Labour party – had taken two fatal steps in the post-war period: first by aligning itself substantially with imperialism in the anti-communist crusades of the post-war years, on the civilian/political fronts even more than the military ones; and, after the rise of Reagan and Thatcher, increasing collaboration with neo-liberalism in country after country, to the point that the social democrats became the left-wing of neo-liberalism itself. This degeneration reached such a point that Francois Hollande, the Socialist President of France, reacted to the terror attack in Paris exactly like George W. Bush, and sought to get embedded in the French Constitution the kind of Emergency powers for the President that had no precedent in the French constitutional tradition. (The Labour party under Blair has of course been far worse.) We should add, though, that this rightward shift in social democracy was not a consequence of the Soviet collapse. The relevant fact is that with its incorporation into overall western imperialism and the neo-liberal order, it had lost all political content that might have otherwise helped it fill the vacuum opened up by the communist collapse all over Europe, East and West.

Any consequential ideological configuration tends to be an incoherent, internally contradictory amalgam of fragments derived from different sources and planes of reality, past and present. As such, it is difficult to identify ideological effects in the contemporary landscape that are derived mainly from the collapse of the communist state system; typically, such effects of a particular development get embedded in larger configurations of various kinds. One broad comment would perhaps be in order, nonetheless.

The largest ideological effect of the collapse of the socialist state system is, not universally but across a large part of the world, a certain decline in the very meaning of the political. Michel Foucault summed up in his own sardonic way the new ideological situation in Europe when he remarked that the prospect of revolution had been the horizon of all politics for some two hundred years, and that it was no longer clear, with that horizon receding beyond sight, just what the meaning of politics would now be. For the first time since perhaps the French Revolution, certainly since the mid-nineteenth century, the word 'communism' has come to mean rather little in the dominant countries of the EU, with the exception of some small groupings and individuals, and has been driven very much to the margins in weaker zones of southern Europe, with the partial exception of Greece. Some of that absence is covered over by the word 'socialism' which, alas, has become something of an all-purpose digit that attaches to all sorts of political streams, from the cynical Mr Hollande to a New Deal Democrat like Bernie Sanders to a classically Bennite Labour politician like Jeremy Corbyn to one of the euphemisms that may, or probably may not, mean some variety of communism: Marxian socialism.

In the ideological domain, 'democracy' is the great fetish on which everyone – Left, Right and Centre – can agree in these post-everything times. Lack of democracy is said to have been the primal sin of communism, and one that eventually brought it to its knees, as if in divine retribution. Democracy is the primary virtue that the US takes to be its historic mission to export to the rest of the world (except to its favourite monarchies and dictators), for which it is willing to invade country after country. Democracy is what gives legitimacy to Modi in India, Erdogan in Turkey, the Muslim Brotherhood in Egypt, and it was in pursuit of democracy that Iraq, Libya and Syria had to be destroyed. 'Democracy' was the great slogan on the lips of everyone in Tahrir Square – and indeed in great many places from Bahrain to Tunisia: elections, the right to vote, the right to what Badiou calls 'capital-o-parliamentarianism'. The New, New Left of the social movements that arose as varieties of post-communism found it necessary to abjure the word 'revolution' with the meaning that the word has had since the onset of the French Revolution. 'Democracy' was now the old/new horizon: capitalism with a human face; not even a radical social democracy, just a decent sort of liberalism, or at best a populism of the Left. That was perhaps an understandable stance in a time when anti-capitalist forces had become fragile after so comprehensive a defeat, while liberal and not-so liberal capitalism was triumphant and the much darker forces of the Far Right were on the ascendant, in the imperialist heartlands as well as globally.

But that is not how the Left experienced that stance subjectively; not as a necessity imposed by defeat and dire threat from the Right and the Far Right. Rather, it was experienced and broadly presented to the world at large as a new wisdom arisen after the dark night of Stalinism. Which also means that almost a century of communist attempts to create a society beyond capitalism is now mostly seen by intellectuals and activists of the New, New Left, aside from some rare exceptions, as a history that teaches us only what not to do. That there might also be some (many?) positive lessons to be learned from that history is made to seem implausible. One is reminded of Walter Benjamin's bleak prediction: 'If they win, even the dead will not be safe; and they are winning all the time.' He said that about Nazis and fascists. But it is much more true about the triumph of liberal capitalism in our time. The ideological hegemony of imperialist power is to be witnessed not only in the shift of most liberalism into economic neo-liberalism and political reaction, not only in the ascendancy of the Far Right across much of the globe, but in the fact that it has so effectively taught so much of today's Left to be ashamed of everything that was communist in its own past – which is to say, a good bulk of its own past, considering that communist parties and communist state systems were cumulatively a much larger part of the history of the Left all through the twentieth century than any other current, including social democracy, which was the largest among those other currents but restricted almost entirely to that larger part of Europe that remained capitalist all through.

Those are the broader ideological currents. It must be added, though, that there are broader, more diffuse but very widespread resistances to the actual functioning of capital in our time. In numerous countries across the planet, there is a new generation of militants who understand the need for revolution, are by and large convinced that the Leninist revolutionary form has had its day, and are busy experimenting with many forms of extra-parliamentary action that liberalism is unable to accommodate. One of Marxism's great achievements is that while it began as a science of politics specifically for the proletarian class struggle against capitalism, it created a revolutionary consciousness and a language appropriate for that consciousness which could then be used by all the exploited and oppressed peoples of the world. The proletariat was the privileged agent of revolution in its own discourse and political action, but it also helped give birth to – or greatly aided the work of – a multiplicity of revolutionary agents: the anti-colonial revolutionary subject, women's movements, revolts against racial or caste justice, and so on. If we listen carefully to left-wing feminists or ecologists, or if we read the documents of the anti-globalization movements – in short, the whole range of radical opposition to exploitation and oppression – the one lexicon that is common to them all is what they have inherited from Marxism. They live in the tense of the interim, militants of a revolution that has not found its appropriate form. This too is an effect of not just the unravelling of the socialist system of states, but also of the manner of that unravelling, the truth of the inner implosion.

The Strategic Triangle: Russia, China, the US

Deng Xiaoping became Paramount Leader in the People's Republic of China (PRC) in 1978, Margaret Thatcher was elected British Prime Minister in 1979, and Ronald Reagan won the US presidential election in late 1980. The fact that neo-liberalism's ascent from enclaves such as

Chile to the imperial centre (on its way to global dominance) coincided with the beginning of the unravelling of the socialist state system is of great significance. The relation between these two processes is not causal but each supplemented the other. Thanks to that unravelling, neo-liberalism found a much more favourable terrain for determination of state policies, not only in virtually all of the rest of the world but in the formerly socialist countries as well. And, the form that the transition back to capitalism took in those countries was also partly shaped by the fact that the Euro-American west which the new rulers of the former COMECON countries wished to emulate was itself gripped by neo-liberal restructuring. The Americans who streamed into Moscow to supervise the transition could now implement those policies in a form far more brutal than was possible either in Western Europe or even the US itself. The Chinese conceded hardly any control and did things much more gradually, but the chief characteristics of their own transition back to capitalism had all the neo-liberalist hallmarks: stripping workers and peasants of the entitlements they had earned during the revolutionary period (1949–78), in terms of job security, health and housing benefits, or regulated prices;[6] export-led growth with abominable work and living conditions for the working class; competition with other lowest-wage countries like Bangladesh and Indonesia for foreign direct investment (FDI) on the most favourable terms and profit rates; and so on. Nor can there be any doubt that the most fundamentalist imposition and equally the most devastating impact of neo-liberal policies – distinctly more devastating and of far greater global consequence than even in Latin America – was in fact in the former COMECON countries, where it came in the condensed and surgical form of 'Shock Therapy', after more than a decade of experience in other parts of the world.

China and the COMECON countries, respectively, occupied very different positions in the world system of power. So, the process of unravelling also came in markedly different forms and with very different intentions and outcomes. The Chinese leadership that initiated the transition to capitalism had itself come out of the revolutionary process (Deng himself had been a famous revolutionary, a close friend and ally of Zhou Enlai and an ally of Mao as often as his critic), and they thought of their radical departures as necessary in view of what they regarded as a blockage and even a failure of Mao's overall policies and especially of the Cultural Revolution. Moreover, their roots were in anti-imperialist nationalism as much as – or perhaps more than – in communism. China had been the largest territorial economy in the world as late as the early nineteenth century and the so-called Boxer Rebellion that ended only in 1901 – and which is known to the Chinese as 'War of Eight Countries on China' – is seared into the memory of every Chinese nationalist. They also knew that for all its revolutionary gains, contemporary China was still largely agrarian, neither wealthy nor significantly industrialized. These communist nationalists who were now supervising a transition to capitalism and national chauvinism did not labour under the illusion, as did Gorbachev and his allies, that they could break into the exclusive Euro-American imperialist club; nor did they have any claim to be Europeans. The most important difference was that they did not set out to immediately dissolve the economic system as such – property relations and social relations of production – but to transform it gradually, year by year. And, equally importantly, they refused to dismantle any of the party–state as institutions of concentrated authority even though any number of millionaires and billionaires were eventually admitted into the party and state apparatuses in the course of changing the very class character of that party–state. Even the word 'communism' was retained, as a legitimating device, even though buried more and more under an avalanche of euphemisms: 'market socialism', 'Socialism with Chinese Characteristics', 'Red Cat/Black Cat', etc. A claim is still made from time to time that this is a phase of accumulation of national capital, a stage leading up to socialism itself, on the way to building a communist future. Legitimacy for the existing system in China is then sometimes sought in Mao's famous theorizations of 'New Democracy' and the 'Block of Four Classes'. Some in the communist movements outside China are persuaded by such claims and invocations.

The Soviet positions – which impacted other COMECON countries decisively – were very different. Unlike Deng and his allies, Gorbachev and his advisors were far younger than the generation that had made the revolution. They initially claimed that they were resuming, after a period of stagnation, the reforms that Khrushchev and Gromyko had initiated (not a very persuasive claim in fact). Like many a Slavic modernizer of the past many generations, they were Europhiles. 'You must recognize that we too are part of the Western civilization', Gorbachev said with desperate pathos in Washington D.C. Variants of this very sentiment one could hear until recently from Putin too, time and again, until the US-sponsored coup in Ukraine, imposition of the sanctions regime, manipulation of oil and gas markets, and destabilization of the rouble cured him of such civilizational fantasies and forced him to turn East, specifically toward China and Iran. It is possible that Gorbachev and his colleagues had initially sought some sort of social democratic reform in the communist system so as to become acceptable to the west, and thought that, as a great power, they would be able to keep intact not only the territorial unity of the state that was the USSR, but also perhaps an economic union of the COMECON countries, roughly on the lines of the European Union. Or, they too may have imagined it realistic to work towards a merger of the COMECON and the EU into a single bloc or, as Mitterand, then French President, suggested with vacuous Gallic aplomb, a confederation from the Atlantic to the Urals (no inclusion, even in that fanciful notion, of either the Asian republics of the USSR or even the Asian bulk of Russia itself; just 'Europe'). The US had some surprises for them on this score, as we shall see.

The COMECON nations were faced with an economy that had begun to stagnate in the early 1970s, just like the western economies. This, at least, was a feature common to neo-liberalism and *Perestroika*; both were responses to stagnation. In the Soviet case, Reagan's decision to go ahead full force with what came to be known as Star Wars technology of offensive military capabilities for the US-led NATO was the latest step in a pattern where the USSR had to keep committing unacceptably high levels of its resources to military readiness in competition with the US, bankrupting itself in the process. Faced with stagnation and this latest escalation in military pressure, the Soviets offered a historic compromise: radical reorganization of their system, even dissolution of some of its most notable features, for the Cold War to end and east–west cooperation to begin. In a radical difference from China, Soviet leaders planned not only to transform the economy much more radically and rapidly (*Perestroika*), but also to dissolve the party–state in its existing form, to be replaced by a classically liberal model (an intention buried under the euphemism of '*glasnost*'). They were men in a hurry. Gorbachev became General Secretary of the Communist Party of the Soviet Union (CPSU) in 1985, then Chairman of the presidium of the Supreme Soviet in 1988. Those three years were obviously ones given to securing position and preparing to take the big leap. It is possible that the process, once begun, just spun out of control.

The last of the Soviet troops withdrew from Afghanistan in February 1989 even as it was quite clear that the Soviet withdrawal was going to spell disaster for that whole region, since it was in Afghanistan that imperialism had assembled a huge multi-national force of Islamic soldiery (the estimated number of *jehadis* brought from outside Afghanistan and Pakistan vary between forty thousand and a hundred thousand), with consequences that would unfold over decades to come. In May that year Gorbachev visited China, the first Soviet head of state to do so since Khrushchev in 1959, to curb military hostilities between the two countries, and also perhaps in a homage to the Chinese version of *Perestroika*, but inadvertently in the midst of a tense time when liberal intellectuals (mostly students) were demonstrating in Tiananmen Square and holding up Gorbachev's portraits as a champion of democracy. Communist states were dissolved across the Warsaw Pact region all through the year, with the exception of Romania, and demolition of the Berlin Wall began in November. Official dissolution of the Soviet Union took another two years, when Gorbachev resigned on 25 December 1991, and the dissolution was announced the next day, to be fully formalized on 1 January 1992; all the individual republics had seceded from the union over the previous six months. No gunshots were required to peacefully dissolve the great experiment that had preoccupied much of the twentieth century.

How did US imperialism react to this sudden, voluntary disappearance of the adversary that Reagan had called 'the evil empire'? Its reactions to China and to the former COMECON countries were remarkably different – mainly because China was not then seen as a serious adversary in the past or for the near future, except in local conflicts such as the one in Korea, whereas the Soviet Union had been the great enemy that had to be subjugated, dismembered and weakened so sharply as to never again be able to aspire for equality. The courting of China had begun earlier and it was rewarded more handsomely when it began disavowing its communist past while the Soviet system was still intact. Kissinger had been invited to visit Beijing secretly for comprehensive talks in February 1971, and then again in October. In recognition of an evolving rapprochement, China was admitted to the United Nations and its Security Council in October that year. Recognition and full diplomatic relations came much later, however, only on 1 January 1979, perhaps in recognition of the direction China was expected to take under Deng. Even so, internal changes were gradual and almost entirely on Chinese terms, and it was only much later, well after the suppression of the Tiananmen Square protests of 1989 and in the wake of Deng's famous Southern Tour of 1992, that it became clear how far the PRC's transformation of the relations of production and strategies of accumulation were going to go. The ensuing policies were viewed much more favourably by transnational corporate capital, and by the US bourgeoisie and its state in particular. The PRC's strategy was to seek growth through exports not of primary goods but mainly of industrial products, and to use that growth for technological transformation of its own industrial base across all departments of production, all of which needed very large doses of foreign investment and technological inputs. The PRC's ability to provide a very large mass of relatively much more skilled labour to high-tech industries at wage rates corresponding to levels of the most primitive kind of accumulation brought in huge investment to build a highly diversified set of industrial plants, for a great number of the biggest corporations. Thanks to the profit rates it offered, it was able to attract staggeringly high volumes of investment from all regions of the imperialist bloc – the US, Japan, EU – which in turn facilitated high rates of accumulation within China, which then transformed its productive capacities, technological levels and infrastructure, from Shanghai to Tibet.

China has served imperialist interests most conspicuously in three different ways. First, it has been by far the most important source for cheap products all across the supply chain that feed the US consumer market, and thus has contributed greatly to the maintenance of social stability in a society where real wages have been stagnant for some forty years, and real unemployment rates run between 15 and 20 per cent. Without these cheap, mainly China-made products, the bulk of the US population would not have been able to maintain anything close to the standards of living it has become historically accustomed to. By now, with constantly expanding productive capacity, China has begun to play a similar role in the EU as well, to the extent that Chinese exports to the EU now surpass its exports to the US. Second, the Chinese economy accounts for sustained high profit rates for many of the highest-ranking US corporations, such as Apple and Walmart, in production as well as distribution. Thirdly, US public debt, calculated at $13.62 trillion as of January 2016, accounts for roughly 75 per cent of its GDP; China and Japan together account for some 20 per cent of it in roughly equal amounts, close to $1.3 trillion each. In short, China plays a crucial role in the US economy in terms of providing cheap consumption goods and helping maintain social stability in a crisis-ridden society, making high rates of corporate profits possible for key players in the US economy, and for sustaining a crucial chunk of the US deficit financing so necessary for the daily functioning of the US economy and its imperialist actions across the globe. Needless to add, the relations are unequal and reciprocal. The US consumer market has been crucial for rapid growth rates in China's export-led model of industrialization, modernization and technological advance. It is primarily on the basis of sustained exports to the US that China has been able to cover its vast import needs, diversify its export destinations, and provide cash and technology to a range of countries – from neighbouring Pakistan to far-flung territories in Africa and Latin America – that provide China with strategic raw materials. Since China was so much poorer, since it pursued mainly economic but hardly any geostrategic interests beyond its borders, and because it did not threaten any of the key US interests across the world, the US was until recently far less hostile toward China than toward Russia. For, its move towards peaceful coexistence with Taiwan and highly accommodative ways of reabsorbing Hong Kong and Macau into its national territory are examples of China's cool and level-headed diplomacy. And, unlike resource-rich Russia, China has had serious deficits in its internal resources in energy and other strategic raw materials, which makes it in some respects more vulnerable.

The Soviet Union – alongside COMECON and the Warsaw Pact – was always the US's main adversary, the other superpower, the competing military giant with a rough parity even in the nuclear field. And it always had the geopolitical advantage of occupying so much of the Eurasian land mass, adjacent to Western Europe at one end and to Japan at the other, with an interminably long border with China and looming over production and underground deposits of oil and gas in the Caspian and Gulf regions as well as the larger Middle East. Western Europe had been taken under America's hegemonic shelter on the pretext of protecting it from the 'Red Menace'. The overt rationale for the creation of NATO was a US-led joint defence against that Menace but, structurally, it served to guarantee Western Europe's own military inferiority in relation to the Big Brother and the Big Brother's iron grip over Western Europe's strategic choices, as de Gaulle well understood. On the other hand, whenever a Soviet or West European leader proposed a serious initiative for *entente* between the blocs of East and West – Khrushchev's 'Peaceful Coexistence' or the '*Ostpolitic*' of Egon Bahr and Willy Brandt – the nightmare in Washington was a unity of purpose between Germany and Russia that bypassed the US. That nightmare still remains.

As we saw, China sought to make a transition at a measured pace; by contrast, Gorbachev and his cohorts executed, wittingly or not, a swift and gigantic internal collapse. China managed to sidestep imperialism's ire and the possibility of self-destruction; the Soviet leaders walked right into it. Dismantling the socialist system of the centrally planned economy as well as the party–state and even the territorial unity of the Soviet Union all at once – together with the break-up of the COMECON which had developed highly sophisticated mechanisms of joint economic planning – rendered all those countries, including the Soviet Union, incapable of overseeing the construction of a viable alternative or defending themselves against predations by either the multilateral institutions or, above all, the US. Gorbachev, the chief architect of this systemic transformation, was set aside in the very moment of the dissolution of the USSR as Yeltsin, a drunken but cunning and vicious buffoon, had already taken over as President of the newly confected Russian Federation, and proved pliable to pressure from his American handlers. Managers of not just a capitalist but a remorselessly neo-liberal transition, to be named 'Shock Therapy', just walked in.

The US had some specific anxieties that it needed to ward off. First, that the new states emerging from the collapse of the Soviet Union – from

Estonia to Georgia to the former Asian Republics of the USSR – along with the former members of the COMECON – e.g. Hungary, Czechoslovakia, what now became Russia – not be permitted to resurrect some kind of an economic bloc. Russia had to be isolated and the others absorbed into capitalist Europe one by one, separately. Second, that the dismantling of the Warsaw Pact ought not to become the occasion for weakening of NATO or for Western Europe to be hearkening for its own security arrangements free of US dominance. One of the functions of the protracted war over various regions of Yugoslavia, from Kosovo to Serbia, was to reinvigorate NATO and to reincorporate Western Europe into US-led wars, this time on European soil itself. Third, that the unification of Germany should not become the occasion for a more generalized mutual accommodation and unity between Eastern and Western Europe, as Gorbachev had been proposing and something that would also be a great theme for Putin during his first tenure as Russian President. This the US addressed, first of all, by incorporating German interests into its own. The ruling Christian Democrats in West Germany, predisposed towards neo-liberalism and hostile to the possible social democratization of the former Soviet bloc, were anyway sympathetic to the US standpoint, and, in addition, needed US assistance in negotiating Soviet withdrawal from the GDR and reintegration of it into a reunited greater Germany (something of a colonizing takeover as it turned out to be). Furthermore, German capital was already dominant in Europe, strong in its productive base and in its own export drives, and it aspired to dominate south-eastern Europe itself, not share it much with a more generalized European capital. If successful in this, Germans could then pick up vast properties and assets in the former socialist bloc for a song, and also gain huge pools of a cheap, well-trained labour force in their very backyard, as the US had found in China. Between the US leadership and the German agreement, the fate of Eastern Europe in the near future was sealed. Not the shibboleth of Franco–German unity but the much more solid reality of the US–German alliance prevailed.

Western Europe had a choice to make. Given the bizarre collapse that Gorbachev, his cohorts and successors had supervised, the former COMECON countries needed a rescue mission. The west, and Western Europe in particular, could have opted for the kind of rescue mission that was undertaken after World War II, when the multilateral London Agreement of 1953 symbolically reduced the German debt but in real terms just abolished it, and, more importantly, the US crafted the ambitious Marshall Plan for West European economic recovery. The aim behind the latter was of course to incorporate the whole of Western Europe, including its social democrats, in the US project for the containment of communism, and to roll back West European communism itself, not to speak of creating a prosperous market for the export of US goods from a US industry overflowing with productive capacity. However, what this also entailed was transferring enough resources for a reconstruction even beyond the levels that had existed before, with brand new industrial plants incorporating the latest technologies. The former COMECON countries were now gripped by a double disaster: the accumulated problems of what came to be known in the Soviet Union as the 'period of stagnation' (formally the Brezhnev years, but really from the early 1970s till the very end), and, on top of it, the manner in which the collapse was executed. They needed a similar rescue: transfer of resources from Western Europe to the East for stabilization and reconstruction. But with the proliferation of neo-liberalism across the western world, times had changed radically.

The Marshall Plan was crafted in the 1950s, at a point in history when even Eisenhower, a Republican President and former commander of the Allied Forces in the European theatre during World War II, could off-handedly say that anyone who did not support the New Deal was way beyond the political spectrum – and, in his famous 'Farewell Address', warn against the rising 'military–industrial complex' that could become a threat to American democracy itself. That was a five-star general speaking in the founding years of the Cold War. Now, in the heyday of neo-liberalism, even the thought of so massive a transfer of resources from one bloc of countries to another would have been treated as some extreme form of madness or even conspiracy, perhaps a last attempt to give communism a new lease on life even after the suicide. Social democratization of post-Soviet East Europe was in any case a pipe-dream. In the world that had emerged after World War II, European social democracy had already made a fatal choice: in becoming part of a vast western coalition of forces in the anti-communist, anti-Soviet crusade, it simply kept moving further and further to the Right. As neo-liberalism rolled across the world, they became its left-wing under the slogan 'There Is NO Choice' (the famous TINA principle). Nor does it seem plausible that the dominant figures in the higher echelons of the various communist parties who executed the dissolution were themselves keen to save enough of the system to try and transit into a social democratic direction. The temptation to benefit from conversion of public properties into private assets at nominal prices seems to have been much too strong.

Consenting to every tenet and prescription of neo-liberal globalization was the precondition for cooperation between the former socialist countries and the west – and 'the west' in practice meant the US and a handful of institutions such as the International Monetary Fund (IMF) that worked as its proxies. Privatization of public assets in these countries was of an entirely different magnitude than the famous and highly destructive privatizations of Latin America – or elsewhere, for that matter – where most assets were in the private domain anyway, and because the market price for those assets in the public domain that were to be privatized could be calculated easily because their mode of functioning was already modelled very much on the patterns of capitalist corporations, since they too existed within a fully functioning capitalist economy. Not so in the former COMECON countries. The magnitude was immense and even the monetary basis for privatization entirely arbitrary, designed to greatly devalue the public assets before they were given over to private ownership. We shall offer just one little example to illustrate how the process worked. It was stipulated that new corporate entities had to be established for disposing of those public assets and that those assets could only be sold for cash or against a collateral, which in turn greatly favoured those who had already accumulated wealth under the previous system, especially during its last years – in other words, the corrupt bureaucrats, the oligarchs, the blackmarketeers and racketeers in general, and who were then also in a position to collaborate with foreign financiers.

This is not the place to go into the practical specifics of the transition or its social consequences. All of that is very well known. We have recalled some basic features of that transition, contrasting the process in China and the COMECON countries respectively, and also contrasting the differential responses of US imperialism to that process in the respective regions. A certain paradox of course is that China, which continues to call itself communist and is officially ruled by a party of that name, has been treated relatively more kindly and collaboratively, whereas the ones who renounced everything and went over to a much more savage form of capitalism have been met with far more domineering hostility. The encirclement of China has been far more gradual in practice and more muted since Dengist policies first came into force; the US has sought to make it more urgent recently (the ill-termed 'Asian pivot'), as China's economic power gets more consolidated and less dependent on US markets. The focus on Russia and on states in its environs has been far more ferocious, not just in terms of the strategic decision to bring NATO to Russia's very borders, and to fight for control over such countries as Georgia, Ukraine and what were once the Asian republics of the Soviet Union.

Why this contrast in treatment of China and Russia respectively? Perhaps the key to understanding this lies in the respective strengths and vulnerabilities of the two countries. China has two strengths in relation to the US: it has vast wealth resources which the US state needs for its own debt financing; and it has vast resources of cheap and mostly very skilled labour (and now also the infrastructure) that US capital needs. Between needs of the state and needs of its capital, the US is forced to bargain with China more soberly. Internally, China has a coherent and well-integrated central authority within which there can be policy disputes and factional struggles over distribution of institutional power but nothing that can drastically shift the nature of its relationship with US imperialism. It also has so much liquidity and so much control over its own financial institutions that it has greater (though not infinite) capacity to survive a cyclical crisis in the global system than virtually any other of the major economies; this is a strength worth noting when crises are looming in the global economy as well the bubble-inflated sectors of the national economy. And, Japan is the only great centre of capital accumulation to which China is geographically proximate; it is far from Europe and far from the great resource-rich regions of the world, which too makes the US less hostile to China than to Russia. Thus, its relative isolation is a blessing of sorts. China's great weakness is that its ambitious economic strategies require far, far more natural resources than are available within its own territory, and it must therefore perennially rely on external sources to meet those requirements. The US can concentrate on building capacities for resource denial, while China stays focused very much on securing those supplies reliably by building an international network of economic alliances and by financing the global infrastructure required for that resource integration (the multiple 'Silk Roads' and equivalents thereof). That is going to be the crux of the now-developing Asian segment of the new Cold War (I don't think the metaphor of 'the new Cold War' is analytically coherent, but it is a useful shorthand).[7] Furthermore, China's religious diversity is its vulnerability: Buddhist subversion in Tibet, Islamic terrorism in western China. Imperialism has invested a great deal in both.

Russia is in some ways the opposite. Contrasted to China, Russia can offer neither fabulous credit finance nor great pools of cheap labour. And, the US views Russia's great natural resources not as a temptation but as a threat to its own interests. The US is rich enough in natural resources and it dominates a majority of the resource-rich countries; it does not need Russian resources and would like the EU to import as little of them as possible. For the rest, Russia is far too powerful in any case; it can neither be a client-state like Saudi Arabia nor can it be bombed into becoming a client-state like Iraq. Nor is it Qatar or Bahrain or even Nigeria. Russia is a different kind of country and has therefore been assigned enemy status. The strategic resources within Russia's own territory are fabulous, its demographic pressures the opposite of China, its financial resources usually enough for its own needs but far inferior to those of China, its military capabilities superior to not only that of China but to that of every other country except the US itself; the size and quality of its nuclear force as well as the capacity for technological innovation in weapons systems gives it, effectively, a rough parity with the US in this arena. Its proximity to Europe is both an advantage and a vulnerability. The surplus capital of resource-poor Europe and the resource-rich but capital-deficient Russia is an obvious ground for alliance and integration. That integration is America's nightmare, since that would make Russia strategically secure and Europe secure in its access to strategic fuels. In such an eventuality Europe could become more independent of the US, needing the US less for guaranteeing a reliable supply of key resources, and Russia more secure, economically and strategically. We shall not detail the strategies the US has pursued in preventing Western Europe from getting closer to Russia economically and strategically. However, it is worth remarking that Western Europe's full compliance in America's bid to isolate Russia and surround it militarily, even though closer relations with Russia would be good for its own economy, is a sobering illustration of how central the US is, and how peripheral and dependent the EU is, in the structure of imperialist power as a whole. The paradox, of course, is that in pursuing inordinately aggressive and successful policies in preventing Russia from developing closer ties with Europe, the US has actually driven Russia and China into something of a long-term partnership in matters economic as well as strategic.

Let us conclude the argument by summarizing some of the key realities detailed above. First, the unravelling of the socialist system has been the central event in the history of imperialism since, let us say, 1990 – over the past quarter-century. It shifted the balance of class forces around the world radically, most particularly in making available vast labour resources to global capital in countries where they had previously been highly protected, at wage rates so low as to depress the wage rate and employment prospects everywhere else. By the same token, it went some distance in resolving the problem of corporate profits for numerous corporations, large and small, that got involved in that transition, and managed to profit from it very substantially over the past quarter-century. Out of the nine million or so jobs that are said to have migrated out of the US into low-wage countries over the past two decades, the majority went to China; that would not have been possible if the socialist system had prevailed there through those years. Second, there is a structural link between the demise of the socialist state system and the onset of universalization of the capitalist mode of production that was given the name of 'globalization' – a correlation that is evident from the fact that there were hardly any books prior to 1990 with the word 'globalization' in their titles, but such books began to proliferate since then and became a flood over the next decade or more, so that the word just got naturalized as a habit of speech with a self-evident meaning. Third, that unravelling greatly shifted the balance of force between imperialism and all the forces opposed to it, of whatever kind, whether socialist forces, or forces of national liberation, or even just national-bourgeois states of the tricontinent that had previously won some space in their dealings with imperialism thanks to an alternative source of possible support. The TINA (There Is No Alternative) effect was felt even more strongly at the level of the system of states than at the socio-economic level within the national economies; the two levels I mention here were of course inter-related and inter-dependent.

As noted above, a striking fact is that, leaving aside the very special case of the Arab world, the imperialist strategies for global dominance are still very largely focused on what were the two big (and competing) centres of power in the erstwhile socialist world: Russia and China. The irony of course is that while the US did manage to take decisive advantage of the fissures between China and the Soviet Union in the 1960s and 70s, the extremity and desperation in its policies over the past decade served to bring these two adversaries together in grand global designs, in defensive response to US belligerence. This paradox reflects a shift in the material basis of the American power of coercion globally. During that earlier period, the productive economy of the US, its military power and the strength of its currency seemed to balance each other more or less harmoniously. Cumulatively, these three factors served as pillars of what was called 'American hegemony'. Under pressure of that overwhelming power and already reeling under the negative impact of the proletarian Cultural Revolution, China sought a reprieve as early as 1971, and, in the bargain, all but gave up its military support to Vietnam. Today, a significant part of America's productive capacity has migrated to China, thanks to America's own promotion of globalization, while the strength of the US currency is owed partly to China's financing of US deficits. Today, 67 per cent of the world's wealth is held in dollars, which is still a high but declining percentage, and the yuan/renbinmi is the first non-European currency to have become a significant instrument for international trade.

Aside from the accumulated size (not just yearly output) and institutional depth of the US economy, what remains above all is the US military might and its unique presence in every corner of the world. The US power is not to be underrated, but its structural imbalance must be taken into account; military power already overshadows the economic power, and the Pentagon now occupies a more central place among departments of the US government than the treasury. However, the nature of this military power is also paradoxical. The US armed forces, more powerful than any that the world has ever known, seem able to destroy one non-nuclear country after another but unable to win a single war. In the Arab world alone the US military has led makeshift alliances of all sorts and destroyed at least four countries – Iraq, Libya, Syria and now Yemen[8] – but anything resembling a victory has eluded it everywhere, unless a dance of death in the ruins of nations be construed as victory.

By contrast, the rapid growth in China's economic might is historically unprecedented and grounds enough for it to start responding, albeit very calculatedly and without bluster. Forming far-reaching alliances and bilateral partnerships is part of that response, especially the growing alliance with Russia, but also a network of economic relationships in different parts of the world based on trade and China's financial capacities. The Sino–Russian alliance has a strong chance of survival because it is based on a sense of weakness of each, as both countries face a highly belligerent adversary. Like the US system of alliances, this too is gathering more and more countries into its various groupings: the Shanghai Cooperation Organization (SCO), a BRICS bank and so on. At present, BRICS (alliance of five emerging economies: Brazil, Russia, India, China and South Africa) seems to have lost much of its steam, thanks to serious economic troubles in South Africa and now even in Brazil; India is of course hamstrung by its alliance with the US while it is tempted by China's economic strength. By contrast, the developing Sino–Russian alliance and institutions related to that alliance (the SCO and the like) seem to have more real substance, not only for those two countries but also for several other countries in the region, notably Iran and other resource-rich countries of the Caspian region. That is how it stands at present, but that is not how it was until about a decade ago. The full implications of Chinese economic strategies and persistently high growth rates started becoming clear only over the last few years, and the Russian economy began its slow climb out of the post-communist abyss well after Putin took over as Prime Minister. These trends in China and Russia have emerged precisely during the years when the economic crisis in the US was deepening – the 2007–08 crisis was very largely the globalization of a crisis that began in the US – and even as the US has been sinking deeper into military quagmires of its own making.

In the evolving structure of what was once called 'containment', it has become very clear that while the US is executing its military encirclement of both countries more strongly than before, the economic warfare against Russia is already well advanced but not visibly so against China.

Thus, the US is doing its best to start denying markets to resource-rich Russia, especially in Europe, whereas the crux of economic warfare against China will of course be denial of resources (and markets to a lesser extent), which is still not aggressively under way. The main theatres for immediate confrontation with Russia are in Europe and the Caspian Sea basin; Syria becomes important only for the reason that it is the only place in the Middle East where Russia has a military base, because Russia chose to intervene there in retaliation for the US-sponsored coup and its aftermath in Ukraine, and because Syria is crucial in Russia's evolving relations with Iran. In this confrontation, the placing of advanced weapons systems close to Russia will be used to disrupt normal relations, including trade and investment relations, between the NATO countries and Russia; and there will be ferocious struggle over routes and directions of new gas and oil pipelines that can bypass Russia and supply Western Europe directly. The main theatre of confrontation with China will be all along the Eastern Pacific, right down to the Malacca Straits. Militarization of these new rivalries in Europe as well as Asia is of course good for the armament industries of numerous countries, from the US to Japan to Sweden; even Germany may feel the pressure to build military strength for itself, alongside Britain and France. A sort of a new Asian NATO is already planned for the US, Japan, Australia and, it is hoped, India as well as Vietnam. Among these, only Japan is particularly keen because this opens up the ground for rearmament and, with that, a huge big jump for the Japanese armament industry, which is envisioned as a great boost for the country's stagnant economy; a recent constitutional coup from the Right has already paved the way for adoption of such policies. The problem is that all the other countries that are to be brought into the military alliance, and are informally already there, are at the same time much too interested in profiting from economic cooperation with China. Even within Japan there is a very considerable opposition to such a degree of confrontation with China and even to the militarization of that scope.

Literature on the subject of these new 'containment' strategies is voluminous. Let me offer just one example. Soon after the Soviet collapse, in 1992, a 'Defence Planning Document' for the US was leaked which said that: 'Our first objective must be to prevent the re-emergence of a new rival . . . we must maintain the mechanisms for deterring potential competitors from even aspiring to a larger regional or global role.' No particular country was named at that time but the tone had changed by 2006 when the *Quadrennial Document Review*, which the Pentagon issues every four years, had this to say: 'Of all the emerging powers, China has the greatest potential to compete militarily with the United States.' Two features of this thinking are notable. First, no other country is to be allowed to have even a *larger regional role*: not China in Asia, not Russia in Europe (but perhaps India in South Asia as a certified US client). Second, the very idea that China could, as of 2006, even dream '*to compete militarily with the US*' is simply in the realm of the absurd. So, one wonders what the US means by military competition; it perhaps means that China may not stake, without US permission, territorial claims to an offshore island that Japan, a US ally, also claims. In other words, the US must remain so very much more powerful that it be acknowledged the arbiter in the smallest of local disputes between any two countries in the world.

One only has to study the nature of the most advanced weapons systems that the US continues relentlessly to build. The extraordinary degree of naval build-up, for instance, is a cause for wonder as to who it is aimed against. Russia, for instance, does not even have a kind of coastline where serious naval warfare, nuclear submarines and all, could be imagined. In a different direction, the rapid rate of increased expansion in American military bases and other forms of military presence in all parts of Africa is of course related to ambitions of the US to dominate the resource-rich continent as much as possible for its own use and profit, but, negatively, this presence is also designed to build the foundations for denying African resources to China whenever it is so desired. This particular strategy goes back to colonial times when European powers set out to compete for acquisition of colonies so as to have privileged access to the resources and markets of those colonies for themselves, but also, equally, to deny those resources and markets to their rivals. The US itself has been so focused on strategic resources of the Middle East since World War II precisely for this reason: replace the former colonial powers, deny those resources to the Soviet Union, and make much of the world, including its NATO allies, dependent on the ability of the US to guarantee the security of oil supplies across vast distances. With respect to the Arab world, that policy continues. Something analogous may now transpire in Africa.

Conclusion

This is by no means a comprehensive analysis of imperialism in our time, even in its political and ideological dimensions. We have said nothing of the great challenges to imperialist domination that have emerged in much of Latin America, which too now seems to be on a retreat that is already visible in Argentina and Brazil and on the defensive in Venezuela. Nor have we taken into account the waves upon waves of resistance to neo-liberal austerity in several parts of Europe – nor of the stirrings within the US of various shades of the Left: Bernie Sanders, in reality a New

Deal Democrat, has had the great merit of reintroducing 'socialism' as a legitimate term in mass politics on a scale unknown since World War I. Above all, we have kept out of our analysis the central imperialist crime of our time: the destruction of millions of human lives in the name of 'War on Terror', 'Humanitarian Intervention', 'Responsibility to Protect', etc., while all the time unleashing *jehadi* terror against its own adversaries. There is no space for a global mapping of that magnitude. Instead, we have deliberately focused on a single logic within the larger design, and we have done so because, despite all the barbarity of imperialist designs in the Arab world, the 'containment' of Russia and China may well come to define the central confrontation in the coming decades of this young century.

Notes

1 For the Far Right in Europe, see the very informative and thoughtful articles by Liz Fikete and Walter Baier in the same issue of *Socialist Register*: Panitch and Albo, eds (2016).

2 Literature on the Far Right's conceptions of state power is considerable and we don't have the space to develop our thesis here. Carl Schmitt's *Political Theology: Four Chapters on the Concept of Sovereignty* is the primary text for so absolute a juridical concept of sovereignty. A close reading of Schmitt's arguments and precepts can clarify many things about the kind of claims the US has made about its rights of absolute imperial sovereignty.

3 I take this phrase from Tugal (2007).

4 European Command, Africa Command, Pacific Command, etc., and, most fascinatingly, the Special Operations Command that works through all other commands and is designed for secret warfare in every corner of the globe, beyond the reach of any law except that of US military law itself. Even a cursory reading of the briefs given to these commands is fascinating and sobering.

5 The Oslo Accords were signed roughly at the same time when Mandela was forming the first post-apartheid government in South Africa. Both events were greeted with high hopes, though in different ways and by different people. Those hopes were to be dashed to a considerable degree, in both cases.

6 By the early 2000s, roughly half of the urban population and some 80 per cent of the rural population had no health insurance, and roughly 30 per cent of household income was now said to go towards covering medical needs.

7 My conceptual difficulty in talking about a 'new Cold War' in the present context is that (the old) 'Cold War' was a euphemism for confrontation between the US and the USSR that was systemic in nature. Today, there is no clash of world systems. Today's clashes – between the US, let us say, and Russia or China or both – are in the nature of rivalries and alignments of the kind known since the nineteenth century as 'balance of power' (among leading powers within the same system of states).

8 In Yemen, the US culpability has at least three layers. First, the US has fought a fierce drone war, ostensibly against al Qaeda, while planting clients and supplying them with weapons of all kind. Second, the Saudi–Emirati alliance that has invaded Yemen and destroyed so much of it relies on the most advanced US-supplied war equipment. Third, as the invading armies are incapable of fighting a ground war on their own, US-based corporations such as Blackwater/Xe and Dyncorp are supplying mercenaries to do the fighting. In short, if some US

corporations provide the weaponry, other such corporations supply the personnel to use much of that weaponry. The main beneficiary so far seems to have been al Qaeda, which seems to be aligned with the US-supplied Saudis.

References

Ahmad, Aijaz (2004), 'The Imperialism of Our Time', in Leo Panitch and Colin Leys, eds, *Socialist Register*; reprinted in Aijaz Ahmad, *Iraq, Afghanistan and the Imperialism of Our Time*, New Delhi: LeftWord Books.

Ahmad, Aijaz (2016), 'India: Liberal Democracy and the Extreme Right', in Leo Panitch and Greg Albo, eds, *Socialist Register*, London: Merlin Press.

Kalecki, Michael (1972), 'The Fascism of Our Time', in *The Last Phase in the Transformation of Capitalism*, New York: Monthly Review Press.

Panitch, Leo and Greg Albo, eds (2016), *Socialist Register*, London: Merlin Press.

Schmitt, Carl ([1985] 2005), *Political Theology: Four Chapters on the Concept of Sovereignty*, English translation (German original 1922, revised 1934), Chicago: Chicago University Press.

Tugal, Cihan (2007), 'NATO's Islamists: Hegemony and Americanization in Turkey', *New Left Review*, 44, March–April.

The Institutional Architecture of Imperialism in the Twenty-first Century

Jayati Ghosh

A central focus of Prabhat Patnaik's work, and a major component of his analytical contributions, has been on the evolution and continued relevance of imperialism. The innovation and profundity of his discussions have shed much clearer light on the nature of imperialism over the past century. He has shown how imperialism continued to be a significant force even after the disintegration of colonial power in the second half of the twentieth century and the resulting lack of direct political control, which changed the landscape in terms of how control could then be exercised. He has highlighted the impact of the domination of finance, globally and nationally, which has dramatically changed the ways in which imperialism has played out particularly in the period since the 1990s. This essay does not pretend to any further development of these important concepts; rather, it provides what could be considered as empirical footnotes that elaborate on how some of these have evolved since the beginning of the current century in terms of the international legal and institutional architecture, thereby generating new ways in which imperialist economic relations are expressed and enforced.

Just after World War II, in the Bretton Woods period, the undisputed dominance of the United States in the capitalist world order played a central role in ensuring that many of the earlier requirements were met through a combination of global policing and economic rules of the game set by the global leader. By the late twentieth century, however, the world had become much more complex geopolitically and economically. The United States had become the sole superpower, but one enfeebled by over-extension (as the wars in Iraq and the subsequent inability to control events across the Arab world showed clearly) and its own increasing economic dependence on capital inflows across the world. Competitive threats from Western Europe and Japan were short-lived due to rampant internal contradictions in both, but the emergence of new powers in the developing world, and in particular the economic rise of China, created a more complex global dynamic. The growing power of multinational corporations was matched by a proliferation of originating countries of such firms, and the technological changes that enabled production relocation along with the vertical disintegration of production led to the emergence of value chains in which the requirements of multinational corporations became somewhat different.

In so far as imperialism is about the struggle over and capture of economic territory (which must be broadly defined to include not just geographical territory such as land and natural resources, but also the creation of new markets, new sources of labour and new forms of surplus transfer such as are reflected in intellectual property), these changes have created new demands upon imperialist structures and processes. In the absence of a world state, and in a much more complex and constantly changing global politico-economic environment, how can capital (which is increasingly global in orientation) generate the superstructures through which the transfers of value are ensured and the investment risks are moderated and contained? It is argued here that much of this has been sought to be resolved by refashioning the global institutional architecture in ways that operate to increase the conditions of 'stability' for large capital, while increasing its bargaining power vis-à-vis working people and citizens as well as nation-states and even smaller capitalist enterprises.

International Trade and Economic Partnership Agreements

One important way in which this has evolved has been in terms of international agreements and treaties that create a legal basis for the enforcement of particular types of economic relationships. The past two decades have witnessed an explosion in the treaties, agreements and other mechanisms whereby global capital imposes rules, regulations and modes of behaviour upon governments and their citizenry. It is true that the post-war international financial system created by the Bretton Woods agreement also specified rules for member countries, and the conditionalities imposed by the International Monetary Fund (IMF) and the World Bank also severely limited the autonomy of countries that were forced to turn to them for assistance. But the recent proliferation of trade agreements (multilateral, regional and bilateral), investment treaties and more comprehensive economic partnership agreements imposes such a plethora of conditions that those almost pale into insignificance. What is more significant is that these rules operate even for countries that are not in the position of being debtor-supplicants to international financial institutions, and so they require all countries to restrict their policies in ways that are directly related to the possibilities of generating autonomous development in periphery countries.

Consider how the multilateral trading system has evolved. Earlier rounds of GATT (the General Agreement on Trade and Tariffs) recognized special and differential (S&D) treatment for developing countries, which required less than full reciprocity and was couched in developmental terms. The Uruguay Round (signed off in 1994) moved to a single-tier system of rights and obligations, under which developing countries have to fully implement all rules and commitments, with flexibility only in longer transition periods. This was seen as *quid pro quo* for market access in agriculture and textiles and clothing, sectors that were highly protected in the developed countries.

But this affected the possibilities of autonomous development in the periphery by constraining the policy choices open to them, and denying them some of the most important instruments that had been used by the current capitalist core in its own industrialization and development process. For example, the Agreement on Trade-Related Investment Measures (TRIMS) does not allow practices like local content specifications to increase linkages between foreign investors and local manufacturers, or foreign exchange balancing requirements or restrictions on foreign exchange use by foreign investors. The Agreement on Trade-Related Intellectual Property Rights (TRIPS) allows for the concentration and privatization of knowledge as noted above, and, additionally, severely restricts reverse engineering and other forms of imitative innovation that have historically been used for industrialization. It has forced the extension of patent life in many countries, allows patenting of life-forms, and puts the burden of proof on the defendant rather than on the claimant seeking to monopolize control over knowledge. The Agreement on Subsidies and Countervailing Measures (SCM) prohibits subsidies that depend upon the use of domestic over imported goods or are conditional on export performance. Ongoing negotiations in the World Trade Organization (WTO) on Non-Agricultural Market Access (NAMA) are currently based on requiring much deeper tariff cuts in developing countries, which will further deprive them of a crucial trade measure that can support infant industry.

The Agreement on Agriculture (AoA) contained fine print that effectively allowed the developed countries to continue with their massive subsidization and protection of their own agriculture and agri-businesses, but it prevents the developing countries from doing even a small fraction of this. Most developing countries are allowed only 10 per cent *de minimis* support, unlike most developed countries which have to ensure only 36 per cent reduction of certain subsidies and limit some others, while maintaining and even increasing others. Developing countries (like India) that attempt to provide some protection to farmers to ensure food security are coming up against this constraint, because, according to the AoA, all such subsidies even in the developing countries must be measured in relation to 1986–88 prices, not current prices! Instead of recognizing the ridiculous nature of this clause, the developed countries have resisted any change and have only agreed to provide a 'Peace Clause' for a limited period to certain countries. There are many other elements of the AoA that are inherently unjust and biased against developing countries, yet have effectively been given a legal basis that prevents change or grievance redressal.

However, if the WTO has created rigidities and constraints on policy space in developing countries, the many Regional Trade Agreements (RTAs) that have been signed in the past two decades are often even worse on this front. There are nearly 400 such agreements in operation, and they have become more comprehensive over the past twenty years. Most (especially the North–South agreements) tend to be 'WTO-plus', i.e. they augment provisions already covered by the multilateral trading regime, or 'WTO-extra', i.e. they contain provisions that go beyond current WTO agreements. Thus they often require reductions of actually applied tariffs rather than of 'bound' tariff rates. They demand more deregulation in services trade. They typically require more stringent enforcement of intellectual property rights (IPRs): they reduce exemptions (e.g., allowing compulsory licensing only for emergencies); prevent parallel imports; extend IPRs to areas like life-forms, counterfeiting and piracy; extend exclusive rights to test data (e.g., in pharmaceuticals); and make IPR provisions more detailed and prescriptive. They have been known to forbid demands for the transfer of technology and knowledge, and disallow conditions on the nationality of senior personnel, even extending treaty provisions to cover taxes and charges. They also enter into a range of areas that the WTO still leaves open to individual countries' policy choices, such as competition policy, rules on investment and capital movement, government procurement, environmental standards, and even labour mobility. Further, unlike the WTO, most RTAs do not provide exceptions to countries in the case of serious balance-of-payments and external financial difficulties.

In addition to these plurilateral and regional treaties, there are the Bilateral Investment Treaties (BITs), of which there are more than 4,000 in operation in the world at present. These are not at all concerned with the regulation of private investment across borders. Rather, they are about protecting and promoting private investment of all types, and effectively privileging the rights of investors over the rights of citizens in the host country – therefore inhibiting states' abilities to control or regulate investment. Furthermore, in such treaties there is typically a very broad, asset-based definition of investment that includes foreign direct investment (FDI), some types of portfolio investment in equities, and real estate and even intellectual property rights. Most of these treaties typically incorporate a very strong and expansive view on what constitutes 'expropriation' for which compensation can be demanded. As a result, it is not just nationalization of assets that has been interpreted as 'expropriation', but even various rules and regulations affecting all domestic investors as well as foreign ones, including even those designed for environmental protection or labour protection, and taxation.

All this matters greatly because BITs, and increasingly RTAs, are subject to dispute settlement mechanisms, both between states and between an investor and a state, that tend to be highly arbitrary, opaque and not open to public scrutiny, and generally pro-investor in their judgments. Since they are legally based on 'equal' treatment of legal persons with no primacy for human rights, they have become known for their pro-investor bias, partly due to the incentive structure for arbitrators and partly because the system is designed to provide supplementary guarantees to investors, rather than making them respect host countries' laws and regulations.

The significance of these treaties and binding legal arrangements is so important for large capital today that new agreements are being lobbied for, that further push the boundaries in terms of constraining regulation and inhibiting measures and policies that would ensure the social and economic rights of citizens. Thus, the Obama administration in the United States joined with Republicans in Congress, with whom otherwise there was great antipathy, to push for a fast-track negotiating authority in order to conclude two major trade agreements: the Trans-Pacific Partnership (TPP) between the US and some countries in Latin America and Asia, and the Trans-Atlantic Trade and Investment Partnership (TTIP) between the US and countries in Europe. President Obama made clear why this was so important: 'We have to make sure America writes the rules of the global economy. We should do it today while our economy is in the position of global strength. . . . We've got to harness it on our terms' (available at http://www.theguardian.com/us-news/2015/may/08/barack-obama-free-trade-tpp-democrats-nike).

The signing of the TPP in late 2015 was more than part of a US attempt to 'encircle' China economically. It was much less about trade liberalization (even though it could well lead to more production relocation to some Asian countries without necessarily increasing employment there) and much more about enforcing other aspects of economic control through IPRs and investment rules. The TTIP similarly would have had only minor implications for trade *per se*; rather, it was oriented towards cementing other aspects of control by large capital. The up-ending of these treaties by President Trump of the United States may appear to have changed all that, but in fact it is quite likely that the Trump administration will push for similar changes in IPR and investment rules, even as it exercises more protectionist policies with respect to trade in goods and services. Meanwhile, other agreements between various different groups of countries (such as the Regional Comprehensive Economic Partnership in Asia) are in the pipeline, and they still tend to use a similar template.

The important point to note here is that all these various trade and economic partnership agreements operate to increase competition *at the production stage*, thereby generating much greater competitive pressure among the various producers in the global South, especially those who are incorporated into global value chains driven by large multinationals. At the same time, by strengthening IPRs, they increase the monopoly power and bargaining strength of the agents controlling the *pre-production and post-production stages* of the value chain – design and branding/marketing in particular. This generates much greater rents from these elements of the value chain and so increases the incomes of large firms based in the North, and simultaneously pushes down wage components in the middle (or production) stage of the value chain. So, there are clear distributional implications of these legal and institutional frameworks at both global and national levels. Recent work by John Smith (2015) and Lauesen and Cope (2015) have brought out very clearly how this has resulted in a massive increase in value and surpluses accruing to companies in the North, even as competitive pressure ensures low wages and low incomes of primary producers in the global South. This is increasingly an important mechanism through which metropolitan capital imposes income deflation upon workers and producers in the South, as has been repeatedly stressed by Prabhat Patnaik (Patnaik 1992; Patnaik and Patnaik 2015).

New Forms of 'Economic Territory'

The growing significance of control over knowledge generation and dissemination as a central element of imperialism – as is being emphasized through IPR rules that are increasingly being put in place in most countries – is evidence of one of the more intriguing aspects of recent capitalist evolution. This is its ability to create new forms of economic territory, and to bring them within the ambit of capitalist economic relations and therefore also subject to imperialist contestation. The previous section highlighted the role of international trade and economic partnership agreements in strengthening IPR rules and the associated monopolies, but there are also internal pressures in many countries for such tendencies. The privatization of knowledge and its growing concentration, through the proliferation and enforcement of intellectual property rights, have become significant barriers to technology transfer and social recognition of traditional knowledge that would be necessary for any kind of economic diversification as well as greater economic justice. They also matter greatly in determining the relative power of profits over people within countries as well as between countries. This is clearly evident in terms of access to medicines (even essential and life-saving drugs) and crucial technologies for food cultivation. But it is also very much the case with respect to industrial technologies as well as the transfer of critical knowledge required for mitigating and coping with adverse environmental changes that themselves result from the production systems created by global capitalism. The national and international institutional structures that should provide checks and balances to the privatization of knowledge, and ensure that knowledge production and dissemination are not subservient to a small elite but are directed towards social goals, have become more fragile and less effective in recent times. Indeed, in many cases they in effect work in the opposite direction, as is evident from the earlier discussion.

Another prominent, new form of economic territory that has become significant as an arena for imperialist penetration and competition today covers the basic amenities and social services, that were earlier seen to be the sole preserve of public provision. A major feature of our times is the privatization of much of what was earlier generally accepted as the basic responsibility of public provision, such as amenities like electricity, water, essential transport infrastructure, and social services such as health, sanitation and education. Of course, the fact that these were seen as public duties does not mean that they were fulfilled: indeed, expanding public provision and enabling wider (and ideally universal) access to good-quality amenities and infrastructure have only come about historically as the result of prolonged mass struggles, and social and political mobilization to demand these. And issues of inequality in such provision have always existed. Nevertheless, the fact that provision is no longer necessarily in the public domain, and that private providers are increasingly seen as the norm, has opened up huge new markets for potentially profit-making activity. This may have been a crucial way of maintaining markets and effective demand, given the saturation of markets in many mature economies and the inadequate growth of markets in poorer societies. The prising open of such markets has occurred through a combination of inadequate and reduced public delivery (the expansion of the global bottled water industry, for example, is a result of the failure of public delivery of potable water) and changes in economic policies and regulatory structures that not only enable but actively encourage private investment in these areas. These changes, in turn, have been pushed by global institutions – formal organizations such as the Bretton Woods institutions and the WTO through its various agreements, as well as more informal but increasingly influential bodies such as the World Economic Forum. This is a more complicated playing out of the imperialistic drive for control over economic territory than can be expressed through purely national mechanisms, but that does not make it any less consequential.

Rules Governing International Finance and Debt Restructuring

The rules governing international finance and debt are now generally recognized to work in ways that reinforce the unequal global power relations between large capital and people across the world. Nowhere is this more evident than in the rules and legal structures governing sovereign debt. The lack of any coherent system to deal with debt default and to enable the viable restructuring of sovereign debt has led to situations in which countries and their populations are bled over years and even decades, merely to service debt generated in the past and through the piling up of earlier loans at ever-higher interest rates. 'Austerity' measures that reduce public spending on social essentials are forced upon unwilling societies on the basis of supposedly 'technocratic' notions that are in fact deeply ideological and elite-serving. Developing countries have known this for some time, but this is now also being experienced by some developed countries such as the crisis-ridden economies of the European periphery. Countries that somehow manage to restructure some of their debt, or that unilaterally decide to renege on some patently unfair debt taken on in the past, arc punished through complex and unbalanced legal systems that do not even accord to entire populations the minimum conditions of debt workout that are routinely accorded to private and corporate debtors within national systems. And here too, the arbitrations and other legal proceedings tend to be excessively biased towards investors and show little recognition of the minimum rights of the citizenry in affected countries. The fact that legal systems and other institutional structures in the core countries tend to support such biases and investors in general reinforces the point that this is another way in which contemporary imperialism is expressed.

This is starkly shown by the travails of the government of Argentina in US courts in lawsuits brought by financial vulture funds. A case that deserves some elaboration had its origins in the 1990s, when the government of Carlos Menem fixed the Argentine peso at the value of one US dollar, through a currency board arrangement that restricted base money supply to the amount of external reserves and sought to increase its spending through the build-up of external debt. This was obviously an unsustainable strategy and it exploded in a financial crisis in 2001, bringing on a major devaluation of the currency and a default on around $100 billion of external debt. In 2005, the government of Nestor Kirchner, which had managed to revive the economy to some extent, offered its creditors debt swaps that significantly restructured the debts. Since Argentine bonds were anyway trading at a fraction of their face value in the secondary market, this deal, which reduced the value of the debt by nearly 75 per cent, was acceptable to most of the multinational banks and other creditors. (Since unpaid interest is added on to the principal and compounded, the actual face value of the debt in such cases is typically much more than the amount originally borrowed or lent out.) Indeed, creditors holding 93 per cent of government bonds participated in the debt swaps of 2005 and 2010.

However, a tiny minority of creditors held out and refused to accept the negotiated settlement. These then sold their holdings to hedge funds (in this case known as 'vulture funds', that take on distressed assets in the hope of recouping a higher value from them), including NML Capital, a subsidiary of Elliot Capital Management, which is run by US billionaire and major Republican party donor Paul Singer. This fund bought Argentine bonds at around 20 per cent of the face value in 2008. It pursued the case both legally and physically: hiring mercenaries to detain and try to seize an Argentine ship where it was docked off the coast of Ghana; grabbing the Argentine presidential plane from an airport as 'collateral' for its supposed holding of debt. NML Capital and another vulture fund, Aurelius Capital Management LP, fought a case in a New York district court, demanding full payment on their debt, of the value of around $1.5 billion. (This amounted to a return of more than 1600 per cent on the initial investment made by these vulture funds.)

In 2012, US District Judge in New York, Thomas Griesa, ruled in favour of the hedge funds, and an appeal by the Argentine government was then dismissed by the US Supreme Court. The judgement was based on a peculiar and unprecedented interpretation of the *pari passu* (equal treatment) clause, which holds that all bond-holders must be treated alike, to mean that a sovereign debtor must make full payment on a defaulted claim if it makes any payments on restructured bonds. So, if the bondholders who agreed to restructure 93 per cent of the Argentine debt were paid according to their agreement, then the other resisting bond-holders would also have to be paid the full value of their debts. The ruling also insisted that any third party – including banks facilitating such transactions – that attempted to pay these bond-holders would be held in contempt of court. This effectively disabled Argentina from repaying debts to other bond-holders (who had already received around 90 per cent of their dues) unless it also paid the hold-outs in full, thereby forcing the country into technical default.

Interestingly, this judgement made a mockery of all debt renegotiation agreements, since there would be no incentive for any creditor to accept less than full value of the debt if some other creditor will be paid in full. No credit system can function, or has ever functioned, with zero default. The possibility of default is embedded into credit contracts through the interest rate, with interest rate spreads operating as the market estimate of the probability of a default. So, those who are seen as less likely to be able to repay are forced to pay higher interest rates, in both formal and informal credit transactions. A creditor who has been demanding and receiving a higher interest rate based on this probability cannot then demand full repayment as a right, since the contract reflected that very likelihood. So, the ruling actually negates the basic principles upon which all credit markets function.

Another extraordinary feature of the US court judgement is the requirement that banks involved in handling the payments made to Argentine bond-holders must turn over information to hold-out bond-holders on all the assets that the Argentine government holds worldwide. This is a major violation of banking secrecy laws everywhere, including in the United States. Even Justice Ruth Bader Ginsburg, a member in the Supreme Court's group of Justices deciding the case, was constrained to ask: 'By what authorization does a court in the United States become a "clearing house for information" about any and all property held by Argentina abroad?' This also severely erodes sovereign immunity, which can even have adverse effects on the US and may be illegal under other US laws.

In fact, this judgement was also in contradiction to the United States' own bankruptcy laws under Chapter 9 and Chapter 11. Yet the US government continued to pressurize Argentina to meet these ridiculous requirements. With the change of government in Argentina in late 2015, the new government headed by Mauricio Macri actually caved in to the demands of the vulture funds led by Elliott Management, agreeing to pay the hold-out creditors as per their demands. Since this would imply breaking the country's own laws which provided that all creditors would be dealt with equally (a prerequisite for most debt restructurings), it further required Argentina's Congress to lift those laws, which it did in March

2016. These moves were speedily met by the same Judge Griesa in New York lifting the injunctions he had passed against Argentina servicing restructured debt.

This entire episode provides one more example of how institutional arrangements have taken the form of legally binding constraints that generally privilege the interests of large capital over all other concerns. It also indicates how difficult it has become for individual countries to take on this system on their own, because of the complex web of legal, financial and institutional arrangements that are in play to punish any 'transgression' of rules, however unjust and unprincipled these rules may be in practice.

New Global Forms of Capitalist Organization

The rise of the multinational enterprise as the dominant and defining feature of global capitalism is arguably one of the most significant processes of the past century. Yet this was remarkably presaged by Lenin and Bukharin a century ago. As Bukharin noted, vertical integration of production tends to be combined with geographical disintegration of production processes.

> There is going on a continuous process of binding together the various branches of production, a process of transforming them into one single organization. This expresses itself, first of all, in the form of combined enterprises, i.e. enterprises combining the production of raw materials and manufactured goods, the production of manufactured goods with that of unfinished products, etc., which process can and does absorb the most diverse branches of production, since under the prevailing division of labour in our times every branch depends upon the other to a larger or lesser degree, directly or indirectly. (Bukharin 1915: 70)

This he saw as operating in tandem with 'the growing internationalization of economic life', in which competition and centralization of capital are reproduced on a world scale.

Yet he was obviously not able to anticipate the sheer extent to which this would occur. The technological changes of the past half-century in particular, particularly the advances in shipping and container technology that dramatically reduced transport costs and time involved, as well as the information technology revolution that enabled a much more detailed breakdown of production into specific tasks that could easily be physically separated, were critical in this. Together, they enabled the emergence of global value chains, which are typically led by large multinational corporations but involve both regional and global networks of both competing and cooperating firms. The large corporation here is not necessarily in direct control of all operations – and indeed, the ability to transfer control over production as well as the risks associated with production to lower ends of the value chain are an important element in increasing the profitability of such activities. This adds a greater intensity to the exploitation that can be unleashed by such global firms because they are less dependent upon workers and resources in any one location, can use competition across suppliers to push down their prices and conditions of production, and are less burdened by regulatory processes that would seek to reduce some of their market power.

These changes in production organization are combining with other incentives to create what has been called a 'downsize and distribute' model that is driving more of the global production chain investment by multinational corporations. Thus, the focus in many developed and developing countries on judging the performance of companies by 'shareholder value' creates incentives for cost reduction and short-termist behaviour that greatly exceed similar tendencies in the past. The lead firms are therefore subject to the discipline of financial markets that demand rapid profits, forcing the global value chains to be constructed in ways that are much less likely to enable or benefit a programme of industrial development in peripheral countries, and also less likely to provide a viable platform for successful economic diversification.

The Rise of New Powers

It is often argued that the rise of new powers – most particularly China, but also India, Brazil and others – means that notions of imperialism are no longer valid. Yet, the imperialist phase of capitalism has been characterized throughout by the emergence of 'new kids on the block', some of which have gone on to become the neighbourhood bullies as well. At the time when Lenin wrote his famous pamphlet, the emergence of the United States as the dominant global power was far from evident, and it is therefore clear that his claim that the phase of imperialism is one in which 'the territorial division of the whole world among the biggest capitalist powers is completed' is the weakest link in his argument, and one that was belied by history almost immediately. So, the US, which seemed at that time to be only a minor player among the major European actors, emerged to dominate the world scene for nearly a century. Similarly, the rise of Japan, particularly in the second half of the twentieth century, by no means signified a weakening of imperialist power generally; it merely necessitated a more complicated assessment of such power.

Currently, the recent emergence of China is being projected as a sign that the global economic landscape is completely transformed.

Certainly, it is true that the growing weight of China in world trade and investment has had a major effect on terms of trade and volumes of exports for many primary producing countries, and has brought in more countries into manufacturing value chains, even as it has also become the most significant source of manufactured goods imports for most countries. Yet there are dangers of overplaying its current significance. Even now, China accounts for less than 9 per cent of global output (measured at constant 2005 prices); its per capita GDP is less than half (around 45 per cent) of the global average and still many multiples below the average of the so-called 'developed' capitalist economies that form part of the imperialist core. In relative terms, China remains a 'poor' country, but it is also true that Chinese capital in various forms is a significant player in the ongoing struggle for control over economic territory that is occurring across the world. It is worth noting that many of the currently hyperbolic mainstream analyses and predictions with respect to China are eerily similar to the descriptions and predictions for Japan in the 1970s, as the emerging giant soon to take over the role of global economic leadership from the United States.

A similar point can be made even more forcefully for several of the other nations that were ecstatically described as 'emerging markets', which supposedly provided proof that forces of imperialism are no hindrance to the rise of developing countries. Together, the 'BRICS' nations (Brazil, Russia, India, China and South Africa) account for less than 15 per cent of world GDP in current prices terms, even though their share of global population is just under half. This is still so small as to mean that announcements of these countries as the new imperialist powers may well be very premature, especially when global institutional structures are still very much balanced in favour of the established powers.

One reason why the newly emerging economies are often thought to be more significant is because many analyses are not based on nominal exchange rates to compare incomes across different countries, but rather on the purchasing power parity (PPP) exchange rates, which seek to establish the relative purchasing power of each currency in terms of prices of a common basket of commodities. However, the use of PPP exchange rates can be quite dubious, as they are based on prices of a basket of average representative consumption goods in the United States, which may not be so relevant to consumption elsewhere, especially the poor in much of the developing world. They are unchanging over time, even though consumption patterns tend to shift with technological change and evolving preferences. PPP exchange rates are also notoriously imperfect because of the infrequency and unsystematic nature of the price surveys that are used to derive them, which can make them quite dated or even misleading. An even more significant conceptual problem with using PPP estimates is that they implicitly inflate the incomes of the poor. In general, countries that have high PPP – that is, where the actual purchasing power of the currency is deemed to be much higher than the nominal value – are typically low-income countries with low average wages. It is precisely because there is a significant section of the work force that receives very low remuneration that goods and services are available more cheaply here than in countries where the majority of workers receive higher wages. Therefore, using PPP-modified GDP (gross domestic product) data may miss the point, by seeing as an advantage the very feature that reflects greater poverty of the majority of wage earners in an economy.

All this does not mean that there have been no changes in global economic and political power: it is evident that there have been, and will continue to be, significant and even transformative changes. However, these changes in the position of countries in the economic and geopolitical ladder do not mean that the basic undercurrent of imperialistic tendencies that drives the global system has disappeared – indeed, it may even become more intense as the struggle for economic territory becomes more competitive, and as the legal and institutional framework within which international economic relations play out becomes more rigid.

References

Bukharin, Nikolai (1915), *Imperialism and the World Economy, with an Introduction by V. I. Lenin*, London: Martin Lawrence Limited.

Lauesen, Torkil and Zak Cope (2015), 'Imperialism and the transformation of values into prices', *Monthly Review*, Vol. 67, No. 3, July–August: 54–67.

Patnaik, Prabhat (1992), *Accumulation and Stability under Capitalism*, Oxford: Clarendon Press.

Patnaik, Utsa and Prabhat Patnaik (2015), 'Imperialism in the era of globalization', *Monthly Review*, Vol. 67, No. 3, August–September: 68–81.

Smith, John (2015), *Imperialism in the Twenty First Century: Globalization, super-exploitation and capitalism's final crisis*, New York: Monthly Review Press.

Mega-Regional Trading Blocs

Implications for the Multilateral Trading System

Biswajit Dhar

Over the past few years, the multilateral trading system governed by the World Trade Organization (WTO) has been in the throes of a crisis brought on by developments both inside and outside the organization. The most obvious source of the crisis has been the inability of the WTO member states to make meaningful progress in the Doha Round negotiations, which was an attempt to make the organization more development-friendly. In the negotiating mandate of the Doha Round, the trade ministers of the WTO member states emphasized that '[i]nternational trade can play a major role in the promotion of economic development and the alleviation of poverty', and that all countries must 'benefit from the increased opportunities and welfare gains that the multilateral trading system generates'. They therefore decided to '*continue to make positive efforts* designed to ensure that developing countries, and especially the least-developed among them, secure a share in the growth of world trade commensurate with the needs of their economic development' (WTO 2001: paragraph 2; emphasis added). Embedded in this mandate was the objective to make the WTO rules more responsive to the needs of the lesser developed countries in a world where national economies were getting more integrated. This was indeed an important prerequisite to ensure that the multilateral trading system acquired a more inclusive character.

This development agenda was included in the negotiating mandates of most of the key areas as well. Thus, while laying down the mandate on agriculture, WTO members agreed that

> special and differential treatment for developing countries shall be an integral part of all elements of the negotiations and shall be embodied in the Schedules of concessions and commitments and as appropriate in the rules and disciplines to be negotiated, so as to be operationally effective and to enable developing countries to effectively take account

> of their development needs, including food security and rural development. (WTO 2001: paragraph 13)

Further, the negotiating mandate on market access of non-agricultural products was 'to reduce or as appropriate eliminate tariffs, including the reduction or elimination of tariff peaks, high tariffs, and tariff escalation, as well as non-tariff barriers in particular on products of export interest to developing countries'. And, the negotiations were expected to 'take fully into account the special needs and interests of developing and least-developed country participants, including through less than full reciprocity in reduction commitments' (ibid.: paragraph 16). In the services negotiating mandate, it was emphasized that the negotiations would be conducted with a view to promoting 'the development of developing and least-developed countries' (ibid.: paragraph 15). Finally, in the area of intellectual property rights (IPRs), the negotiations included two issues in which developing countries had articulated their concerns. The first was regarding the impact on access to affordable medicines arising from the strengthening of the patent regime resulting from the introduction of the Agreement on Trade-Related Aspects of Intellectual Property Rights (TRIPS).[1] The second was the issue of protection of genetic resources and traditional knowledge by introducing mandatory requirements on entities seeking patent rights on products and processes using such resources and knowledge (WTO 2001: paragraph 19). These requirements entail sharing of benefits with the countries and communities providing the genetic resources and arising from the commercial exploitation of the products and processes developed using these resources. However, the Doha Round negotiations were effectively stalled at the height of the global economic downturn in 2008, and they remain mired in differences between the developed and the developing countries with little prospects of revival. The crisis facing the Doha Round increased manifold when WTO members were unable to reach an agreement over the continuation of work within the organization based on the Doha mandate at the conclusion of the 10th Ministerial at Nairobi in December 2015 (WTO 2015: paragraph 30).

But while the Doha Round remains paralysed, three groups of countries have initiated processes of economic integration by forming so-called mega-regional trade blocs (hereafter mega-regionals). Until a couple of years back, the focus on the mega-regionals was entirely on the Trans-Pacific Partnership (TPP) Agreement, the proposed formation led by the United States that currently includes eleven other countries. In 2013, two mega-regionals were announced, namely the Regional

Comprehensive Economic Partnership, and the Trans-Atlantic Trade and Investment Partnership (TTIP). The former is an initiative taken by the Association of South East Asian Nations (ASEAN) to consolidate the free trade agreements (FTAs) the grouping has entered into with six partner countries in its immediate neighbourhood, namely, China, Japan, South Korea, Australia, New Zealand and India. The latter is an economic partnership agreement proposed between the US and members of the European Union (EU). Besides the above-mentioned, members of the Asia Pacific Economic Cooperation (APEC) decided at their Beijing Summit in November 2014 to work towards the Free Trade Area of Asia Pacific (FTAAP). With China strongly endorsing the FTAAP, this formation could bear its imprint in the future.

What unites the mega-regionals is their quest to create favourable market access conditions for dominant players in global markets. This is sought to be achieved by eliminating tariffs and adopting rules and regulations that would enhance the control of these players in the marketplace. Under these circumstances, new players, especially from the developing and least developed countries, would find it difficult to compete, especially because the mega-regionals would not provide an enabling environment for them, which the WTO had agreed to create in the Doha Round negotiations.

The mega-regionals currently being negotiated are developing frameworks for trade governance, whose implications for the multilateral trading system under the WTO is emerging as a major issue. This essay is an attempt to explore some of the areas in which these trade blocs will challenge the WTO. The essay has two parts. At the outset, it discusses the key elements of the three mega-regionals. The second part discusses the implications of these agreements for the future relevance of the WTO.

The Mega-Regional Trade Agreements

The mega-regionals have emerged as formations that include almost all the major economies.[2] Currently, twenty-two economies (counting the EU as a single economic entity) are negotiating the mega-regionals, whose combined share in global trade was more than 76 per cent in 2014. These proposed trading blocs have two prominent features. First, they are seeking to set rules for trans-boundary transactions between countries covering a wide range of areas, many of which are not included in the existing WTO framework. Members of the mega-regionals have initiated negotiations in a number of areas that the WTO has not been able to discuss given the lack of consensus among its members. The more prominent of these are labour standards, environment, investment and competition policy.

Apart from these, there is another set of issues concerning regulations and standards, especially IPRs, technical barriers and food safety standards, on which the WTO members have had low levels of engagement because of opposing ambitions. While the developed countries have been pushing for ratcheting up of regulations and standards, most of the developing countries have been seeking ways to address these issues keeping in view their development imperatives. But these issues are high on the agenda of the mega-regionals.

A second feature of the mega-regionals is that at least two out of the three that are currently in the process of being ratified or are under negotiations, namely, the Trans-Pacific Partnership (TPP) and the Trans-Atlantic Trade and Investment Partnership (TTIP), are being driven by the agendas of the major economies. The third, the Regional Comprehensive Economic Partnership, too has the possibility of adopting the broad framework of the TPP, since there is a significant overlap of membership between the two proposed blocs. The mega-regionals could, therefore, introduce rules for the conduct of cross-border transactions that are used by the developed countries as tools of domination of the global economy.

In the following discussion, we shall elaborate on the distinctive features of the three mega-regional trade blocs.

Trans-Pacific Partnership Agreement

The Trans-Pacific Partnership Agreement or TPP is effectively an attempt being made by the US to establish its footprint in East Asia, economically the most dynamic region of the world during the past quarter-century. This move is a part of the expansionary strategy that the US administration has adopted in the post-downturn phase, an integral part of which is to seek new markets. More recently, the Obama administration officially announced intensification of its role in the Asia Pacific region.[3] The TPP is viewed as an important element in the US 'rebalancing' toward the region (Fergusson 2015a: 5). Twelve countries participated in the TPP negotiations, which concluded in October 2015. The current membership of the TPP accounted for just over 29 per cent of the total global trade in 2014.

The idea of the TPP took shape in 2008 when the US decided to provide leadership to an initiative taken by Chile, New Zealand, Singapore and Brunei (the so-called P-4) to form an FTA. The US has therefore driven the negotiating agenda of the formation as well as its process. The US has viewed the TPP as a trade agreement that would 'unlock opportunities for American manufacturers, workers, service providers, farmers, and ranchers – to support job creation and wage growth' (Office of the United

States Trade Representative, n.d.). Its negotiating objectives have been articulated thus:

> TPP will be a comprehensive deal, providing new and meaningful market access for goods and services; strong and enforceable labour standards and environmental commitments; groundbreaking new rules designed to ensure fair competition between state-owned enterprises (SOEs) and private companies; commitments that will improve the transparency and consistency of the regulatory environment to make it easier for small- and medium-sized businesses to operate across the region; a robust intellectual property (IP) rights framework to promote innovation, while supporting access to innovative and generic medicines and an open Internet; and obligations that will promote a thriving digital economy, including new rules to ensure the free flow of data. (Ibid.)

One of the more pertinent observations that has been made in this regard is that the TPP 'provides the United States with the opportunity to project its trade interests by negotiating a "comprehensive and high standard" FTA with provisions that build on those in FTAs the United States concluded throughout the 2000s, especially the most recent FTAs, such as the US–Korea FTA (KORUS)' (Fergusson 2015a: 6).

The insistence that the TPP be a trade agreement bearing the distinctive footprint of the US was a legislative imperative for the Obama administration. Under the US Constitution, Congress has the authority for regulation of foreign trade. But while Article I of the Constitution states that Congress has the power to 'regulate commerce with foreign nations', and to 'lay and collect taxes, duties, imposts, and excises', thus assigning no specific responsibility for trade to the President, Article II gives the President the exclusive authority to negotiate treaties and international agreements, and exercises broad authority over the conduct of the nation's foreign affairs. The US Congress addresses this chasm between the powers of the executive and the legislature in the realm of trade by authorizing the administration to engage in trade negotiations. This authority is granted through the Trade Promotion Authority (TPA) and is better known as 'fast track approval'.[4] The most recent of these authorizations from the Congress, granted to the Bush administration,[5] expired in 2002. Significantly, the Obama administration was not granted Congressional authorization to negotiate trade deals. Therefore, while engaging in the TPP negotiations, the Obama administration tried to convince the Congress that these would not require the US to change its laws and regulations; in other words, the administration conveyed the message that the TPP would accept the norms and standards that US legislations had adopted.

This was also a signal to the TPP partners that they would be negotiating under the broad directions of US laws and regulations.

The TPP framework was adopted in the 2011 meeting of trade ministers. Accordingly, it was to include the following broad areas: (i) comprehensive market access – removal of both tariff and non-tariff barriers in all areas; (ii) a regional agreement that facilitates trade and the development of production and supply chains among TPP members; (iii) holistic, agreement-wide approach to specific areas: regulatory coherence, competitiveness and business facilitation, small- and medium-sized enterprises, and development; and (iv) emerging trade issues such as those caused by new technology.

The weight of US interests in the TPP negotiations held thus far is clearly visible in the texts on IPRs and investment. As regards IPRs, the overarching objective of the US was to conclude an agreement that reflected a 'standard of [intellectual property] protection similar to that found in US law'.[6] This implies that the US is seeking to introduce standards of IPRs that are significantly higher than those available under the TRIPS Agreement. More specifically, the US is seeking to ratchet up the TRIPS standards in the following areas: (i) expand the coverage of patentable subject matter through the inclusion of patenting of plants and animals; (ii) extend the term of patents beyond twenty years; (iii) eliminate the use of flexibilities that are currently available under the TRIPS Agreement that governments may like to use to protect public interest.

The chapter on protection of [foreign] investment that TPP members have agreed to is generally 'based on the current iteration of the US model bilateral investment treaty (BIT)'.[7] Of all the elements included in this chapter, the investor–state dispute settlement (ISDS) mechanism is the most contentious. The ISDS mechanism allows a foreign investor to litigate against its host government using private international arbitration mechanisms under the rules of the International Centre for Settlement of Investment Disputes (ICSID)[8] or the United Nations Commission on International Trade Law (UNCITRAL).[9]

A significant trigger for the disputes that the investors have brought against the states has been actions by government authorities to prevent abuse of public interest by foreign investors, which have been labelled as 'indirect expropriation'. The investment chapter of the TPP clarifies that '[n]on-discriminatory regulatory actions by a Party that are designed and applied to protect legitimate public welfare objectives, such as public health, safety, and the environment, do not constitute indirect expropriations, except in rare circumstances'.[10] Although this definition provides some policy space to the public authorities to challenge the investors' actions in their territories on grounds of public interest, some observers have commented that the threat of disputes that an investor could initiate may have a 'chilling effect' on nation-states, and they would therefore desist from taking any action against the foreign investor (Tienhaara 2011).

Several other substantive issues that the TPP includes are labour standards,[11] environmental regulations, and government procurement and competition policy, which make it clear that this agreement will eventually restrict the policy space for more than the WTO. Inclusion of these areas was rejected by the WTO members, and it seems unlikely that a majority of developing country members of the organization will consider including these areas. Even in the two conventional areas of market access, namely for goods and services, the ambition levels for removal of trade barriers set by the TPP members are considerably higher than those seen in the WTO negotiations. The likely exceptions in this regard could be agriculture and trade in services. While Japan has been resisting unfettered liberalization of agriculture, in the latter instance, movement of people as one of the modes of service delivery (the so-called Mode 4) is not a part of the US template for FTA negotiations.[12]

At the same time, however, participating countries may not readily find common ground in the ambitious area of 'regulatory coherence', which aims to 'ease the conditions and costs of trade between TPP countries while affirming the rights of TPP countries to regulate their economies to promote legitimate policy objectives'.[13] This area was included with the explicit objective of promoting regional value chains within the TPP member states, but its eventual outcome will once again depend on how proactively two larger countries of the grouping, namely the US and Japan, are able to provide direction.

Trans-Atlantic Trade and Investment Partnership

The Trans-Atlantic Trade and Investment Partnership (TTIP) was launched in 2013 with the objective 'to increase trade and investment between the EU and the US by realizing the untapped potential of a truly transatlantic market place, generating new economic opportunities for the creation of jobs and growth through increased market access and greater regulatory compatibility and setting the path for global standards.[14] Clearly, setting global regulatory standards would be the key objective of the TTIP.

The TTIP was being posed as a formation that would address the economic woes of the two economies. At least this was the message sent out by the High Level Working Group (HLWG) on Jobs and Growth, which provided the contours of the agreement. The final report of the HLWG states that the TTIP could generate new business and employment by significantly expanding trade and investment opportunities in both economies. Such opportunities are to be created, on the one hand, through ambitious reciprocal market opening in goods, services and investment, and by modernizing trade rules and enhancing the compatibility of regulatory regimes, on the other. Critical to the negotiations would be elimination, reduction or prevention of unnecessary 'behind the border' non-tariff barriers to trade in goods and services, and enhanced compatibility of regulations and standards, since the tariff barriers in both economies are already quite low.

The issue of 'behind the border' barriers to trade are particularly important for the US and the EU, for they have clashed over the policy measures adopted by their respective governments, which were seen as providing unfair commercial advantage to domestic enterprises. The most celebrated of these cases involved the disputes over the grant of subsidies to Boeing Company and Airbus Industrie, that are being adjudicated by the dispute settlement mechanism of the WTO.

Grant of subsidies has also been a major issue of contention in the area of agriculture. The US and the EU are the largest providers of agricultural subsidies, but they have differed over the manner in which their respective governments have provided subsidies to producers. History has it that once these economic powers papered over their differences, they were able to secure outcomes that gave them enormous advantage. Twenty years ago, they were able to resolve their differences over farm subsidies, which helped break the impasse in the Uruguay Round negotiations, paving the way for the establishment of the WTO. Today, the TTIP provides an ideal platform for the EU and the US to resolve their differences not only over farm subsidies but in other areas as well. This strategic coming together can be used by them to leverage the Doha Round negotiations, notwithstanding the drastic change in global economic dynamics over the past two decades.

The objective to achieve compatibility of regulations and standards is another ambitious dimension of the TTIP. In recent decades, both the US and the EU have provided tacit protection to their domestic enterprises by adopting strict product and process standards. Alive to the fact that the issue of standards could be a potential deal breaker, standard-setting organizations in both jurisdictions are discussing ways in which they can find acceptable solutions. The American National Standards Institute (ANSI) together with the three European Standards Organizations – European Committee for Standardization (CEN), European Committee for Electrotechnical Standardization (CENELEC) and European Telecommunications Standards Institute (ETSI) – have taken up the issue of their collaboration in emerging areas of technology, such as cloud computing, machine-to-machine communication and 'Smart Cities'. A successful outcome of these discussions could have a far-reaching impact, for it could produce industry-wide standards that can be harmonized globally. This would undoubtedly be the first major step towards addressing the problem of non-tariff barriers and the consequent easing of cross-border trade.

The HLWG has identified 'rules addressing shared global trade challenges and opportunities' as one of the major areas to be included in the TTIP. According to the Working Group, the proposed agreement will be 'developing rules in several areas that would not only be relevant to bilateral commerce, but would also contribute to the progressive strengthening of the multilateral trading system'. These rules will cover intellectual property rights, environment and labour, raw materials and energy, customs and trade facilitation, and competition policy, among others.[15] The strategy that has been adopted by the EU and the US thus far is to carve out new rules in these critical areas through the TTIP, and to have these accepted at the global level subsequently.

Regional Comprehensive Economic Partnership

The Regional Comprehensive Economic Partnership (RCEP), which brings together the ASEAN and its six FTA partners, is seeking to establish 'ASEAN centrality' through the consolidation of all ASEAN+1 FTAs. When they initiated the negotiations, the sixteen-member RCEP set the end of 2015 as the targeted date for concluding their negotiations. This date coincides with that of the formation of the ASEAN Economic Community (AEC).

Of the three mega-regionals that are currently being negotiated, it is the RCEP that lacks a distinct identity, on account of two contrasting dimensions. The first is that this agreement was proposed as a model of development partnership aimed at promoting trade between the participating countries, which is unlike any trading arrangement that has ever been seen, including the WTO. Given this framework, the RCEP could end up with low ambitions on trade liberalization and focus more on the economic partnership pillar.

The negotiating mandate of RCEP, which was elaborated in the 'Guiding Principles and Objectives for Negotiating the RCEP' adopted by the ministers of the proposed regional forum in August 2012, mentions at least two features of the proposed agreement that make it quite different from conventional trade agreements. The first of these is that 'RCEP will recognize . . . interests of ASEAN's FTA partners in supporting and contributing to economic integration, equitable economic development and strengthening economic cooperation among the participating countries'. In other words, economic development and cooperation were expected to be the building blocks of RCEP.

The second contrasting feature is that the RCEP negotiating mandate includes economic and technical cooperation as one of its negotiating planks, which 'will aim at narrowing development gaps among the parties and maximizing mutual benefits from the implementation of the . . . agreement'. The Guidelines further clarify that 'economic and technical cooperation provisions in the RCEP will build upon existing economic cooperation arrangements between ASEAN and ASEAN's FTA partners participating in the RCEP'.

It is important to note here that the ASEAN members have viewed 'technical and development cooperation' as a *sine qua non* for economic integration not only within their region, but between ASEAN and other parts of the world as well. This was highlighted in the Initiative for ASEAN Integration (IAI), launched in November 2000. The IAI stated that technical and development cooperation would 'address the development divide and accelerate the economic integration of the less developed ASEAN Member Countries so that the benefits of ASEAN integration are shared and enjoyed by all ASEAN Member Countries'. When it was launched, the IAI identified the following as its priority areas: infrastructure, human resource development, information and communications technologies, capacity building for regional economic integration, energy, investment climate, tourism, poverty reduction, and improvement in the quality of life.

In contrast, seven out of the sixteen participants in RCEP, who are also participating in the TPP negotiations, could raise the ambitions on trade liberalization. As mentioned earlier, the TPP members are seeking to remove most of the barriers in the trade in goods and services. The advanced countries and some of the more open economies, like Singapore, Brunei and Malaysia, could be a part of this grouping. By so doing, RCEP could lend support to the two other mega-regionals in altering the rules of engagement between countries away from those that the multilateral trading system has put in place.

Challenges for the WTO

The challenges for the multilateral trading system under the WTO arising from these mega-regionals are two-fold. The first is the ability of the organization to institutionally monitor these trading blocs and bring them under some discipline in terms of their functioning. A second set of challenges would be to address the concerns of WTO members that would not benefit from these mega-regionals: after all, the founder members of the organization did recognize that trade should seek to address the development needs of these countries.[16] In addition to countries that do not belong to any of these mega-regionals, this group could potentially include those developing country members of the mega-regionals that are not likely to gain because the developed countries driving them would be imposing high regulatory barriers.

Since the implementation of the General Agreement on Tariffs and Trade (GATT) in 1948, bilateral and regional trade agreements entered into between GATT/WTO members are subjected to the discipline of the GATT/WTO. The architects of GATT had provided an opportunity for members of the organization to enter into preferential trading agreements, as long as they conformed to a set of rules elaborated in Article XXIV of GATT. For services, the relevant disciplines are provided in Article V of the General Agreement on Trade in Services (GATS). Thus, as long as the bilateral and regional trading agreements conformed to the above-mentioned provisions of GATT or GATS, their formation was considered legal.

However, the WTO would fall short of similarly monitoring the mega-regionals, for the latter would be dealing with a number of 'WTO-plus' issues. Some observers have suggested that the WTO needs to respond to this situation by engaging more actively with the mega-regionals. The obvious intent behind this suggestion seems to be that the WTO should recognize the changing landscape and begin ways of 'multilateralizing' the mega-regionals.

But this approach would put the multilateral trading system in a situation it has never before faced in its nearly seven-decades-long existence. 'Multilateralizing' the TPP or TTIP would effectively end the practice of negotiated outcomes between WTO members, and would be tantamount to accepting the writ of the major economic powers to explicitly influence the global trading system – the first time such a phenomenon would occur in the post-colonial world.

Although the multilateral trading system, governed first by GATT and followed by the WTO, was not entirely attuned to the development needs of the lesser economic players, the two institutions did recognize the intrinsic link between trade and development. As was mentioned at the outset, the founding members of the WTO had recognized this critical linkage while establishing the organization, and they had reinforced this link while agreeing to the negotiating mandate for the Doha Round. The mandate tried to address the development imperatives of the developing countries in two ways. First, by seeking to amend the existing agreements through the inclusion of development-oriented provisions, as for example, by mandating that the WTO Agreement on Agriculture (AoA) should allow developing countries to address their concerns relating to food security, rural livelihoods and rural development. Secondly, and perhaps more importantly, the Doha mandate addressed the problem of rent-seeking in critical areas like agriculture and IPRs. Thus, the Doha Round was expected to reduce the overhang of agricultural subsidies and to reduce excessive rent-seeking through patent rights by allowing developing countries specific instruments for bringing down the prices of medicines. In contrast, the mega-regionals would allow perpetuation of these market-distorting policies, thus allowing the dominant players to strengthen their control over global markets.

The framework of economic integration agreements adopted by the mega-regionals is, without doubt, driven by short-term sentiments. Taking cognizance of development imperatives does not seem to be part of the DNA of these agreements. It is therefore important for the excluded to actively consider a path that does not follow the one traversed by existing economic integration agreements, which have encouraged countries to trade on the basis of their initial comparative advantage, but have not provided opportunities to participating countries to climb the development ladder and hence defy their comparative advantage.[17] While the development experiences of the present-day advanced countries are rife with examples where countries have defied their comparative advantage over time, the mega-regionals are challenging a historical truism.

This essay was written before the election of Donald Trump as President of the United States and the subsequent decision to pull the US out of the Trans-Pacific Partnership Agreement. – Editors

Notes

1 This was elaborated in the Ministerial Declaration on the TRIPS Agreement and Public Health. See, for details, WTO (2001).

2 Of the emerging economies, only Brazil, Russia, South Africa, Nigeria and Turkey are not participating in any of the mega-regionals.

3 The ultimate goal, according to the then National Security Advisor, Tom Donilon, is to promote US interests by helping to shape the norms and rules of the Asia-Pacific region, to ensure that 'international law and norms be respected, that commerce and freedom of navigation are not impeded, that emerging powers build trust with their neighbours, and that disagreements are resolved peacefully without threats or coercion'. See Donilon (2011).

4 The first of these approvals came in the aftermath of the Smoot Hawley Tariff Act of 1930. In order to overcome the damaging impact of this legislation on US commerce, the Congress enacted the Reciprocal Trade Agreements Act and authorized the President to enter into reciprocal trade agreements that reduced tariffs within the range approved by it. In 1974, the remit of this authorization was expanded to cover non-tariff issues as well.

5 The authority was included in the Bipartisan Trade Promotion Authority Act (BTPA) of 2002. For details see, Fergusson (2015a): 7.

[6] This was the objective included in the Bipartisan Trade Promotion Authority Act (BTPA) of 2002, the last 'fast track approval' that an administration had received from the Congress in 2002.

[7] The authority was included in the Bipartisan Trade Promotion Authority Act (BTPA) of 2002. For details see, Fergusson (2015a): 7.

[8] ICSID is an autonomous international institution established under the Convention on the Settlement of Investment Disputes between States, and nationals and legal persons of other states. It is a multilateral treaty formulated by the Executive Directors of the World Bank, which came into force in 1966.

[9] UNCITRAL provides the rules for commercial arbitration, including investor–state dispute resolution. These rules were first adopted in 1976.

[10] Trans-Pacific Partnership, Chapter 9, pp. 9–35, available at https://ustr.gov/sites/default/files/TPP-Final-Text-Investment.pdf.

[11] The Chapter on Labour is among the most contentious. The key objective herein is to introduce the mandatory requirement to implement four Core Conventions of the International Labour Organization (ILO), also called 'Labour Standards'. Besides, the US has concluded three bilateral agreements with Malaysia, Brunei and Vietnam on the implementation of Labour Standards, which makes it mandatory for the three countries to implement the ILO Conventions before they join the TPP. For details, see Trans-Pacific Partnership, Chapter 19: Labour, available at https://ustr.gov/sites/default/files/TPP-Final-Text-Labour.pdf.

[12] No US FTA negotiated after the agreements with Chile and Singapore includes provisions on the temporary movement of personnel. Fergusson (2015a): 19–20.

[13] Fergusson (2015b): 42.

[14] Council of the European Union, 'Directives for the Negotiation on a Comprehensive Trade and Investment Agreement, called the Transatlantic Trade and Investment Partnership, between the European Union and the United States of America', 2013.

[15] One major area in which the two economic entities have considerable divergence of views is in respect of the inclusion of the investor–state dispute settlement (ISDS) mechanism in the TTIP investment regime. The EU has developed scepticism over the ISDS mechanism, especially the inability of the sovereign state to protect issues relating to public interest when the foreign investor invokes the ISDS mechanism.

[16] While adopting the Marrakesh Agreement for establishing the WTO, founder members of the organization recognized that 'that their relations in the field of trade and economic endeavour should be conducted with a view to raising standards of living, ensuring full employment and a large and steadily growing volume of real income and effective demand, and expanding the production of and trade in goods and services, while allowing for the optimal use of the world's resources in accordance with the objective of sustainable development, seeking both to protect and preserve the environment and to enhance the means for doing so in a manner consistent with their respective needs and concerns at different levels of economic development'.

[17] See Ha-Joon Chang's arguments in Lin and Chang (2009).

References

Donilon, Tom (2011), 'America is back in the Pacific and will uphold the Rules', *Financial Times*, 27 November.

Fergusson, Ian F. (2015a), *Trade Promotion Authority (TPA) and the Role of Congress in Trade Policy*, Congressional Research Service, report no. RL33743, available at https://fas.org/sgp/crs/misc/RL33743.pdf.

Fergusson, Ian F. (2015b), *The Trans-Pacific Partnership (TPP) Negotiations and Issues for Congress*, Congressional Research Service, report no. R42694, available at https://www.fas.org/sgp/crs/row/R40502.pdf.

Lin, Justin and Ha-Joon Chang (2009), 'Should Industrial Policy in Developing Countries Conform to Comparative Advantage or Defy it? A Debate Between Justin Lin and Ha-Joon Chang', *Development Policy Review*, 27 (5): 483–502.

Office of the United States Trade Representative (n.d.), *Trans-Pacific Partnership: Summary of U.S. Objectives*, available at http://www.ustr.gov/tpp/Summary-of-US-objectives.

Tienhaara, Kyla (2011), 'Regulatory chill and the threat of arbitration: a view from political science', in Chester Brown and Kate Miles, eds, *Evolution in Investment Treaty Law and Arbitration*, Cambridge: Cambridge University Press, available at SSRN: http://ssrn.com/abstract=2065706.

WTO (2001), 'Ministerial Declaration', Ministerial Conference, Fourth Session, Doha, 20 November WT/MIN(01)/DEC/1).

WTO (2015), 'Nairobi Ministerial Declaration: Adopted on 19 December 2015', paragraph 30.

Neo-liberalism, Authoritarianism and the Contemporary Polity

Prakash Karat

Prabhat Patnaik is a public intellectual *par excellence*. He is not only a distinguished economist, but also an able exponent of Marxist theory who has made valuable and incisive contributions to the study of political economy, politics and society. An important part of his work pertains to the consequences of neo-liberalism in India, and he has argued persistently that neo-liberalism is not just a set of economic policies but an entire policy framework that characterizes the era of global finance capital. He has pointed out that the 'pursuit of neo-liberal measures in the realm of economy also requires an appropriate restructuring of the polity' (Patnaik 2012). This concern with the restructuring of the polity in the present historical conjuncture is the guiding theme of my essay.

I

In a series of essays, Prabhat Patnaik has spelt out how neo-liberalism leads increasingly to the attenuation of democracy and constriction of the democratic rights of the people. Starting from the basic Marxist position that democracy and individual freedom 'cannot be authentically realized under capitalism', Patnaik has written of the constraints on bourgeois democracy as capitalism develops in societies like India, contending, in a thought-provoking formulation, that the '*totality of unfreedom* [in the contemporary polity] *has a tendency to get accentuated over time as a condition for the consolidation of bourgeois rule*' (Patnaik 2011: 26).

This tendency of the bourgeois ruling class to curb and erode bourgeois democratic rights gets accentuated and enters a qualitatively new phase with the advent of imperialist globalization, the hegemony of globalized finance capital and the imposition of the neo-liberal order. In Patnaik's view, three features of globalization attenuate democracy and restrict the democratic rights of the people. The first is the tremendous growth in income and wealth inequality, which proceeds, in his opinion, through the process of the 'primitive accumulation of capital'. This process of accumulation is accompanied by a minimal increase in employment. The second feature is the accentuation of social inequalities, a process that, Patnaik contends, contributes to a 'rolling back' of the democratic gains of the people. This is connected to a reduction in the role of the state sector and increasing privatization of education and other basic services. The third feature is the rise of identity politics and the consequent exacerbation of religious, regional and ethnic divisions. Neo-liberalism and globalization thus spawn virulent communal forces that seek to suppress minorities and their democratic rights.

Given the authoritarianism required for a neo-liberal regime, the advent of the growing threat of the Hindutva forces leads Patnaik to see a creeping fascism developing in India. While he has clarified that 'such creeping fascism, however, does not mean that a fascist state is on the horizon', it is nevertheless, according to him, instrumental in the creation of the neo-liberal polity.

Such a polity, to repeat, is marked by an effective strangling of democracy despite the continuous formal existence of democratic structures; a pervasive practice of 'identity politics' that sustains multiple fascist tendencies, including the overarching tendency of communal-fascism; rampant 'corruption'; and the pursuit of policies which, apart from the impoverishment they bring to the people and the oppression of the progressive political forces they unleash, also roll back the social and political gains made by hitherto excluded groups like Dalits and women, and reduce the minorities to a subservient status (Patnaik 2012).

Patnaik has thus made a significant contribution to a crucial task, no less than that of conceptualizing the political economy of contemporary India. While accepting the basic premise that contemporary capitalist economic policy 'requires an appropriate restructuring of the polity', I differ in that I do not characterize it as 'creeping fascism'. It is, I believe, more appropriate to term it creeping *authoritarianism*. What is developing in India is a form of authoritarian political rule. The anti-democratic trends and the narrowing of democracy should be seen as an authoritarian response emerging from within the constitutional-democratic framework and from forces without. What needs to be considered is how neo-liberalism is reshaping the existing political system by whittling down its bourgeois-democratic features and bringing about an authoritarian version of constitutional democracy.

With regard to the transition in advanced capitalist countries from bourgeois democracy to authoritarian forms of rule, Ralph Miliband writes of less extreme alternatives than fascism, 'which do not require the wholesale dismantling of democratic institutions, the total subversion of all liberties, [and] certainly not the abandoning of democratic rhetoric' (Miliband 2006: 198).

In the present era of globalized finance capital, the ruling classes institute authoritarian rule in order to consolidate their class rule or to tackle intractable contradictions in society. According to Miliband, after the universal revulsion at the horrors of fascism in Nazi Germany, it is difficult for the bourgeoisie to consider fascism as an option even in a situation of extreme crisis. Social contradictions, both external and internal, can be tackled with degrees of authoritarianism and by resort to a variety of national chauvinism. Miliband, therefore, saw authoritarian capitalist states as a substitute for fascism. Prabhat Patnaik, as we have said, has written that 'creeping fascism' does not mean that fascism is 'on the horizon'.

Thus, for our purposes, it would be more useful to analyse the anatomy of an Indian variant of authoritarianism.

II

In India, where capitalist development occurred within a context where the tasks of the bourgeois-democratic revolution remained incomplete, the tendencies to constrain democracy and curb the democratic rights of the people were always immanent in the social formation. But with the global changes brought about with the hegemony of finance capital, and the resultant attacks on national sovereignty and the weakening of the capacity of nation-states to defend national and popular interests, the erosion of democracy and democratic rights is manifested in the degradation of formal democratic institutions, in the hollowing of democracy, in the transformation in the role of political parties and in the political system itself. The ruling classes' inherent interest in accession to the demands of finance capital and in privatizing all spheres of the economy have been primary motives for the state to serve market forces.

As far as the rights of the people are concerned, the parliamentary democratic system adopted under the Republican Constitution represented a major advance. The parliamentary democratic system acquired its legitimacy and validity through popular acceptance of and participation in the electoral process, through the associated mass mobilization by political parties. Political parties have had constantly to keep the people's democratic aspirations in mind when shaping their programmes and political positions.

Neo-liberalism and the sway of finance capital in the domestic sphere has led to a growing homogenization of bourgeois political parties. It has widened the gap between what parties profess and what they actually do. The pre-eminent demand of the neo-liberal regime is that governments may change but the 'reforms' process must go on. This understanding has been in effect over more than two decades. Ever since the Narasimha Rao government unleashed the new liberalization policies in 1991, successive governments – whether Congress-led coalitions, BJP-led coalitions or a non-Congress secular coalition (United Front) – have shown striking similarities and continuity in the economic policies they have pursued.

Protecting the interests of finance capital, and ensuring hospitable conditions for capital flows and investment, became the *sine qua non* of any government in power. How quickly this became the priority for the central government was evident in stark manner in May 1996, during the thirteen-day government of Atal Behari Vajpayee. That government was sworn in without a majority in the Lok Sabha. On the day (27 May) that it faced a confidence vote, when it became evident that the government would fall if there were to be a vote, the Cabinet was hurriedly convened during the lunch-break in parliament. The sole item on the agenda was to approve a sovereign counter-guarantee to the Enron Corporation in connection with its project at Dabhol in Maharashtra. Faced with the imminent downfall of the government, the priority for the ruling party was to provide a counter-guarantee to the Enron Corporation to enable it to raise funds from Indian banks and other financial institutions. The Dabhol project of Enron went on, of course, to become a classic tale of corporate chicanery and governmental corruption.

All bourgeois political parties have taken a more or less uniform stand in support of issues vital to the interests of finance capital and imperialism; these include financial sector liberalization, disinvestment of shares in public sector enterprises and privatization of basic services. Even where there is a particular policy that a party initially commits itself to reverse – as was the case with foreign direct investment in multi-brand retail by the Bharatiya Janata Party (BJP) – it has been unable to do so after coming to power. Bourgeois political parties have unquestioningly embraced the macroeconomic policies dictated by neo-liberalism. The Enron case, in fact, showed in microcosm the culpability of all these parties in foisting neo-liberal policies on the people. The regime has further been consolidated by the suborning of the bureaucracy and the support of the corporate media.

The political consensus on neo-liberal policies is accompanied by changes in the role and character of the bourgeois political parties themselves. The compulsion for all political parties to respond to popular aspirations for a better life, for food, housing, education, employment, health and basic services, gives their election manifestos and promises a peculiar two-facedness. While bourgeois parties adhere to neo-liberal nostrums in their economic policy platform, they promise also to meet the people's needs and aspirations. If elected to government, a bourgeois party has to undertake a certain number of social welfare measures and hand out doles in order to maintain the façade that it is responding to people's needs. At the same time, a free run is given to big capitalists and the rural rich to accumulate capital, while the nexus of big business–ruling politicians–bureaucrats ensures that some of the spoils are distributed to the political rulers too.

The regional parties, which are in government in roughly one-third of the states of India, have been transformed in the neo-liberal age. The regional bourgeoisies they represent have prospered and grown under liberalization. The parties themselves have undergone a transformation. The main leaders and their family members get involved in business and capitalist entrepreneurship. Increasingly, those who get elected to district local bodies, assemblies and parliament are themselves businessmen or capitalists. The rural rich, liquor merchants, contractors and big traders are well represented at all levels in the bourgeois parties.

The vocation of politics is increasingly seen as a business – and persons in business themselves join politics. This intertwining starts at the level of the local bodies and extends up to parliament. This has brought about a change in the composition of the bourgeois parties and their class interests. While the big bourgeoisie is still mainly represented by the BJP and the Congress party, significant sections of big business at the regional and state levels support and utilize the regional parties too.

These changes in the neo-liberal regime have accelerated the process of homogenization of bourgeois parties and are a reflection of the ruling-class consensus that there is no other option but the neo-liberal path. The role of political parties as representatives of various sections of the people is getting steadily eroded. The absence of inner-party democracy in most bourgeois parties undermines their representative character. Many parties are becoming family-run outfits, reflecting the overall orientation of politics as a business. Party leaders seek to protect and bequeath the properties and assets earned through their political positions to their family members by appointing them or grooming them to be successors to political leadership.

The reach of the business–politician nexus is still not fully appreciated, because, with the tremendous proliferation of capitalism, it is happening from the ground upwards. For instance, in the Karnataka assembly elections of 2013, a survey by a leading newspaper found that the 'real estate sector has funded the assembly polls'. Further, 'most of the candidates, irrespective of the political parties they represent, and independents contesting from Bangalore and Mysore, have a direct or indirect hand in land transactions'.[1] The report further points out that in the previous elections, the mining lobby was dominant, just as in an earlier period the liquor lobby prevailed.

The degeneration in the political system is manifested in parliamentary institutions too. Pervasive high-level corruption fostered by the neo-liberal order strikes at the root of the democratic system. Corruption subordinates public policy-making to private interests. In the neo-liberal polity, more and more businessmen and entrepreneurs of all sorts are becoming Members of Parliament (MPs) and legislators. Several ministers in the previous, Congress-led UPA (United Progressive Alliance) government were businessmen–politicians, and conflicts of interest and corrupt practices stemmed from this nexus.

To begin with, international treaties and agreements with foreign countries do not require the approval of parliament. A government can barter away bits of sovereignty of the country through treaties, and parliament has no say in the matter. The WTO (World Trade Organization) agreement, the Indo–US nuclear deal and the Indo–US Defence Framework Agreement were all signed without parliamentary approval. Vital economic policy decisions, such as opening multi-brand retail trade to foreign capital, are taken by the executive without parliamentary sanction.

The importance of parliament has declined. Between 1952 and 1972, the Lok Sabha worked for an average of 120 days a year. In the decade 1991–2010, the corresponding figure fell to 70 working days a year. And this is not only due to disruptions of proceedings; the executive has consciously tried to curtail parliament, increasing resort to ordinances being just one example of such curtailment.

The hollowing out of democracy and the denuding of political parties of any ideological and programmatic content have been witnessed in Western Europe under neo-liberalism. 'The widespread drift towards forms of decision-making that eschew electoral accountability and popular democratic control, in Europe and elsewhere, furnishes us with a context in which the European Union's democratic deficit may best be understood' (Mair 2013: 222). Some of these trends have become visible in India's parliamentary democracy and party system as well.

III

The authoritarian thrust emanating from the neo-liberal process has found expression in the demand to change features of the political system by amending the Constitution. 'Stability' and 'strong government' have become major preoccupations. The demand for a presidential form of government arose more sharply in the 1990s than before; the proposal was backed by the BJP and articulated most vigorously by L.K. Advani. Vasant Sathe, a veteran Congressman, explained the salience of the demand in the new circumstances:

> It is realized on all counts that political stability is a condition precedent for sustained economic growth. [The] direction of liberalization, which has received acclaim throughout the world and which is attracting foreign investment, is likely to receive a severe setback if the political stability of government at the national level is shaken. There is a feeling of urgency to find a solution to this problem. (Quoted in Karat 1995)

The Speaker of the Tenth Lok Sabha, Shivraj Patil, circulated a discussion paper on reviewing the system. Among the changes suggested were a guaranteed term of five years for the Lok Sabha with no dissolution of the house mid-term; and the formation of a government with a two-thirds majority by means of a coalition of parties, failing which the President was to form a government with persons outside parliament or with the help of 'constitutional authorities'. The thrust of these proposals was to undermine a parliamentary system based on political parties. The essence of the presidential form of government is a more authoritarian set-up which would be inherent in the executive authority of the President.

The BJP demand for a review of the Constitution, first contained in its 1991 election manifesto, finally took shape when a National Commission to Review the Working of the Constitution was set up by the BJP-led NDA (National Democratic Alliance) government on the fiftieth anniversary of the Constitution. The Commission did not, however, recommend the presidential system that the BJP desired so greatly.

A decade of efforts to alter the parliamentary system through constitutional means did not make headway. Having a person like Narendra Modi as the President of India with executive powers would have been ideal for the RSS–BJP combine. But the deep-rooted parliamentary democratic system and its capacity to accommodate vast diversities has thwarted moves for an authoritarian replacement. The efforts for a constitutional exercise to instal authoritarianism were given up for the time being. Instead, there began a multi-pronged effort to incrementally introduce authoritarian measures in multiple spheres, including the political system.

The architecture of a national security state has also been taking shape. As Home Minister in the NDA government, L.K. Advani, in a lecture to the Federation of Indian Chambers of Commerce and Industry (FICCI), spoke of creating an 'effective state' by initiating far-reaching reforms in the administration, judiciary and the internal security system. Though he deliberately avoided the term 'strong state' because 'it may be construed to have some undemocratic connotations', what he envisaged was in fact a strong state in place of what some consider to be a soft and debilitated state structure.

The growth of terrorist activities in the 1980s provided a further justification for a strong national security state. Provision for preventive detention already existed in the Constitution (Article 22). Legislation was enacted immediately after the Constitution was promulgated. Since the Preventive Detention Act (1950), there have been a series of Acts prescribing preventive detention, and imposing curbs on safeguards and legal rights provided in the criminal justice laws. Whatever misgivings surfaced from time to time, as in the case of the Prevention of Terrorist Activities Act (POTA), which was allowed to lapse in 2004 by the UPA-I government, the demand for a stringent law against terror brought back a draconian law in the form of the Unlawful Activities Prevention Act in 2008. The National Security Act still exists in the statute book. These laws have been used to arrest trade unionists and activists of opposition parties. Thousands of people have been detained under these laws, and very few of them were eventually tried and found guilty by the courts. Sedition clauses in the Indian Penal Code (that is, in respect of acts of waging war against the state) are routinely used to arrest people protesting against state policies or projects that affect the lives and livelihoods of the people.

Authoritarian laws have targeted Muslim youth and tribal people. Hundreds of Muslim youth have been rounded up in terror cases and falsely implicated, or kept in detention for long periods and then released. In the name of combating Maoist violence, Adivasis are swept into custody and then detained under such laws. The authoritarian ethos has strengthened so much that police and security forces act against the people with impunity. In the name of tackling terror and Maoist violence, false encounters, illegal detention and torture in custody have become commonplace. The Armed Forces Special Powers Act (AFSPA), which is in force in Jammu & Kashmir and parts of the North East, gives the armed forces powers outside the purview of the Penal Code and has enabled them to act with impunity, killing several innocent civilians.

The demand for 'flexibility of labour' has been a priority of the neo-liberal regime. Its corollary is the weakening of trade unions. As part of the authoritarian thrust of the Narendra Modi government, proposals to amend labour laws to curtail the rights of workers and restrict trade unions have been mooted. The BJP state governments of Rajasthan and Madhya Pradesh have already legislated these changes.

The space for public protests and political mobilization has been shrinking steadily. There has been a drastic increase in curbs on assembly, protests and political campaigning with the advent of the neo-liberal regime. And it can be said that where the executive does not intervene, the higher judiciary has been active in placing curbs on people's rights. In 1997, the Kerala High Court declared *bandhs* illegal, a decision endorsed by the Supreme Court. A year later, *hartals* were prohibited. Courts have banned assembly and demonstrations in many public spaces that were traditional venues for mass mobilization. Courts of law invariably issue injunctions against strikes and assembly near workplaces. At present, there is hardly any big public ground that can be used for political rallies and mass demonstrations in the state capitals near the legislative assemblies. In Delhi, the right to assemble in the Boat Club grounds near parliament has been prohibited since 1993. Even the Election Commission would prefer election campaigning to be confined to television studios.

The overall result has been a curbing of democratic rights, erosion of civil liberties and a shrinkage of space for public protests. These measures go beyond the exercise of the repressive powers legally vested in a bourgeois-democratic state. Authoritarianism provides the legitimation for the repressive measures *beyond* the normal repressive apparatus of the state.

IV

The Hindutva communal forces, with their attacks on minorities and fascistic methods of suppressing democratic rights and dissent, have emerged as a major source of authoritarianism. The vicious identity politics spawned by the impact of globalization and neo-liberalism have infused them with a new vigour. The rise of Hindutva communalism coincides with the advent of liberalization in India, and these twin forces have fuelled authoritarian trends. The Rashtriya Swayamsevak Sangh (RSS) believes in an authoritarian Hindu *rashtra*.

The six-year rule of the BJP-led government in 1998–2004 saw concerted efforts by the RSS to infiltrate institutions of the state, and to reshape educational and cultural policies. With the BJP acquiring an absolute majority in the Lok Sabha a decade later, the RSS has begun a calibrated plan to refashion the educational, cultural and social set-up and different institutions on majoritarian lines. The soil for authoritarianism is being cultivated not only in the political sphere, but also in the social and cultural arenas. The ban on beef consumption; moral policing; the denunciation of artists and cultural productions as anti-Hindu; attacks on elite educational institutions, demanding that they conform to Hindutva values; censorship of the arts and intimidation of artists – all of these are features of this authoritarian onslaught.

A parallel can be found in the Turkish experience, where the ruling AKP (Justice and Development Party) and Prime Minister (now President) Erdogan set out to reshape the Turkish state and institutions on Islamist lines, away from the secular framework founded by Kemal Ataturk. A necessary corollary for this has been Erdogan's attempt to establish an authoritarian presidency by amending the Constitution, a project that has been temporarily stalled after the failure of the AKP to win a substantial majority in the Turkish parliament in the elections of May 2015.[2]

The axis between neo-liberalism and communalism is the most potent stimulant for authoritarianism. The pace of authoritarianism has speeded up since the Modi regime took office in May 2014. The fight to defend democracy and bourgeois-democratic rights has to be waged by Left and democratic forces. The classic Marxist position has been that when the bourgeoisie trample upon democracy, it is up to the working class to defend bourgeois democracy. Rosa Luxemburg has stated this position lucidly:

> If democracy has become partially superfluous and partially troublesome to the bourgeoisie, it is necessary and indispensable to the working class. It is necessary, first of all, because it creates the political forms (self-government, electoral rights, etc.) that will serve the proletariat as springboards and fulcrums in its transformation of bourgeois society. Second, however, it is indispensable because only in it, in the struggle for democracy, can the proletariat become conscious of its class interests and its historical tasks. (Luxemburg 2015: 85)

The critical question is how to link the struggle for democracy and against authoritarianism with the struggle against neo-liberal capitalism. In India, the corrosion of the representative form of democracy, i.e. the parliamentary system, is well under way. With the influx of big capital in the electoral system, neo-liberalism is strangling the democratic space for the Left. The reverses that the Left have suffered in the recent elections to parliament and to the assemblies in states such as West Bengal are not unconnected to this phenomenon.

It would be wrong, however, to conclude that all democratic potential in the parliamentary electoral system has been exhausted. The struggle for democracy has also to be waged in the formal parliamentary system. The defeat of the Indira Gandhi regime in the 1977 elections, after the imposition of internal Emergency, is a reminder that people will not easily give up their rights in a parliamentary democratic system, however restricted these may be. But it would be a major mistake and a reformist illusion to restrict the fight for democracy to the confines of the parliamentary system, especially at a time when formal parliamentary democracy is getting hollowed and delinked from the people's expectations.

The main arena has to be the struggle against neo-liberalism – that is, to rally the working people around an alternative programme that is a radical departure from the neo-liberal path. This will be the terrain on which authoritarianism can be fought and defeated, since neo-liberalism provides the essential wellspring for authoritarian power and ideology.

The fight against the other source of authoritarianism, mainly Hindutva communalism and the lesser varieties of identity politics, requires the integration of the struggle in defence of the livelihoods and rights of the working people with the fight against communal forces. Severe social and economic inequalities and unemployment provide cannon-fodder for communalism. Without addressing the real economic problems of the people, popular mobilization against disruptive communalism cannot advance.

Electoral battles to isolate and defeat the BJP, while necessary, are totally inadequate to combat communalism, which is active in the ideological, social and cultural spheres. It is in these spheres that more determined interventions are called for. The neo-liberal and Hindutva dispensation is inimical to the interests of all socially oppressed sections. The rights of Dalits, Adivasis, women and minorities are under siege, and their right to equality, in particular, is denied. The vital link is between class-based struggles and social struggles, and this link must be strengthened.

Neo-liberal capitalism has brought about many changes in society, amongst classes and in the sphere of ideology. We need to study, analyse and understand these changes for a better praxis. Neo-liberal politics and changes in the polity are one part of the new dispensation. There is also need for new slogans, tactics and forms of struggle in the socio-economic sphere, a matter that needs separate discussion. But what is undisputable is that the Left, being the only consistent force against neo-liberal imperialism and communalism, has to play the crucial role in the popular-democratic mobilization against Modi-style authoritarianism.

Notes

[1] 'Real Estate Sector Funding the Assembly Polls', *The Times of India*, Bangalore edition, 1 May 2013.

[2] See Ghosh (2014) for an interesting comparison of the path taken by the two countries.

References

Ghosh, Amitav (2014), 'Erdogan and Modi: Parallel Journeys', *The Times of India*, 30 November.

Karat, Prakash (1995), 'Altering Parliamentary Democracy: Stability and the Ruling Classes', *People's Democracy*, 14 May.

Luxemburg, Rosa (2015), *Reform or Revolution*, New Delhi: LeftWord Books.
Mair, Peter (2013), *Ruling the Void: The Hollowing-Out of Western Democracy*, London: Verso Books, London 2013.
Miliband, Ralph (2006), *The State in Capitalist Society*, reprint, New Delhi: Aakar Books.
Patnaik, Prabhat (2011), 'Capitalism, Freedom and Democracy', in *Re-Envisioning Socialism*, New Delhi: Tulika Books.
Patnaik, Prabhat (2012), 'Ways of Neo-Liberalism', *Frontline*, 15–28 December.

'Fascists in positions of power'
In Search of Resistance

Teesta Setalvad

India and its national consciousness are being driven today by a force that is not only simply fascist in its ideological moorings and inclinations, but one that has – from its birth in 1925, through its evolution and now, 90 years later – clearly shown contempt for the fundamental principles of India's parliamentary democracy, the Constitution of India. The involvement of the Rashtriya Swayamsevak Sangh (RSS) in aggravating aggression and violence among different sections of Indians through official writings and interventions by its leadership, and in directly contributing to such violence through active participation in bouts of communal violence, has been systematically and fairly well documented over the decades: from the pre- and post-partition violence between 1936 and 1947, until as recently as the lynch-mob killings at Dadri (2015), Muzaffarnagar (2013) and Atali (2014).[1] A pamphlet of the undivided Communist Party of India issued in 1947, says it all. Written by P.C. Joshi, it analyses the partition-driven violence, and lays the responsibility squarely at the door of the communal RSS, the Muslim League and the Akalis.[2] The RSS's unabashed defiance of a hard-earned Indian consensus endorsing not just the rule of law, but equality of all Indians before the law, is a carefully aimed strategy to gain reflective support from those amongst its fellow thinkers who are already entrenched in positions of governance that are fit to undermine fair application of the existing laws (based on equality and non-discrimination contained in the Indian Constitution) and more.[3] In true-to-form fascist style, their continued assertions test the waters, garnering support for the ultimate goal, silencing ineffectual opposition while seeking to intimidate or even eliminate real and meaningful resistance. Recently, at a press meet organized by the Safdar Hashmi Memorial Trust (Sahmat) in New Delhi, Professor Prabhat Patnaik, to whom this volume is dedicated, summed up the challenging situation thus, 'though we may not (yet) have a fascist government in power, we do have fascists in positions of power'.[4]

Given this pre-eminent threat to the very existence of India as a socialist, secular, democratic republic, given the brazen incursions on rational thought and education and culture, and given the fact that a pervasive sanction of targeted hate and violence appears to now flow from the very pinnacle of Indian power at the centre, where, we must ask, is lasting resistance to this politics that has consolidated firmly since the 1980s likely to emerge, and what form is it likely to take? This question begs some deliberation.

The clear shift of India's national economic policy away from a previously socialist orientation towards one that promotes a 'free market' economy, and encourages monopolies and consolidation of capital, began in the 1990s. Along with this came a fashionable public discourse, promoted significantly by sections of the privately-owned Indian media (since the early 2000s the electronic Indian media have tended to dominate public consciousness and the visible, urban political discourse), to rubbish all services, especially health and education, that were hitherto publicly-owned and run in ways meant to ensure access for a large number of Indians. This orchestration in favour of the private sector and privatization pushed rash, and not necessarily sound, economic decisions. An interesting footnote or prefix to this narrative comes from the cold facts relating to the structure of the Indian media itself, not just in terms of ownership but also in terms of forms of employment. Journalists, managements contemptuously told their 'employees' in the early 1990s as the wave of 'liberalization' swept through the corridors of the Indian media too, are expendable parts of the business, and the real meat lies in advertising (revenues). News and editorials were to fit (if there was space) between the pages of advertising, which was no more just revenue for the newspaper but actually shaped its concerns and thrust.[5]

Thus, the duality that has shaped Indian political economy over the past quarter of a century is a pervasive majoritarianism accompanied by a drastic over-emphasis on public outlays on corporate subsidies, while rural employment, health, education and other such sectoral budgets experience systemic cuts, though the burdens they pose on the exchequer are a fraction of the former. A hardened hate politics ensures periodic bouts of intense and ghastly violence against the targeted sections deemed inimical to the homogeneity of a Hindu *rashtra*,[6] with a sustained public discourse of 'otherness' that facilitates this periodic bloodletting. The concomitant reorganization within the working class, its shift to the unorganized sector and the atomization of sections of the population that were earlier organized, as, for example, teachers and journalists, almost ensured that the resistance to the politics of majoritarianism got splintered or muted.

The current Indian parliament (elected in 2014), with 545 seats, has MPs (Members of Parliament) with assets worth Rs 10 million (*crorepatis*) occupying 353 seats; in comparison, the previous parliament had 145 MPs worth Rs 10 million each. Among these 353 MPs are mining barons, owners of telecom companies and, last but not the least, television media barons with controlling shares in the news networks.[7] This reflects a rare convergence of corporate, political and media interests, hitherto unparalleled, a triangulation of interests, in a sense a stranglehold that is choking India's parliamentary democracy.

Unsurprising, then, was the brazen campaign of sections of Indian corporates to back the Narendra Modi campaign in the lead-up to the 2014 elections.[8] If the lower house of the Indian parliament today is strangulated by these predominant interests, hope lies in the role played by the parliamentary opposition over the sessions since the winter of 2014 in the upper house, where all attempts by the current political dispensation to push through a regressive land acquisition law were defeated. Barely two years ago, the previous UPA (United Progressive Alliance) government, consulting all shades of political opposition, overturned a 150-year-old central law that disempowered the farmer and the tiller, and gave unfettered rights to the government to seize productive, agrarian land. Displacement and impoverishment were the result, with much of the land acquired by corporates not even being put to the use it was ostensibly acquired for.[9] Labour laws are the next target of this regime, as is the Forest Rights Act, again enacted after years of struggle and demands by mass movements – years that saw the Indian adivasi/tribal population held to ransom to a corporate–forest officer–bureaucracy nexus, which deprived us of much forest cover and rendered us vulnerable.

Similarly, the gains of two hundred years of the labour movement are sought to be taken away under the guise of 'economic reforms'. Barely 7 per cent of India's labour force today is organized while 93 per cent work in sub-human conditions; if this existing 7 per cent is made vulnerable to the 'market' – as journalists were when their salaries were trebled and they were put on annual contractual employment – compliance to the existing regime is guaranteed as resistance will be crushed.

Within the organized Left, the Communist Party of India (Marxist) (CPI[M]), with its mass and front organizations, boasts a membership of 1 million – nationally a not-so insignificant number, until one asks the rather slippery question of where do the votes of these 1 million members (10 lakh individuals) go?

As the results of the last general elections were deconstructed and discussed, especially in states like West Bengal and Kerala, the immediate analyses spelt doom. As subsequent elections (local) took place, however, a more nuanced assessment began to creep in. In the lower house of the present parliament, the Left presence is a total of 12 seats. All of these MPs are from Kerala, West Bengal and Tripura. The national vote-share of the Left in 2014, at 4.18 per cent, was almost half of that a decade earlier (2004), when the Left secured as many as 62 seats in parliament. Since not much has changed drastically in terms of the challenges to the political economy, this decline in terms of seats won and vote-share lost must be seen in the context of a vastly splintered opposition, regionally and nationally. The situation does not in any way lessen the gravity of the challenge faced by the organized Left, especially if it needs to carefully and systematically stage a comeback on the national stage.

This, however, need not be the case in principle. A stray conversation with Professor Patnaik comes to mind repeatedly: what he found encouraging during his continued and unabashed association with the CPI(M), he said, were instances such as when he was visiting Chennai, and, while travelling in an autorickshaw, he discovered that the driver was a member of the CITU (Centre of Indian Trade Unions, affiliated to the CPI[M]). It is this sense of belonging to a vast, wider and larger brotherhood (not excluding the sorority of course) that Patnaik says means so much to him even today in terms of transformative and committed politics. The consciousness that governs this wider brotherhood is rich and challenging; it is a consciousness not simply based on a basic understanding of the class structure, the mode of production and the attendant forms of exploitation that go with accumulation of capital, but one that reflects, or must reflect, the means and methods of conveying the conditions of joy, sorrow, living and work, whether it be through language, song, music, food or drink.

A consciousness that is the essence of being and living, in a sense – of culture and, of course, faith. The relationship of culture and faith with a vibrant socialist consciousness and the ability of a political organization to negotiate these complex areas were what made the experience of the Indian People's Theatre Association (IPTA) so memorable. It brought issues that concern a vast majority of Indians, rural and urban, to the centre stage of cultural consciousness across generations. The fact is that it was not just IPTA on its own, but its association and relationship with a mass working-class movement, rural and urban, embodied then in the undivided and unified Left (the Communist Party) that made this possible. There were some tensions between leaders of the political wing and cultural practioners always, but the sheer depth and scale of this phenomenon was huge, as seen in its impact, for instance, on mainstream Indian cinema; for decades, talent that emerged from this wider and more rooted consciousness scripted several of India's early films. Conversations with many of the creative luminaries of that time record how this sense of reality was reflected not just in the choice of subject or script of cinema, as may be obvious, but also, as in the making of *Garm Hawa*, the production set.[10]

A few months back, while I was on one of my several trips to meetings organized by state units of the CPI(M), this time in Kannur in Kerala, a living example of this sense of collective being and consciousness greeted me. I was graciously hosted at the state guest-house and after the large meeting at the city centre, was given dinner by the young caretaker there. Soon after the meal, Sunil, who by now was a familiar face because he had been plying me with tea and food since the afternoon, knocked on the door and sought to introduce the cook, Nasser, to me. Both were young and in their twenties, both were party members, and both had attended the meeting at the city centre, which had addressed the issue of 'Creeping Communalism and the Threat from Fascist Forces'. When, after a charming request for a photograph, they left, I again recalled Professor Patnaik's words. Kannur has seen innumerable real-life battles to preserve cultural and economic freedoms, with party workers at the forefront. Kannur is also where violent battles have been fought between the RSS and the CPI(M).

Yet the challenge faced by the organized Left today – be it nationally at the electoral level, or regionally, or locally where a young and youthful electorate is looking for strong, progressive alternatives – is one of form, approach and language. Technology and creativity need to be understood and appropriated with the vast knowledge of historical experience. At a recent meeting in Mumbai, where one of India's renowned historians was speaking, a veteran trade unionist insisted that the problem was one of being able to 'connect'. Power, capital and technology have enabled a draconian personality to 'connect' to 31 per cent of India's voters, ensuring support for a dream presented as messianic reality, as if a What'sApp image or slogan can ensure realization of a promise. In such a scenario, how and where do we begin to capture the imagination of those whom we organize and work with, so that their political choice is reflected in a democratic and inclusive culture?[11]

Towards the end of 2012, no less than 33,000–35,000 *Anganwadi* and *Balwadi* workers were brought, by CITU, for a sit-in *(dharna)* to Delhi, a protest that lasted three days. It was winter and we visited the venue, in solidarity. No television cameras covered the event though the number of day-care nurturers who look after pre-school children, and who were present there to protest their pathetic working conditions, was in no way insignificant. Attempts to get television anchors of 'national' (read privately-owned) channels to hold a news-hour discussion on the issues these day-care workers brought to the protest were unsuccessful. Comrade Hemlata Kandikuppa (CITU) detailed how these women work for a pittance, sometimes as little as Rs 300 per month, while more and more demands are placed on them. The demand at the protest was that they be treated as regular employees (which they are not) and that details of all work assigned to them be acknowledged. Similarly, the remuneration given to mid-may meal cooks-cum-helpers cannot be dignified by calling it a salary. CITU had made efforts to include the conditions of workers in the scheme as an agenda item in the forthcoming session of the Indian Labour Conference.[12] The narrative of the protest (working conditions and overall payback to this section of Indians) ought to have gravely impacted us. Even the effort of getting 33,000 women workers from across India to Delhi was a historic endeavour. The overall fragmented nature of the response, and absolute scorn displayed by television news networks and even the print media towards such issues of the working class in India, has rendered most Indians immune to their condition. Moreover, the fact that not only are primary care-givers treated this way by our governments, but that we do not care enough to know about their work and life conditions is truly a matter of concern, even shame, for any society or country that wants to guarantee secure and quality care for all its children, poor and rich – leave alone one that wishes to see itself an economic power-house.

The fact that it is CITU, one of the mass-based trade unions, that is organizing this section of the work force is heartening. What begs exploration and action, however, is whether this political engagement of organizing also consists of a rigorous political education on caste, on communalism, on discrimination, with a healthy dose of shared histories, music and culture.

The story of agricultural workers is even more complex. An example of the resistance of this migrant and moving work force was seen in the vibrant efforts made by the All India Agricultural Worker's Union (AIAWU) and the Bharatiya Khet Mazdoor Union (BKMU), in the wake of violent attacks against Dalits and Muslims in Haryana and Uttar Pradesh, to confront the issue of caste conflict head-on.[13] The circular and appeal issued by the office bearers of these organizations, dated 24 October 2015, reportedly led to 60 protests all over Haryana and Uttar Pradesh.

This is a rare and much-needed example of once again bringing back a politically sensitized working class to centre stage for combating engineered political conflict, a strategy that could provide a useful buffer to the refashioning of aggressive religious and caste identities amongst them. It is only if and when alternate identities related to active political engagement emerge for the working class that large sections of it will become a buffer against the insidious spread of both majoritarian and minority communalism. Time-tested and shared histories of past collective experience, the involvement of these sections in present, local and past resistances, could provide a creative buffer to the poison of hate and division. Today, free and invasive social media technologies are being used to turn young populations against each other. What if these were used instead to guard against bloodletting, at all times telling and sharing more inspirational historical narratives of inclusive resistance?[14]

Three lakh sugarcane workers in Maharashtra comprise the state's migrant work force, living in poor and exploited conditions. Maharashtra is a high sugar-producing state. The pattern of migration moves from the state's economically backward districts of Beed, Osmanabad and Latur to the sugarcane belt comprising Sangli, Satara, Pune, Solapur and Kolhapur districts in the western part of the state. The Sugar Commissioneriat of the state has no official record of the migrant labourers, but social and advocacy groups fighting for their rights put their number at more than three lakhs. A local *mukadam* or contractor awards them the contracts for sugarcane-cutting, which includes a payment of Rs 50,000 to Rs 70,000 to the labourer for the entire season. But the unit 'labourer' is actually a pair: either husband and wife, or two men. So, each harvester gets half the amount. A large chunk of the money, though, is paid before the season. Poor work conditions and unregulated working hours make for an insecure life. Absence of any formal education and alternate sources of employment force the labourers to return to this source of earning, however restrictive the life and work conditions. Again, this is an invisible reality. Neither the print nor the electronic media really informs, educates or involves the rest of India in looking at or resisting this exploitation. The constant flow of their movement as labour makes conventional organizing a challenge. What happens to the communal or casteist imaging that is part of the contemporary discourse? Can the migrant labourer remain immune in the absence of any alternate rigorous political and popular culture and imagination?

The qualitative collapse or absence of visionary, inclusive and progressive values from the working class movement in India has allowed, and even made easy and possible, the insidious creep of majoritarian, aggressive, macho, communal politics. In India, as is increasingly clear, but as was articulated decades ago by a man who became India's first Prime Minister, Jawaharlal Nehru, 'Fascism will come under the garb of majority communalism.'

It is no wonder, and certainly not a coincidence, that even before Gujarat it was Maharashtra, with its far more progressive base and polity, that not only gave birth to the Shiv Sena, but was the historical location of a solid and sustainable alliance between the Shiv Sena and the parliamentary wing of the RSS, namely the Bharatiya Janata Party (BJP), from 1995 to 1999. The RSS was born in Maharashtra with its headquarters in Nagpur (in 1925), but its policies have always been dictated from the neighbourhood of Shaniwar-peth in Pune dominated by Brahmins. As Ashok Dhawale of the CPI(M) puts it:

> The Shiv Sena, during nearly three and a half decades of its existence, has always symbolized a semi-fascist face of reaction. Amongst all the regional parties that are today opportunistically supporting the BJP-led regime at the Centre, it is only the Shiv Sena (SS) that has a clear ideological affinity with the RSS-controlled Sangh Parivar. That is precisely why the SS has been the BJP's earliest and oldest political ally in the country . . . since 1989, the two have had an unbroken alliance at both national and state levels. Despite rough patches, this alliance is set to continue for the near future. (Dhawale 2000)

Bal Thackeray, the supremo of the Shiv Sena had attended an RSS *shakha* in his childhood; though in a different fashion from the RSS, he openly espoused contempt for any democratic consciousness or politics, using violence and intimidation as a strategy and tactic.

Today, as the RSS-dominated NDA-II (National Democratic Alliance-II) regime at the centre has come to symbolize a direct threat to India's rich and multifaceted understanding of the past, public memory has relegated the Shiv Sena's early assaults on free expression to the sidelines. Recent actions of the Shiv Sena (its crude attacks on visiting Pakistani bureaucrats and musicians, for instance) appear aimed at recapturing political ground lost to the RSS. The media today delve little into the history of violent political movements, giving a new and even more banal meaning to the term 'sensationalism'.[15] It has been said that when Adolf Hitler reigned strong in Germany with the founder of the Gestapo, Hermann Goering, whenever he heard the word 'culture', his hand went to his pistol. The faithful Shiv Sena hordes that Bal Thackeray groomed with his individualistic demagoguery faithfully followed this example. Very early in its existence, the Shiv Sena had attacked two radical plays by Vijay Tendulkar, *Sakharam Binder* and *Ghasiram Kotwal*. The latter exposes the degenerate ways of the Peshwas, Brahmin rulers of Maharashtra who had succeeded the Maratha reign.[16] This exposure was resented by the brahminical Sena, which, ironically, had drawn many cadre from the agrarian OBCs (Other Backward Classes) and EBCs (Economically Backward Classes). In the 1980s it was the turn of the film *Tamas*, made for television by Govind Nihalani based on the novel by Bhisham Sahni. The theme was the catastrophic communal inferno at the time of India's partition, and the film began with the apt sentence, 'Those who forget history are condemned to repeat it.' The Shiv Sena, BJP, RSS and Vishwa Hindu Parishad (VHP) began a violent campaign demanding a ban on the film. At the time the campaign did not succeed and *Tamas* was telecast every week on Doordarshan, though at the rather late hour of 10 pm on Mondays. Maharashtra has also been the scene of violent brahminical outpourings against Gandhi and is the birthplace of his assassin. It was during the first NDA government that the play *Mee Nathuram Godse Boltoy*, based on a manipulation of Godse's speech after his conviction, was crafted. Since its inception – and again today with a majoritarian government firmly in place in Delhi – this creation has seen several new leases of life. Today, it is not just a play but a call for temples to be built in the name of the killer of Gandhi, much akin to calls for temples in the name of Narendra Modi, a man who still carries the burden of responsibility for the communal carnage of 2002 in Gujarat.[17]

Bombay then and Mumbai now have sat comfortably with this brand of ethnocentric, communal fascism. The 1980s were pivotal to the Sena's entrenchment in not just the public sphere (where its violent, criminal assertions simply did not attract legal action by the police and government[18]) but in its politics, fashioned and encouraged by Bombay's elite. If Amitabh Bachchan and Jaya Bachchan and a host of other Bollywood bigwigs proudly announced their business association (and hence protection from extortion and threat!) with the Sena, leading industrialists felicitated the Sena supremo in the rooms of the iconic Taj Mahal hotel in south Bombay. Post 2007–08, it was the same noted names of Indian (Mumbai) business that heralded the metamorphic start of Narendra Modi's election campaign when they hailed him as 'prime ministerial material'.[19]

In Bombay, even before it was re-named Mumbai during the Shiv Sena–BJP regime of 1995–99, sections of the elite engaged in business, film and law openly declared allegiance through obeisance to the 'fuhrer'.[20] As significant was the communal violence – read pogrom – of 1992–93, in which Bombay's Muslims and some Christians[21] were targeted in violence that was apparently orchestrated from the offices of the Shiv Sena's trade union, Bharatiya Kamgar Sena (BKS). This bout of communal violence also signalled the outright communalization of the criminal underworld, with Bal Thackeray openly giving a call to this effect,[22] to which, significantly, sections of the Dawood Ibrahim gang retaliated with stabbings of *mathadi* workers (Maharashtrian Hindu load-bearers from the unorganized sector), and finally, by allegedly having a hand in the multiple/serial bomb-blasts that rocked the city on 12 March 1993.[23] During the rule of the Sena–BJP government, Mumbai saw 150 deaths in what have come to be known as 'police encounters'. In the first ten months of 1997 there were 70 deaths in 45 such incidents. The appearance of this phenomenon in Mumbai then marked a new stage in the criminalization of politics and the politicization of crime.[24] For each new death the police invoked 'self-defence' as justification, and insisted (without any independent evidence) that the miscreants had opened fire first. Not surprising, since the law allows the police to use arms against anyone charged with an offence for which the punishment is death. Interestingly, however, as P.A. Sebastian has written, there were some strange coincidences: not one police officer was killed or even injured in these 'encounters', though in their affidavits submitted in court the police claimed that the criminals carried sophisticated weapons that had been imported or smuggled into the country, usually AK rifles. The ruling regime of the time did not merely accept the police version of events, but sought to use the machinery of the state to settle disputes with its rivals.[25]

It was Maharashtra, then, that first ceded its legacy of a strong, sound and resilient working class culture to majoritarian fascism, almost a half century ago. The emergence of the Shiv Sena in 1965 redrew the contours of this consciousness when it injected a sharply exclusivist sense of belonging and cultural identity into Bombay's working class. The murder of trade union stalwart and elected Member of the Legislative Assembly (MLC), Krishna Desai, of the Communist Party of India, was one in a series of clashes that sharpened this division. Repeated use of violence and intimidation (Katzenstein 1979), deliberately left untackled by the state government, emboldened the Sena that had always voiced contempt for democracy, promoted authoritarianism as opposed to democracy and legitimized the use of violence. Despite its aggressive appeal with undertones of exclusive regionalism and even communalism (ibid.), the Parel assembly by-election in 1970 was contested by Desai's widow, a woman who, like the Shiv Sena's candidate, was a Maharashtrian from the coastal district of Ratnagiri. Many of Bombay's mill workers hailed from the Konkan coast. In the election, all the right-wing parties – including the Jana Sangh, Swatantra, Hindu Mahasabha and Congress (O) – supported the Shiv Sena. The communist candidate had the support of the Congress (R) and Socialist Party. When the results were declared and the Sena candidate won, it was by a miniscule margin of 1,679 out of the total of 62,662 votes cast (ibid.). The election rhetoric of the Sena included slogans like 'the red flag will never again fly in Bombay', the 'anti-national character of the Communist Party', etc.

The cynical hand of the ruling V.P. Naik government of the Congress, in allowing the violent nature of this mobilization to grow unchecked, has informed and haunted the Sena–Congress relationship that now extends to the former Congress bigwig and presently head of the Nationalist Congress Party (NCP), Sharad Pawar. The outcome of this combination of regionalism laced with communalism in the 1960s was reflected in the sharp polarization of the polity on the issue of religious identity in not just working-class Bombay, but in Jalgaon, Mahad and even Bhiwandi, leading to state-wide incidents of violence in 1970.[26]

This phenomenon took on new proportions during the post-Babri Masjid demolition pogrom in Mumbai, when purportedly offices of the Shiv Sena trade union (Bharatiya Kamgar Sena) were used as launching pads for attacks on Muslim lives, homes and properties. The communalization of the public sphere in Bombay/Mumbai between the 1960s and 1990s was informed by sharp hate-filled rhetoric that not only went unchecked by the executive and its law enforcement arm, the police, but worse, was implicitly legitimized by the higher judiciary that turned a blind eye to it.[27] The battered state of the Communist Party during this period was reflected in a splintering of its working class base. Tragically that base, through a significant shift in orientation and consciousness, became, and has been since, the underbelly of the Shiv Sena. The early 1980s also saw the collapse of the textile mills, once the seat and bedrock of the working class movement, and it was a man called Datta Samant, individualistic and economistic in his approach, who filled the vacuum thus created. He too hailed from the coastal Konkan belt and was arguably a rare example of a working class leader who made it to parliament, championing the lost cause of his supporters who were organized under the Kamgar Aghadi (Worker's Front).

Soon after the demolition of the Babri Masjid on 6 December 1992, a meeting of trade unions was held in Mumbai in which I participated as office bearer of the Bombay Union of Journalists (BUJ). There was an overwhelming sense of the need for a protest from India's premier working class bastion against the criminal and unconstitutional act that had taken place in full public view at Faizabad–Ayodhya – a lumpen act that signalled the criminalization and communalization of not just Indian politics but the country's public sphere, and legitimized both the demonization of India's religious minorities and physical attacks on their life and property. We were witnessing the 'democratic' defiance of the rule of constitutional law by self-avowedly majoritarian and fascist forces. With this and every such act, their electoral popularity consolidated. Today they rule India, to India's peril.

Coming back to the trade unionists' meeting in that faraway December of 1992, after the issue was discussed and deliberated upon for over three hours, with some of us pushing the agenda of a strong workers' protest, Datta Samant made a reluctant admission, 'My workers are Kamgar Aghadi in the day but Shiv Sainiks at night; I cannot guarantee any enthusiastic participation.' This remark concluded the meeting, and the much longed-for march of, and for, the working class in Mumbai against the politics of hate and division never took place. It is that absence of visible articulation of opposition that has continued to guide the overall responses of working class representatives in western India to the politics of division and aggressive communalism.

In the 1960s and 1970s, the backs of the communist unions in India's financial capital were sought to be broken, and the brutal murder of unionist Krishna Desai was epochal. While the Shiv Sena, suspected of committing the act, was never brought to book, the role of the state's Congress leadership in allowing rampant communalism to spread and grow cast a shadow over the state's politics, which has lasted till today. Though the Sena, through the BKS, made inroads among sections of existing trade unions using parochialism, violence and intimidation in a heady mix, it was the patronage extended by key industrialists in Bombay's manufacturing sector that gave the Shiv Sena its much-needed vindication. The textile mill sector remained out of reach for the Sena, however. The historic strike of textile workers was led by Datta Samant – previously with the Congress-led INTUC (Indian National Trade Union Congress) – who was known for his economistic, single-issue approach: high wages with no compromise. Though the workers swore by his leadership, the refusal of the Indira Gandhi-led central government to concede to their demands not only led to the collapse of the strike but the disintegration of working class solidarity, allowing a free and easy entry for the Shiv Sena. Samant was killed in May 1997. The police claimed he was murdered by a criminal gang, instigated by one Guru Sattam, who was paid $500,000 and is now in Hong Kong. Those responsible were alleged to have been connected with Premier Automobiles, where Samant was organizing the workers (Seabrook 1998).

Samant, an icon in terms of his fight for the economic well-being of his workers, did not concern himself much with the culture of working class identity. It is this abdication of the working class from active involvement in discourses on socio-democratic politics and the direction of the political economy that has vitally contributed to the erosion of the parliamentary system of democracy and its transformation into its present-day manifestation of majoritarian electoral politics.

Creative engagement with larger organizations of labour and the working class today needs to draw on history, the social sciences and the rich experiences of our culture. Through this engagement they need to counter the deliberately manipulated versions of history, and communalist renderings of Tipu Sultan, Shivaji, Aurangzeb and Akbar.[28] This has to be combined with creative methods of engaging with a fractured and restructured working class not conventionally positioned for easy organization.[29] Raising the political consciousness of today's youth, who have been rendered apolitical by the sustained take-over of a large number of institutions of higher education and technical education by student outfits belonging to the right-wing, poses a further challenge.

We are, in a sense, witnessing a kind of discontent within our system of parliamentary democracy, especially in the specific political conditions of a first-past-the-post electoral system and absence of proportional representation. Dr Babasaheb Ambedkar addressed the implications of such a crisis eloquently in a speech delivered at the concluding session of the All India Trade Union Worker's Study Camp, held in Delhi from 8 to 17 September 1943, under the auspices of the Indian Federation of Labour. He said, 'Social and economic democracy are the tissues and the fibre of a political democracy', the absence of which causes an acute crisis.[30]

A crucial issue at this historic moment that poses an acute challenge is how far India's corporate capital will bend and go.[31] It is fairly well-documented that Hitler's rise was enabled by sections of the German and international corporate sector. Some of them – Volkswagen, Ford and Coca Cola, among others – saw his demonic solutions as the way forward for a battered Germany. The national political scene with the Weimar Republic was portrayed, hysterically (and disproportionately), as being a sea of chaos. A cultivated sense of despair was promoted. It was this kind of discourse that enabled the Nazi takeover of Germany. Are we seeing such a situation emerging in India today? And if this is indeed the case, we need to ask: where will the resistance come from?

Notes

1 'Who Cast the First Stone', *Communalism Combat*, March 1998, available at http://www.sabrang.com/cc/comold/march98/document1.htm; 'RSS Mouthpiece calls Dadri lynching a "natural reaction"', available at http://www.dnaindia.com/india/report-dadri-lynching-rss-mouthpiece-calls-it-a-natural-reaction-editor-says-they-do-not-support-violence-2136055; 'Hindu Rashtra – Village by Village, Understanding Atali', available at http://kafila.org/2015/06/24/hindu-rashtra-village-by-villageunderstanding-atali/

2 'What happened in the Punjab cannot be called a riot. It was a regular war of extermination of the minorities, of the Sikhs and Hindus in Western Punjab and

of Muslims in East Punjab. It cannot be compared to Calcutta or Noakhali, Bihar, or even to Rawalpindi, for in all these cases it was mobs of one community that took leading part in killing, looting and burning the minority in the area, their communal passions being roused to a pitch of frenzy and savagery. In the Punjab, however, in the recent biggest killing ever seen, it was the trained bands equipped with firearms and modern weapons that were the main killers, looters and rapers. These were the storm troops of various communal parties such as National Guards of the Muslim League in the Western Punjab, and the Shahidi Dal of the Akalis and the Rashtriya Swayamsevak Sangh of the Mahasabha in the Eastern Punjab. They were actively aided and often actually led by the police and the military in committing the worst atrocities . . . in violence and in brutality, in the numbers killed (which Shri Prakasha, India's Ambassador to Pakistan, places at 1½ lakhs), in the use of plenty of modern deadly weapons, in the devastation spread over 14 districts of the Punjab and in the way in which the police, the military and the entire administration was geared not to stop the riots but to spread it – the Punjab tragedy is without parallel.' Joshi and Dhanwantri (1947): 5–6. (Comrade Dhanwantri was a comrade of Bhagat Singh, president of the Lahore District Congress Committee, and a communist leader of Punjab.)

[3] Appointments of persons with ideological moorings in the RSS, be it in the police force, administration or judiciary, ensure that discrimination and not the rule of law prevails.

[4] 'Assault on Reason – The Re-writing of History', press conference held by Sahmat at the Press Club, New Delhi, on 5 September 2015, addressed by Irfan Habib, Prabhat Patnaik, Anil Nauriya and Teesta Setalvad.

[5] Senior journalist P. Sainath has been analysing the ownership structures of the Indian media. In an interview given to *Communalism Combat* (Sainath to Setalvad), he reminds us that the detailed work undertaken by India's independent Press Commissions foresaw the danger and threat of privately-owned media with no secure working tenure for journalists. He urges that a movement for implementation of secure jobs for journalists (Working Journalists law) that has been subverted by the contract system should be undertaken. P. Sainath on 'Convergence of Media, Business and Politics', Part III, available at https://www.youtube.com/watch?v=dUKIxl6r7yc&feature=youtu.be; P. Sainath on 'Media's Private Treaties', Part V, available at https://www.youtube.com/watch?v=YlcJigJ7nXU&feature=youtu.be

[6] 'Muslims can live in this country, but will have to give up eating beef, says Haryana CM Manohar Lal Khattar': 'Democracy has freedoms, but those freedoms have limitations . . . can't hurt another', Manohar Lal Khattar said: available at http://indianexpress.com/article/india/india-news-india/muslims-can-live-in-this-country-but-they-will-have-to-give-up-eating-beef-says-haryana-cm-manohar-lal-khattar/#sthash.DfKNG39w.dpuf. 'Hindu Women Must Have At Least 4 Children, Says BJP's Sakshi Maharaj, available at http://www.ndtv.com/article/india/hindu-women-must-have-at-least-4-children-says-bjp-s-sakshi-maharaj-645239. These are only a couple of the more obnoxious examples.

[7] P. Sainath on 'Corporate Media', Part IV, available at https://www.youtube.com/watch?v=oUttt4_HjPs&feature=youtu.be

[8] Ibid.

[9] 'Can't blame UPA Land Acquisition Bill for stalled projects: RTI', available at http://articles.economictimes.indiatimes.com/2015-04-28/news/61616398_1_land-acquisition-law-stalled-projects-consent-clause

[10] Teesta Setalvad interview with Zaidi and Sathyu: 'Understanding the truth of

Partition is a must to combat Communal Forces symbolized by the Current Regime: M.S. Sathyu, Film Director', available at http://www.sabrang.com/cc/ccinterviews/MSSathyu.htm

[11] Veteran Mumbai-based trade unionist M.J. Pandey at a meeting that hosted historian Romila Thapar in Mumbai on 26 October 2015. She spoke on 'Indian Society and the Secular'.

[12] The issues brought to the table by CITU related to *Anganwadi* workers and helpers, and ASHAs (Accredited Social Health Activists), and the remuneration for mid-day meal cooks-cum-helpers. In addition to the jobs specified, the *Anganwadi* workers are compelled by the district programme officers, as per the orders of the District Collectors, to conduct surveys of different types –of disabled persons, of hand pumps in the area, etc. They are also given the responsibility of collecting census data, election duties, etc. The job of implementing the Kishori Shakti Yojana, which was not there earlier has been included now. Similarly, the government has decided to implement the Indira Gandhi Matritva Sahayog Yojana (IGMSY) from *Anganwadi* centres. The remuneration for IGMSY is nominal. They have to maintain registers and records for each and every activity – altogether around twenty or so; the number differs in different states. This too takes up a lot of their time. Further, they are asked to attend different types of meetings and training programmes, and are made part of village-level committees. The government has decided to extend their working hours to six hours a day: five hours for running the *Anganwadi* centre and one hour for home visits. But in practice they have to work longer hours. The ASHA's duties include accompanying the pregnant woman in labour to the hospital and ensuring that her name is recorded in the registers; otherwise she does not get her incentive. This means that she has to be available round the clock including through the night; that is why she is provided with a mobile phone in some states. She has to work for at least six to seven hours in a day to discharge the responsibilities allotted to her. The mid-day meal workers – cooks and helpers – have to buy the materials, clean and cook, clean the vessels and the premises. These jobs too take at least five to six hours in a day. This means that they cannot take up any other job for some additional income while working as mid-day meal workers. The same is the case with the ASHAs. The 2010 Circular issued by the Govt. of India, MHRD, Department of School Education and Literacy, MDM Division Dt. 30.04.2010, Lr.F.No.5-1/2010-MDM-2-1, outlines the abysmal working conditions – including the directive that they should be treated as temporary workers (Rs 1,000–1250 is all that is paid to them).

[13] In the demands made by the AIAWU and BKMU, Suneet Chopra and V.S. Nirmal, joint and national secretaries of the two organizations, demanded the following: (1) the Prime Minister should present a white paper on the failure of the BJP government to prevent attacks on Dalits all over the country and especially in states governed by the BJP. (2) The Chief Minister of Haryana should take immediate steps to protect Dalits and minorities in the state from attacks by taking action against the Haryana police that has failed miserably to protect them, or should resign. (3) In the cases of the murders in Faridabad and Sonipat districts, the Haryana government should immediately invoke the provisions of the SC/ST Act both in Sunpedu and Gohana against the murderers, including members of the Haryana police force, who should be arrested and proceeded against. (4) Compensation of a minimum of Rs 10 lakhs per victim killed and immediate rehabilitation of the families concerned as well as those of Gohana and Mirchpur. (5) Both unions have decided to individually and jointly cam-

paign against the threat that the BJP government represents to the Dalit community of Haryana and conduct protests all over the state.

[14] KHOJ education for a plural India, an initiative towards dissemination of a shared plural and inclusive history among Maharashtra's teachers, is trying, even though faced with a hostile political environment, to regularly reach over 3,000 teachers at the zilla parishad and municipality levels, through the creative use of technology.

[15] Bal Thackeray's funeral in November 2012 saw the then UPA-II government allowing a state funeral and senior political commentators hailing him as a political hero. The fact that an innocuous Facebook post by two girls in rural Thane drew the response of a physical threat and arrest punctured the eulogies somewhat.

[16] Vijay Tendulkar remained a trenchant critic of the Shiv Sena and the RSS. In a wonderful first person account to *Communalism Combat* in April 1997, he recounted how little those growing up as Maharashtrians experienced of Muslims in real life or as historical figures: 'During this very period, another Muslim entered my life. He was leading the cultural squad of the undivided Communist Party in my state. He was Amar Sheikh Shaheer (the bard), popularly called Amar Sheikh. He came from a poor rural Muslim family and sang songs with a political message. He had a strong booming voice which thrilled an audience of thousands. You did not have to be a communist to feel charged by the magic in his voice. The "revolutionary" message did not mar the lilt and the roar of his singing.' Tendulkar was founding president of Citizens for Justice and Peace (CJP), a post he held until his death on 19 May 2008.

[17] The Shiv Sena's attacks on free thinkers have extended to M.F. Husain's paintings and Deepa Mehta's film, *Fire*. The abuse and demonization heaped by the Sena mouthpiece, *Saamna*, and its two editors, Sanjay Raut (Marathi) and Sanjay Nirupam (Hindi), in the 1980s have been documented: secularists are snakes in the grass, and Dilip Kumar and Shabana Azmi, *Pakistanis*. Sunil Dutt, a man of principle in politics, was a particular enemy for the Shiv Sena (he won his elections from the Bombay North West Constittuency). It was the height of irony, therefore, that, devastated by his son's incarceration in the Bombay bomb-blasts case, Dutt pleaded with Bal Thackeray, whose party was then in power, for mercy when the Congress–NCP combine did not, or chose not to, help. During the Sena–BJP rule in Maharashtra between 1995–99, P.L. Deshpande, Maharashtra's most popular writer, was awarded a Maharashtra Bhushan. During his acceptance speech he criticized the lawless and violent ways of the regime. An infuriated Thackeray asked why he had accepted the award in the first place. Historian Y.D. Phadke publicly criticized the Sena leadership and its involvement in the murder of Ramesh Kini, and Thackeray used *Saamna* to incite his cadres to beat Phadke with shoes. Similarly, Vasant Bapat strongly ciritcized the Sena–BJP's lumpen ways, for which he received public abuse and vitriol. This author has been featured no less than a dozen times in editorials in the *Saamna*, reviled and threatened. The first time the Wankhede cricket stadium was dug up to 'prevent' Pakistani cricketeers from playing was in 1989, and the fact that in 2015 the same tactics and same persons were used to 'disrupt' the meeting of the BCCI in Mumbai reveals how comfortably the Shiv Sena sits, or is allowed to sit, within Mumbai's ethos. Worse, echelons of the political and police leadership negotiate this relationship easily.

[18] It was during an S.B. Chavan-led Congress government that this author, along with Javed Anand, Sajjid Rasheed, Nikhil Wagle, P. Sainath and others, had

formed a group, Journalists Against Communalism, and tried – albeit unsuccessfully – to get Bal Thackeray booked under the law for systemic use of hate speech threatening violence against sections of Indians. Vivek Monteiro (CITU) was a regular and inspirational participant at these meetings to mobilize citizens against communalism. A historic meeting of Sabrang, then in a loose organizational form, at the Kurla railway station in 1989, to protest the brutal killing of a young Muslim boy on the eve of elections, had attracted speakers like Ahilyatai Rangnekar, Ramdas Athawale and Amol Palekar. The motive behind the killing was simple: scare away the minority voters who were likely to vote for a secular Janata Party candidate. At the time, journalist Sajjid Rasheed was standing from the constituency.

[19] See the interview of this author with P. Sainath on www.sabrang.com, that eloquently explains this collapse of corporate media–political interests.

[20] A *Time* correspondent openly recorded Thackeray's admiration for Hitler post the 1992–93 violence; see page 243 of the Justice B.N. Srikrishna Commission Report.

[21] '*Aaj kasaai, Kal Isaahi*' was scribbled on a blackboard of the Sena at Vakola in Santacruz East.

[22] In 1990, Thackeray had hailed as a hero his friend Arun Gawle – 'our boy', as he called him – the Hindu answer to the notorious Muslim gang controlled by Ibrahim Dawood. See Seabrook (1998).

[23] Ibid.

[24] Ibid.

[25] The Committee for the Protection of Democratic Rights (CPDR) then filed a writ in the High Court which challenged the executive in its attempt to assume judicial powers. Mr Sebastian, advocate and secretary of the CPDR, was quoted as stating that in Bombay a significant section of the elite had been criminalized.

[26] Annexure to the Justice B.N. Srikrishna Commission Report, Sabrang Communications & Publishing Private Limited, 1998, Chapters 103 and 106.

[27] 'Crime and Punishment', *Communalism Combat*, January 1995.

[28] S.A. Dange, veteran trade union leader of the Communist Party of India, made a historic and oft-quoted speech, '*Shivaji Tyancha and Amcha*' (Shivaji, Theirs and Ours), reproduced in full in Lok Vangmangya's *12 Speeches*, published in three editions, 1967, 1976 and 2012. The speech was delivered on 3 May 1959 at the gates of the Amar Hind Mandal, Dadar. Govind Pansare's booklet, *Shivaji Kon Hota?* (Who Was Shivaji?), was first published by the same publishing house in 1988. Pansare, who was brutally shot dead on 16 February 2015, used to hold large meetings contesting communalist renderings of history and Shivaji as an icon of Hindutva.

[29] Today, the services sector poses a huge challenge to labour organization. Retail branches of multinational fast-food outlets employ slickly dressed young women and men, whose work conditions involve 16-hour working days and low wages. The recent success of the Fast Food Workers' strike in the USA, the Occupy Wall Street agitation, or, closer home, Occupy UGC to protest the discontinuation of research fellowships by the University Grants Commission, are welcome signs. These need to be built upon.

[30] In this speech, Ambedkar elaborated: 'With all this, there is immense discontent against Parliamentary Democracy even in countries pledged to Democracy. The reasons for discontent in such countries must obviously be different from those assigned by the dictator countries. There is no time to go into details. But it can be said in general terms that the discontent against Parliamentary Democracy is due to the realization that it has failed to assure to the masses the right to liberty,

property or the pursuit of happiness. If this is true, it is important to know the causes which have brought about this failure. The causes for this failure may be found either in wrong ideology or wrong organization, or in both. I think the causes are to be found in both. As an illustration of wrong ideology which has vitiated Parliamentary Democracy I can only deal with two. I have no doubt that what has ruined Parliamentary Democracy is the idea of freedom of contract. The idea became sanctified and was upheld in the name of liberty. Parliamentary Democracy took no notice of economic inequalities and did not care to examine the result of freedom of contract on the parties to the contract, should they happen to be unequal. It did not mind if the freedom of contract gave the strong the opportunity to defraud the weak. The result is that Parliamentary Democracy in standing out as protagonist of Liberty has continuously added to the economic wrongs of the poor, the downtrodden and the dis-inhcrited class. The second wrong ideology which has vitiated Parliamentary Democracy is the failure to realize that political democracy cannot succeed where there is no social and economic democracy. Some may question this proposition. To those who are disposed to question it, I will ask a counter question. Why Parliamentary Democracy collapsed so easily in Italy, Germany and Russia? Why did it not collapse so easily in England and the USA? To my mind there is only one answer – namely, there was a greater degree of economic and social democracy in the latter countries than existed in the former. Social and economic democracy are the tissues and the fiber of a Political Democracy.'

31 There is an interesting piece of research by Sam Greenspan on 'Eleven Companies that Surprisingly Collaborated with the Nazis'. In this he tells us, among many other details about Hugo Boss, Volkswagen, Bayer, Coca Cola, Chase Bank, IBN and Siemens, that Allianz actually 'insured Auschwitz, their CEO was one of Hitler's advisers, and, during the Holocaust, instead of paying life insurance benefits to Jews, they sent that money straight to the Nazis'. After World War II ended, Allianz officially apologized for its role in the Holocaust and paid several million dollars in restitution; see http://www.11points.com/News-Politics/11_Companies_That_Surprisingly_Collaborated_With_the_Nazis

References

Dhawale, Ashok (2000), 'The Shiv Sena: Semi-Fascism in Action', *The Marxist*, Vol. 16, No. 2, available at http://www.cpim.org/marxist/200002_marxist_sena_dhawle.htm

Jayarajan, P. (2012), *When the Wheels of Fascism Run: a brief account of the rise and fall of the RSS in Kerala*, Thiruvananthapuram: Deshabhimani Book House.

Joshi, P.C. and Dhanwantri (1947), *Bleeding Punjab Warns*, Communist Party of India, September.

Katzenstein, Mary Fainsod (1979), *Ethnicity and Equality: The Shiv Sena Party and Preferential Policies in Bombay*, Ithaca: Cornell University Press.

Seabrook, Jeremy (1998), 'Very political crimes in Bombay', *Le Monde Diplomatique*, June, available at https://mondediplo.com/1998/06/10india2

Democracy after Modi

Hindu Nationalism and the New Public Discourse

Zoya Hasan

India's sixteenth general election, held in April–May 2014, represented a tectonic shift in Indian politics. For the first time since independence, India elected a Hindu nationalist party to power with an absolute majority. The Bharatiya Janata Party (BJP) became the dominant political force in the country backed by a decisive mandate, as Narendra Modi led his party to a sensational win. Its victory was so complete that it captured all or most of the seats in some of the states, and reduced the Indian National Congress (INC) to merely 44 of the 543 seats in the Lok Sabha – a shocking comedown for a party whose history is integral to India's founding narrative. Coupled with the near-obliteration suffered by parties on the Left, which were until recently an influential presence in parliament, it is easy to conclude that the centrist, secular and progressive voices have lost out (Sharma 2014). The dramatic fall of the Congress party and Modi's arrival on the centre stage signals a shift in the political landscape to the Right. The election of the Right to dominance has drastically changed the discursive and ideological space in vast areas of culture, society, economy and politics.

The existence of a BJP government at the centre with a stable majority has set off a public debate about the nature of the government in power and its implications for the future of democracy in India. So far, the debate has been dominated by a tendency to ignore regime differences, arguing that there is very little difference between political regimes – the only noteworthy difference is the position on communalism. This approach ignores the basic issue, which is the uniqueness of the BJP. The BJP is not a normal right-wing party like the British Tories or even the US Republicans; its uniqueness in the general configuration of right-wing parties in the world is because of its organic links to the Rashtriya Swayamsevak Sangh (RSS), dedicated to making India a Hindu state. There is no parallel to this on the side of parties in the opposition, which means we cannot argue as if there is some kind of equivalence here. In this light, it is important to consider the effect of the forces of the right on the trope of secularism, nationalism and majoritarianism, to mention the three major challenges we have to cope with in India today, and how in turn these will shape the cultural, social and political foundations of our democracy.

Rise of the Right

Modi's spectacular success in the 2014 general election was due largely to widespread disillusionment with the United Progressive Alliance (UPA) government that ruled the country for two terms, from 2004 to 2014, led by the Congress party. A loss of public faith in the UPA government, resulting from endless corruption scandals, incompetent handling of issues like inflation and complacency in the face of mounting public discontent, shaped the specific context for the rise to power of the BJP. But more than anything else, it was Modi's well-crafted, resource-rich, aggressive and single-minded campaign, bankrolled by corporate India and heavily supported by the Indian diaspora community, which defined the 2014 election as an election for change, and Modi as an answer to India's problems of poor governance and weak leadership.[1] He was not just riding anti-UPA anger; as a polarizing figure, he actually ignited this anger by pushing a politics of antagonism and confrontation.[2] The grassroots efforts of 45,000 nation-wide branches of the RSS played a decisive role in favour of Modi through a massive mobilization of Hindus, urging and motivating them to come out and vote against the UPA, which it was determined to push out of power.

The greatest success of Modi was his ability to refashion his image and that of his party by projecting a 'developmentalist' stance 'redefined as both aspirational and nationalist', in the words of Arvind Rajagopal (2015), which proved to be highly successful. Frequently used expressions like 'development', 'Gujarat model', 'governance', 'decisive', etc., succeeded in deflecting attention from mass violence and the involvement of Hindu extremists in it, and other negatives such as the centralization of power, authoritarian tendencies and so on, which are essential features of the Gujarat model. The effort to dovetail religious nationalism with economic progress led to a widespread belief that in the trade-off between Hindutva and development, the BJP had opted for the latter (Desai 2014). In the event, the corporate sector, the middle classes and the media readily accepted the propaganda line that Modi has gone beyond the communal agenda, as though there is a contradiction between economic growth and the communal agenda, when in fact, Hindutva and 'development' have always been inextricably intertwined. In reality, the alliance of the two is not unusual, since neo-liberalism is usually allied with and promoted by socially reactionary forces such as religious nationalism. Praful Bidwai has noted how the nexus between big business and Hindutva was confirmed:

> When Narendra Modi arrived in New Delhi to be sworn in as India's prime minister, he flew in a private aircraft belonging to the Adani group, although he could have taken a commercial flight or a chartered plane. On landing, he was greeted with a communal–military slogan, 'Har Har Modi'. The two events showed where Prime Minister Modi's loyalties and priorities would lie: with Big Business and Hindutva, both of which he had served with pious zeal in Gujarat since the anti-Muslim pogrom of 2002 and through crony-capitalist deals later. (Bidwai 2015)

This blend of neo-liberalism and religious chauvinism lacked electoral legitimacy previously, but has gained wide acceptability since thanks to the popular mobilization efforts of the Modi campaign which attracted substantial mass support, especially from the youth, all of which serves to justify it as an expression of the will of the majority.

Never before had the corporate sector so explicitly supported a single party. Never before had corporate India contributed so massively to a party's election campaign and its victory, which led the *Economic and Political Weekly* to call it 'the biggest corporate heist in history'.[3] In the past, the corporate elite hedged their bets by not openly associating with one powerful party or its rival. This changed in the last general election with the corporate sector endorsing one candidate who received unequivocal endorsement and financial support from them (Kumar Vikram 2015).[4] Not surprisingly, the election saw an unprecedented amount of funds flow to one party, which, 'according to one independent estimate, ended up spending more than Rs 5,000 crore on just advertising, only a little less than the $986 million that United States President Barack Obama spent on his 2012 presidential campaign in a country where the per capita income is more than 30 times that in India' (ibid.).

Pluralism and Secularism

India is by far the most heterogeneous society in the world. Few can disagree with the view that India has thrived due to its diversity, and, indeed, much of its progress in the first few decades after independence was closely tied to its preservation of pluralism and cultural breadth. Its stunning linguistic, cultural and religious diversity has been supported by a Constitution that emphasizes equal rights for all, and protects liberties of religion and speech. But a good Constitution does not implement itself and challenges to these core values repeatedly arise, not least in the present when communal movements and communal politics threaten to overturn the core values.

The rise of the Right challenges secularism with its emphasis on democracy, religious neutrality (or equal standing for all citizens, regardless of religion) and social justice, but it also seeks a communal reconstruction of national identity and derides the principle of minority rights, a key feature of Indian secularism, as an unwarranted privilege. For the BJP secularism means nothing more than the strategy and practices of a non-theocratic state through which it is possible to maintain peace between communities and protect the religious liberty of individuals (Bhargava 2002: 92). Its notion of 'secularism' derives from its belief that Hinduism is the most tolerant of all religions and consequently most conducive to secularism. In other words, it is not constitutional principles or the laws of a secular state but the natural tolerance of Hinduism and Hindus that can make secularism safe in India.

While secularism has been integral to India's democracy for the past seventy years, its practice over the last two decades or more has led to its gradual erosion. Secular parties have found the idea of scoring quick electoral gains by tampering with secular principles and institutions too tempting to avoid. In the quest for electoral advantage, the once dominant Congress made a series of choices from the mid-1980s to the mid-1990s that compromised India's secular ethos. Despite, or some would say because of, the concessions to demands of religious groups by Congress governments on the Ayodhya and Shah Bano issues in 1986, the polity has been riven by competitive communalism and sectarian conflict. The social and political space that the Right seized was created by the retreat of secularism during Congress rule and the six years of BJP-led NDA rule (1998–2004), and, most crucially, by the ambivalence and contradictions in secular political practice. These compromises enabled the BJP to dramatically expand its political base in north and north-western India, and, above all, to discredit the secular project. All in all, the secular constitutional dispensation has been under immense pressure from various quarters.

Despite the difficulties into which it has run, secularism, however imperfect, is not an option; it is an absolute necessity in the context of India's diversity and pluralism. Basing politics or governance on religious principles would be fundamentally wrong. Consequently, India has maintained a constitutional commitment to secularism. The Congress government had the words 'socialist' and 'secular' written into the preamble of the Constitution in 1976 to emphasize the importance of these concepts to the Indian nation. In the lead-up to the 2015 Republic Day celebrations, the BJP government placed an advertisement in a national newspaper that included the original version of the Constitution's preamble, which excluded both words. The government faced severe criticism for this omission, but justified itself by saying that it was commemorating the original preamble and not the one that is currently used. To make matters worse, in the aftermath of the controversy, the Minister of Communications and Information Technology, Ravi Shankar Prasad, asked for a debate on whether the words 'socialist' and 'secular' should be included, fuelling speculation that the BJP wants to officially end decades of secular policy. This is despite the fact that in the *S.R. Bommai* case, the Supreme Court held that 'secularism is an integral part' of the Constitution's basic structure. Dropping the word secular would weaken equal citizenship. Secularism alone can create equal rights for all citizens, regardless of religion, ethnicity or culture. Besides, dropping it can weaken the resolve of subsequent governments, and possibly the judiciary, to protect and extend the rights of the vulnerable and the deprived. Of greater danger would be attempts by the Modi government to dismantle actual constitutional provisions or laws that give meaning to those rights.[5] This would be all the more disturbing as key assurances of the Constitution, such as equality before law and fair opportunity, have been breached repeatedly by successive governments and without any redress from the state.

Dilution of the term secular would weaken democracy since secularism and democracy are not mutually exclusive concepts; rather, the interconnections between the two in the Indian context are obvious.[6] This can be confirmed by a quick look at the specific provisions pertaining to secularism and fundamental rights, and the debates in the Constituent Assembly on the rights of religious freedom. These debates underline the intrinsic link between democracy and secularism, based on a recognition that India can build national unity and survive only on the basis of secularism. Any attempt, therefore, to distance secularism from democracy could change the specific meanings of these terms. In today's circumstances, it is perhaps even more important to emphasize the constellation of concepts – secularism, democracy, equality and justice – as their interconnection is an outstanding achievement of India's freedom struggle and had defined the political project of independent India.

When the Indian state framed its policies to accommodate diversity, most of the western and third world states had not consciously acknowledged in their policy frameworks the internal diversities in their societies. It is notable that those countries of South Asia, such as Sri Lanka and Pakistan, which have not accommodated minority groups, have witnessed high levels of conflict. However, it is precisely this process of accommodation that many in India now worry will be undermined by Hindu majoritarianism.

One essential test of a true democracy is whether it protects the rights of minorities, especially when these are in tension with the political majority or government. Far from providing assurances, religious minorities in India have been subjected to discrimination, intimidation and repeated violence (and this includes unlawful detention) in the recent past. Communal politics and attacks on minorities, combined with the state's discrimination in the administration of justice and longstanding problems of police bias, have created a pervasive climate of impunity where minority communities feel increasingly insecure with no recourse when religiously motivated crimes occur. Even police officials concede that inherent inequalities in the criminal justice system have limited Muslims' access to justice and space to protest peacefully.

Modi has been careful not to speak the language of division and polarization, and chosen that of development and nationhood. But there has been a plethora of statements by BJP leaders who have used divisive and polarizing language to inflame tensions and spread religious discord. At the same time, there are also several government decisions that seek to bring habits of eating, of worship, of linguistic preference, of diverse religious practices into a structure of homogeneity, since only a select band of people attribute to themselves the right to dictate and evaluate the culture and lifestyle of individuals and groups at large.

Erosion of pluralism is a slippery slope that ends up targeting not just minorities and outsiders, but dissenting insiders too. The growing culture of intolerance and forcible suppression of political views that are different from those of the ruling dispensation were reflected in the assassination of writers and mob killings of people over issues of cow and beef, and in the attempts by the government in power to impose a legislated and monolithic history of India that seeks to glorify some aspects and denigrate others. The space for free speech, thought and politics is shrinking at the same time as right-wing vigilante groups target freedom of expression and freedom of religion. A pervasive atmosphere of self-censorship born out of fear of reprisals has grown, which threatens to silence the critical voices of authors, journalists and artists.

Nation and Nationalism

It is not just communalism that is being promoted but a homogenizing ideology of unity that more readily conforms to exclusivist notions of religion and nation. Since Modi came to power, this ideology has entered the centre stage of Indian politics. At the heart of it are questions of nationalism, the relationship between Hindus and Muslims and other minorities, reworking policies in the area of education and culture, etc.

The BJP's takeover of the national government in May 2014 allowed the Sangh Parivar – the umbrella group of Hindu nationalist organizations that includes the BJP, the RSS and the Vishwa Hindu Parishad (VHP), among others – to entrench itself in state power.[7] The BJP has close links with these organizations, a relationship that helped the party fund-raise in the US for a Modi victory. While they differ in tactics and strategy, they are all grounded in the philosophy of Hindutva ('Hinduness'), and feature prominently on the national political scene. They support the assimilation of Hindu culture and traditions into state policies and institutions, and generally oppose the secular agenda.

These organizations are the direct descendants of a political tradition dating from the pre-independence period that had sought to anchor Indian nationalism in Hindu ethno-religious identity. Its origins go back to the early days of British colonialism, which saw not just the emergence of Hindu nationalism but the construction of Hinduism as it is known today. Despite its development and growth, Hindutva did not play a significant role in either the freedom struggle or in creating the secular Constitution of independent India. During the first four decades after independence in 1947, the BJP was unable to gain substantial political influence. It met with stiff resistance in the 1950s and 1960s; it was blocked by the dominant political forces, the political Left and liberal middle classes, from influencing the state away from secularism and state-led economic development. The BJP failed to gain any momentum because of an overwhelming consensus in favour of secularism and secular nationalism.

The secular consensus held dominant sway over public life well beyond the Nehru era, meeting serious challenge only in the late 1980s. This coincided with an erosion of the Congress model of centrist accommodation of the earlier decades; the breakdown of this consensus paved the way for the emergence of the BJP's brand of politics, as increasing numbers of middle class Hindus bought into the idea that the majority community had been denied its due dominance of the public sphere. To them, the enshrinement of secularism as India's governing doctrine had not given enough political space for the affirmation of a Hindu identity, and therefore they regarded secularism as little more than a proxy for anti-Hindu politics.

Although efforts to make India a predominantly Hindu nation are not a new phenomenon in India's political life, the defining moment for the BJP's rise to power came in 1992, with the destruction of the Babri Masjid, a centuries-old mosque in Ayodhya that many Hindus believe is the birthplace of Lord Rama. Between 1992 and 1998, other Sangh Parivar members took advantage of the crumbling secular fabric of the country to advance their Hindutva agenda. In 1998, the BJP was elected to power at the centre for the first time (although without an absolute majority as in 2014). Four years later, in 2002, communal tensions once again exploded when over a thousand Muslims were massacred in Gujarat after a train of Hindu pilgrims travelling back from Ayodhya was attacked. At the time, Modi was Chief Minister of the state, and was widely accused of not doing enough to prevent the massacre. That alone should have 'permanently disqualified him from reaching where he now has', remarks Achin Vanaik (2014).

Until the 2014 electoral mandate, the BJP did not have the power or the heft to pose a serious challenge to secularism or communal harmony. The success of the BJP in these recent elections has radically changed the situation. Most importantly, the RSS has used this opportunity to work towards the creation of a Hindu *rashtra* (a Hindu state). Setting the tone for this political agenda, the RSS chief, Mohan Bhagwat, has repeatedly affirmed that India is a Hindu country; he has declared that 'India is a Hindu state and citizens of Hindustan should be known as Hindus.'[8]

The philosophy of the Right stands in stark contrast to the path chosen by modern India, which started its journey in 1947 on the basis of a broader concept of inclusive nationalism. Indian nationalism is not based on a particular language, a particular geography, a particular religion or a particular ethnicity. India opted for the secular idea of a nation and rejected the Hindu ethno-religious identity of the RSS particularly after the assassination of Mahatma Gandhi. By adopting this nationalism, India set itself apart from Pakistan – which effectively committed itself to being a state for Muslims. The first Prime Minister of India, Jawaharlal Nehru, believed in composite nationalism and scrupulously avoided defining the nation in terms of the majority community.

Hindu nationalism, on the other hand, actively promotes an idea of India that conflates religious identity with national identity. It seeks to create a binary of national and anti-national through an insistence that slogans such as '*Bharat Mata ki Jai*' are the litmus test of being national. Anyone who refuses to shout these slogans becomes anti-national. However, nationalism is not expressed merely by raising a flag or shouting a slogan, but by safeguarding equal rights guaranteed in the Constitution and ensuring good governance. The greatest irony is that the forces now most vociferous in laying claim to true nationalism were completely absent in the freedom struggle. At the same time, there is a conspicuous attempt to appropriate political figures from the freedom struggle, even those whose views are incompatible with their own majoritarian ideology.

The new nationalism is defined and identified as a doctrine of uniformity which brooks neither difference nor dissent. By creating a new official vocabulary of patriotism it has made dissent an act of sedition which becomes the heart of defining the nation. As a consequence, reasons of the nation-state become even more sacrosanct than democracy (Visvanathan 2016). The arrest of student activists at the Jawaharlal Nehru University in New Delhi on 9 February 2016 on charges of sedition came in handy to further these plans of circumventing intellectual freedoms and crushing dissent as anti-national. The use of sedition as a test of loyalty is spurious (Kapila 2016). The test of popular sovereignty is democracy, as power and authority in independent India rests with the people. Nehru's speech on the Objectives Resolution at the inaugural session of the Constituent Assembly in 1946 made this clear. 'Obviously we are aiming at democracy and nothing less than a democracy. . . . The House will notice that in this Resolution, although we have not used the word "democratic" because we thought it is obvious that the word "republic" contains that word . . .'. Given that democracy is synonymous with the experience of freedom in India, questioning or criticizing the government is not anti-national. At any rate, criticism of the country or the nation is distinct from that of the government or state's acts and policies. The intensifying clash of ideas of nationalism hides a deeper set of contestations about India's culture, democracy and its past.

As for all the strident promises of rapid industrial expansion and millions of jobs for the mass of unemployed youth, not much has been delivered; we have seen instead an explosion of a cultural politics of the Right, and a strong attempt to create legitimacy through cultural and ideological domination (Banaji 2015). Tensions over the national and religious identity of India have also been played out in the cultural and educational fields. Since gaining its historic electoral mandate, the BJP and its allies within the Sangh Parivar have worked to exert greater influence over the historical national narrative within educational curricula. This focus has at times been perceived to be a higher priority for the government than developing and implementing much-needed institutional reforms within education.

In several states, changes in school and college textbooks have been pushed through that emphasize Hindu nationalist interpretations of India's ancient history which is being assiduously remodelled to bring it closer to the Sangh Parivar's grandiose myths about India's hoary past. Acutely aware of the failure to provide a credible account of India's past and present, the Sangh has attempted to reorganize educational syllabi to reflect a historical narrative perceived to be a composite of mythology and Hindu religious texts, as well as appropriate conservative icons from the freedom struggle to compensate for its own lack of participation in the anti-colonial struggle. In the same manner that ancient and medieval Indian history is being rewritten to suit the political demands of the present, so modern Indian history must also be rewritten, for example, to portray Nehru as a leader who failed India because of the decision to declare that a Hindu-majority India would be governed by a secular state defined by equal citizenship and not religious considerations even after the creation of Pakistan as a homeland for Muslims (Sanghvi 2014).

The larger agenda of the Sangh Parivar includes substantive changes both to the content of education by engineering long-term changes in their programmes and priorities, and by making key appointments of personnel who will execute such changes (Bidwai 2014). To achieve this end, the Modi government was purging some institutions and making suspect appointments in others, in particular bodies that deal with education and culture. Apart from interference with the governance of universities and academic institutions, questionable appointments were made to important institutions. These were not the first instances of appointment of persons in positions of power and influence with proximity to the ruling party. Still, the Modi government's approach appears to be different because in the past government nominees had a semblance of professional attainment to their credit, whereas the record of most individuals appointed by the present government is dismal in the absence of academic credentials or achievement, and seems driven by a mix of loyalty to the RSS and intellectual downsizing by a mediocre regime.

Majoritarianism and Majority Rule

Running parallel to the new definition of nationhood are majoritarian notions of democracy, which have gained momentum after the BJP won an absolute majority in 2014 – the first party to do so in thirty years. This, combined with the sustained ideological work of the RSS/BJP, is shifting the constitutional meaning of democracy in the direction of majority rule – a system of political rule by a political/ethnic/religious group elected under a system of universal suffrage. Ruling groups, especially those inspired by religious nationalism, often claim to be the majority parallel to ethnic or demographic majorities, but they never are. Apart from assuming uniformity in the politics of the majority, it appears to leave no room for Dalit politics or minority politics, or the cultivation of backward constituencies. Democratic politics, moreover, is not about the dominance of numbers; otherwise, the winning party claiming majority support can ride roughshod over minorities, large sections of the majority too and the opposition, and trample dissent.

One consequence of majority rule is the political marginalization of minorities. This is evident in the inadequate representation of minorities, especially Muslims, in both the executive and the legislature since the 2014 elections. The current Lok Sabha is not a complete aberration in this regard, but with 23 Muslim members out of the total strength of 543, 'the representation of Muslims is the lowest since 1952' (Adeney 2015). For the first time, the ruling party does not have a single Muslim MP in the Lok Sabha. The fact that India's largest minority community does not have an effective voice in its elected assemblies does not augur well for India's democracy.

The result of this marginalization is that the widest range of interests is no longer adequately represented in decision-making arenas, and the needs of individuals and minority communities need not be discussed or accommodated (Bhargava 2002). The exclusion of certain communities from the system and the violation of individual and community-specific rights result in an infringement of equality of citizenship (ibid.). Taken to its extreme, this would entail the political and cultural subordination of the country's Christian and Muslim populations. However, the Indian Republic prohibits the majority from running roughshod on the basis of its numerical strength. The Constitution limits the power of governments and groups in order to protect the individual's rights.

The argument of majority rule rests on the false assumption that permanent majorities exist from the start, and are fixed forever, in every group, community or nation. This mistaken notion is based on a conflation of ethno-religious majority with a political majority. The critical distinction between the two gets lost as both are invariably treated as the same. Consequently, religious majoritarianism often masquerades as democracy. The dangers of this proposition have been evident in the attempts to impose the preferences of the upper castes on Dalits and minorities, for example, in food choices. Implicit in the growing political importance of the cow and cow vigilantism was the rejection of habits and beliefs that were different from the majority. Through these measures the ruling dispensation seeks to translate the religious majority into a political majority.

What is more, the political majority is not nearly as impressive if you consider the BJP's vote share: 31 per cent of the national vote, but under the magic of the first-past-the-post system it translated into an absolute majority in the Lok Sabha. The BJP converted its 31 per cent vote share to 282 (52 per cent) seats, as compared to the Congress's 19.3 per cent converting to just 44 (8 per cent) seats. The democratic form of government based on such a mandate, in a strict political sense, is not the rule of the majority.

The drawbacks of majority rule are most apparent in the adversarial relationship between the government and the opposition in the past decade or so. Modi has frequently spoken of governance based on consensus without relying on his party's majority in the Lok Sabha.[9] But counting the unprecedented 282 seats that his party had garnered, he reflected that 'earlier one needed to form a coalition in order to head the government. Now, just to form the opposition one needs to coalition-build.' The very first act of the government was to reject the Congress's claim to the post of leader of the opposition in the Lok Sabha, as it did not have the requisite number of 55 members to be recognized as a parliamentary party. The rejection of this claim, though legally sound, underlines an unwillingness to accommodate the opposition. For its part, the BJP thinks that winning an absolute majority in the general election protects it from making any compromises. Perhaps because (unlike its predecessor) it enjoys a majority in the Lok Sabha, the party believes that democracy means majority rule (Palshikar 2014).

Political majorities are constituted and reconstituted in changing historical and political circumstances. It is evident that political majorities are contingent and do not last, at least in part because opposition parties make adjustments to capitalize on opportunities. The Mandal (caste) and Mandir (religion) interregnum of the early 1990s signified the arrival of identity politics, which upstaged the religious politics that had been catapulted to centre stage by the Ayodhya movement (Kapila 2015). This produced a major confrontation between the upper castes and the backward castes which displaced the Congress from its position of dominance in Uttar Pradesh, and this had a cascading effect on the party's declining political fortunes in most states. It also prevented the BJP from reinforcing its emergence as the principal opposition to the Congress despite unprecedented public support for Hindutva in north India for the first time since independence. A major consequence of that moment was that religious politics could not consolidate its popular mandate. Twenty-five years later the 2014 mandate has given what Sruti Kapila calls a 'second electoral incarnation' to the BJP by closing 'the gap between the new economy and the political sphere' (ibid.).

Major shifts in the approach to secularism, nationalism and majority rule under the Modi regime have emasculated democracy and pushed it towards majoritarianism. While all the formal appurtenances of democracy exist, they are distorted by the primacy given to promotion of the interests of the majority community and the excessive focus on electoral calculations and political machinations to seize power in state after state. The most insidious aspect of the rise of the Right is the normalizing and mainstreaming of Hindu nationalism and its domination of the public arena. To avoid the pitfalls of majoritarianism, a system of checks and balances is considered necessary so that a temporary legislative majority does not lead to unchecked and arbitrary executive power; hence the need for an independent judiciary, a free press, and protection of individual freedoms and collective rights of assembly, association and protest (Pandey 2014). More importantly, a strong opposition and continuous struggle is required to check the monopoly of political, economic or social power by those who find themselves temporarily in charge of the state even as they push the constitutional arrangement of democracy in the direction of authoritarian rule.

Notes

1 'NRI Indians are BJP's biggest donor', *Indian Express*, 26 February 2014, available at http://indianexpress.com/article/cities/ahmedabad/nri-indians-are-bjps-b...

2 Editorial, 'Anger, Aspiration, Apprehension', *Economic and Political Weekly*, Vol XLIX, No. 21, 24 May 2014.

3 Ibid.

4 Analyses by Association for Democratic Reforms (ADR) and National Election Watch (NEW) found that the BJP cornered about 69 per cent of total donations made to political parties in 2013–14 even though it was not in power at the centre when it gained the most. Kumar Vikram (2015).

5 The Citizenship (Amendment) Bill, 2016 is an example of this approach. The Bill seeks to make drastic changes in the citizenship and immigration norms of the country by relaxing the requirements for Indian citizenship. The issue here is the applicability of the amendments on purely religious lines. The Bill is a furtherance of its agenda of making religion the consideration for the conferral of citizenship to Hindus from Muslim majority countries. For a discussion of this, see Garg (2016).

6 For a pertinent analysis of this interconnection see Sumit Sarkar (2001).

7 Sangh Parivar refers to the constellation of Hindu nationalist organizations started by members of the RSS and inspired by its ideas of Hindu nationalism.

8 'RSS Chief Does it Again, Says "Hindutva is the Identity of Our Nation"', available at http://www.ndtv.com/india-news/rss-chief-does-it-again-says-hindutva-is-..., accessed on 17 August 2015.

9 'In first I-Day speech, PM Narendra Modi underlines need for a pact between government and citizen', *The Indian Express*, 16 August 2015.

References

Adeney, Katherine (2015), 'A Move to Majoritarian Nationalism? Challenges of Representation in South Asia', *Representation*, 51 (1): 7–21; published online 7 April 2015.

Banaji, Jairus (2015), 'Reclaiming India's democracy', *The Hindu*, 1 December.

Bhargava, Rajeev (2002), 'Liberal, Secular Democracy and Explanations of Hindu Nationalism', *Commonwealth & Comparative Politics,* Vol. 40, November.

Bidwai, Praful (2014), 'How the Sangh Parivar is taking over education and culture institutions', *Scroll.in*, 25 December.

Bidwai, Praful (2015), 'Modi's disastrous first year', *The International News*, 23 May.

Desai, Radhika (2014), 'A latter-day fascism', *Economic and Political Weekly*, No. 35, 30 August.

Garg, Lovish (2016), 'If India Wants to Remain Secular, the New Citizenship Bill Isn't the Way to Go', *The Wire*, 21 September.

Kapila, Sruti (2015), 'The Majority of Democracy', *Social Text*, 27 February.

Kapila, Sruti (2016), 'Once Again, Sedition is at the Heart of Defining the Nation', *The Wire*, 28 February, accessed 19 September 2016.

Kumar Vikram (2015), 'BJP coffers bulged with corporate cash in Financial Year 14', *Mail Today*, 25 February.

Palshikar, Suhas (2014), 'The making of a "neo-Hindu" democracy', *Seminar*, 665.

Pandey, Gyanendra (2014), 'Democracy, in India as elsewhere, is not a tyranny of the majority', *Outlook*, 22 August.

Rajagopal, Arvind (2015), 'The reinvention of Hindutva', *The Hindu*, 4 March.

Sanghvi, Vir (2014), 'A view of India based on hatred', *The Hindustan Times*, 20 November.

Sarkar, Sumit (2001), 'Indian democracy: the historical inheritance', in Atul Kohli, ed., *The Success of Indian Democracy*, Cambridge: Cambridge University Press.

Sharma, Pratul (2014), 'The Indian Right Arrives in Official Policy Prime,' *The Sunday Standard*, 7 December, available at http://www.newindianexpress.com/thesundaystandard/The-Indian-Right-Arriv...

Vanaik, Achin (2014), 'India's Landmark Election', *Socialist Register*, Vol. 51.

Visvanathan, Shiv (2016), 'The paranoid art of nationalism', *The Hindu*, 26 August.

Scientific Temper and Our Current Concerns

Amiya Kumar Bagchi

The first and the most obvious point to make about what is called 'scientific temper' is that it does not concern only professional scientists and technologists but also the attitude of mind of all members of society. One of the best definitions of this attitude was given by Rabindranath Tagore in his *Religion of Man* (1930/1931: 11), when he postulated that since the generation of life out of the inert part of nature, 'It was made conscious not of the volume but of the value of existence, which it ever tried to enhance and maintain in many-branched paths of creation, overcoming the obstructive inertia of Nature by obeying Nature's law.' So, the ability to engage creatively in life and enhance its value by obeying Nature's law is a principal characteristic of a scientific temper.[1]

Moving in life creatively starts with curiosity. Every child starts with the beginnings of a scientific temper. She learns how to use her hands, how to avoid fire, how to grasp things, and once she begins to learn from books or orally from her friends, parents and teachers, her curiosity grows. A child who has learned that plants absorb energy through a process of photosynthesis naturally asks, 'How do the trees get their food when they shed their leaves in winter?' Some of the enemies of the growth of a scientific temper are the stifling of a child's curiosity by rote-learning, authoritarian diktats to silence a child who asks too many questions, or the pushing of a child into a competitive rat race irrespective of her preferences.

I will illustrate the point of how engaged curiosity leads to the making of a scientist by telling the story of Gopal Chandra Bhattacharya, a leading entomologist of India in the first half of the last century. His book in Bangla, *Banglar Keet-Patanga*, is considered to be the authoritative book in its field, but he became a scientist without any formal scientific training to begin with.

Bhattacharya was born in 1895 in a poor family in the small village of Lonesing in the district of Faridpur (now in Bangladesh) in British India. His education did not proceed beyond school-leaving (Entrance) examination. While he was still living in the village, there arose a scare that a forest bordering the village had become infested with ghosts. A fire had been noticed in the forest after nightfall. People avoided paths near the forest after dark. Bhattacharya, along with two friends, decided to challenge the theory of haunting by ghosts and claimed that the fire must be due to natural causes. On the way to the place of the fire one friend got cold feet and fell away. Ultimately Bhattacharya alone went up to the place where the fire was seen. He found a rotten and wet tree trunk, and when he touched the trunk, his fingers glowed because they were covered with the fungi that emitted light. After coming back, he made experiments with the fungi which were emitting light: they would emit light only when they were wet and not when they were dry. In 1918, he wrote an article on all this in the famous Bangla magazine, *Prabasi*. That attracted the attention of Sahay Ram Bose, a leading specialist on fungi, who used Bhattacharya to collect specimens for him. Bhattacharya in the meantime continued his observations of bioluminosity, as well as the behaviour of insects and frogs and other small aquatic animals. All these activities led to Jagadis Bose giving him a place in the Bose Institute where he worked for the rest of his life. (Goswami 2011).

This is the aspect of Bhattacharya's scientific temper as an individual: without intense curiosity and a determination to test your beginning hypothesis against the cold steel of facts, you cannot be a scientist. But there is also a public aspect of science – the need to banish cobwebs of the mind among people which impede the acceptance of logic and evidence, and clutter up social interaction. Meghnad Saha, along with other Bengali scientists, had in the 1930s established the journal *Science and Culture* with this objective. Many of Saha's pioneering articles on river valley projects were published in this journal. This was followed, after independence, by the establishment of *Bangiya Bigyan Parishad* for popularizing science. When that body decided to bring out a magazine, *Gyan o Bigyan*, Bhattacharya became its editor. Along with *Science and Culture*, it became a vehicle not only for propagating received scientific theories, but also for changes in those theories. It may be mentioned here that realizing the importance of the diffusion of a scientific attitude among the general public, Oxford University has created a Professorship for the Popular Understanding of Science. I am glad to see that Vigyan Prasar, under the auspices of the Department of Science and Technology, is performing a similar function in India.

The Bose Institute was originally privately funded, because the colonial government rarely spent money on research outside some of the official Surveys it ran for gathering information about India's resources with a view to exploiting them for the benefit of the Empire. In Calcutta University, Ashutosh Mukherjee started postgraduate teaching and research with the help of private endowments. The Indian Institute of Science was established by Jamsetji Tata with his company's funds. But in every independent country, public funding is the primary source of finance for scientific research.

In any capitalist country, the incentive for research can be either a desire to make money by finding new products or processes, or the pursuit of new knowledge for its own sake. But if the former becomes the primary motive driving the best brains, especially in a country which is awash in poverty and illiteracy, then scientific research or the diffusion of a scientific temper is likely to suffer badly. In our country, the advent of neoliberal economic policies has severely damaged the incentive for becoming a scientist. Most of the best and the brightest, and their parents, have their attention glued to the careers of Indra Nooyi, Vikram Pandit or Satya Nadella, rather than to the achievements of Venkatraman Ramakrishnan or Roddam Narasimha or Ashok Sen.

In the twentieth century and beyond, even among the leading scientists and innovators, motivations for research have been quite varied, with very different results. The careers of John Bardeen, Walter Brattain and William Shockley, the inventors of the semiconductor effect and of the silicon-based semiconductor chip, illustrate this. They made their fundamental discovery while working for Bell Laboratories. Shockley, the director of the team, wanted the invention to be patented in his name alone. Fortunately, neither Bell Labs nor the Nobel Committee, which awarded the three inventors the Nobel Prize in Physics jointly in 1956, agreed. The three went their different ways. Shockley founded a company in what would later be known as the Silicon Valley and the company flopped. Bardeen went on to make jointly with two other scientists a fundamental discovery in superconductivity, which is the basis, for example, of the MRI technology in medical diagnosis.

The application of medical knowledge, especially its dominant branch, namely allopathic medicine, has been a notorious arena of dogmatism (what is designated alternatively as scientism) and the misapplication of medical technologies. For a long time, doctors and medical researchers believed, for example, that ulcers were caused only by irregular eating habits, spicy foods or stress. Then two Australian scientists, Robin Warren and John Barry Marshall, showed that the bacterium *Helicobacter pylori* (*H. pylori*) is the cause of most peptic ulcers, reversing decades of medical doctrine and leading to new kinds of treatment. Marshall and

Warren received the Nobel Prize for Physiology in 2005, as recognition of the importance of their discovery.

One of the most notorious examples of misuse of advances in technology is that of pre-natal sex determination and the induced abortion of female foetuses. Two of the technologies used for such purposes are amniocentesis and obstetric ultrasonography. Using such sex-selective procedures, female foeticide that had virtually vanished in communist China under Mao Zedong's leadership resurfaced there under market-oriented reforms, and China, along with South Korea, India, Bangladesh, Pakistan, countries of the South Caucasus region (Azerbaijan, Armenia, Georgia) and Albania, became the major killing sites of female foetuses (Guilmoto 2009; UNFPA 2012). On the other side, doctors prescribe MRI and CT scan for many illnesses which do not require such tests. The latter kind of misuse is prevalent in every country in which most of health care is conducted by hospitals and clinics as a profitable venture. Under the rules of the capitalist game of competition, a medical equivalent of the arms race is conducted by such health delivery systems, to the detriment of patients and society as a whole.

The irony is that, unlike most other professionals, doctors trained in the allopathic system of medicine have to take the Hippocratic Oath, which should guide their behaviour as medical professionals. A modernized version of the Hippocratic Oath, written in 1964 by Louis Lasagna, Academic Dean of the School of Medicine at Tufts University, and used in many North American medical schools today, includes the following:

> I will apply, for the benefit of the sick, all measures [that] are required, avoiding those twin traps of overtreatment and therapeutic nihilism.
>
> I will remember that there is art to medicine as well as science, and that warmth, sympathy, and understanding may outweigh the surgeon's knife or the chemist's drug.
>
> I will not be ashamed to say 'I know not,' nor will I fail to call in my colleagues when the skills of another are needed for a patient's recovery.
>
> I will remember that I do not treat a fever chart, a cancerous growth, but a sick human being, whose illness may affect the person's family and economic stability. My responsibility includes these related problems, if I am to care adequately for the sick.
>
> I will prevent disease whenever I can, for prevention is preferable to cure.
>
> I will remember that I remain a member of society, with special obligations to all my fellow human beings, those sound of mind and body as well as the infirm. (Tyson 2001)

Already in 1993, a survey conducted among the same medical schools found that 'fewer than half of the oaths taken today insist the taker be held accountable for keeping the pledge'. From President Obama's enormous difficulties in getting a minimal public health care bill passed by the US Congress, it can be easily seen that the situation may have got worse rather than better in the technologically most advanced nation of the world.

The misuse of science by doctors has been enormously aggravated by privatization of higher education, especially medical education, and of the health care system, in the USA, India and in most countries in which the state refuses to spend the requisite amount of money on education and health care, and leaves the regulation of medical practice entirely to doctors (Angell 2009; Angell 2011; Bagchi 2007; Tilak 2009). Drug companies enter into corrupt deals with doctors, as happened in the Harvard Medical School (Wilson 2009). Many psychiatrists prescribe drugs which can have deleterious effects on the patient's physical and mental health, because the biggest drug companies finance their research, their conferences and distribute various freebies to them. In India, the chairman of the Medical Council accepted a bribe to give recognition to a private medical college. Accusations of similar malpractice have been made against some other members of the Medical Council, and yet many of them continue to be associated with the central government's health policy (Ravi 2010; Nagarajan 2014).

The misuse of science occurs with the most visibly lethal effects in times of war. Fritz Haber, a German Jew, was the inventor of the Haber process for synthesizing ammonia, which has been the foundational invention of today's artificial fertilizer industry. But during World War I, as a patriotic German, he invented poison gases which killed tens of thousands of soldiers of the enemy, including a large contingent of Indian soldiers who had been sent by the British to fight on the Franco-Belgian border. Unable to stop Haber from carrying on with his genocidal inventions, his wife committed suicide (Britannica 2014). Tragically, during the Nazi rule of Germany, Haber's inventions were used to kill millions of Jews in gas chambers. The heinous use of science to kill fellow humans reached another peak when atom bombs were dropped by the US authorities on Hiroshima and Nagasaki in Japan on 6 and 9 August 1945. The second bomb was dropped almost wantonly, just because it had been made. The consequences of that crime against humanity have stretched across generations, since, apart from radiation deaths, the exposure to radioactivity has led to the birth of malformed babies.

That criminal act led to some of the greatest scientists in the world, led by Albert Einstein and Hans Bethe, to try and stop the proliferation of atomic weapons, but so far to no avail. Again, it was the US military authorities and their political masters who misused science to commit genocide and ecological destruction. This happened during the US–Vietnam war from the 1960s to 1975. Apart from other acts such as the use of carpet bombing and heavy shelling to destroy whole cities,[2] the US authorities used Agent Orange to defoliate hundreds of thousands of acres of farmland, and the consequences of that are still being felt in Vietnam today.

Besides the deliberate use of technology for purposes of war, the unregulated and competitive use of non-renewable energy and accelerated depletion of biodiversity have jointly led to the irreversible accumulation of greenhouse gases and climate change. But so-called climate change sceptics aligned with big business who do not want to stop unregulated use of non-renewable resources, have even used threats of violence against climate scientists (Milman 2011).

There is yet another area in which mankind has been playing the devil's game, and that is the use of nuclear power. The use of nuclear energy necessarily means, among other things, the accumulation of nuclear waste which cannot be safely disposed of: its radioactivity will continue to pollute the soil and water for thousands of years. The disaster at the Fukushima plant of the Tokyo Power Corporation has again demonstrated that there is no safe use of nuclear power. This safety will be especially threatened with climate change since the frequency of unforeseen earthquakes, tsunamis and storms will increase. It was a welcome sign that two former Prime Ministers of Japan, Koizumi from the side of the ruling party and Hosokawa from the Opposition, were jointly campaigning for a nuclear-free Japan in the recent mayoral election. But they lost against the candidate of a Prime Minister who wants speedily to turn Japan again into a military power, with the USA backing him.

These examples are enough to show that the nurturing, survival and diffusion of a scientific temper depends greatly on the social and political milieu. A world in which most people feel insecure, many are illiterate, and where there are media, evangelists and godmen often backed by powerful political groups, an irrational belief system can easily trump either scientific truth or a healthy scepticism. When the state apparatus can be used to bolster such irrationality, then not only the scientific temper but the very freedom to think independently becomes endangered. Research into astrology with state funding is one of the dangerous examples of this genre. Astrology might have been a motivating force behind the rise of astronomy, but the observations through the Hubble telescope or experiments regarding the ultimate constituents of matter with the Hadron Collider have nothing to do with astrology.

Unfortunately, a formal training in science is no guarantee against superstitious practices or irrational beliefs about testable phenomena. In the 1980s, I was invited to give a talk at the Central Fuel Research Institute. It was a day or two after a solar eclipse. I was told that a section of the staff, including some scientists, had asked for a holiday on that occasion. When this was refused, some took casual leave, and quite a few of them threw away the burnt-clay utensils in which food was cooked that day.

In 1939, when Nazism and fascism seemed to be poised to conquer the whole of continental Europe, and from there to establish global dominance, Bernal commented on the mysticism and abandonment of rational thought that was being propagated by the news media, saying that this phenomenon was 'not only a sign of popular or political disquiet; it penetrated far into the structure of science itself' (Bernal 1939: 3). With religious preachers being able to use prime time on TV channels to preach various kinds of anti-rational doctrines about the nature of life and the universe, the need to fight that tendentious propaganda has become greater than ever.

The misuse of science, the dogmatic certainty that some scientists have about the finality of the truths of science as they are currently known (which is dubbed scientism) and their inability to scrutinize the morality of particular uses of science have given space for the rise of a peculiar phenomenon, namely, postmodern discourses on science. Fortunately or unfortunately, most of it is just the logorrhoea of social scientists and has little to do with the science that scientists practise. For example, despite the second law of thermodynamics pointing inexorably forwards, with no possibility of anybody dipping in the same flow of water today and tomorrow, most scientific experiments are replicable: the hundred-gram pebble dropped from the top of the leaning tower of Pisa will take the same time to drop to the ground on a calm day today as in Galileo's time, unless the tower has leaned further and the top has come nearer to the ground. For the latter phenomenon, a correction can be made easily by using Newton's formula of gravitational attraction. Most postmodernists simply ignore some of the basic postulates for validation of a scientific hypothesis. While they may criticize some of the biases produced by the Eurocentric or sexist attitudes of some scientists, they in fact give comfort to some of the stoutest defenders of irrationality in the name of one kind of organized religion or other.

Now I turn to my own specialization, namely, social sciences.

The three major or traditional social sciences – political science, political economy and sociology (with its Siamese twin, social anthropology) – were born in particular contexts, to address particular problems of the states or societies they were born in. The theory of the unchallengeable authority of the sovereign state was crafted separately by Jean Bodin and Thomas Hobbes in a context in which their own states, namely Valois France and Stuart England, were involved in bloody civil wars. Ibn Khaldun observed the different Arab states in the Maghreb and in Spain in various states of refinement in the arts and different degrees of social cohesion. He must also have reflected on the decay of the Arab states as contrasted with the Turkish invaders moving in from the East. Such observations and reflections led him to produce his great theories of social cohesion and conflict, and his theory of history encompassing economic, cultural, social and environmental factors (Enan 1979). He was also one of the first scholars to theorize rigorously about a market society which was not yet under the sway of capitalism (Boulakia 1971).

Political economy arose against the background of several European states competing and warring with one another for profit and power. In the heyday of British imperialist liberalism, the liberal political publicists foresaw the end of world history with the establishment of European dominance over the world. In the formulation of Immanuel Wallerstein, in that epoch the former idiographic disciplines were converted into nomothetic disciplines on the model of Newtonian physics (Wallerstein 2011, chapter 5). Political economy became economics, which in the writings of neoclassical economists, sedulously distanced itself from history and the social structure of any particular country. This also produced a kind of scientism, under which the unverified (and sometimes unverifiable) hypotheses of neoclassical economics became etrnal truths in the practice of most mainstream economists. Some correction to this was made by two great economists, John Maynard Keynes and Michal Kalecki, but in mainstream academic studies, their works have been either discarded or distorted to mean something other than what they had meant in their context. The finality of the US dispensation has been in the background of their belief systems. The absurdity of this kind of economics has been well-illustrated by the prize to three economists awarded by the Bank of Sweden (mistakenly called the Nobel prize in economics). Two of these economists have been awarded the prize for spinning out the theory that stockmarkets work efficiently, so that nobody can make an extra rupee by out-guessing the market. The third economist has been awarded the prize for tearing that theory to shreds with empirical evidence (Öncü 2013).

The absurdity of this is further heightened by the fact that anybody who has studied the working of stockmarkets and their periodic crashes, from the time of the Tulip mania in the Netherlands in the 1630s, through the working of English stockmarkets from the times of Daniel Defoe and the South Sea Bubble, to the New York and global stockmarket crash of 1929, and read Keynes's canonical analysis of how they work, could not possibly believe for even a second in the efficient market theory for which these two inventors of the absurdity were rewarded by the bankers. But after all, the bankers are there to serve the rich and so are most of the mainstream economists. As Paul Krugman, an earlier recipient of the same Swedish Bank prize, wrote recently, much of the world is being run by persons with hard hearts and soft heads. While more than a third of Indians are suffering from malnutrition, women are dying in their millions prematurely in childbirth, millions of infants are dying of malnutrition and respiratory diseases, controllers of finance babble about bringing down fiscal deficits without touching the wealth of the super-rich because lower inflation at any cost will keep the real value of that wealth intact. And there are economists with their theories detached from contact with the dirt of the real world to support them.

The cure for the nonsense penned by the postmodern scribblers on science,[3] or the absurd and far more dangerous nonsense peddled by economists at the service of the rich and the powerful, is not less science but more – a science that is rooted in facts of nature, of lived human lives and the relation of man as a cognitive part of nature to the environment in which he/she has her being. A scientist, like any other worker, has to work for a living, and he is paid by a university, a research institution, by a government department or by a company. As in the case of any other worker, the rest of society labours in order to pay him. So, common morality would indicate that he has responsibility towards the rest of society.

With greed yoking new technology to its purpose, global warming is already portending the end of the world as we know it earlier than scientists had imagined even a hundred years back. J.B.S. Haldane, a great biologist who had chosen to live in India, had written: 'Man's little world will end. The human mind can already envisage that end. If humanity can enlarge the scope of its will as it has enlarged the scope of its intellect, it will escape that end' (Haldane 1940: 286).

Despite all the scientific evidence about the purely material origin of the world and of life, and ancient philosophers such as Carvaka, the author of *Sankhya*, expressing scepticism about the existence of a conscious mind as creator or monitor of the world, perhaps the majority of the people of the world believe in some form of institutionalized religion. Such beliefs often lead them to behave in a manner which defies logic or the evidence of the senses or scientific data. What is far more dangerous is that systems of institutionalized religion have been used in the past, and continue to be used in today's world, for political purposes. Thus political Judaism, political Christianity, political Islam, political Hinduism and political Sikhism have been used not only as instruments for people's minds in a democracy, but also for generating hatred against fellow human beings, leading to myriad murders. There are now evangelists of atheism, such as Richard Dawkins and Lawrence Krauss, who are on a mission to get rid of what Dawkins has famously called the 'God Delusion'.

However, as Karl Marx wrote 170 years ago:

> Religion is the sigh of the oppressed creature, the heart of a heartless world, and the soul of soulless conditions. It is the *opium* of the people.
>
> The abolition of religion as the *illusory* happiness of the people is the demand for their *real* happiness. To call on them to give up their illusions about their condition is to call on them to *give up a condition that requires illusions*. The criticism of religion is, therefore, *in embryo, the criticism of that vale of tears* of which religion is the *halo*. (Marx 1844, 'Introduction')

For ordinary people in India and the majority of mankind, life remains a vale of tears. So, along with fights against superstition and the political use of religion, the campaigners for sustenance of a scientific temper in society must also fight the root causes of poverty, illiteracy and ill health, and try to eradicate them.

Acknowledgement: I am greatly indebted to Sarvashri Hamid Ansari, R. Ramachandran, R. Gopichandran, T.V. Venkateswaran, Gauhar Raza, Vinod Wadhawan and Gurdeep Singh Sappal for discussions and comments that facilitated the writing of the paper, and to Jasodhara Bagchi for incisive comments on its first draft.

Notes

[1] Better technologies have been the result of applications of science since the maturing of the industrial revolution in Western Europe and the USA. In the following I am therefore assuming that invention and application of new technologies are intimately associated with advances in scientific knowledge.

[2] A US Admiral who was in charge of the shelling and destruction of the ancient city of Hue in North Vietnam quipped later, 'We had to destroy it in order to save it.'

[3] For a critique of the postmodern views of science propagated by Ashis Nandy, Gyan Prakash and their like, see Dasgupta (2014).

References

Angell, Marcia (2009), 'Drug companies & doctors: a story of corruption', *New York Review of Books,* 15 January.

Angell, Marcia (2011), 'The illusions of psychiatry', *New York Review of Books*, 14 July.

Bagchi, A.K. (2007), 'Governing the market in health care: The social and political requirements', in Di McIntyre and Gavin Mooney, eds, *The Economics of Health Equity*, Cambridge: Cambridge University Press: 36–58.

Bernal, J.D. (1939), *The Social Function of Science*, London: George Routledge & Sons.

Boulakia, Jean David C. (1971), 'Ibn Khaldun: A Fourteenth-Century Economist', *Journal of Political Economy*, 79 (5): 1105–18.

Britannica (2014), Fritz Haber, *Encyclopaedia Britannica* (online), http://www.britannica.com/EBchecked/topic/250759/Fritz-Haber/260673/Chemical-warfare#toc260675, accessed on 15 March 2014.

Dasgupta, Subrata (2014), 'Science studies *sans* science: Two cautionary postcolonial tales', *Social Scientist*, Vol. 42, Nos 5–6, May–June: 43–61.

Enan, Mohammad Abdullah (2007), *Ibn Khaldun: His Life and Works*, New Delhi: Kitab Bhavan, available online at https://archive.org/stream/IbnKhaldun-HisLifeWorksByMohammadAbdullahEnan#page/n1/mode/2up, accessed on 26 March 2014.

Goswami, Parimal (2011), 'Panchabhut banam ek bhut', in Parimal Goswami, *Samagra Smritichitra*, Kolkata: Ananda: 145–46.

Guilmoto, Christophe Z. (2009), 'The Sex Ratio Transition in Asia', *Population and Development Review*, 5 (3): 519–49.

Haldane, J.B.S. (1940), 'The last judgment', in *Possible Worlds*, London: Evergreen Books: 264–86.

Marx, Karl (1844), 'A contribution to the critique of Hegel's Philosophy of Right', *Deutsch-Französische Jahrbücher*, 7 and 10 February, available at http://www.marxists.org/archive/marx/works/1843/critique-hpr/intro.htm, accessed on 15 March 2014.

Milman, Oliver (2011), 'Australian climate scientists receive death threats', *The Guardian*, 6 June.

Nagarajan, Rama (2014), 'Eminent persons write to PM, allege health secretary transferred for taking on corrupt MCI, Ketan Desai', *Times of India*, 22 February.

Nobel Prize (2005), 'Press release: The Nobel Prize in Physiology or Medicine 2005', 3 October, available at http://www.nobelprize.org/nobel_prizes/medicine/laureates/2005/press.html, accessed on 16 March 2014.

Öncü, T Sabri (2013), 'Faith and Scepticism in Markets: Sveriges Riksbank Prize 2013', *Economic and Political Weekly*, 45 (46), 16 November.

Ravi, Thilaka (2010), 'Medical Council of India: the rise and fall', *Medindia*, 20 May, available at http://www.medindia.net/news/indiaspecial/Medical-Council-of-India-The-Rise-and-Fall-69144-1.htm#ixzz2w6ZQx5wU , accessed on 16 March 2014.

Tagore, Rabindranath (1930/1931), *Religion of Man: Being the Hibbert Lectures of 1930*, available at https://archive.org/details/religionofmanbei027987mbp, accessed on 15 March 2014.

Tilak, J.B.G. (2009), 'Private sector in higher education: A few stylized facts', *Social Change*, 39 (1): 1–28, doi: 10.1177/004908570903900101.

Tyson, Peter (2001), *The Hippocratic Oath Today*, available at http://www.pbs.org/wgbh/nova/body/hippocratic-oath-today.html, accessed on 18 February 2014.

UNFPA (2012), *Report of the International Workshop on Skewed Sex Ratio at Birth: Addressing the Issue and the Way Forward*, The United Nations Population Fund Workshop, Hanoi, Vietnam, 5–6 October 2011.

Wallerstein, Immanuel (2011), *The Modern World System*, Vol. IV: *Centrist Liberalism Triumphant*, Berkeley, California: University of California Press.

Wilson, Duff (2009), 'Harvard Medical School in ethics quandary', *New York Times*, 3 March.

Capitalism and 'Labour Reserves'
A Note

Praveen Jha, Sam Moyo, Paris Yeros

Professor Prabhat Patnaik is widely recognized, both in India and abroad, as an intellectual giant with an enormous range. Equally important is his unwavering commitment to the politics of progressive socio-economic transformation backed by extremely persuasive theoretical discourse, and involving the creative development and extension of the Marxist framework of analysis, which distinguishes him as an organic intellectual. His sustained and powerful critique of mainstream economics has been critical in undermining its hegemony and in illuminating alternative, radical ways of understanding and engaging with the world.

One of the major themes running through Professor Patnaik's work is the stress on the 'spontaneity' of capitalism as a system and its implications for the mass of the working population. An aspect of that spontaneity is the logic of absorption versus repulsion of labour in relation to capitalist accumulation processes, a theme central to Marxian political economy. This note attempts an engagement with this theme and explores some related issues that may be of interest at the current juncture. Sections I and II of the note constitute its analytical core. Section III flags some of the important indicators from the world of labour in the contemporary global economy to substantiate the arguments sketched in the preceding sections. Section IV concludes the note.

I

As is generally acknowledged, one of the most profound differences in conceptual frameworks of competitive capitalism between classical political economy and almost any other paradigm in economics[1] relates to utilization of all the resources on offer; in the former, there is no guarantee that the competitive mechanism will ensure full utilization of all the available resources, whereas the mainstream models subscribe to the so-called 'Say's law', according to which 'supply creates its own demand', ensuring full employment. Of course, theoretical innovations in mainstream economics during the last half a century or so, such as incorporating imperfect information, missing markets, etc., in an otherwise competitive framework, can accommodate possibilities of excess supply, underutilization, unemployment, discrimination or segmentation in one or the other market. However, whereas in the 'perfectly' competitive equilibrium framework of mainstream economics there is no way that the resources on offer can remain unemployed, in the 'free' competition equilibrium framework of classical political economy there is no guarantee that the resources will be fully utilized. Sure enough, equilibrium models of competitive economy across different paradigms have a number of differences with respect to underlying structural and behavioural assumptions, which we need not go into here. For our purpose, it is adequate to highlight the above-noted profound difference in what may be considered seemingly analogous models of competitive frameworks under capitalism.

In fact, specifically with reference to labour, differences across analytical frameworks are particularly stark, and the Marxian model of competitive capitalism stands in sharp contrast to any other conceptual framework in economics. To restate the differences with respect to the core conclusions *in a context of competitive capitalism*: for Marxism, continuous production of 'labour reserves' is a necessary feature; for mainstream economics, there is no question of unutilized or underutilized labour; and for a whole range of heterodox models, 'surplus labour' may be a transitory feature. We do not wish to get into a detailed discussion of alternative analytical paradigms here and our focus is almost entirely on the Marxist framework; however, a couple of brief comments on non-Marxist traditions may be in order, in due course, to put into sharper relief the conclusion highlighted above.

The core of Marx's analysis, whether in his early work such as the *Communist Manifesto* or his magnum opus, *Das Kapital*, is based on a model in which capitalism is an incessantly competitive[2] and 'spontaneous' system, i.e. a system which is governed by its own immanent tendencies or, as Marx often put it, 'laws of motion', independent of the volition, will and consciousness of individual economic agents, with everyone being coerced into playing their respective roles by the defining logic and trait of the system, which is: '*Accumulate, Accumulate! That is Moses and the Prophet!*' There are a number of laws, or immanent tendencies, which Marx highlighted as powerful drivers of such a spontaneous system, but there is one that is particularly relevant for our discussion here, and possibly the most useful starting point for comprehending 'labour reserves' under capitalism as discussed in Chapter 25 of *Capital*, Volume 1, titled 'The

General Law of Capitalist Accumulation'. The crux of Marx's 'absolute general law of capitalist accumulation', as he put it, is:

> The greater the social wealth, the functioning capital, the extent and energy of its growth, and, therefore, also the absolute mass of the proletariat and the productiveness of its labour, the greater is the industrial reserve army. The same causes which develop the expansive power of capital, develop also the labour power at its disposal. The relative mass of the industrial reserve army increases therefore with the potential energy of wealth. But the greater this reserve army in proportion to the active labour army, the greater is the mass of a consolidated surplus population, whose misery is in inverse ratio to its torment of labour. The more extensive, finally, the lazarus layers of the working class, and the industrial reserve army, the greater is official pauperism. *This is the absolute general law of capitalist accumulation.* Like all other laws, it is modified in its working by many circumstances, the analysis of which does not concern us here. (Marx 1976: 798; emphasis added).

In other words, Marx's claim is that with the incessant development of the productive forces under capitalism, an inevitable outcome is a strong tendency towards labour power repulsion, which is not a transitory phenomenon but a durable feature.[3] As Marx put it in his inimitable style, while generals won battles by recruiting armies, capitalists won them by discharging the army of workers. To put it differently, the process of capitalist accumulation necessarily makes segments of labour redundant and results in a *permanent* presence of what Marx calls 'relative surplus population', which is absolutely critical to both the secular and cyclical aspects of the capitalist dynamic.[4] Thus, one of the organizing principles in Marx's narrative of the onward march of capitalism is an organically connected dialectical process of 'valorization of capital' along with 'devalorization' of labour power. It is this dialectic that provides the conceptual peg to examine and analyse the issue of 'labour reserves' under capitalism.

Such a reading of a competitive capitalist system – that the permanent presence of a labour reserve is not only an effect of capitalist accumulation, but in fact a general condition for such accumulation – puts the Marxist framework in sharp contrast to any other paradigm in economics (including the Keynesian paradigm).[5] As is well known and mentioned earlier, the perfectly competitive neo-classical model of capitalism is characterized by full employment of all 'factors of production', and the 'marginal productivity' of the factor in question, at the point of full employment, determines its 'rate of return' or share in the value of output.

In such a framework, any exogenous increase in labour force is absorbed through instantaneous adjustment via substitution and 'efficient' changes in factor proportions. Again, as is well known, in Robert Solow's famous 'steady state' model of growth, it is an exogenously given rate of growth of labour force (in efficiency units, by taking into account 'labour-augmenting technical progress') that determines the rate of growth. In other words, *a low rate of growth of labour force is in fact a constraint on the overall growth rate of the system, and unutilized labour, thus, is not visualized as a problem at all.* Of course, there have been all kinds of innovations in the neo-classical framework over time, yet there is no explanation whatsoever for the genesis and persistence of unemployment (except as short-term, frictional, deviations, etc.) *in a competitive framework*, with its idealist conception of well-functioning markets and rational economic actors.

Similarly, models of competitive economy in the heterodox tradition, in general, even while acknowledging the presence of substantial labour reserves at particular junctures, do not visualize their persistence as being 'intrinsic' to the logic and dynamics of capitalism, as is evident from extremely influential contributions by a number of economists of repute who played a seminal role in the founding of 'development economics'. Of course, most of them accorded a leading role to the state in influencing the capitalist dynamic either through 'state capitalism' or 'mixed economy frameworks' which would lead to a disappearance of 'surplus labour' through a virtuous cycle of rising capitalist profit, investment and growth over time. For instance, the 'stylized' model in the justly famous 1954 paper by W. Arthur Lewis tried to show that under conditions that were conducive to the fast growth of profits (relative to population growth), it must happen that capital accumulation finally catches up with labour supply. In fact, the so-called 'Lewisian turning point' continues to be an extremely influential metaphor in much of the literature on economic transformation even in contemporary development economics. It refers to a stage in the process of transfer of surplus labour from traditional to modern sectors when the said surplus disappears and real wages start rising.[6] *Such a metaphor, whatever its significance under very specific contexts, is hardly of substance in understanding the dynamics of labour reserves under capitalism.*

Needless to say, the models in the heterodox tradition are generally far more realistic with respect to their core assumptions, and, of course, appropriate policy interventions are central features of such models. But *the point being emphasized here is that they are characterized by the absence of any intrinsic tendency that would explain the presence of permanent labour reserves.* In other words, there is no organic linkage between their stylized frameworks of capitalism and relative surplus population. With these brief remarks on non-Marxist paradigms of competitive capitalism, let us now turn to the Marxian framework.

Although in Marxian political economy, as indeed in Marx's writings, 'relative surplus population', 'labour reserves' and 'industrial reserve army' are often used interchangeably, there has been some debate as to whether, for the sake of conceptual clarity, it is appropriate to do so. We do not wish to enter into a detailed discussion on this debate here, except to note that there is little in Marx's work that makes a clear distinction between these three terms, and that, going by the discussions in the first volume of *Capital*, Marx seems to have had a marginal preference for the term 'relative surplus population'. The distinction that Marx did make, in reasonably sharp fashion, was between the different components of the 'relative surplus population', categorizing them as *floating*, *latent* and *stagnant*.

The first of these consists of those who are sucked in and out of the capitalist production process as per its routine requirements, and are capable of adapting to the demands of changing accumulation. As Marx put it:

> In the centres of modern industry – factories, manufacturers, iron works, mines, etc. – the labourers are sometimes repelled, sometimes attracted in great masses, the number of those employed increasing on the whole, although in a constantly decreasing proportion to the scale of production. Here the surplus population exists in the floating form. (Marx 1976: 794)

The 'latent' category consists of those components not fully integrated into the circuit of capital, such as parts of the population in pre-capitalist activities who may find a place in the circuit of capital as and when the need arises. It is as if this segment is waiting in the wings. Marx here considers the example of the agricultural population constantly at the point of passing over into an urban or manufacturing (in the sense of all non-agricultural industries) proletariat; thus the countryside becomes a constant source of latent surplus population.[7] Finally, the third segment, namely the 'stagnant', consists of those who constitute almost 'an inexhaustible reservoir of disposable labour power', but suffer from extremely irregular employment and are almost unemployable. In fact, this segment almost merges with those who dwell 'in the sphere of pauperism'. Thus the last of the three forms of relative surplus population identified by Marx is obviously at the bottom of the economic/social hierarchy, and includes 'vagabonds, criminals, prostitutes', the malnourished, the elderly, etc., constituting more or less a class of 'dangerous' paupers. In other words, this third segment or the 'lowest sediment' effectively consists of, to quote Marx:

> the demoralized and the ragged, and those unable to work, chiefly people who succumb to their incapacity for adaptation, due to the division of labour, people who have passed the normal age of the labourers; the victims of industry, whose number increases with the increase of dangerous machinery, of mines, chemical works, etc., the mutilated, the sickly, the widows, etc. (Marx 1976: 797).

Further, pauperism

> is the hospital of the active labour-army and the dead weight of the industrial reserve army. Its production is included in that of the relative surplus population. Its necessity is theirs; along with the surplus population, pauperism forms a condition of capitalist production and of the capitalist development of wealth. It enters into the *faux frais* of capitalist production; but capital knows how to throw these, from the most parts from its own shoulders on to those of the working class and the lower middle class. (Ibid.: 797).

Having briefly discussed the meaning and components of relative surplus population (henceforth RSP), we may now recall the major insights emerging from Marxian political economy as regards the dialectics of absorption versus repulsion of labour power in capitalist accumulation. As is well known, there is a large literature on the subject and it is near-impossible to pull together all the significant strands in our overview discussion here. Rather, our purpose is to highlight some of the core arguments to outline what may be considered a perspective at best.

II

Capitalism, left to its own spontaneous mechanisms, generates a number of immanent outcomes, such as a permanent labour reserve as mentioned above; however, as Marx emphasized, capitalism in its long march is also about relentless class struggle and changes in the balance of class forces nationally and globally. Thus, to understand the trajectories of the world of labour one has to engage with the complex intertwining of the regimes of accumulation and class contestation in the *longue durée* of the capitalist dynamic. A major analytical task has been to understand the evolution of capitalism as a 'combined and uneven' global system through its various stages (e.g., mercantilism, competitive industrial capitalism, monopolistic financial capitalism, etc.), and to make sense of the differences in trajectories of accumulation across different regions of the world.

The role of powerful mechanisms such as primitive accumulation, and the importance of colonialism and imperialism in the genesis and consolidation of the uneven world system have been investigated systematically, rigorously and in great detail. From this vast literature, we highlight below a couple of stylized facts that are relevant to our discussion.

The first of these is the division of the world into a 'core' and a 'periphery', where the latter is shaped, in large measure, by the requirements of the former. As is well known, during the mercantilist phase itself the 'west' managed to get an economic stranglehold over the 'rest', typically through colonization or at least partial political control. The beginning of this phase is dated to the conquering of the Americas in the sixteenth century, and parts of Asia and Africa in the seventeenth century, by European powers. Marx highlighted some of the significant episodes in this process of rapacious mercantilist accumulation as follows:

> The discovery of gold and silver in America, the extirpation, enslavement and entombment in mines of the aboriginal population, the beginning of the conquest and looting of the East Indies, the turning of Africa into a warren for the commercial hunting of black-skins, signalled the rosy dawn of the era of capitalist production. These idyllic proceedings are the chief momenta of primitive accumulation. (Marx 1976: 915.

As the pillage and the plunder deepened and widened, the three continents of Asia, Africa and Latin America were impoverished on a gigantic scale.[8] The second phase of this process is associated with the advancement of industrial capitalism in Europe and countries of white settlement – North America, Australia, New Zealand – which threw the 'losing' continents even deeper, through a variety of mechanisms under the overall framework of colonialism/imperialism, into the vortex of unprecedented exploitative traps and left them structurally deformed. The net result was that capitalist accumulation in the metropolitan countries received a massive boost, whereas the periphery was largely appended to the former to serve its requirements.[9]

The other point worth highlighting here is the significant role of mass migration, much of which was in the nature of 'forced entry' into the temperate regions of white settlement, *which was critical in taking care of the labour reserves* in Britain and continental Europe. The so-called great frontiers of white settlement were grabbed from indigenous populations after their large-scale decimation, and countries in Asia, Africa and Latin America also came in very handy for absorbing a part of the huge reserve army that had built up in Europe. Cecil Rhodes captured this situation very well in 1895 when he said:

> I was in the East End of London [a working-class quarter] yesterday and attended a meeting of the unemployed. I listened to the wild speeches, which were just a cry for 'bread, bread!' and on my way home, I pondered over the scene and I became more than ever convinced of the importance of imperialism. . . . My cherished idea is a solution for the social problem, i.e., in order to save the 40,000,000 inhabitants of the United kingdom from a bloody civil war, *we colonial statesmen must acquire new lands to settle the surplus population*, to provide new markets for the goods produced in the factories and mines. The Empire, as I have always said, is a bread and butter question. If you want to avoid a civil war, you must become imperialists. (Rhodes, quoted in Lenin 1969: 93–94; emphasis added)

To get a sense of the significance of exodus: the extent of emigration from Britain, on an annual basis, was more than half the increase in the British population between 1820 and 1915 alone. For Europe as a whole, the estimates of total emigration were staggering and well in excess of 50 million between 1870 and 1914. Such transfer of surplus labour, on a scale comparable to colonial/imperial Europe, is of course impossible in the contemporary world.

In short, for almost four to five hundred years, i.e. from the onset of the capitalist mode of production to the decolonization of countries in Latin America, Asia and Africa, one of the most significant economic outcomes on a global scale was the division of the world economy into 'core' and 'periphery'. In large measure, this was facilitated by the former's 'comparative advantage in violence' (to use Findlay's expression), through primitive accumulation under colonial and imperialist regimes. The global combined and uneven development of capitalism bound together, more than ever before, different regions of the world in a hierarchical network of the dominant and the dominated. This was indeed a most powerful vindication of Marx's 'polarization' thesis on a global scale.

Thus, at a high level of generality, the global economy around the middle of the twentieth century could be characterized in terms of two distinct accumulation regimes: one applicable to the metropolitan system and the other to peripheral capitalism. Samir Amin (1974) made a stylized distinction between these two regimes, highlighting their core features as a 'self-centred system' and a 'peripheral system' respectively, drawing analytically on the well-known departmental schemes in Marx's illustration of accumulation and reproduction in *Capital*, Volume 2 (Chapter 19). Amin's central argument is that, in the self-centred accumulation regime, there is a virtuous synergy between the 'capital goods' and the 'mass consumption goods' departments (Marx's first and second departments in his reproduction models), whereas in the peripheral accumulation model, the dominant economic relation is between the exports sector (almost entirely consisting of primary goods) and the luxury goods consumption sector. Thus, in the former, there is a relatively robust and viable accumulation dynamic (of course, depending on the strength of the linkages between the two departments noted above) and this also has relatively better implications for labour absorption, as a greater proportion of workers can hope to be a part of the active work force and with better working conditions. In the peripheral model, according to Amin's formulation, the impulse for capitalist accumulation is largely linked to export demand from the metropolitan countries and the income originating from exports is largely spent on luxury goods consumption. As he puts it,

> Under these conditions the domestic market, born out of the development of the export sector, will be limited and distorted. The smallness of the internal market explains the fact that the periphery attracts only a limited amount of capital from the centre although it offers a better return. The contradiction between the consumption and production capacities is completely removed on a world scale (centre and periphery) by a widening of the market at the centre, the periphery – fully deserving its name – merely fulfilling a marginal, subservient and limited function. This dynamic process leads to an increasing polarization of wealth at the centre. (Amin 1974: 14)

Thus, in Amin's model of peripheral capitalism, the dominant internal classes are basically parasitic in nature: 'Latifundists in some places, Kulaks and others, comprador commercial bourgeoisies, state bureaucracies, etc.'. This model is characterized by a much stronger tendency towards marginalization of the masses and extreme inadequacy of opportunities to get absorbed properly in the ranks of the active labour army. Thus, 'unemployment in this case differs from unemployment of the central model of development. Underemployment, in general, will have the tendency to increase instead of being relatively limited and stable (as in the central model), cyclical variations apart' (ibid.: 15).

Whether or not one finds Amin's stylized model of dualism in the global accumulation of capital persuasive is not a moot issue for our discussion.[10] The purpose of recalling it here is basically to point to the linkages between regimes of accumulation and labour absorption. In the *longue durée* of capitalism, at different levels of generality, one can identify a variety of regimes of accumulation, each characterized by a particular mode of incorporation of labour power. The Marxist literature on modes of production in general and varieties of capitalist modes of production in particular, on uneven development, unequal exchange, 'articulation versus disarticulation', etc., is an extremely rich terrain that explores the relevant issues in great detail and with considerable insight. It may, therefore, be foolhardy for us to attempt a typology to examine the linkages between capitalist accumulation and labour incorporation in any comprehensive sense, and we desist from doing so here.

Nonetheless, for illustrative purposes, one may think of the long march of combined and uneven global capitalism since its inception, at a high level of generality, as consisting of three broad phases: the first phase, which witnessed a protracted push towards a *laissez-faire* capitalism in the centre, along with colonial and imperial domination in the periphery; the second phase with relatively regulated capitalism on a global scale, including in the newly independent countries, mostly after World War II (although in the metropolitan countries, some significant regulations had started emerging soon after World War I itself), and up to the 1970s; and the third phase, which has witnessed the ascendancy and dominance of neo-liberalization during approximately the last four decades. Similarly, focusing on the post World War II era, *dirigisme* in most third world countries was characterized by a strategy of relatively autonomous development and 'import-substituting industrialization'. In some countries the core strategy was 'export-oriented industrialization'. Each of these strategies, or accumulation regimes, had specific consequences for the dynamics of 'labour power absorption/repulsion'.

For instance, the strategy of state-led economic transformation and often public sector-led industrialization, adopted in varying degrees in several countries of the third world, resulted, in many cases, in growth outcomes that were unprecedented and quite respectable with reference to any appropriate benchmark.[11] In countries where such a strategy unfolded with a degree of seriousness, such as India, there was accelerated capital accumulation, which laid the foundation for a well-diversified industrial structure within a reasonably short period, and this was a major achievement (for further details, see Chakravarty 1987, contributions in Byres, ed. 1997, among others). However, due to the absence/weakness of structural reforms (in particular land reforms), the development of the 'home market' was seriously compromised and the links between Departments 1 and 2 remained quite weak. This also had serious adverse implications for labour absorption.

In the so-called 'East Asian miracle' cases, during the *dirigiste* era, where in a few countries the emphasis was on 'export-oriented industrialization' and in some others on 'import-substituting industrialization', but with relatively less 'export pessimism', the trajectories of accumulation and labour absorption showed significant differences as compared to, for instance, countries in South Asia. In most of the East Asian cases, radical, redistributive land reforms and/or substantial government investment in infrastructure for agricultural production played a critical role in facilitating rapid and broad-based growth of the 'home market', resulting in relatively better synergy between Departments 1 and 2, and, consequently, a relatively robust phase of labour absorption. The point worth noting here is that the so-called miracle cases were indeed exceptional cases which could not be replicated easily elsewhere. Much of the third world found it extremely difficult to rise to the challenge of creating decent livelihood and employment for the masses in general. In other words, even during the *dirigiste* era, the structural conditions in most of these countries were such that, despite respectable GDP growth rates, levels of unemployment and underemployment – in short, the problem of acute labour reserves – seemed insurmountable. Sure enough, a fuller account of the relationship between capital accumulation and labour absorption requires detailed discussion of several other important factors and of the specificities of the countries in question, which we cannot take up here; however, the foregoing brief remarks illustrate some of the analytical issues that require careful investigation.

In particular, the core argument we wish to reiterate here, drawing on a rich legacy of Marxist analyses, is: capitalist accumulation in peripheral social formations cannot have the same synergy with labour absorption dynamics as in the case of metropolitan countries (except in exceptional circumstances) precisely because the historical advantages the latter enjoyed cannot be replicated by the former, whether, *inter alia*, with respect to the resource question, the market question or the emigration question. One major outcome in the *differentia specifica* with respect to the overall accumulation trajectory between the core and the periphery is that the extent of proletarianization in the latter is seriously constricted, creating a situation where most producers are in the ranks of the semi-proletariat/proto-proletariat/lumpen proletariat, etc., and there are no easy exit routes for them. To put it differently, *the balance between the active army and the reserve army in the two instances is dramatically different, with the weight of the latter being substantially higher in the case of the periphery*. Further, this also means that the overall nature and function of the reserve army or surplus labour in the periphery is not quite the same as in the case of the metropolitan countries, although its broad forms and segments (e.g., floating, latent, stagnant), suggested by Marx, continue to remain relevant.

Thus, even though one may argue that the constitutive segments within the broad spectrum outside the active labour force conceptualized in the context of the evolution of capitalism in England in particular (or the European trajectory in general) are substantially different from their counterparts in the periphery, the analytical significance of Marx's components of the reserve army of labour is still persuasive, given his *stylized model* of the capitalist mode of production. It is obvious that large segments of workers outside the active labour army are 'economically active' (in a range of petty production, such as subsistence farmers, peasant producers, artisans, etc., or in household reproduction), but clearly, they cannot be considered the *proletariat* in Marx's sense; in his *problematique* of the evolution of the capitalist mode of production, such segments of an economically active population constitute a *potential proletariat* at best, and hence are analytically similar to the three components of the reserve army of labour mentioned above. Of course, if one takes the view that the classical or the metropolitan trajectory of capitalist development cannot be replicated in the periphery, the relationship and linkages between active and 'surplus' workers are obviously different in the two cases, and possibly far more complex for the periphery; in particular, both conceptually and empirically the extent of fuzziness between the two may be substantial in the case of peripheral accumulation. Nonetheless, even for the periphery, the analytical significance of the three components of the surplus labour population should be obvious.[12]

Thus, the differences in the nature of accumulation dynamics have huge implications for the balance between active and surplus workers, the nature of class formation, class action, etc. All these issues, of course, need to be examined carefully in particular economies and societies in their specificities. Much of the foregoing discussion is pegged at a high level of generality, taking the Marxian conception of *spontaneous* capitalism and *absolute general law of capitalist accumulation* as reference points. However, as Marx repeatedly pointed out, the *laws of capitalism* were modified in their working by many circumstances, which detailed and grounded analysis must take into account. With these brief remarks, we now turn to a snapshot of global labour surplus population at the current juncture.

III

Of course, for both conceptual and empirical reasons, operational measures to map the world of work and labour have always been contentious, and are likely to remain so. Nonetheless, with all these limitations, it may be instructive here to draw at least a kind of reasonable sketch; and in what follows, we highlight some of the relevant trends at the current juncture using data from the International Labour Organization (ILO). Sure enough, there are limitations and uncertainties with respect to the ILO data which we do not discuss here, and there is no simple, one-to-one correspondence between the Marxian conceptions discussed above and their operational counterparts in the said data-sets; however, our claim is that the empirical picture emerging from these broadly conforms to our foregoing analysis.[13]

Going by ILO data, the global labour force increased from approximately 2.26 billion to 3.09 billion between 1991 and 2010–12. Over the same period the number of unemployed persons increased from approximately 150 million to 195 million. Employed persons are distributed by the ILO into two main categories: wage and salaried workers (also known as employees) and self-employed workers (consisting of self-employed workers with employees, called employers; self-employed workers without employees or own-account workers; members of producers' cooperatives and contributing family workers, also known as unpaid family workers). Another distinction made by the ILO is between 'non-vulnerable' workers (consisting of employers, as well as wage and salaried workers) and 'vulnerable' workers, consisting of all those who work but cannot be considered wage and salaried workers; basically it comprises of 'own-account workers' and 'contributing family workers'. Information for the period since the early 1990s in respect of the above-noted classification is provided in Annexure Tables 1A and 1B, and 2A and 2B. As is evident from these tables, throughout this period, the proportion of wage and salaried workers, which may be taken as a proxy for the active labour force in the spirit of Marx's formulation, was well below 50 per cent of the global labour force. Thus, the greater part of world labour consists of those who are 'vulnerably employed' as per the ILO classification, which, along with unemployed, may be considered a proxy for the size of the relative surplus labour at any given juncture.

As should be obvious, a high proportion of wage and salaried workers in a country is indicative of 'advanced' capitalist development, i.e. a metropolitan country. On the other hand, a substantial share of own-account workers (self-employed without hired employees) and a large share of contributing family workers are typically associated with a small 'formal sector'[14] and a large agricultural sector along with a variety of informal livelihood options outside agriculture, which is common to the periphery in general. Thus, as per recent ILO estimates, in the developed economies and the European Union as a whole, the proportion of wage and salaried workers was more than 80 per cent, whereas the share of own-account workers has been around 9 per cent during the last couple of decades, and the percentage of contributing family workers has been negligible (around 2 per cent). In the case of the erstwhile socialist countries and some of the southern and central European (non-EU) economies, there has been some decline in the share of wage and salaried employment in total employment in recent years, although it still continues to be more than 75 per cent, alongside an increase in own-account workers, which is around 16 per cent as per the recent estimates.

More than 60 per cent of total employment in Latin America and the Caribbean, and the Middle East, is made up of 'wage and salaried' workers, whereas for North Africa the comparable figure is around 50 per cent. In East Asia, Southeast Asia and South Asia, the proportions for wage and salaried workers are 48, 36 and 21 per cent, respectively, as per the recent count, and the larger proportion of workers are contributing family workers and own-account workers. In the case of Sub Saharan Africa, the proportion of wage and salaried workers is just around 20 per cent. Thus the overall work force in the developing world as a whole is dominated by 'own-account and contributing family workers'. (It should be noted that this excludes the significant number of workers engaged in work related to social reproduction, who are dominantly but not exclusively women.)

In the world as a whole, the share of wage and salaried workers in total employment is currently about 48 per cent, while the proportion of contributing family workers is around 15 per cent, and that of own-account workers is close to 35 per cent. Thus the proportion of workers in what has been termed vulnerable employment by the ILO remains quite high, at about half the proportion of the total number employed, while wage and salaried workers together with employers, constituting 'non-vulnerable employment', account for the other half. Clearly, in many of the developing and low-income regions, the share of vulnerable employment is between 70 to 80 per cent of the work force, which is characterized by significant levels of underemployment/disguised unemployment.

The other notable feature of work force distribution (for details of the global occupational structure, see Annexure Tables 3A and 3B), as one would expect, is that the lion's share of employment in the case of the peripheral economies is accounted for by the agricultural sector. For instance, for South Asia and Sub Saharan Africa, the respective shares were about 51 and 62 per cent on average over 2010–12; even in the case of East Asia, the share of the work force in agriculture was around 34 per cent on average over 2010–12, which was close to the global average for this sector. It is also worth emphasizing here that the services sector tends to be generally bloated in most peripheral economies as it often becomes a kind of 'parking lot' for those expelled from agriculture but unable to get absorbed in the formal industrial sector, constituting the overwhelming proportion of the urban informal economy, described famously as the 'Planet of Slums' by Mike Davis.

In fact, the share of the industrial sector has been stuck at around a little over 20 per cent for the global economy as a whole since the early 1990s; it increased from 21.6 to 22.5 per cent between 1991 and 2010–12, whereas the share of the services sector went up from 33.9 to 44 per cent over the same period for the global economy as a whole, and similar rising trends are reported for all the sub-regions. The decline in employment in the industrial sector (from 31 per cent in 1991 to 22.5 per cent over 2010–12) for the developed economies and the European Union, and the concomitant increase in the share of employment in the service sector from 62 to 74 per cent over the same period, may partly be along expected lines; however, for the rest of the world, a great deal of the explosion of the services sector may simply be diversification of distress due to accelerated primitive accumulation in the recent decades of neo-liberal globalization.

As regards unemployment rates, which seek to capture the proportion of the labour force that does not have a job but is available and actively looking for work, the figures reported for the developing countries tend to be extremely fuzzy if not unreliable, as these do not capture the extent of underemployment and disguised unemployment. Without entering into a discussion of the notions of work, employment, unemployment, etc., which is a conceptually slippery terrain even for the advanced capitalist countries, let us simply note here that as per the ILO measures, gainful employment has been a serious problem for most sub-regions of the global economy. For the last couple of decades the open unemployment rate has hovered around 6 per cent, and the global count of the unemployed has increased in absolute numbers. In fact, for the sub-regions constituting developed economies, as per the ILO estimates, rates of unemployment are generally considered a serious problem at the current juncture, along with the worsening quality of overall working conditions and labour relations. Compared to its 'golden age' in the heyday of the 'welfare state' in the post-World War II era, the world of work in recent years has been characterized by growing 'precariousness' for the majority of workers in advanced capitalist countries; the extent of this appears so hard-hitting that researchers like Guy Standing interpret it as the emergence of a 'new class, viz., the precariat'. It would seem as if the 'west' is trying to catch up with the 'rest' in the race to the bottom with respect to overall conditions of work globally.

The ILO also notes that a major policy issue, associated with the growing employment crunch, that has emerged during the last couple of decades is that of youth (defined as persons aged between 15 and 24 years) unemployment (for details of the global pattern, see Annexure Tables 4A and 4B). In almost all regions of the world, the rates of youth unemployment (as a percentage of the youth labour force) have increased over the years; in the developed economies and the European Union, the total youth unemployment rate increased from 14.6 per cent in 1991 to about 18 per cent during 2010–12, which happens to be the highest incidence in any sub-region. In the world as a whole, the unemployment rate among the youth increased from 11.7 per cent in 1991 to 12.5 per cent during 2010–12. Further, in most regions the youth unemployment rate was higher among females than among males, with the discrepancy between them being the highest in the Middle East, followed by North Africa, whereas in the developed economies and the European Union the incidence of youth unemployment among males and females was similar.

Although country-specific enquiry goes beyond the scope of this paper, it may be of some interest to note in passing a couple of features relating to the world of labour in India (a country which has been a 'poster child', along with China,[15] for its growth performance for almost four decades), which are relevant for our discussion here. Going by the conventional official definitions of the organized/formal and unorganized/informal sectors,[16] it is quite clear that the overwhelming majority of workers in India belong to the latter. As is evident from Table 5, of approximately 485 million workers, as per the most recent estimate, more than 447 million (i.e. over 92 per cent) are categorized as informal workers. Further, it is also quite clear that there is a significant trend of 'informalization' of the work force in the formal sector; in fact, most of the incremental increase in employment in recent years in manufacturing, services and other non-agricultural activities consists of informal and flexible contracts. In general, jobs and social security in India's formal sector are on a downward slide. It is also worth noting here that socially disadvantaged workers tend to be over-represented in the informal economy (Table 6), and even in the so-called 'modern' sectors, e.g. industry and services, the overwhelming bulk consists of informal workers and, as mentioned, there is an increase in the share of informal contracts from already extremely high base levels (Table 7).

In sum, the foregoing snapshot of the global labour scenario clearly shows that the world of work for the majority in the contemporary world economy is characterized by fragile and vulnerable conditions. The proportion of regular wage and salaried employees (which can be taken as a proxy for the 'active labour army', as suggested earlier) is a minority globally, its spread is quite uneven (in conformity with the combined and uneven development of global capitalism) across sub-regions, and this segment of the formal/regular sector has been under pressure in the recent years. The majority of workers in the peripheral economies fall in the category of the vulnerably employed, which is a collection of very diverse economic activities, and these workers have little prospect of joining the ranks of regular wage workers. One may, justifiably, quibble over the fine-tuning of the relevant concepts, but it would be hardly off the mark to consider this large and heterogeneous segment as being coterminous with Marx's reserve army of labour.

IV

The obvious conclusion that emerges from our foregoing discussion is a reiteration of the well-known Marxist position regarding a durable labour reserve under capitalism. As discussed in section II above, the nature, texture, and ebb and flow of RSP are organically connected with the dynamics of accumulation and class contestation. Further, at a very high level of generality, the long march of global capitalism, since its inception, may be divided into three broad phases with respect to major implications vis-à-vis the world of labour in general and labour reserves in particular. Sure enough, within each one of these, as well as across countries within particular phases, detailed and grounded accounts throw up a large spectrum of regimes of accumulation as well as regimes of labour with significant differences, which we have abstracted from in our brief account here.

The current phase of neo-liberal globalization, which started its ascendancy approximately four decades ago, has been characterized by ever-greater unshackling of capital in most countries around the world (with very few exceptions) and severe setbacks to the working classes almost everywhere. The vision of an inexorable capitalist system driven by its own immanent laws, sketched in the *Communist Manifesto* with eloquent, broad brush-strokes, has possibly materialized for the first time as a truly global order. In fact, with the advantage of hindsight, one might wonder how easily what Polanyi visualized as the 'great transformation' has unravelled so fast! As is well known, in his justly famous and profound work, *The Great Transformation*, Karl Polanyi advanced the claim that a *laissez-faire* market system 'could not exist for any length of time without annihilating the human and natural substance of society' (Polanyi 1944: 3). As he put it:

> While on the one hand markets spread all over the face of the globe and

> the amount of goods involved grew to unbelievable proportions, on the other hand a network of measures and policies was integrated into powerful institutions designed to check the action of the market relative to labor, land, and money. (Ibid.: 76).

Essentially, he theorized the capitalist project as a 'double movement' where the unbridled tendency of the market towards total commodification was kept in check by a counter-movement by the society and the net outcome was 'embedded capitalism'. The long post-World War II boom accompanied by the rise of the welfare state in the advanced capitalist countries may have lulled many into taking Polanyi's claim as serious and almost self-evident. One may note in passing that Polanyi's contribution was also an attempt to engage critically with Marxism and offer an alternative perspective on socio-economic transformation. It is not possible to get into a discussion of his contribution or his critique of Marx here, but it should be evident, in the light of the resurgence and consolidation of the neo-liberal order during the last few decades, that Polanyi seriously underestimated, if not misunderstood, powerful insights central to Marxian political economy relating to the capitalist dynamic.

As is well documented, neo-liberal globalization, or 'disembedded global capitalism', has had huge adverse implications for the world of labour even in advanced capitalist countries. Hence, the notion of precariousness is back to the centre stage. As noted by Magdoff and Foster (2013), with respect to almost all indicators of the labour market, such as employment, working conditions, wage rates, wage shares, etc., workers in the most advanced and powerful economy in the world, viz., the United States of America, are in a very difficult situation and have become worse-off over the last four decades or so. As Warren Buffett put it eloquently, 'There's class warfare, all right, but it's my class, the rich class, that's making war, and we're winning.'[17] Facts and figures emerging from almost every country in the 'west' are possibly a confirmation of Buffett's loud boasting! In southern Europe, official unemployment rates are in the range of 25 to 30 per cent and workers retrenched from formal jobs have found a variety of part-time parking lots, including vulnerable self-employment.[18] Inequalities of income and wealth have risen dramatically in the neo-liberal era, along with a widening of the gap, at unprecedented rates, between the managerial class and average workers. In developing countries, there are a handful of cases where some dimensions of the well-being of workers have shown improvement (connected with the logic of combined and uneven development of global capitalism, which we cannot discuss in any detail here); but these may well be temporary and, if the neo-liberal regime continues to hold sway, the limited gains may get reversed in no time. As has been emphasized frequently, a strategy of 'beggar thy neighbour' is at the core of the neo-liberal order; we would rather qualify it as '*beggar thy worker and thy neighbour*'.

In any case, as discussed in section III, the global economy in general, and the developing world in particular (including its 'poster children' such as China and India), are characterized by a huge labour reserve with little prospect of any significant reduction in it; on the contrary, one may expect a deterioration in this respect, both because of changes in the 'productive forces' (e.g., the information and communications technology revolution) and increasing neo-liberal 'production relations'. Thus a scenario of higher levels of disguised unemployment, more part-time work and increases in the length of the working day, in short, persistent and rising informality for the working classes, may well be the order of the day. Of course, neo-liberal capitalism is not cast in stone, and any prognosis must be open-ended to take account of the likely strategies of capital and the resistance of labour.

Finally, for the periphery in the contemporary global capitalist order (which constitutes the overwhelming share of humanity), the prospect of emulating the nineteenth-century European trajectory of socio-economic transformation, and to imagine a comparable trajectory and similar fate for its labour reserves, is an illusion. Policy-making during the *dirigiste* era in the developing countries often showed at least an awareness of the relevant challenges confronting them in this respect, and, *inter alia*, tried to provide some protection to petty production so that the swelling of RSP is contained. As has been shown by Prabhat Patnaik in several of his illuminating contributions (e.g., Patnaik 2009), neo-liberal capitalism unleashes powerful forces, including the dismantling of any such protection, which tend to worsen the prospects of diminution of labour reserves.

Recent Global Trends

ANNEXURE TABLE 1A: **Status of Employment of Global Work Force** (percentage)

Year	*1991*				*1992–94*				*1995–97*				*1998–2000*			
Region/Status in employment (in %)	*WSE*	*EMP*	*OAW*	*CFW*	*WSE*	*EMP*	*OAW*	*CFW*	*WSE*	*EMP*	*OAW*	*CFW*	*WSE*	*EMP*	*OAW*	*CFW*
Developed Economies and European Union	83.0	4.4	9.9	2.7	83.0	4.4	9.8	2.7	83.5	4.3	9.7	2.5	84.2	4.3	9.3	2.2
Central and Southeastern Europe (non-EU) and CIS	79.5	1.5	13.1	6.0	78.5	1.5	13.5	6.5	75.2	1.7	16.1	7.0	74.0	1.7	17.5	6.8
East Asia	31.7	1.9	30.9	35.5	31.5	1.7	32.1	34.6	34.8	1.7	32.4	31.1	38.8	1.8	31.6	27.7
Southeast Asia and the Pacific	29.3	2.5	36.9	31.3	30.2	2.5	37.1	30.2	31.5	2.4	37.9	28.2	33.1	2.5	38.2	26.2
South Asia	17.3	1.9	60.3	20.6	17.0	1.8	60.0	21.1	16.3	0.9	60.8	21.9	17.4	0.9	60.9	20.8
Latin America and the Caribbean	60.3	4.8	27.3	7.6	58.6	4.2	28.8	8.4	59.4	4.3	28.1	8.2	59.8	4.3	27.9	8.1
Middle East	55.9	7.3	21.3	15.5	57.3	7.2	21.2	14.3	59.4	6.0	22.3	12.3	60.7	5.6	22.7	11.0
North Africa	44.8	9.4	20.1	25.8	46.3	9.9	20.5	23.3	47.1	9.1	20.0	23.8	47.8	9.5	19.3	23.3
Sub Saharan Africa	16.1	0.7	41.7	41.6	16.0	0.8	43.0	40.2	16.7	1.0	45.5	36.9	17.0	1.0	47.2	34.8
World	42.7	2.7	32.1	22.4	42.2	2.6	33.0	22.3	42.8	2.4	33.9	21.0	44.2	2.4	34.0	19.4

Note: WSE: wage and salaried workers (employees); EMP: employers; OAW: own-account workers; CFW: contributing family workers.

ANNEXURE TABLE 1B: Status of Employment of Global Work Force (percentage)

Year	*2001–03*				*2004–06*				*2007–09*				*2010–12*			
Region/Status in employment (in %)	*WSE*	*EMP*	*OAW*	*CFW*	*WSE*	*EMP*	*OAW*	*CFW*	*WSE*	*EMP*	*OAW*	*CFW*	*WSE*	*EMP*	*OAW*	*CFW*
Developed Economies and European Union	85.0	4.1	8.9	2.0	85.3	3.8	9.2	1.6	86.0	3.8	8.9	1.3	86.2	3.7	9.0	1.2
Central and Southeastern Europe (non-EU) and CIS	75.3	1.8	17.0	5.9	76.0	1.8	17.5	4.6	77.7	2.1	16.5	3.7	77.9	2.1	16.3	3.7
East Asia	41.4	1.9	31.2	25.5	42.2	1.8	31.9	24.1	45.3	1.8	31.7	21.2	48.2	1.8	31.3	18.7
Southeast Asia and the Pacific	32.6	2.5	39.0	25.9	34.6	2.4	39.2	23.8	35.5	2.3	39.5	22.6	36.3	2.3	39.5	21.9
South Asia	18.1	1.3	58.6	22.0	18.3	1.2	58.6	21.9	19.9	1.1	59.4	19.6	21.2	1.2	59.4	18.2
Latin America and the Caribbean	59.2	4.4	28.1	8.2	61.3	4.6	26.6	7.5	63.4	4.6	25.7	6.3	63.7	4.6	26.1	5.5
Middle East	61.7	5.3	23.2	9.8	63.3	5.2	23.2	8.4	66.4	4.8	22.0	6.7	68.1	4.7	21.4	5.8
North Africa	48.7	10.2	20.0	21.1	48.2	9.4	23.2	19.2	49.2	9.3	24.8	16.7	49.4	9.5	25.8	15.3
Sub Saharan Africa	17.8	1.1	48.4	32.7	19.2	1.1	50.4	29.2	20.2	1.3	50.4	28.0	21.0	1.4	50.5	27.2
World	44.8	2.5	33.9	18.7	45.3	2.4	34.6	17.7	47.0	2.4	34.6	16.0	47.9	2.4	34.8	14.9

Note: WSE: wage and salaried workers (employees); EMP: employers; OAW: own-account workers; CFW: contributing family workers.
Source: *Key Indicators of Labour Markets*, ILO.

ANNEXURE TABLE 2A: **Vulnerability and Employment of Global Work Force**

Year	*1991*			*1992–94*			*1995–97*			*1998–2000*		
Region/Status in employment	*STE (in '000)*	*SPVE (in '000)*	*SSVE (in %)*	*STE (in '000)*	*SPVE (in '000)*	*SSVE (in %)*	*STE (in '000)*	*SPVE (in '000)*	*SSVE (in %)*	*STE (in '000)*	*SPVE (in '000)*	*SSVE (in %)*
Developed Economies and European Union	414,125	52,176	12.6	413,568	51,886	12.5	425,173	51,659	12.1	440,005	50,679	11.5
Central and South-eastern Europe (non-EU) and CIS	148,828	28,304	19.0	149,210	29,903	20.0	145,300	33,577	23.1	144,647	35,079	24.2
East Asia	672,383	446,121	66.3	694,857	463,693	66.7	715,887	454,724	63.5	734,186	435,410	59.3
Southeast Asia and the Pacific	199,025	135,774	68.2	207,413	139,546	67.3	223,320	147,548	66.1	236,449	152,363	64.4
South Asia	419,848	339,547	80.9	441,599	358,474	81.2	471,296	390,025	82.7	502,691	410,588	81.7
Latin America and the Caribbean	162,657	56,743	34.9	176,959	65,810	37.2	188,861	68,558	36.3	203,542	73,193	36.0
Middle East	30,057	11,066	36.8	32,176	11,406	35.5	35,453	12,273	34.6	39,396	13,255	33.7
North Africa	37,532	17,217	45.9	39,203	17,174	43.8	42,592	18,644	43.8	46,317	19,746	42.7
Sub Saharan Africa	175,359	145,956	83.2	186,201	154,883	83.2	203,192	167,311	82.4	220,263	180,569	82.0
World	2,259,814	1,232,904	54.6	2,341,186	1,292,775	55.2	2,451,074	1,344,318	54.9	2,567,496	1,370,879	53.4

Note: STE: sum of total employment; SPVE: sum of persons in vulnerable employment; SSVE: sum of share of vulnerable employment in total employment.

ANNEXURE TABLE 2B: Vulnerability and Employment of Global Work Force

Year	*2001–03*			*2004–06*			*2007–09*			*2010–12*		
Region/Status in employment	*STE (in '000)*	*SPVE (in '000)*	*SSVE (in %)*	*STE (in '000)*	*SPVE (in '000)*	*SSVE (in %)*	*STE (in '000)*	*SPVE (in '000)*	*SSVE (in %)*	*STE (in '000)*	*SPVE (in '000)*	*SSVE (in %)*
Developed Economies and European Union	447,179	48,697	10.9	460,183	49,696	10.8	472,597	48,402	10.2	467,314	47,434	10.2
Central and South-eastern Europe (non-EU) and CIS	149,153	34,157	22.9	153,453	33,989	22.2	159,471	32,192	20.2	163,771	32,752	20.0
East Asia	759,538	430,744	56.7	788,307	441,733	56.0	809,267	428,352	52.9	825,604	413,045	50.0
Southeast Asia and the Pacific	250,135	162,307	64.9	263,538	165,973	63.0	279,926	173,975	62.2	297,065	182,476	61.4
South Asia	541,423	436,403	80.6	583,733	470,070	80.5	603,730	477,147	79.0	626,000	485,961	77.7
Latin America and the Caribbean	216,290	78,572	36.3	234,258	79,754	34.1	250,534	80,192	32.0	266,856	84,507	31.6
Middle East	44,325	14,639	33.0	51,322	16,210	31.6	56,593	16,268	28.8	62,063	16,856	27.2
North Africa	49,528	20,354	41.1	55,295	23,452	42.4	60,573	25,169	41.5	64,495	26,504	41.1
Sub Saharan Africa	240,045	194,673	81.1	263,076	209,517	79.6	286,399	224,730	78.5	311,346	241,746	77.6
World	2,697,616	1,420,546	52.7	2,853,163	1,490,393	52.2	2,979,091	1,506,429	50.6	3,084,514	1,531,282	49.7

Note: STE: sum of total employment; SPVE: sum of persons in vulnerable employment; SSVE: sum of share of vulnerable employment in total employment.
Source: *Key Indicators of Labour Markets*, ILO.

ANNEXURE TABLE 3A: Employment Pattern of Global Work Force (percentage)

Year	*1991*			*1992–94*			*1995–97*			*1998–2000*		
Region/Employment by sector (in '000)	*Agri.*	*Ind.*	*Services*	*Agri.*	*Ind.*	*Services*	*Agri.*	*Ind.*	*Services*	*Agri.*	*Ind.*	*Services*
Developed Economies and European Union	6.9	31.0	62.1	6.5	29.8	63.7	6.1	28.6	65.3	5.6	27.7	66.8
Central and Southeastern Europe (non-EU) and CIS	28.6	29.7	41.7	27.1	28.6	44.3	26.5	26.3	47.2	25.9	25.1	49.0
East Asia	56.9	22.9	20.2	53.8	23.6	22.6	48.5	24.5	27.0	47.7	23.9	28.4
Southeast Asia and the Pacific	58.6	13.6	27.8	56.5	14.6	28.9	50.7	16.5	32.7	49.7	15.9	34.4
South Asia	61.8	16.0	22.2	61.5	15.6	22.9	60.3	15.5	24.2	59.7	15.5	24.8
Latin America and the Caribbean	23.6	23.1	53.3	24.2	22.2	53.6	22.6	21.3	56.1	20.9	21.6	57.5
Middle East	23.1	24.1	52.8	23.0	23.9	53.1	22.9	24.0	53.1	22.6	24.3	53.1
North Africa	34.0	20.9	45.2	35.5	19.6	45.0	34.3	19.9	45.9	32.5	19.9	47.7
Sub Saharan Africa	67.5	8.5	24.0	67.7	8.1	24.1	67.1	8.0	24.8	66.5	7.9	25.5
World	44.5	21.6	33.9	43.6	21.3	35.1	41.3	21.2	37.6	40.6	20.6	38.8

ANNEXURE TABLE 3B: Employment Pattern of Global Work Force (percentage)

Year	*2001–03*			*2004–06*			*2007–09*			*2010–12*		
Region/Employment by sector (in '000)	*Agri.*	*Ind.*	*Services*	*Agri.*	*Ind.*	*Services*	*Agri.*	*Ind.*	*Services*	*Agri.*	*Ind.*	*Services*
Developed Economies and European Union	5.0	26.3	68.8	4.2	25.3	70.5	3.8	24.3	71.9	3.6	22.5	73.8
Central and Southeastern Europe (non-EU) and CIS	23.2	25.7	51.1	21.0	25.9	53.1	18.8	25.9	55.4	19.3	25.5	55.1
East Asia	47.3	22.7	30.0	42.7	24.5	32.9	37.6	27.6	34.7	34.0	29.3	36.7
Southeast Asia and the Pacific	48.2	17.3	34.5	45.7	17.9	36.4	43.6	18.2	38.2	41.4	18.8	39.8
South Asia	57.1	16.9	26.0	54.4	18.5	27.1	52.6	19.9	27.6	51.1	20.9	28.0
Latin America and the Caribbean	19.4	21.5	59.1	18.5	22.0	59.5	16.6	22.4	60.9	15.9	21.7	62.3
Middle East	21.9	24.7	53.4	20.6	25.6	53.8	18.0	26.1	55.9	16.5	26.4	57.1
North Africa	31.5	19.2	49.3	32.0	20.0	48.0	30.0	21.6	48.3	28.4	23.2	48.5
Sub Saharan Africa	65.7	8.0	26.3	64.2	8.2	27.6	62.7	8.6	28.7	62.0	8.7	29.3
World	39.7	20.3	40.0	37.4	21.1	41.5	35.0	22.1	42.9	33.6	22.5	44.0

Source: *Key Indicators of Labour Markets*, ILO.

ANNEXURE TABLE 4A: Youth Unemployment Rate

Year	*1991*			*1992–94*			*1995–97*			*1998–2000*		
Region/Youth unemployment as a percentage of youth labour force	*Total*	*Male*	*Female*	*Total*	*Male*	*Female*	*Total*	*Male*	*Female*	*Total*	*Male*	*Female*
Developed Economies and European Union	14.6	14.4	14.7	16.2	16.4	16.0	15.7	15.4	15.8	14.0	14.0	13.9
Central and Southeastern Europe (non-EU) and CIS	20.9	20.9	21.0	18.0	18.0	17.9	19.1	18.6	19.7	21.1	20.4	22.0
East Asia	8.8	10.4	7.1	8.1	9.6	6.5	8.9	10.6	7.3	9.5	11.3	7.8
Southeast Asia and the Pacific	8.9	8.7	9.3	9.4	9.0	9.9	10.1	9.8	10.4	12.8	12.8	12.8
South Asia	9.3	9.0	9.9	8.9	8.9	9.1	9.2	9.2	9.4	9.5	9.4	9.6
Latin America and the Caribbean	16.1	13.4	20.9	12.7	10.9	15.9	14.6	12.3	18.5	15.5	12.9	19.7
Middle East	23.8	21.4	35.7	23.9	21.5	35.5	24.2	21.4	36.1	24.1	21.2	35.8
North Africa	23.5	20.5	31.1	24.8	21.9	32.5	25.3	22.8	31.8	24.6	22.7	29.2
Sub Saharan Africa	13.3	12.6	14.1	13.2	12.6	14.0	13.2	12.4	14.0	13.1	12.4	13.9
World	11.7	11.8	11.5	11.3	11.5	11.0	11.9	12.0	11.9	12.5	12.5	12.6

ANNEXURE TABLE 4B: Youth Unemployment Rate

Year	*2001–03*			*2004–06*			*2007–09*			*2010–12*		
Region/Youth unemployment as a percentage of youth labour force	*Total*	*Male*	*Female*	*Total*	*Male*	*Female*	*Total*	*Male*	*Female*	*Total*	*Male*	*Female*
Developed Economies and European Union	14.3	14.9	13.8	14.1	14.5	13.5	14.4	15.3	13.3	17.9	19.1	16.5
Central and Southeastern Europe (non-EU) and CIS	19.2	18.8	19.6	18.5	18.1	19.3	18.3	18.1	18.6	18.0	17.7	18.6
East Asia	9.2	10.9	7.5	8.6	10.2	7.0	8.7	10.3	7.1	9.2	10.9	7.4
Southeast Asia and the Pacific	15.8	15.2	16.7	17.2	16.3	18.4	14.3	14.1	14.6	13.0	12.5	13.8
South Asia	9.4	9.4	9.5	9.5	9.4	9.8	9.3	9.1	9.8	9.9	9.5	11.0
Latin America and the Caribbean	16.8	13.9	21.3	16.2	13.2	20.8	14.5	11.9	18.4	13.7	11.5	16.9
Middle East	26.3	23.4	37.2	25.2	21.9	36.7	25.2	21.7	38.3	27.7	24.0	42.0
North Africa	25.3	23.2	30.5	23.7	20.4	32.0	20.5	16.9	29.7	22.4	17.3	35.0
Sub Saharan Africa	13.3	12.6	13.9	12.1	11.6	12.7	11.9	11.4	12.5	11.9	11.4	12.4
World	12.9	12.9	13.0	12.6	12.4	12.8	12.1	12.0	12.2	12.5	12.4	12.8

Source: *Key Indicators of Labour Markets*, ILO.

Recent Indian Trends

Annexure Table 5: India's Work Force, Formal versus Informal, 1999–2000 to 2011–12

Sector/Worker	*Total Employment (million)*		
	Informal/ Unorganized Workers	*Formal/ Organized Workers*	*Total Workers*
1999–2000 (NSS 55th Round)			
Informal/Unorganized sector	341.3 (99.6)	1.4 (0.4)	342.6 (100.0)
Formal/Organized sector	20.5 (37.8)	33.7 (62.2)	54.1 (100.0)
Total	361.7 (91.2)	35.0 (8.8)	396.8 (100.0)
2004–05 (NSS 61st Round)			
Informal/Unorganized sector	393.5 (99.6)	1.4 (0.4)	394.9 (100.0)
Formal/Organized sector	29.1 (46.6)	33.4 (53.4)	62.6 (100.0)
Total	422.6 (92.4)	34.9 (7.6)	457.5 (100.0)
2009–10 (NSS 66th Round)			
Informal/Unorganized sector	388.0 (99.6)	1.6 (0.4)	389.6 (100.0)
Formal/Organized sector	36.9 (52.3)	33.5 (47.6)	70.5 (100.0)
Total	425.0 (92.3)	35.1 (7.65)	460.2 (100.0)
2011–12 (NSS 68th Round)			
Informal/Unorganized sector	403.8 (99.7)	1.4 (0.3)	405.2 (100.0)
Formal/Organized sector	43.4 (54.4)	36.1 (45.5)	79.5 (100.0)
Total	447.2 (92.2)	37.5 (7.7)	484.7 (100.0)

Notes: 1. Data from the following four rounds of the Employment–Unemployment Surveys of the National Sample Survey Organization, Government of India, have been used here: 1999–2000, 2004–05, 2009–10 and 2011–12.
2. Figures for the 55th (1999–2000) and 61st (2004–05) rounds are adopted from the *Report on Conditions of Work and Promotion of Livelihoods in the Unorganized Sector*, 2007.
3. Figures for the NSS 66th (2009–10) and 68th (2011–12) rounds of Employment–Unemployment Surveys are based on unit-level data.
4. Figures in brackets are percentages.

ANNEXURE TABLE 6: Extent of Informal Sector and Informal Workers by Various Social Groups (per cent)

Social Group	*66th round (2009–10)*		*68th round (2011–12)*	
	Informal Sector	*Informal Workers*	*Informal Sector*	*Informal Workers*
Scheduled Tribe (ST)	89.10	96.05	88.91	95.52
Scheduled Caste (SC)	85.60	94.39	84.56	94.32
Other Backward Class (OBC)	86.82	94.04	85.89	93.89
Others	79.13	86.95	77.32	86.93
All	84.67	92.35	83.62	92.25

Source: Computed from NSS unit-level data of the 66th and 68th Employment–Unemployment Surveys.

ANNEXURE TABLE 7: Extent of Informal Workers in Each Industrial Division from 1999–00 to 2011–12 (per cent)

Industrial Division	*55th round (1999–2000)*	*66th round (2009–10)*	*68th round (2011–12)*
Agriculture	98.7	99.53	99.57
Industry	85.5	91.20	91.77
Services	75.83	78.01	79.20
All	91.7	92.35	92.25

Source: Computed from NSS unit-level data of the 66th and 68th Employment–Unemployment Surveys.

Notes

[1] The Keynesian framework being the well-known exception.

[2] Inexorable, ceaseless competition and generalized alienation are central to Marx's conception of capitalist commodity production, where all economic actors are subjected to external coercive force of the system, organically connected to its immanent tendencies. Thus, as Marx put it in *Capital*, Volume 1, chapter 24: 'competition makes the immanent laws of capitalist production to be felt by each individual capitalist, as external coercive laws. It compels him to keep constantly extending his capital, in order to preserve it, but extend it he cannot, except by means of progressive accumulation'. (Marx 1976: 739)

[3] In fact, pre-capitalist modes of production, in contrast to the capitalist mode of production, are characterized by a tendency to put a lid on relative surplus population.

[4] To quote Marx: 'the industrial reserve army, during the periods of stagnation and average prosperity, weighs down the active labour army; during the periods of overproduction and paroxysm, it holds its pretension in check. Relative surplus of population is therefore the pivot upon which the law of demand and supply of labour works. It confines the field action to this law within the limits absolutely convenient to the activity of exploitation and to the domination of capital.' (Marx 1976: 639).

[5] To quote Marx: 'But if a surplus laboring population is a necessary product of accumulation or of the development of wealth on a capitalistic basis, this surplus population becomes conversely the lever of capitalistic accumulation, nay a condition of existence of the capitalistic mode of production. It forms a disposable industrial reserve army that belongs to capital as absolutely as if the latter had bred it at its own cost. Independently of the limits of the actual increase of population, it creates for the changing needs of the self-expansion of capital, a mass of humans always ready for exploitation.' (Marx 1976: 784).

[6] It is interesting to note that in his well-known subsequent work, Lewis was much less sanguine about transfer of labour out of agriculture. To quote him: '*Our agricultural economics is based on the assumption that number in agriculture will decline as economic development proceeds: Our policies are therefore set towards helping to reduce the number of men per acre, instead we shall need for the next three or four decades agricultural policies aimed at absorbing men per acre.*' (Lewis 1978: 241).

[7] In fact, it may be better to conceptualize latent as not being limited only to pre-capitalist sectors but also segments of population, e.g., housewives or home-based women in general, at particular stages, which constitute a potential proletariat.

[8] The exact estimate of plunder is obviously a difficult task. However, Patnaik notes that a very conservative estimate of such an appropriation through different channels would exceed a billion pound sterling by 1800, which was 'more than the capital of all the industrial enterprises operated by steam which existed in Europe around that date'. (Patnaik 1995: 23).

[9] For detailed discussions on these issues, see Bagchi (1982), Baran (1957), Galeano (1973), Magubane (1979), Habib (1995), Williams (1966), Rodney (1972), Inikori (1982), Marx (1976), Patnaik (1995), Patnaik (1999), Blomstrom and Hettne (1984), among others.

[10] In fact, in spite of our substantive appreciation, we have some issues with Amin's formulation, beginning with the nomenclature used in the model; the expression 'self-centred' appears quite misleading as from almost its inception, metropolitan capitalism has hardly been self-centred. Further, in the post World War II

era, we have had examples of models of accumulation in the non-metropolitan regions where the linkage is relatively more robust than suggested by Amin.

11 This point has been made repeatedly by several researchers; for further details on this, see contributions in Ranis and Schultz, eds (1988); Chang and Rowthorn, eds. (1995), among others. Lewis (1988) and Williamson (1988) take the strong view that the growth performance in many of the third world countries, based on the above-noted strategy, was not only respectable but very impressive by historical standards. Europe's per capita per annum growth rates happened to be 0.74, 1.27 and 1.35 for the periods 1800–50, 1850–1900 and 1900–50, respectively. In the case of the third world countries, where a concerted push towards industrialization and economic transformation had to wait until after World War II, at least half of them had a per capita per annum growth rate of over 2 per cent between 1960 and 1982. The problem with these countries was not the lack of growth but, as Lewis and others have pointed out, very uneven distribution of the fruits of growth.

12 Patnaik makes a very useful distinction between two broad segments of the reserve army in highlighting some of the central features of the global capitalist dynamics; the two broad segments, viz., 'the pre-capitalist sector reserve army' and 'the internal reserve army', play very different *sui generis* roles, and their significance for metropolitan and peripheral accumulation are very different (for details, see Patnaik 2009).

13 Using ILO data, somewhat similar attempt to quantify the global reserve army of labour has been attempted by Foster *et al.* (2011).

14 Strictly speaking, Marx's conception of ALA is not quite identical with formal and secure employment. However, going by the analytical intent, it may not be far off the mark to treat the informal segment as a segment characterized by pervasive underemployment and disguised unemployment, and hence very much similar to the latent and stagnant segments of RSP.

15 Although the labour scenario in China is better than in India, for a variety of historical and contemporary processes, yet, going by standard indicators such as share of wages in output, current wage rates, work conditions, the size of labour reserves, etc., the overall world of labour is characterized by serious concerns (for details, see Yao 2010).

16 According to the National Commission for Enterprises in the Unorganized Sector (NCEUS), the definitions for informal/unorganized worker and informal/unorganized sector are as follows. *Informal/Unorganized Sector*: The unorganized sector consists of all unincorporated private enterprises owned by individuals or households engaged in the sale and production of goods and services operated on a proprietary or partnership basis and with less than ten total workers. *Informal/Unorganized Worker*: 'Unorganized workers consist of those working in unorganized enterprises or households, excluding regular workers with social security benefits, and workers in the formal sector without any employment/social security benefits provided by the employers'. The definition of the *Informal Economy* adopted by ILO is as follows: 'The term "informal economy" refers to all economic activities by workers and economic units that are – in law or in practice – not covered or insufficiently covered by formal arrangements. Their activities are not included in the law, which means that they are operating outside the formal reach of the law; or they are not covered in practice, which means that – although they are operating within the formal reach of the law, the law is not applied or not enforced; or the law discourages compliance because it is inappropriate, burdensome, or imposes excessive costs.' On the face of it, although the above-noted definitions are clearly different, yet

in a substantive sense they are not dissimilar, and, for the working population, more or less capture those who belong to the segment of regular wage and salaried workers.

[17] As quoted by Ben Stein in 'In Class Warfare, Guess Which Class Is Winning', *The New York Times* (26 November 2006).

[18] Those who take the 'Lewisian turning point' as a serious metaphor may do well to consider the possibility of a 'Lewisian *counter-turning* point' while analysing the world of labour in different phases of capitalism!

References

Amin, Samir (1974), 'Accumulation and Development: A Theoretical Model', *Review of African Political Economy*, No. 1, August–November: 9–26.

Bagchi, A.K. (1982), *The Political Economy of Underdevelopment*, Cambridge: Cambridge University Press.

Baran, Paul (1957), *The Political Economy of Growth*, New York: Monthly Review Press.

Blomstrom, M. and Bjorn Hettne (1984), *Development Theory in Transition*, London: Zed Books.

Byres, T.J., ed. (1997), *The State, Development Planning and Liberalization in India*, New Delhi: Oxford University Press.

Chakravarty, S. (1987), *Development Planning: the Indian experience*, New Delhi: Oxford University Press.

Chang H.J. and R. Rowthorn, eds (1995), *The Role of the State in Economic Change*, Oxford: Clarendon Press.

Foster, J.B., R.W. Mc.Chesney and R.J. Jonna (2011), 'The Global Reserve Army of Labour and the New Imperialism', *Monthly Review*, Vol. 63, Issue 06, November.

Galeano, Eduardo (1973), *Open Veins of Latin America*, New York: Monthly Review Press.

Habib, Irfan (1995), *Essays in Indian History: Towards a Marxist Perception*, Tulika, New Delhi.

Inikori, J.E. (1982), *Forced Migration: The Impact of the Export of Slave Trade on African Societies*, New York: African Publishing Company.

Lewis, W.A. (1978), *Growth and Fluctuations 1870–1913*, London: Allen and Unwin.

Lewis, W.A. (1988), 'Reflections on Development', in G. Ranis and T.P. Schultz, eds, *The State of Development Economics*, UK: Basil Blackwell.

Magubane, B.M. (1979), *The Political Economy of Race and Class in South Africa*, New York: Monthly Review Press.

Magdoff, Fred and J.B. Foster (2013), 'Class War and Labor's Declining Share', *Monthly* Review, Vol. 64, Issue 10, March.

Marx, Karl (1976), *Capital: A Critique of Political Economy*, Volume I, Harmondsworth: Penguin.

Marx, Karl (1978), *Capital: A Critique of Political Economy*, Volume II, Harmondsworth: Penguin.

Patnaik, P. (1995), *Whatever Happened to Imperialism and other essays*, New Delhi: Tulika Books.

Patnaik, P. (1984), 'The Market Question and Capitalist Development in India', *Economic and Political Weekly*, Vol. 19, Nos 31/33, Annual Number: Focus on Industry, August.

Patnaik, P. (2009), *The Value of Money*, New York: Columbia University Press and New Delhi: Tulika Books.

Patnaik, U. (1999), *The Long Transition: Essays on Political Economy*, New Delhi: Tulika Books.

Polanyi, Karl (1944), *The Great Transformation: The Political and Economic Origins of Our Time*, Boston: Beacon Press.

Ranis, G. and T.P. Schultz, eds (1988), *The State of Development Economics*, UK: Basil Blackwell.

Rodney, Walter (1972), *How Europe Underdeveloped Africa*, Dar es Salaam: Tanzania Publishing House.

Williams, Eric (1966), *Capitalism and Slavery*, New York: Capricorn.

Williamson, J.G. (1988), *Comments on 'Reflections on Development'*, in G. Ranis and T.P. Schultz, eds, *The State of Development Economics,* UK: Basil Blackwell.

Yao, Yang (2010), 'No, the Lewisian Turning Point Has Not Arrived', *Economist*, 16 July.

Some Reflections on Marxism and an Aesthetic of Resistance

An Essay

Anil Bhatti

I

It is a truism to say that a systematic Marxist aesthetics does not exist. Instead we have something much more productive and relevant for our times: a series of interlinked expressions of concerns and debates, all of which try to establish a connection between artistic production and political commitment based on an integral view of the liberation of humankind from the oppressive incompleteness of the present. This has necessarily entailed deep differences of opinion on the shape (*Gestalt*), forms and methods of artistic production in general, and literary production in particular.

The difficulty with the view that literature should have generated a greater corpus of debate lies in the overemphasis, in the past, on the role of the medium of language and its place in human communication. In a seminar held in Kasauli in 1979 on 'Marxism and Aesthetics' there was an awareness of this, and discussions on literature were linked to reflections on architecture, art and cinema, among other visual art forms, which were discussed in the context of cultural movements in India.[1]

The underlying tension between the 'Party' and the arts is always at the back of such discussions. In his introduction to the collected papers of the seminar, G.P. Deshpande characteristically quoted from a speech by Zhou Enlai in 1961 which emphasized the interdependence of political criteria and artistic criteria in cultural production. Socialist freedom, ideological remoulding, unity among literary and art workers are tasks and work that 'should be carried out in the manner of a gentle breeze and mild rain. It cannot be done with haste. It should be done over a long period and done patiently. Only thus can people have ease of mind' (Deshpande 1979–80: 5).

Given the unease of the present, 'ease of mind' can only be a utopian perspective, which nevertheless is the foundation for the double relationship between the artist's committed cultural praxis and the revolutionary party. This was part of the thinking process in the Kasauli seminar:

a creative form of relationship which admitted the Brechtian autonomy (but not autarchy) of the different logics according to which a political party functions and how cultural praxis organizes itself in relationship with, but not in being subsumed by, the revolutionary party. This relationship of being *with* but not *of* the party is perhaps one of the important lessons that have emerged internationally from critical engagement with the history of Marxist political and cultural practice, and the question of cultural intervention. It has taken a long history to achieve this form of democratic relationship in which there is, as it were, an osmotic exchange between the party and the committed artistic collective (cf. Moss and Rahman, eds 2013).[2]

The difficulty lay partly also in the truncated nature of the revolution itself, and in the disjunction of the political and the artistic avant-garde. The necessary dialectical unity of both was envisioned by Peter Weiss in his great novel *Ästhetik des Widerstands* (*Aesthetics of Resistance*, 1975–81) by the historical reference to the Spiegelgasse in Zürich.[3] This is one of the great themes in Peter Weiss' visionary novel about the emancipation of the working class through the appropriation of art and the struggles for a united front in Weimar Germany to oppose the rise of fascism in Europe; the juxtaposition of the simultaneous presence of the political and artistic avant-garde in a socio-temporal configuration which, however, never fused together or congealed.

The avant-garde is an artistic and political concept relevant to both fields and processes in art and politics. In the Spiegelgasse, or Mirror street – the name itself is suggestive – Lenin lived at one end in 1916 and at the other end a revolutionary group of poets and artists, the Dadaists, congregated in the legendary Café Voltaire in Zürich. These two avant-gardes never met. But if they had, then the imagination of the revolution, the struggle against fascism, would have achieved that level of concentrated interconnectedness which would have emphasized the wholeness of revolutionary transformation of every element of social existence, and shown that the political and the artistic struggle do not exist in separated fields.

The novel brings together an anonymous proletarian narrative voice in constellations with real historical figures from the Weimar period. In one such constellation the revolutionary Willi Münzenberg who was a key figure on the cultural front of the KPD, the German Communist Party, recreates the connected field for the reader. He points out that the Dadaists established themselves in the Spiegelgasse in February 2016 after the Zimmerwald conference (September 1915). But the artists were as unaware of their true role, which was to supplement the revolution, as were the politicians, who did not concede any revolutionary potential to the

© Christoph Steier

© Christoph Steier

artists. But, as of spring 1916 the Spiegelgasse accommodated the whole revolution because by then Lenin too had moved to it. The narrative voice in the novel asks Münzenberg about the location of the Spiegelgasse. In Peter Weiss' evocative language, the way to the street in Zürich assumes the quality of historical enchantment. You approach it, we read, from the Limmat Quai, go through the Marktgasse, turn into the Münstergasse and there it is rising to your left.

The first house on the left with a few steps before it is the Cabaret Voltaire: a place that emits enough noise in the evening to make the walls shake. One continues along the steep path to the crossing where the Napfgasse meets it, and there you find the house where the pastor and founder of physiognomy Lavater lived. Goethe visited him, probably in 1775. The young Hölderlin visited him too before Lavater became a counter-revolutionary opponent of the French Revolution. Georg Büchner lived nearby in the Brunnenturm. Next to it was Number 14 on the second floor, where Lenin and Krupskaja had rented a room from the shoemaker Kammerer whose shop was in Number 12.

If you opened the windows at night, Münzenberg tells us, you could hear the sound of drumming from the Cabaret. At this time Lenin (struggling with illness in the novel) was working on his imperialism study.

The two poles of the revolution related to each other since they were both concerned with liberation – liberation of forms and of movements, the renewal and reconstruction of language, of ways of seeing

© Christoph Steier

© Christoph Steier

and looking. This revolution had an influence on our senses and our search for a transformed existence. Weiss lets Münzenberg speak of a comprehensive social and artistic revolution demonstrating the cohesive togetherness of the elements which had hitherto always been treated separately. The point was to recognize both forces in their specificity and equality (*Gleichwertigkeit*), and to bring their parallel development to a common denominator. The complementarity of the two revolutionary intensities lay in their shared neighbourhood. But neither recognized the other yet. The two lines remained rigidly separate offering the possibility of an asymptotic convergence only in an infinitely remote dimension.

© Christoph Steier

The Spiegelgasse thus becomes one of those spatio-temporal domains which are the signature of a utopian symbolic order. The French Revolution is present with the reference to Lavater, Goethe and Büchner, whose play *Dantons Tod* (Danton's Death) remains crucial for the debate on revolution and revolutionary terror in the French Revolution. This domain contains a latency which allows the 'wholeness' and 'completeness' of the full revolutionary transformation to emerge as a vision, as a lightning flash, which allows us momentarily to become aware of what the whole, complete revolution might mean when its twin liberations resulting from the conscious (awake) and dreamt revolution ('*wache und geträumte Revolution*') were intertwined.

This is also a cognitive flash that lights up against the darkness of our times and illuminates the 'resistible rise' (Brecht's term) of fascism. New juxtapositions and configurations emerge. The names evoke this. In such a constellation we remember that the significance of Goethe's *West–Eastern Divan* lies in the attempt to establish connections between Europe and the Orient at a time when colonialism is blocking these connections by erecting essentialized boundaries and borders. Goethe's concept of world literature as a vision bases itself on solidarity directed against the order of colonialism. On the basis of this Marx and Engels could imagine a development where, in place of the

> old local and national seclusion and self-sufficiency, we have intercourse in every direction, universal inter-dependence of nations. And as in material, so also in intellectual production. The intellectual creations of individual nations become common property. National one-sidedness and narrow-mindedness become more and more impossible, and from the numerous national and local literatures, there arises a world literature. (*Communist Manifesto*)

World literature, it must be emphasized, never meant a collection of 'great books'. The concept refers to the emergence of a new quality of literary production that is liberated from national bondage. It challenges the assumed inevitability of the fusion of language, myth, territory in a nationalist configuration, and thus makes us see the possibility of a utopian emancipation of the whole of mankind. This makes it possible to read past literatures against the grain, realize the force of translation and grasp the inherent interconnectedness, wholeness of the creative enterprise of literary and artistic production.

The narrative voice in Weiss' novel wonders why the suppressed of the earth had not been able to establish their own power for two thousand years. It speaks of the 'October' of liberation which was the proof that all the attempts to establish one's own power had accumulated an energy that was seeking release. The spiral-like development of history made it possible to see oneself in the immediate proximity of the defeated of past centuries, their rage and their lethargy. We, the narrative voice says, were close to the slaves and bonded labourers. We were no longer groups but a class. The continuation of subjugation of past generations and in the colonies showed us that the yoke was the same everywhere. We did not share a country but a responsibility. This led to the consciousness of solidarity, of internationalism.

The novel emphasizes that this solidarity and internationalism were different from the rise of exoticism in the context of colonial expansion, and the increasing exposure to new, strange and far-off worlds. We read that one speaks of the exotic and praises it whenever one wants to hide the social and economic background of a country. The stranger or more remote or more secret the country presents itself as, the greater the injustices and the poverty and the misery. In all the continents the awareness of material factors generates tension in one's encounter with a city or a landscape. The crucial point is that one does not look for the differences in the customs and myths, in dance and music, but for *similarities* with what one was familiar with, and for connecting lines to the same origins.[4] There was nothing incomprehensible. Instead, this affirmation of a basic comprehensibility based on similarities is directed against the myth of impenetrability, of a secret hidden behind a veil.

The slogan that the worker has no country had been valid earlier. Lenin in October 1917 saw the immediacy of the presence of India, China, Latin America and Africa. The revolutionary continuity was broken by the rampant growth of the power of imperialism, and one now only mentioned separate uprisings. The anger here is that the freedom struggle now remains confined to one's own country; the idea of internationalism is forced into the background, gets lost and we start fighting each other because there is no agreement about the meaning and understanding of the revolution as a whole, says Münzenberg.

We have to remember that we are dealing with the comprehensive connectedness of the struggle. It is a matter of how things hold together or cohere or find coherence (*Zusammenhang*).[5] The destruction of the awareness of solidarity is a result of the splitting up of the struggle, splitting up of solidarity. It then becomes a form of specialization, and the discreteness of experience wins over the connectedness of reality.

Awareness of the connectedness enables us to think in terms of constellations (Walter Benjamin) rather than systems of influences, and to remember that solidarity and similarity are rooted in real social praxis.[6]

II

This way of looking at the revolution has an immediate echo if we look back on our own practice.

The period after 1947 in India was not the end of an era but a period of transition. Transfer of power meant that we lived in a process of partial liberation. The twin aspects of liberation – freedom from external domination through anti-colonialism and freedom from internal subjugation by overcoming the feudal casteist order – could never be completely resolved.

How does one inherit the past under such circumstances? In transition times one inherits that element in romantic capitalism which, as the philosopher Ernst Bloch always emphasized, points to a lack, to something missing in the given life-world and unclear dreams of another life. Transition and the meaning of anti-feudal and anti-imperialist struggle implies forging new blocks, new fronts.

Consider Sahmat (the Safdar Hashmi Memorial Trust). This can be seen as a formation that combines what might be seen as the avant-garde of artistic protest with the avant-garde of politics. It represents an aesthetic practice for times of transition. Sahmat (meaning 'in agreement') is not a movement in art in the conventional sense. It is not a secessionist group with a programmatic manifesto. Rather, it is a loose, unprogrammed collective with an interventionist praxis which is infused by the conviction that the rise of fascism and communalism in India is resistible, and that the values of secularism and creative expression can be defended. All this would not be necessary if we were living in good times; in times where 'ease of mind' is possible. But the world in general, and India in particular, are passing through dark times. Different places and different times have different terms for these dark times. But the general impulse is similar. The Turkish migrants' protest against a neo-fascist attack in Köln (Cologne) in Germany led to the formation of *Birlikte*. The term, like Sahmat, means together or standing together, and the actions of *Birlikte* are based on a combination of aesthetic and political resistance.

Sahmat adopts the secular stance of singing in and of dark times. For Sahmat this means occupying the spatial and temporal domains which are threatened by the forces of reaction with the artistic, political and organizational means that emerge collectively out of these *dark* times.

Sahmat's name also signifies the readiness and openness for alliances which are forged in the struggle of being in history, making history: broad fronts in a political conjuncture that is characterized by an increasing retreat from the ideals and the promise held out by the anti-colonial freedom struggle. Fronts for a struggle against the fascism of our times to defend the key areas in which the promise of the anti-colonial struggle as documented in India's Constitution was being compromised, attacked, violated. A resistance searching for forms of struggle.

In other words, Sahmat does not implement a given theory. Rather, theory and practice, abstraction and concrete manifestation cannot be separated. No linearity. Or, to put it differently, the practice of Sahmat becomes the materiality for reflection. And this is striking. Complex, largely self-organizational practice produces art which resists cooption and exists in a highly articulated field of reflection about art and commitment. It is sufficiently complex to allow episodic involvement as well as the directional commitment of the whole-timer.

It is important to emphasize that Sahmat inherits and defends the values of the freedom struggle. Precisely because successive governments at the centre move away from these values in the turn towards neo-liberalism, Sahmat affirms the role of being inheritor of the freedom struggle.

What is Sahmat defending, what is it attacking? It becomes immediately clear that the defence of values is an attack on the violation of these values and the concrete, real, dream of freedom from colonial oppression, feudal bondage. The unleashing of the imagination is a negation of the leash, the fetters of bondage, narrow-mindedness and fascist fundamentalisms. The key themes of secularism, diversity, freedom of expression are also meant to be taken literally as the desire to take the promise of the Constitution seriously; to show once again through creative activity that the gap grows between the promise of the Constitution and the daily violation of it.

These are part of the project of India as envisaged in its Constitution. Rather than an idea, India is an unfinished project, the contours of which were sketched during the freedom struggle. Sahmat revitalizes it by defending it against the daily violation of it and the abdication of responsibility. So that even if bourgeois parties as governing parties resile from it and pay only lip service to the aims, Sahmat affirms it. Thus Sahmat constitutes not a mechanical but a dialectical continuity of the freedom struggle. And this is based on its Aesthetics of Resistance.

Fascist ideology causes confusion. Clarity vanishes, things flicker in an unclear haze. It feeds on the unrest that is immanent in crisis. The carnivalesque celebration of creativity is an answer to the terror of the authentic. The aesthetic of the multiple, the assemblages, the various overflows through syncretic experimentation signal a struggle against that ideology of the authentic and the pure which is at the ideological core of fascism and fundamentalism.

It rapidly develops a heightened sense of the need for alliances. Of interactions with the community to fight communalism. An artistic version of the organic intellectual. Except that here the complexity is heightened because of the material of art. Sahmat becomes the material.

Sahmat also sees itself in an international context of struggles against fascisms. Sahmat becomes the condition enabling art in dark times. It asks the Brechtian question posed in the 'Solidarity' song: Whose street is the street, whose world is the world? A question that *Birlikte* in Cologne also asked.

Sahmat's ability to establish links and connections, its basic syncretic drive, is directed against the opposing fundamentalist drive towards separation, partitioning and the ideologization of difference. As against the obsession with separation, the insistence on seeing similarities, constellations and the search for affiliations, allegiances and alliances is coupled with an affirmation of solidarity that is based on establishing an alliance and a unified front which cuts across those categories that fundamentalism and fascism privilege explicitly through homogenization: language, race, territory.

The distinguished Marxist scholar D.D. Kosambi once called India a country of long survivals:

> 'a country where contemporary society is composed of elements that preserve the indelible marks of almost every historical stage'. India was a country of long survivals. People of the atomic age rub elbows with those of the chalcolithic. The vast majority of countryside gods are still daubed with a red pigment that is a palpable substitute for long-vanished blood sacrifices – which also survive in a few cases, although the very idea of blood sacrifices would now come as a shock to many devotees. (Kosambi [1956] 1968: 8)

The notion behind this is that of a palimpsest. India, it must be emphasized, is a palimpsest. Affirmation of the simultaneity of its historical formations is an affirmation of this palimpsestic order which necessarily negates any primordial purity and validity of simple origin. It fights against the logic of erasure that is contained in the drive for purity of an original, authentic, homogeneous order of society. The only logic of erasure would lead to emptiness since then the original sheet is blank. The only authenticity is in emptiness. The canvas is empty. Hence also the insistence of inscribing on to this a protest through writing, art, performance, praxis, because the logic of fascist homogenization would lead to erasure: erasure through riots, pogroms, terror. But if we only see the verticality of the palimpsestic order, we would shorten its perspective and be unable to see that we are concerned with meshes, weaves and webs equally.

This notion – used by Jawaharlal Nehru, among others – characterizes the historical complexity of large states and empires to negate the essentialization imposed by the concept of authenticity and the primacy of pure origins. The validity of the palimpsest lies in its connected completeness (*Zusammenhang*) and not in any particular layer. Thinking in terms of simultaneities, similarities and palimpsests enables us to move away from thinking in simple linearities and trajectories in order to emphasize fields, archives, constellations and configurations with differing rhythms, different paces. The image of the palimpsest corresponds in many ways with the notion of 'non-synchronous simultaneity' which Ernst Bloch formulated in the context of his study of fascism in *Heritage of Our Times* in 1935. In a palimpsest, the layering can be seen as a form of enrichment, which leads to the dominance of the multiple. Any attempt to ascribe authenticity to one particular layer, to some mythical original, some *Urtext*, leads to an impoverishment because it destroys the totality of the process of inscription. In any case, the original layer would logically have to be an empty surface. Thus do fundamentalists affirm the doctrine of complete erasure, of *tabula rasa*, in order to ensure the ascendancy of homogenization against the presence of the pluricultural. The desire for the supposedly authentic and the corresponding search for '*Urtexts*' and roots generate strong tensions in the pluricultural formation. The idea of an *Urtext* which permits of no variations, which considers different interpretations, different arrangements of mythological epics as blasphemous, is essential to the fundamentalist desire for purity and authenticity.

III

Fascism is based on the obsession with purity and origins. This leads to the desire for the *erasure* of memory and to a programme of obliteration of the impure. As against this, a left-wing perspective in our dark times is based on the development of the critical art of inheritance (Bloch). How to find, rehabilitate, critically inherit and appropriate cultural heritages, combining past and present, establishing links and, out of the plenitude of the world, deriving that critical assemblage which will enable us to shape a better world. This is based on mingling, mixing, emphasizing affiliations, alliances and similarities in the complex search for a possible united front of aesthetics against the rise of fascism.

In this sense pluricultural and heterogeneous societies can be viewed as complex webs and palimpsests of overlapping similarities. *Similarity* (*Ähnlichkeit*) with diversity would then be the goal of the historical process based on a universalist humanist perspective. It is based on solidarity which ignores particularist bonding in order to project a pluricultural society of communication characterized by fuzzy borders and transcended boundaries. We could indeed see the signature of the pluricultural form of life in the affirmation of *similarity in diversity* as against absolutization through homogenization. (In any case the older slogan, unity in diversity, was never intended to suggest uniformity in diversity.)

The affirmation of similarity in social praxis would help us to defend secular, democratic principles. Only objects frozen in time and space can be identical and remain the same. Processes involving individuals and their social configurations, alliances, allegiances explore ranges of similarities emphasizing the fluidity of borders and the fuzziness of identities. These processes lead to social and cultural weaves. It would be more important now to assess the nature of the weave (and the process of weaving) achieved as an outcome of the tension between processes of creating heterogeneities and homogeneities.

It is the weave and not the thread that is important. Kabir's poetry brings this out:

> *jhini jhini bini chadariya*
> *kah ke tana, kah ke bharni,*
> *kaun taar se bini chadariya*
> *ingla pingla taana bharni,*
> *sushumna tar se bini chadariya*
>
> Subtle, subtle, is the weave of that cloth.
> What is the warp, what is the weft,
> with what thread did he weave that cloth?
> Right and left are warp and weft,
> with the thread at the centre he wove that cloth.

We could read this with James Joyce's vision of Ireland:

> Our civilization is a vast fabric, in which the most diverse elements are mingled, in which Nordic aggressiveness and Roman Law, the new bourgeois conventions and the remnant of a Syriac religion are reconciled. In such a fabric, it is useless to look for a thread that may have remained pure and virgin without having undergone the influence of a neighbouring thread. (Joyce 1907: 165–66)

And to make our constellation fuller, this could be formulated in Wittgenstein's terms. He writes that we can expand our concept of number

> as in spinning a thread we twist fiber on fiber. And the strength of the thread does not reside in the fact that a fiber runs through its whole length, but in the overlapping of many fibers. But if someone wished to say: 'There is something common to all these constructions – namely the disjunction of all their common properties' – I should reply: Now you are only playing with words. One might as well say: 'Something runs through the whole thread – namely the continuous overlapping of those fibers.' (Wittgenstein 1975)[7]

The weave allows partial and temporal overlaps, and thus a more experimental praxis and resultant solidarity, namely, the translation of its passionate engagement through a communication process to generate the empathy (Gramsci's *con-passionalità*) of a mass engagement for the common defence of values which are violated daily by fascism, communalism and fundamentalism.

IV

The revolutionary surrealistic dream of a coalescence of art and life envisages a new form of community bringing together the disparate on the basis of similarity and solidarity which creates the new alliances, and which is directly in confrontation with the homogenized community of race, language, territory, religion so beloved by fundamentalists.

In Bloch's perspective, the multiversum of culture expresses the incompleteness of the '*Humanum*'. The only tolerant point of time which is utopian-tolerant lies in its ever-growing incorporation of nations and national cultures in the humanist camp. This incorporation is the incorporation of the whole of human history. This '*Humanum*' is comprehensive enough in the real possibilities of the intended goal to encompass *all* movements and forms of human cultures in the togetherness of different times. Thus one can say, as a result of a realistic view of the shared history of colonialism and the freedom struggles: '[t]he western concept of progress implied in its revolutions *no* European (and, indeed also *no* Asian or African) point, but *another* better world' (Bloch 1964: 200; emphasis added). The world-historical perspective implies a rejection of all culturalist viewpoints, and a rejection of parallel and organically authentic logics of separated trajectories. Instead, Bloch's perspective reinforces the polycentricity of pluricultural, shared histories in which the plurality ensures the retention of multiple but deeply interconnected, interwoven paths of world history as a great experiment. The aesthetic of resistance is a struggle in this direction.

Notes

[1] 'Marxism and Aesthetics': Special Number, *Social Scientist*, Vol. 8, Nos 5–6, December 1979 – January 1980.

[2] In this essay I have drawn on my review of Moss and Rahman, eds (2013), published in *Frontline*; see Bhatti (2013).

[3] In India the novel was discussed in Bhatti (1983). The novel was frequently referred to in the panel discussion on 'Schiller and Aesthetic Education Today', in the Yearbook of the Goethe Society of India. See also 'Andreas Wiebel Die wache und die geträumte Revolution: Kritische Weltliteratur in Peter Weiss' Ästhetik des Widerstands', in the Yearbook of the Goethe Society of India

(2012). I thank Dr Christoph Steier, University of Zürich for the images of the Spiegelgasse.

4 'Nicht nach Verschiedenheiten suchte ich in Sitten und Gebräuchen', in *Mythen, Tänzen und Musik, sondern nach Ähnlichkeiten mit dem, was mir bekannt war, nach Verbindungslinien zu gleichen Ursprüngen*' (I, 272).

5 The notion of '*Zusammenhang*' and the concept of 'Totality' are related but not identical. Totality conceives of a greater degree of theoretical structuredness than the interconnectedness of '*Zusammenhang*'.

6 Cf. E.V. Ilyenkov, *Dialectical Logic: Essays on Its History and Theory*, translated by H. Campbell Creighton, Indian edition, 2008, on Marxian analogy. 'The "similarity" of commodity fetishism and religious estrangement is rooted in the connexion of people's social ideas and their real activity, and the forms of practice, in the active role of the ideal image (notion)' (ibid.: 280). And: 'Universality so understood is by no means a silent, generic "sameness" of individuals but reality repeatedly and diversely broken within itself into particular (separated) spheres mutually complementing each other and in essence mutually dependent on each other and therefore linked together by bonds of community of origin no less firm and no less flexible than the organs of the body of a biological specimen developed from one and the same egg cell. In other words, theoretical, logical determination of the concrete universality of human life can consist solely in disclosing the necessity with which the diverse forms of specifically human life activity develop one from the other and in interaction of the one on the other, the faculties of social man and his corresponding needs' (ibid.: 360).

7 Translation available at http://www.voidspace.org.uk/psychology/wittgenstein/eight.shtml (accessed 4 May 2015).

References

Bhatti, Anil (1983), 'Peter Weiss and the Aesthetics of Resistance', *Journal of Arts and Ideas*, Vol. 3, No. 5 New Delhi; Hindi translation, 'Peter Weiss aur Pratirodh ka saundarya shastra', *Aalochana*, No. 69, New Delhi, 1984.

Bhatti, Anil (2013), 'Mapping Sahmat', *Frontline*, 19 May; available at http://www.frontline.in/books/mapping-sahmat/article4705568.ece (accessed 4 May 2015).

Bloch, Ernst (1986), *Tübinger Einleitung in die Philosophie*, Frankfurt am Main: Büchergilde Gutenberg.

Deshpande, G.P. (1979–1980), 'Introduction', *Social Scientist*, Vol. 8, Nos. 5–6, 'Marxism and Aesthetics': Special Number, December–January.

Ilyenkov, E.V. (2008), *Dialectical Logic: Essays on its History and Theory*, translated by H. Campbell Creighton, New Delhi: Aakar Books.

Joyce, James (1959), 'Ireland, Island of Saints and Sages' [1907], in Ellswoth Mason and Richard Ellman, eds, *The Critical Writings of James Joyce*, New York: The Viking Press.

Kosambi, D.D. ([1956] 1968), *An Introduction to the Study of Indian History*, Bombay: Popular Book Depot.

Moss, Jessica and Ram Rahman, eds (2013), *The Sahmat Collective: Art and Activism in India since 1989*, Chicago: Smart Museum of Art, University of Chicago.

Weiss, Peter (1975–1981), Ästhetik *des Widerstands*, Frankfurt a. M.

Wittgenstein, Ludwig (1975), *Philosophische Untersuchungen,* third edition, Frankfurt am Main: Suhrkamp Taschenbuch.

Culture in the War of Position

Mihir Bhattacharya

This essay is about speaking and listening, especially listening, which lies at the core of a certain notion of cultural practice. This notion is at the same time deeply political, as it involves questions of democracy and tolerance and equality and dignity, among other things. The specific range of issues taken up in this essay involves a consideration of left-wing movements and party organizations at various stages in history and in different parts of the world; but the major concern happens to be the place of culture, including people's culture, both in organized movements and in the long-term struggle for hegemony. Gramsci's notion of a war of position seems to fit the dynamics of this struggle; hence the title. The focus will be on India, however, but not all parts of India, and a certain aspect of the Russian Revolution will come into the story. But first things first, as the saying goes, and let's consider speaking and listening as culture and as politics.

Speech and Power

A little child discovers an odd thing in an imperial progress and blurts out that the emperor has no clothes on. Earlier, an outrageous bluff by a couple of crooks had worked, and official voices had proclaimed the exquisite elegance of clothes which did not exist. But no one spoke up. This speechlessness happened through the internalization of a kind of coercive discipline in the public sphere. Crooks are drop-outs from the system put in place by the ruling classes and operate in the interstices of the disciplinary regime, beating the system at its own game. The system, in whatever kind of class society, has its own rules of the game, and generates a public sphere which is mainly a world of institutionalized discourses, and the more powerful of these discourses ensure compliance through technologies of manipulation, surveillance and terror. This is what explains the speechlessness of the courtiers and the crowd. The cautious optimism of thinkers who saw possibilities of resistance to, and liberation from, class rule through the democratic procedures developed in the public sphere in mature western societies seems tragically misplaced in the new millennium (Habermas 1976). Control of social and political life has been taken over by the global operations of finance capital, aided and abetted by the state (P. Patnaik 2003). Hans Christian Andersen's modern folktale (published 1837) draws upon the accumulated wisdom of the underdog to paint a truer picture; it also brings in the people's own apparatus for the generation of meanings and values. Andersen contrasts the two worlds, the public sphere of official discourse and what I have called the *common world* of seemingly untutored utterance, actually speeches from a different discursive universe, in a neat little parable of power and control. This power and control are manifest in the public sphere of any society, including the present dispensation of parliamentary democracies.

There are of course differing voices, often coming from beyond the confines of official discourse, but such voices have to reach the public sphere through the available organs of circulation – political and social institutions, administrative apparatus, educational network, religious establishment, information and cultural media, publishing houses and so on – and come up against visible and invisible gate-keeping common to all power-determined and/or market-driven circulation of texts and ideas. The large majority of people in a country like India are excluded anyway from its ambit. You can't read books and newspapers if you don't have the money and/or haven't learnt to read. You don't listen to the radio or watch TV or use the internet if you can't invest either the money or the time for the access. The labouring poor are not part of the public sphere even as passive recipients of messages, let alone having their voices heard. All these institutions will listen only selectively and filter out whatever doesn't fit in. The dissenting voices do not, therefore, spread everywhere and reach everybody. Besides, the very reading of any text, whatever the origin, is subject to internal surveillance, because both *acquisition*, which goes on spontaneously in family and society, and *learning*, which comes with one's own effort from institutions, bear upon the production of meaning, bringing into the process the socially available apparatus of uses and gratifications. Variant or resistant readings are subject to agenda-setting (Hall 1997).

But, as in the story, a voice rings out and stays in circulation, as the larger world beyond the public sphere, the *common world* of utterance, takes hold of it and spreads its message throughout the community of speakers. The phenomenon has often found its way into the special world of people's imagination. The story of King Midas and his ass's ears is an example. There are many versions of the story which circulate in the folktale of nations. Kedarnath Chattopadhyay, author and editor in early twentieth-century Bengal, retells the story of Bhabbam Hazam, Bhabbam the barber, who discovers the king's asinine ears and just can't keep it to himself, whispering the truth among the reeds on the lonely riverbank. Flutes made later on from the reeds tell the story aloud to all and sundry ('*Jagannatherkheyalkhata*', 1955; the story first appeared in *Sandesh*, edited by Sukumar Ray in 1913). You can't prevent people from talking to each other. Words spread, often with incredible speed. Voices attack or subvert or bypass the Logos. The listener in the first instance becomes the speaker in turn and talks to others. Mikhail Bakhtin, the epoch-making theoretician of dialogism, has interesting things to say on the civilizational import of the process (Bakhtin 1984, 1986).

The Common World

The common world is the universe of voices which remains an inherent part of human existence throughout history, and it has continued to be so even after the rise of capitalism and the increased dominance of the public sphere through the media. Speech in many forms continues to be a creative and critical practice peculiar to social life, manifest in innumerable ways. Jokes will proliferate, moving fingers will write graffiti, and nowadays people will use the telephone and the mobile and the internet to circulate news and views and gossip, letters and messages and blogs will be written, people will speak and shout and whisper at work and at leisure, mothers will cajole and scold, children will shout, lovers will coo, songs will be sung, stories will be told, conversations will go on forever. The point is not that the common world is inherently transgressive, or that utterance is by nature refractory. It is simply the universal possession of all human beings, perhaps the only one left in your power. Your body has been taken over by the system, extracting labour by various means and invading its interior in the cause of the system; the land and the water and the very air you breathe are all in the hands of expropriators and extractors and polluters. Perhaps only talk is left. People talk because it is a manifestation of their consciousness and part of their 'species-being' (Marx [1844–45] 1975), and they talk with many objectives, mostly beyond the reach of official discourses. It constitutes an immense world of utterance which cannot be institutionally controlled. It is an area of freedom essential to the fulfilment of the possibilities of human existence, even when everywhere human beings are in chains. And because of this irreducible freedom of praxis and because of its inherent creativity – all of us, barring some with impediments, are capable of generating an infinite number of sentences – utterance is *potentially* negative and transgressive. The centres of power can control and manipulate official organs of communication and culture, and can intimidate refractory voices and transgressive texts – not only in totalitarian regimes – by setting up an apparatus of carrot-and-stick. But words will out, if not the truth. This common world and its discourses are linked to labour, essential to the production and reproduction of human existence, and can be theoretically separated from the 'semiosphere' as conceived by Juri Lotman.

'Common' is a historically loaded term, mostly suggestive of the life of labouring people, starting from the primitive economy of hunter–gatherers to more complex systems; and the concept of a common world of material and mental things has been carried over from pre-capitalist times to the present. The 'village common' of the British countryside is a vestigial example of the communal possession of material resources which marked pre-capitalist economies. The common world of utterance is conceived on the same model; it is set apart on the one hand from everyday life, and on the other from the public sphere. Every human being is a member of the common world, and every human being contributes to its praxis by word and deed. A familiar segment of this – since the people in the country are a main consideration here – may be called cultural or ludic or recreational with entertainment being its main *raison d'être* and artistry being its hallmark, approved markers being employed to demarcate its pragmatic address. This is 'people's culture' as opposed to 'popular culture', and the former is often labelled oral culture, though orality is its main and not the only channel of communication, for music, dance, drama, painting, ritual and other matters pertain to its performative universe. Its academic domain-name is 'folklore', and the label has done duty for such a long time that its theoretical inadequacy and dubious origins have now receded into the background. Folklore as a discursive domain is ascribed principally to tribal and peasant societies – though urban folklore is considered these days to be an important part of oral culture – and is generally linked to a distinct world-view and its material foundation, work or labour or praxis.

The Make-Believe Universe

There is, however, another view of the matter. The continuity of the common world is called in question or ignored by many current strands of thought. The truth, many hold, is always in jeopardy; voices are forever under pressure. The idea that voices will subvert official versions of the real is now contested by the postmodern picture of a teeming world of representations which completely engross consciousness in its self-reflexive web. Emile Durkheim had earlier analysed the 'mechanical solidarity' of pre-industrial society as opposed to the 'organic solidarity' of the modern, both imposing a gag-order on deviant expressions. Foucault's famous formulations on discipline and control carry on in the same vein. The more recent proposals of Baudrillard, Debray, Debord and others appear to be based on the relatively simple idea that since the media obliterates all indices to reference from the life of the masses, the world gets lost in an infinitely revolving loop of signs. The universe of representations has expanded enormously through the media, extending further and further beyond your direct experience. You cannot be subjectively present at all places at all times, seeing and hearing things at first hand, but you have access to 24-hour television, and radio and the internet, possibly, and you are therefore surrounded by a second-order reality brought to you by images and texts which build up an alternative world. The building blocks of that order become the master-code for your world-view, subsuming earlier codes. Whatever you see and hear directly, whatever you think of the things around you, whatever seems good or bad to you, have all now become so many functions of the simulated universe being constantly constructed and reconstructed for you. Direct experience is willingly filtered and reassembled to fit into the tutor code of the simulacrum. This media-driven hyper-reality will only have pseudo-references, just as a mirrored folder on a computer (possibly hacked by an expert) does, substituting a doctored copy for the original. Even meta-data will be manufactured. The mirror version will generate texts and images and sounds just like the original, but its source-code would be the hacker's programming, subverting the foundational directive of the original. It sets up therefore a virtual world, possessing all the representational properties of common-sense experience or sensory deductions or hermeneutic schemata. What would formerly be accessed from word of mouth or family talk or local gossip or religious doctrines or cultural texts or school lessons or political judgments or academic discourses is now restricted only to media sources, particularly television, the earlier authorities having been absorbed and integrated into the media universe.

Baudrillard's favourite instance is the Iraq invasion, be it the Papa Bush massacre or the Baby Bush genocide. Since the CNN was the only official witness to what went on in Iraq, its carefully structured texts, visual and auditory, became the virtual authority for what had happened in that part of the world. Night-time bombings were pictured as virtual fireworks, brilliant streaks of silver and gold piercing the dark nightscape on the TV screen. The consequent devastation on the ground was carefully edited to suit the image of the mighty US punishing aberrant Arabs, 'collateral damage' notwithstanding. A small rag-tag crowd in Baghdad pulling on army-issue ropes to topple the Saddam statue is made to represent the entire Iraqi people. With such ubiquitous *son-et-lumière* shows covering the spectrum of representation, the viewer is caught in a web of virtuality and becomes a function in a complex algebra of disciplinary fables. Any discussion of what went on in Iraq is therefore a derivative of what may be called 'mediotic' programming. Discovery procedures are guided by the agenda-setting of the source-code. The particular case of the Iraq invasion is just an example, perhaps a big example, of the mediospheric discipline imposed on human consciousness. But the disciplinary pressure is on day in day out in the advanced capitalist world. The relentless stream of image and sound from Fox News, for instance, charms most of the American public into accepting that greed is good and that rule by corporate capital is the only 'natural' system in the world. The media happens to be the only source of knowledge and ideas and entertainment in the postmodern world, and so its infinitely regenerative universe of signs swallows up any residual appurtenances of older cognitive tools and more traditional knowledge-systems.

The Globalization of Knowledge and Pleasure

In an entry dated 25 August 1938, Walter Benjamin records in his 'Conversations with Brecht': 'Don't start from the good old things but the bad new ones' (Benjamin 1973). Brecht's maxim is a reminder of the grim reality faced by the people of Europe at the time: the rise of fascism and the imminence of World War II, caused by the conflict among competing imperialist powers. Peace and justice and democracy lay in ruins, presaging worse times to come. We are not much better off in the second decade of the twenty-first century, though our crisis is of a different kind. The proto-fascism of the current era is a direct consequence of the hegemony of transnational finance capital, which makes an instrument of the state and of the major political parties, to fragment and weaken the working class by a massive rise in unemployment and underemployment (as a consequence of the phenomenal increase in labour productivity), by casualization of the work force, and by creating a huge army of the lumpen-proletariat from which its stormtroopers are recruited. Added to the process, in countries like India, is the loot of natural and created resources of the people by a stratagem described by Marx as 'primitive accumulation', and the parallel damping down of the viability of small-holding agriculture, leading a section of the peasantry to the ultimate desperation of mass suicide.

This crisis is obfuscated by the kind of theoretical discourse being discussed at this point. The postmodernists are not unduly bothered by the power equations of their source-code nor disturbed by the economic foundations of the media sphere. The all-encompassing media or the overarching discourse of power is something of a given for them, and cannot be comprehended or overcome. Therefore, the best you can do is to wallow in your despair or work up a collective *jouissance* over the mass-produced ingredients of pleasure, displayed in an enormous array of goods and services and images and recreations. But surely, the basic building-blocks of the system can be investigated and uncovered for the people. One can see, for instance, that with the processes of globalization, that is, the neo-liberal imperial order of finance capital, there has been a remarkable spate of synergy and convergence in the sphere of mediated information and ideas and entertainment all over the world. Financial power came from mergers aided and abetted by the advanced capitalist states. 'For example,' says an expert,

> the 1989 merger of Time and Warner created the largest media group in the world with a market capitalization of $25 billion. This was followed in 1995 by Time–Warner's acquisition of Turner Broadcasting (CNN). In late 1993 the merger of Paramount Communications and Viacom, owner of MTV, saw the emergence of a $17 billion company, making it the fifth largest media group behind Time–Warner, News Corporation, Bertelsmann and Walt Disney. . . .
>
> The acquisition by News Corporation of the Hong Kong-based Star TV for $525 million has given (Rupert) Murdoch a satellite television footprint over Asia and the Middle East with a potential audience of 45 billion viewers. When allied to his other television interests . . . his organization (has) a global reach of some two-thirds of the planet. (Barker 1999: 47 –48)

This story is usually hidden from the ordinary viewer, with the result that news and entertainment come to them in waves of a 'natural' order of things, potentially acceptable as a valid picture of the world. This obsession with the new media hides other ways of transmission of texts; these ways operate dominantly in developing societies, but the advanced world has not completely got rid of them.

Culture and the Common World

The *Ramayana* story or *Ramkatha* is available in a large number of Indian languages and in a great many versions, not necessarily derived from the Sanskrit text ascribed to Valmiki. There is a very powerful lobby in the public sphere, led by several large organizations including a political party, which would link a version of Hindutva with one or two central texts; these would serve its interest of political mobilization. These people are seeking the expunction of the divergent *Ramkathas* and the undisputed supremacy of the *Ramcharitmanas* and the *Hanuman chalisa*, and only remotely the Valmiki *Ramayana*. The sanctity of the accepted narrative becomes an instrument of hegemony; any divergence can be made into a public heresy and therefore punished, as happened to Husain for his image of Saraswati. There is a struggle here, first, between two contending groups in the public sphere, one trying to suppress a large body of oral texts and even any mention of such texts, and the other, a smaller segment, defending the right to their entry. The *Ramkatha* exists in hundreds, perhaps thousands, of versions, circulating in most of the Indian languages. It is also known and often quite popular in a large number of cultures outside India: Afghanistan, Cambodia, China, Hungary, Indonesia, Iran, Japan, Laos, Malaysia, Mongolia, Myanmar, Nepal, Philippines, Sri Lanka, Thailand, Tibet and Vietnam.

The usually accepted model for such transmissions – not only for the Rama story, but generally for myths, legends and folktales, and arts and ideas in general – is a set of people-to-people contacts over the *longue durée*, and the historical array of modes of contact involves trade relations, spread of religions, wars and conquests, migrations, scholarly exchanges, diplomatic and dynastic relations, and so on. All this happened in India over millennia. It is assumed that, in the pre-modern world and often in the modern, people will tell stories to other people whenever and wherever they meet, and will also pass on written texts and pictures, as well as music, drama, dance, ritual, arts and crafts, magic, medicine, learned discourses, political ideas, programmes of action, religious doctrines, etc., as occasion arises. The institutional arrangements for such material as well as symbolic transmissions largely carried out by common people, often the labouring poor and sometimes by specialists, are fairly well known. The *caravanserai* would be a centre of gossip, a place where stories are told, news is exchanged, negotiations are carried on, ideas are spread. The court of a potentate would attract artists, soldiers, scholars and other professionals. Patronage was an important instrument of exchange. The place of learning – monastery, library, school or university – would invite, train and send down large numbers of people who would be the bearers of various disciplinary traditions. The pilgrim routes would throw together vast numbers of people from many lands. Migrations and conquests would be powerful instruments of exchange and reconstruction of discursive material. The list need not be prolonged. The exchanges would occur within the borders of a country or empire, and often across boundaries.

The Transactival Text

It is possible to envisage institutions and traditions – most of them long-lasting and continuous – in which common people participate as story-tellers, listeners, performers, viewers, messengers, experts, readers, artists, censors, craftsmen, philosophers, intellectuals, critics, activists, interpreters and so on. Such functions are not very often professionalized and demarcated. Roles would be swapped. The story-teller would also be a listener and possibly a critic. A poor peasant on a pilgrimage would pick up many narratives which he would adapt into his own stock and retell to his village. A young woman married into a distant community would carry her songs and stories and games and jokes with her, and transmit them to her neighbours and her children. This is not an idyllic picture of the so-called 'organic community' or the '*Mir*'. The poor peasant is ruthlessly oppressed and exploited; the young woman is uprooted, enslaved and confined. But the work of creativity goes on in the matter-of-fact way that characterizes the life of the labouring people, including the powerless, the downtrodden and the outcast. And this work is collective. The bulk of the cultural and intellectual transmission which takes place among the poorer people has a way of constructing, reconstructing, storing and circulating texts and ideas which are mostly without authorial signature. The folktale is a particularly telling example of this surge of anonymous traffic across cultures and languages, but its range is actually enormous. Religious or political ideas and programmes would spread far and wide through the agency of selfless converts who would stand down while organic intellectuals are thrown up by the movement. Most of the popular revolts in colonial India spread among the people in this fashion. Buddhism and Christianity and socialism, for instance, have spread further by people-to-people contact than by learned treatises. The movement led by Gandhi is a particular case in point. The cluster of ideas and programmes encapsulated in the term *ganhibawa* in Satinath Bhaduri's magnificent novel *Dhoraicharitmanas* (1949–51) illustrates this kind of passage.

The story of Rama travels throughout a land and across frontiers because many people have liked and retained and retold this story in many versions over generations. This exchange may well be called a flow of alternative politics over millennia, because one other significant mark of this transmission is the large-scale obliteration of political/administrative boundaries. Natural barriers like mountains, oceans and deserts, and cultural divides like language, religion, values and customs, happen to be far more important than politically demarcated frontiers. The active agency of the people either ignores or defies the divisions marked by conquest and political accommodation, often no more than lines drawn on a map and transferred to arbitrary locations. The paths traversed by a story or song or drama may sometimes be lost to later generations, but only because there is no need for the community to remember the modes of transmission, which are always open and direct and person(s)-to-person(s). The people decide what and how and why ideas and stories and songs and dances should move, in which directions and over which period. They accept and naturalize political ideas and programmes emanating from many quarters. The politics of anti-colonial struggles in India before and after the coming of Gandhi shows how the people's participation changes the whole character of a movement. Ideas move far and wide and with incredible speed when people like the ideas and act on them. I have called this traffic, and its texts, *transactival.*

The Transordinal Text

There is another kind of project in textual transmission – in contrast to the people's initiative – which the market initiates and implements. The feature film *Titanic*, released in 1997, was the result of a massive deployment of finance, manpower, technology and organization; it was released in hundreds of theatres across the United States, and thousands of prints were sent rapidly to all corners of the globe. The promotional campaign started long before the film was completed. This is what usually happens these days with a big production; a large part of the budget is earmarked for advertisement and promotion. Ancillary products – T-shirts, toys, mementos – appear on cue. The stars have an image build-up in print and electronic media. Stills, promos, news and gossip create a familiarity with the product long before it appears on the market. The familiar pattern is repeated with other cultural products of finance capital: *Avatar*, for instance, or *Sex and the City*. A need is thus created, a desire activated, and a manufactured demand turns into a craze. Full movie houses and brisk sale of DVDs and discs testify to the efficacy of the massive apparatus which is deployed in order to bring a text to the viewer. This is usually the story with films, television programmes, novels and topical books, magazines, popular music and so on. The market for such material is spread across the globe, and national boundaries as well as natural barriers do not really exist so far as the transmission of such texts is concerned. The power of the market mechanism ensures that the strongest players will always reach the targeted audience. The marketing of the Harry Potter novels is another instance of this process. The same thing happens when ideas and discourses move from centres of power to intended recipients. The state is a major player in this arena and works through what has been called the ideological state apparatus by Louis Althusser. Schools and universities play important roles in pushing ideology down the throats of learners. Power is the key in such transmissions. Organization and mobilization move ideas and programmes down the line in a hierarchical order. Powerful classes and groups alone possess both the material and intellectual resources necessary to induct people into their agenda. This is true of situations where even state power is being challenged and opposed. Nationalism of the kind Tagore criticized so bitterly, in text after text in his mature years, spread in just such a way, relying on machineries of persuasion and coercion. I have called this traffic, and its texts, *transordinal.*

Gender, race, class, caste and colony (imperialism in general, that is) – which may be called the *power pentad* – as major determinants in the production and exchange of culture, ideas and information, play in and out of this binary traffic of texts. The history of the travelling text shows that the transordinal and the transactival are two moments in the construction and circulation of such material, with one text often sharing both moments in different points of time. Voices from the common world decide what is to be done with texts which come their way, positioning their own understanding in the way of the operations of the power pentad. The voices are critical as well as creative, forever making new texts from the inexhaustible resources of people's intelligence and people's imagination. This view, of course, flies in the face of the orthodoxy assiduously propagated by Soviet Marxism – and swallowed solemnly by votaries of 'dialectical materialism' elsewhere – that human consciousness and creativity are wholly determined by the mode of production, and that the idea of a continuity of autonomous renewal and reinvention of mental praxis is theoretically unacceptable. Fortunately for Marxist thinking and leftist culture, this view proved impossible to work with in practice. At a certain point in the history of modern Indian culture, certain vulgar minds tried hard to classify cultural texts and practices as 'feudal' and 'bourgeois' and 'progressive' and 'socialist', and a considerable industry devoted to labelling came up, but there were very few takers of such missionary zeal. The progressives in general accepted that the relationship between the 'base' and the 'superstructure' was important, but, as Brecht pointed out, the specific mode of production of culture was of urgent and immediate concern, for the artist has to solve technical problems of her craft when she is trying to reach her community of reader/auditor/spectator. The artist continuously listens to her community and tries to represent their imaginative and critical drive. Creativity forges ahead and concerted action becomes possible when 'mind-forged manacles' are defied. As history shows, cultural movement and joint action become possible only when voices converge and contest and re-engage and re-converge.

Knowing Sudhi Pradhan (1911–1997) and P. Govinda Pillai (1926–2012)

In considering the recent history of the culture of voices, I may as well start off with our first meeting with P. Govind Pillai (PG), and possibly the second or third with Sudhi Pradhan (Sudhi-da). We first met PG in early October 1979, at our friend Vivan Sundaram's house in Kasauli, where he and Geeta Kapur had started a series of artists' workshops under the auspices of the Kasauli Art Centre. A largish crowd of intellectuals and artists met there in 1979 for what turned out to be something of a path-breaking seminar on 'Marxism and Aesthetics'. The seminar was a departure from the usual run of such things, for it was not a strict academic do, open only to disciplinary participation, nor was it formally structured like innumerable learned occasions which stud the professional calendar of institutions all over the world. There were papers and presentations sprinkled with a few performances, but the discussion went off in all directions, the participants bringing all kinds of ideas and experiences to bear upon the matters at hand, and people talked and argued and often quarrelled far into the night, animated by the overarching concern with the politics of culture. One must remember the times. The trauma of the Emergency was over but the hotchpotch replacement at Delhi had failed the people, and the time seemed right for a left-democratic surge in national politics; a small fraction of the intelligentsia wanted to do their bit for the cause. The Kasauli meet in 1979, and again in June 1982, were the first two of a series of meets which resulted in the birth of *The Journal of Arts and Ideas* in 1983. Some people trace the beginning of Cultural Studies in India with the *Journal*; but for many of the participants the most vital part of the enterprise was its political momentum.

Sudhi Pradhan brought his experience of the Indian People's Theatre Association (IPTA) of the 1940s and 50s to bear upon the new initiatives being thought out by the group, if such a loosely strung network of people can be called a group. P. Govinda Pillai had started a little later than Pradhan and was still vigorously working on the frontline of cultural pursuits in the Left circles, his interests spanning large swathes of intellectual terrain – from orthodox Marxism to the cutting edge of critical theory. Being in a position of responsibility in the Communist Party of India (Marxist) (CPI[M]), PG presumably connected the concerns of the Kasauli crowd with the current dispensation of leftist politics in India, just as Sudhi-da's participation was a reminder of the relevance of the older leftist surge. It turned out that these two veterans were also – then as well as later – a most vital link with the attempt at refashioning the intellectual and cultural practice on the fringes of the political Left. Sudhi-da was a senior adviser on culture to the newly formed Left Front government in West Bengal. His special charge was the resuscitation and revitalization of folk and tribal culture, still the major form of self-expression of the people in the countryside. PG, with his deep interest in cinema and the performing arts, supplemented Sudhi-da on the realist–modernist front. He had brought to the gathering a message of rethinking or, rather, a fresh initiative within the leadership of the CPI(M), consonant with a certain turn of events which had brought the Left into a prominent position on the national political scene.

The general elections in 1977 had seen a decisive defeat for the Congress led by Indira Gandhi. This was not surprising, given her tyrannical aberrations during the previous couple of years of Emergency rule, which itself was a panic reaction to increasing public disenchantment. But what did cause a surprise was the political space that opened up for the Left, particularly the CPI(M); they gained a substantial number of parliamentary seats in Kerala, West Bengal and Tripura, and made significant inroads in some other parts of the country where they had a major presence in people's movements. In West Bengal they formed the state government by an overwhelming majority. The verdict of the people seemed to indicate that the communists were wanted in positions of responsibility and power after three decades of ceaseless people's struggle in independent India. The leadership had not clearly anticipated this result, particularly in West Bengal, and was less than fully prepared to assume governmental responsibility. Two short-term stints in 1967 and 1969 had, however, warned the leadership of both the pitfalls of electoral politics and the necessity of meeting head on the problems of governance. At the end it was the overwhelming enthusiasm of the people which rode over any misgiving or hesitation.

Millions and millions were speaking in the cause of democracy and development and dignity of life, and though these voices were not actually reaching the ruling class and even the Public Sphere through the media, the culture of asphyxia had been decisively subverted through the processes of hard-won democracy, however flawed and truncated and repressed. People spoke through the ballot box and the communists learnt from the experience. An understanding of the state of actually existing democracy in India, existentially arrived at through decades of ceaseless struggle and incredible sacrifices, had already opened up a dialogic space in which the communists encountered the reality of people's needs and aspirations; dogma became much less important than voices, as the Kerala experiment in 1958, and the United Front trials in West Bengal in 1967 and 1969, had shown. This understanding of what the people were demanding secured a vital position of the Left in the national-popular struggle for democracy.

The time seemed right for a further radicalization of politics in independent India. The momentum of the struggle for emancipation from colonial rule had not yet been spent, and India was firmly in the camp of non-alignment and Soviet-leaning third-worldism. Neo-liberalism had not yet spread its virus into the ruling circles of India; a moderate version of *dirigisme* was in practice and a certain aura still clung to the Nehruvian agenda of social democracy. This itself had been an attempt to go forward from the utopian – and regressive – part of Gandhi's vision for India, even though the Mahatma's programme for the massive political mobilization of the people lay at the heart of any subsequent development in Indian politics.

He had listened to the people, and talked to them in their own language, and had invoked their own values in gathering them together in a massive camp of fighting-fit, unarmed warriors. The Mahatma's words and actions became a transactival force of enormous magnitude, and overcame both the apparatus of colonial rule and its ideological underpinnings. The road to freedom was built by deploying their strength of presence against the conventional might of a standing army and a paid security apparatus. Antonio Gramsci's brief comment illuminates the working of the process.

> India's political struggle against the English . . . knows three forms of war: war of movement, war of position, and underground warfare. Gandhi's passive resistance is a war of position, which at certain moments becomes a war of movement, and at others underground warfare. Boycotts are a form of war of position, strikes of war of movement, the secret preparation of weapons and combat troops belongs to underground warfare. (Gramsci 1971)

The movement's combat troops were the masses of labouring people in India, wave after wave of whom joined the struggle over a long period of time. The major factor behind this astonishing mobilization was the organization behind the movement, led by Gandhi with consummate finesse. Nothing much could have been done without an array of focused objectives, and a strategic and tactical plan executed by a credible leadership and cadre. The people had found a mission and an organization they could call their own. This honed the resolve for freedom among the Indian people and prepared them for the impending tasks of democracy in the future. Independence and its newly created institutions meant to the people that the fruit of political democracy was at hand after a long and hard fight; it also meant that they would not let go. This aspect of the Gandhian revolution explains why India had not gone the way of other newly liberated countries into military dictatorship. There was an enormous presence of the people – poor, hard-working and oppressed, but roused through struggle into a deep resentment of authoritarian rule – behind the public sphere and the institutions of democracy. Indira Gandhi's design of absolutism had come up against this hard resolve, and duly crumbled. A radical agenda was set in the years following the upheavals of 1977, especially in the area of human rights and social justice and land reforms. Not a great deal came out of it in most parts of the country. But the two or three state governments run by a Left coalition voted to power through people's mandate – though governance was circumscribed by constitutional and political impediments – made a serious attempt at implementing the agenda within the limits set by circumstances. A great deal of work was done in the first phase. A large promise loomed on the horizon. What happened to the promise in the long run is another story.

Some of the people who met at Kasauli – and some of the others who joined the group later – were linked to the leftist movement and a few were members of the CPI(M). I suppose that the idea of inviting PG was to hold a watching brief so that the intellectuals and the artists did not stray out of line; this was the much-practised cautionary device of all leftist formations, fearful that political control would be lost once the intelligentsia started moving on their own steam. But some of us felt pleased – as faithful members of the party – that a senior party person like PG was with us, which meant that our line of work was being taken seriously; and there was also comfort in the thought that political mentoring was available when needed. Much to our surprise and delight, however, PG joined the discussion like any other participant, full of intellectual queries, eager to argue out point after point, keen to listen to others with his characteristic modesty and courtesy. It often seemed that he was on a learning stint rather than guardianship. Sudhi-da had left the undivided party in the 1950s, but his heart was with the CPI(M), and he delighted in the company of younger leftists who were so keenly engaged with matters of the mind. His path-breaking compilations of documents from the old IPTA were in full swing – the first volume had come out in 1978, and two more were to follow in 1982 and 1985 – and he was hopeful that a new initiative would come about from such meets. It seemed that the infamous instrumental view of intellectual and cultural work – that the 'wet' side of things, matters of arts and ideas, would at best serve to explain and elucidate the party line and bolster the course of political programmes set by higher authority – had been kept at bay. Culture appeared to be important as *politics*; thinking would not only help party work but was in fact party work. In Sudhi-da's and PG's approach, both were perceived as fundamental practices of human life and not derivatives of more elementary particles of politics.

Both these communist veterans thought that one must think and speak up and engage with others in unending dialogues. Difference had to be cherished, and suppression of speech was an impoverishment of politics and a denial of humanity. They were not alone in maintaining this position. Most of the early leaders of the Communist Party had this gift of listening, to intellectuals certainly, but mostly to the working people for whom the party was fighting. Some were famous for patient argument over long periods of time. The iron discipline the party was famous for did not mean an inflexible position on tactics and ideas; the notion of guardianship was there and proselytizing was in vogue, but the living presence of the party among the people saved it from the fate of doctrinaire and authoritarian little groups common in religious and political history. For these early leaders, praxis demanded an enrichment of revolutionary theory from unending dialogues, which meant in turn that utterance is the most precious of human gifts. Listening is the core of praxis; reading is a window to the world. Lenin had read an enormous amount of material, often of bourgeois origin, while composing *The Development of Capitalism in Russia* (1899), which lies at the core of the party's revolutionary understanding of the ground reality. One need not point out the kind of reading Marx had done in his life. PG's life-work was based on this fundamental view of things, and he never deviated from this, whatever the problems he faced inside the party or out. Sudhi-da still straddled the twin worlds of people's culture and labour studies, and he kept harping on the importance of going out to the people and listening to them and learning from them. Malini and I were initiated by Sudhi-da in the world of folk and tribal culture at around the same period, and we shall never forget his insistence that our work was primarily dialogical, not pedagogical; if intellectual work is dedicated to the cause of the people, it is the people who would decide how such work would align with their needs and desires and goals, and how and when the mediation of the mainstream intelligentsia would help them forge links with the larger political movement. This was of course heretical thought for much of the political leadership, particularly in the middle ranks, for whom the party – read the leadership – was the fount of all wisdom, laying down the law on everything; the people were just followers, working faithfully to realize the ever-receding goals of the millennium.

Apart from remembering two of our precious friends and mentors, I have a couple of particular reasons for recalling Kasauli on the happy occasion of honouring Prabhat Patnaik for his life's work. We were close friends – Utsa and Prabhat, Malini and I – for nearly a decade when we journeyed to Kasauli with our young children; other much-loved friends were there and many life-long friendships were made on the occasion. Prabhat was one of the key persons who kept the discussion alive, just as Rajendra Prasad was the prime mover of the whole enterprise. It is lucky for us that the work Prabhat still does day in day out shows no sign of slackening or losing its lustre, for it is not merely academic–institutional work that we are talking about, but a range of activities which includes a direct participation in politics and a *representative* link with the life of the people. The 70s and 80s of the last century were historical, just as the 40s and 50s were; this period, like the earlier one, opened up many fronts on which the artist and the thinker could work side by side with the people, not just spiritually but concretely, involved in actual movements which sought to advance the cause of democracy. Prabhat is one of those who have set the pace for this line of work, and he has illuminated for many whatever subject he has broached on whatever platform. 'Much to the man is due.'

The other reason I recall Kasauli is equally personal, and perhaps, to a degree, historical. Professional intellectuals and artists move in and out of many connected worlds and many institutional set-ups, but they do not very often find opportunities for converging, as artists and intellectuals, on the public stage, and form politically elective affinities and engage in collective practices. Kasauli and after gave a boost to many individual trajectories of political engagement. The group does not any longer have continuity or cohesion, but most of the individuals originally involved and those who converged later on the platform provided by *Social Scientist*, *The Journal of Arts and Ideas*, Jana Natya Manch (Janam), Safdar Hashmi Memorial Trust (Sahmat), and one or two other forums have remained true to the original impulse of the Kasauli meets. One must not, however, exaggerate the importance of what happened in the 1970s. A great deal more happened earlier, in the 40s and 50s, when the need was more urgent and the times more propitious. The Progressive Writers' Association (PWA), and subsequently the IPTA, became a fairly widespread cultural movement during World War II, and soon came under the leadership of the undivided Communist Party; P.C. Joshi was the most dynamic leader from the political side who thought out and led a vigorous cultural programme at the time. The party provided the vital element – an organization and a support structure – but the creative surge was a function of participation and commitment.

The question of leadership and organization inevitably comes up when one thinks back on junctures such as these. It was the movement which unleashed a creativity waiting in gestation; the special way of working together to produce memorable texts and performances was made possible by a sense of belonging and solidarity with the people. The work would have been impossible without the presence of the party. A great many of the most important artists and intellectuals from all over India joined the anti-fascist platform and stayed on to travel in step with the IPTA, knowing fully well that it was linked to the Communist Party. This is well known and much commented upon by both admirers and detractors. But the story of the other side of theoretical praxis, academic as well as popular work by the radical intelligentsia, is not often highlighted. There is a long history of inquiring minds turning to Marxism and communist organizations in the twentieth century, particularly those who became interested or involved in the anti-colonial struggle. Very often the long periods in jail or internment or exile provided opportunities for introspection and dialogue and study, as a result of which a new vista of political action would come up, and deeper links with the people would seem possible in organized struggle transcending the goals and methods of both Gandhian and armed opposition to British rule. Revolution beckoned to the most advanced minds grappling with the vision of a national transformation. And the vision attracted another group of intellectuals, largely professional academics, whose work was to command enormous respect both in institutions and in the public sphere. Marxist studies in India had been largely introspective in the decades after World War I, engaged less in developing theories than in putting together a large and varied national narrative, just as the radical artists sought to probe deep into the lives of the Indian people and the revolutionary activists worked towards a social transformation of the nation. Intellectuals like D.D. Kosambi, Rahul Sankrityayan, D.P. Mukerji, E.M.S. Namboodiripad, D.P. Chattopadhyay, R.S. Sharma, Niharranjan Ray, Sushobhan Sarkar, Bipan Chandra, Ashok Mitra, Irfan Habib and others transformed nothing less than the identity of India in what had previously gone on in Indology, Philosophy, History, Economics, Sociology, Cultural Studies and other human sciences. One sees a significant leftist front emerging from the programme of national liberation across a vast range of activities, mostly linked to the vanguard party of the working people, and definitely putting the agenda of people's democracy on the political, cultural and intellectual map of modern India.

The 1970s and 80s never saw a movement such as this, it is true, but something of a platform came up, and it generated a certain spread of activities all over India. It contributed something to the war of position which still goes on in many parts of the country, and it forged links with the world outside. It is often thought that the leftists exercise a disproportionate influence in the world of intellect and artistry, and that this is due to the stature of a handful of clever and talented people who have somehow deviated into outlandish beliefs. It is forgotten that there are many orders of intellectual work and many kinds of cultural activities all over India – not always perceived by the media or brought into the public sphere – in which millions of leftists are involved. People teaching in schools and colleges and universities – those who do not usually go to big seminars or publish in prominent journals – and white-collar workers in public and private sectors, trade unionists, journalists, lawyers, doctors, engineers, and so on from the ranks of the educated middle class would be obvious examples. But much more to the point would be the intellectual and cultural resources of the vast masses of working people, both urban and rural, who go on producing their own organic intellectuals. Leftism of various kinds had attracted the attention of many of these leaders and stirred their lives, because a certain model of mental work had touched them. Simply put, this model meant that a journey out of your habitual confines, i.e. prescribed models of creativity and criticism which tradition allows, was possible and desirable. It involves freshly acquired insights, derived from dialogic interactions and disciplined acquisition of ideas, into approaches to the lived lives of the people. This process is often spontaneous and uncomplicated and widespread. Gramsci describes the relevance of this group in the war of position in a brief comment on the workers of Turin in his day.

> The proletariat is less complicated than might appear. They have spontaneously formed an intellectual and cultural hierarchy, and reciprocal education is at work where the activity of the writers and propagandists cannot penetrate. In workers' circles and leagues, in conversations outside the factory, the word of socialist criticism is dissected, propagated, made ductile and malleable for every mind and every culture. (Gramsci 1985: 33)

The work done by the IPTA straddled both sectors, people's culture and avant-garde artistry, and brought them together on one platform. Politics was part of it, and even party work, but that is not the whole story.

Politics and Visual Positions

Telling the larger story will mean going back to the period of the anti-colonial struggle and the first couple of decades after independence. The point can be illustrated by the particularities of the new Indian cinema and its context. It is well known that the late 40s through the 50s and the 60s were a time when film societies sprang up all over India, mainly in the cities and mainly through the agency of people from the educated middle class, some of whom were professional intellectuals. All of them were interested in 'good' cinema, as opposed to the 'basket of entertainment' offered by Indian films and the sleek pot-boilers from Hollywood, and wanted opportunities for viewing both classic and modern films from all corners of the globe. A small section of them had been bitten by the film bug and wanted to make films some day; a few had actual experience of filmmaking. Assam is a case in point. Bhupen Hazarika, for instance, belonged to the small section in that part of the country. By 1964 he had made five films, and between 1956 and 1988, he had directed or co-directed fifteen films, some of them documentaries. That makes him a major film personality in Assam, not just a singer and composer known all over India. The legendary Jyoti Prasad Agarwala, who had made the first Assamese feature film, *Joymati*, in 1935, along with another stalwart Bishnu Prasad Rabha, had discovered the young Bhupen, and his first contact with films was made when he sang two songs for Agarwala's *Indramalati* in 1939, when he was just fourteen years old.

But the point to note is that films were just one element in the larger story of Assamese culture, and of Indian culture, in the age of the struggle for freedom; and the story continues subsequently in the early years after independence. Jyoti Prasad and Bishnu Prasad were geniuses of the first order; they gave shape to the performative part of modern Assamese culture, just as literature was transformed by Lakshminath Bezbarua, Hem Goswami, Bholanath Das and others, and fiction took new directions with Padmanath Gohain Barua and Rajani Kanta Bardoloi. The performative part was particularly important when the need of the hour was to represent the masses, many of them illiterate in the formal sense, but culturally and intellectually enriched by the *satriya* traditions and the folk and tribal ways of life. The people, both rural and urban, were ready for the new politics of culture in the era of movements and struggles; the elite and the modernist had to respond to their needs and desires and talk their language before the people would join. That is why the new consciousness of the avant-garde, shaped by aspirations for political, intellectual and cultural modernity, sought to express itself particularly in music, dance, drama and cinema, all of which could be accessed easily by the people, and could be made responsive to their demands. And most important of all, these texts could be read/viewed/heard by everybody in a largely rural and unliterate culture, and reconstructed/re-interpreted on a large scale; messages regarding this new kind of culture spread by word of mouth at incredible speed. This is the reason why the left-wing movement in culture, which started in the 1930s and spread to all parts of India in no time, took up the performing arts in a big way. The IPTA, founded in these turbulent times, had writers and painters in its ranks, but music, dance and theatre were in the core of its repertoire, and most of its epoch-making innovations were in those areas. Cinema was important, but 'poor' cinema was not sustainable under the circumstances. Jyoti Prasad and Bishnu Prasad had gravitated towards the left-wing by the sheer logic of their radical thought and practice. The unforgettable Irabat Singh did his pioneering work in both Assam and Manipur. Hemango Biswas and Bhupen Hazarika followed in their footsteps. When the Assam IPTA came into being, its programme had already been inscribed in actually existing movements and performances. The culture of Assam before and after World War II had been indelibly marked by left-wing politics. Though numerically small and politically less than dominant, the left formations, along with leftist-nationalist thought, exercised a major influence on creative and intellectual work of the period. This happened in many other regions of India; the story is well known, and is skipped here. In Gramsci's terms, the war of position was in full swing.

If cultural and intellectual work is thought of as a practice deeply rooted in the life of the people, and if the people are placed in a historical locus, then the question of *representation* will invariably come up, and so will the artist's place in people's movements. One should not of course fall into the naturalist fallacy and demand a certain kind of Zolaesque slumming from all artists, but if you look at the biographical order of the progressive artists concerned, you will find that at some point their lives meshed with the ongoing movement of history, and that many of them saw the need for marching with the people and representing them in their respective spheres of work. The times were very difficult. Take the case of Bengal, where the Marxist cultural movement grew very strong. War and famine and partition and riots and refugees marked the turbulent 40s and 50s. Resistance to exploitation and oppression grew among all classes of people. The anti-colonial struggle took on new meanings and new dimensions. The communist movement gathered momentum as Bengal lurched from one crisis to another. Many of the best minds of the time stood up for the distressed, the downtrodden and the exploited. It does seem to be the case that the radical moment often enters culture from the movement which sees participation from large masses of the working people. But in most cases that is neither the beginning of the story nor the end.

There is in fact no easy passage from strongly felt unease and anger with the existing scheme of things to solidarity with the most oppressed and/or the most vocal, and then on to a viable and workable means of constructing a cultural text adequate for the representational job. Then there is the business, much discussed in Marxism, of catching the movement of history in your text – something that Marx and Engels had discerned in Balzac, and Lenin in Tolstoy. This links up with Marx's profound idea of class struggle as the principal motive force in history, and the corollary that the great artist – just as the great thinker – sees the birth of a new society in the womb of the old. The large story of determination of consciousness by the relations of production is indeed just that, a large story which demands an enormous amount of gloss in specific cases. There are two determinations at work in cultural history, which is actually a history of consciousness, both at the 'writerly' and the 'readerly' ends. Something happens in the mind of the author to make her aware of things happening in history, just as something happens in the mind of the reader. But to explain just what happens when this awareness takes shape in the work of art, you have to traverse the story of the relations of material production to arrive at the available means of mental and artistic production. This is what Walter Benjamin had pointed out a long time back. He had also introduced the notion of an artistic break in this area of text-making, just as Louis Althusser postulated an epistemic break in philosophy. This is the terrain of overdetermination, an idea taken over from Freud by Jacques Lacan and used fruitfully by other Marxists in philosophy and cultural history. Lacan talks about the worker who agitates for higher wages and the one who realizes that the movement for higher wages is part of the class struggle for the destruction of capitalism. This overdetermination may happen to both authors and readers. Often in history this takes place when a movement is on, and there is passage from the movement to the moment, at which texts are constructed by authors and reconstructed by readers. The progressive cultural movement is a major exemplar of this passage. But this is not the only way in which radical texts are written and read.

There is a strong sense of determination and overdetermination which has marked Marxist thought for a very long time. This position is often more normative than historical, in the sense that the movement is supposed to generate just one exclusive moment, as the Soviet Writers' Congress of 1934 vigorously legislated, declaring Socialist Realism, whatever it may be, to be the only creative principle for the committed artist. In the event, this disastrous piece of prescription generated a great deal of trash; it also caused untold misery to the conscientious artist and the theoretician. The best novelist of the Soviet era, Mikhail Bulgakov; the best poet, Vladimir Mayakovski; the best filmmaker, Sergei Eisenstein; and the best theoretician, Mikhail Bakhtin – all did their job not because of the prescription but in spite of it. It is important, therefore, to propose a weaker sense of determination which allows for a measure of realism in the picture, assuming that a multiplicity of voices and positions can mark the cultural scene both at the creative and the reading end. People do a great many things, singly or together, to respond to a moment. In cultural work, there is a separate trajectory of artistic production, involving themes and conventions and techniques, which meshes with the history of material production at particular points of time. In a sense, linked to the relations of production, there is a separate history of speaking and listening.

Revolution and the Reinvention of Culture

In a short story called 'Misery', written in 1886, Chekhov narrates half a winter's day's events in the life of a St Petersburg cabbie, Iona Potapov, whose only son died three days ago. He does not quite know what caused the death, 'from fever, must be', and does not complain about the hospital where the young man languished for three days. He accepts the bitter cold and snow, the rudeness and meanness of fares, the frightening traffic, the old age which will soon make him unfit, and the death which is not far off; all this is what the poor and the oppressed have endured for ages, and his lot will be no better than that of millions and millions like him. But for the past few days the unbearably horrifying tragedy has taken him to the breaking point, and he feels an overwhelming yearning for a long unhurried talk about his son, the illness, the hospital, the funeral, his daughter left in the village. . . . But no one listens to him: the military gent who abuses him, the gay young men about town who cheat him over the fare, the janitor busy with his own thoughts, the cabbie in the coach-yard who is fagged out with fatigue. So he goes to the stables, unable to sleep, and talks to his horse.

In a sense, culture is a matter of talk, of voices, of representation. Chekhov proposes to explore, in story after story about pre-revolutionary Russia, just how the conditions for the production of voicelessness for large masses of the people have been generated and regenerated. This is a special kind of silence, enforced by class rule. A coachman is just there as a lowly servitor; he is not supposed to have either subjectivity or voice or any kind of biography outside his allotted role in the economy as far as his masters and betters are concerned. But anyone who has read the story will realize, in line with what the narrative voice points out, that Iona a has a definite language of his own which links him with the vast masses of the labouring poor in Russia, and that he shares a life-world and a culture, both in his native village and in the lower depths of life in the city, with the majority of mankind. Culture, then, is a commonality of voices and practices and meanings – with special genres like funeral processions and women's wailings mentioned by Iona – which comes up every so often against the stony wall of repression. The silence of the lambs is not a special case of *aphasia*, as many post-structuralists would hold, but an enforced *asphyxia*, a throttling of voices by class rule. The revolutionary movement in Russia was about the dismantling of class rule and establishing social ownership of the means of production, yes, but one important prerequisite of the process of revolutionary change was the removal of 'mind-forged manacles' (in the words of a revolutionary English poet, William Blake) and liberating the thinking of the people, thus unleashing critical and creative energies on a hitherto unprecedented scale. One of the first things that revolutionary theory and revolutionary practice ensured in the Soviet Union was a free play of voices, a surge of freedom where silence was once enforced. This was a matter of representing those previously unrepresented, and in the process a radical redefinition of culture was taking shape.

Lenin had worked out a programme of sorts in the tricky area of representation in November 1905, in *Party Organization and Party Literature*. He was of course talking largely of utilitarian and interventionist discourses – pamphlets, journals, polemical writings, political economy, party publications and so on – but the position he adopted had implications for creative work as well. In fact, the word 'literature' was being used in communist circles of the day as a hold-all for all kinds of communication, especially writings, and given the urgency of revolutionary tasks on the ideological front, this conflation of kinds of writing was hardly noticed. Lenin was at pains to emphasize that one of the principal tasks of the democratic revolution is to free literature from the 'captivity of feudal censorship', so that 'everyone is free to write and say whatever he likes'. This freedom of speech for all writers must be complete, but Lenin was scathing at the same time about writings in the service of 'bourgeois shopkeeping', careerism and bourgeois-anarchist individualism. The party will want to 'cleanse itself of people advocating anti-party views' and engage in polemics with enemies of progress, but will not try suppression or censorship. After 1917, the most urgent task on the revolutionary cultural front was precisely to ensure that this freedom of the people to speak up was extended to every sphere of life and every stratum of society. Fierce criticism of certain institutions and discourses was one aspect of this freedom. The new culture would give voice to those who had remained silenced in history.

In the old, pre-revolutionary society, a section of those who had been born lucky had found the conditions unbearable and started talking to each other on ways to end this oppression. Reading, discussion, writing, experiments and innovations were the very stuff out of which the ideas and values of one section of the revolutionary vanguard emerged. In the exhilarating years of preparation for the revolution, there was hardly any separation of organizational and intellectual work. You gather the workers together, form party cells, prepare pamphlets, discuss strategy and tactics, form action squads, put up the barricades and fight when necessary, but you are at the same time reading and thinking and writing and keeping in touch with the latest in literature and art. The vanguard was working out, under heavy and constant pressure, some kind of model for life in a socialist society. If I am free, what do I do with my freedom? There are many answers to this complex question, and some were being rehearsed in the preparatory stages. The revolution would bring out into the public sphere many of the problems relating to this range of issues.

Bukharin's prison novel, *How It All Began*, paints a graphic picture of the intellectual processes the middle-class youth of the early twentieth century were going through. The protagonist, Kolya Petrov, is in high school, slogging through the useful liberal training in Greek and Latin, reading Moliere and Goethe and Stendhal, Tolstoy, Chekhov and Gorky and Andreyev, going to the picture galleries, listening to music, and talking, talking, talking about the present and the future of Russia. There is amused rejection of Christianity, even Tolstoy's stripped-down version, and indignant dismissal of liberals and 'legal' Marxists, including the rather obscure Shulyatikov who achieved sorry fame with his *Justification of Capitalism in Western European Philosophy*. Then the two teenagers, Kolya and Tosya, come upon the secret journal, *Iskra*, 'printed on such thin paper', and are riveted by a quote from Marx: '. . . the proletariat, which does not wish to allow itself to be treated as riffraff, needs courage, consciousness of its own worth, pride and independence, far more than it needs bread'. This is the notion of freedom that promised a common ground for the working class, and the intellectuals and artists, to meet on. Gorky's *Mother* is the classic text illustrating this process of the proletariat finding its feet as a class-for-itself through informed revolutionary struggle, and the de-classing of the intellectuals through theoretical practice. When these two strands come together you find the arrival of the organic intellectual of the working class.

It is easy to see with hindsight that the heady sense of liberation after the revolution would have led to excesses by artists and intellectuals. Lenin was upset that Lunacharsky had passed the printing of 5,000 copies of Mayakovski's *150,000,000*. He was puzzled and pained by the new 'proletarian' art which sought to produce such specimens as *Karl Marx Standing on Four Elephants*. He was deeply suspicious of Proletkult and especially of Futurism. The theoretical argument is very interesting. Lenin was of the view that a genuine proletarian culture could not be produced as if in an incubator or hot-house. He maintained that proletarian culture could come into being only on the basis of universal literacy under Soviet power, when there would be millions and millions of educated people and the conditions for the production of a new kind of culture would be laid. This new culture will have deep links with the best flowers of bourgeois culture, which would be the foundation of a new proletarian culture. His advice to the workers, 'Learn, acquaint yourselves with bourgeois culture', is imbued with a deep theoretical vision and not simply conservatism of personal taste. One can see that his views were formed under the influence of nineteenth-century realism, as indeed were the views of Karl Marx himself. This deep link between Marxism and realism, mediated by the splendid visions of the Enlightenment, would be worked out in vigorous excursions by Georg Lukacs later on, leading to very interesting debates with Brecht and Benjamin. It is obvious that many artists and intellectuals wanted hectic modernist experiments under the aegis of revolutionary rule, and people like Gorky and Lunacharsky were wholly in favour of such avant-gardism, much to the puzzlement and despair of the political leadership. Gorky's argument was perhaps a little paternalistic, but he was of the firm view that his own version of realist art was not the only option available to the new cultural workers. He and his kind were against any censorship and repression, perhaps recalling the harsh days of tsarist autocracy. If one looks at the first couple of decades of Soviet cultural and intellectual work, one can see both the strength and the weakness of the Leninist position. You learn from the previous age, yes, and your work as an organic intellectual of the working class is incomplete unless the members of that class are there, so to speak. But just as the revolutionary party has to work as an avant-garde in the beginning, the revolutionary artistic community too has to be bold in their experiments and explore the available means of cultural production to find their proper idiom. If one looks at the disastrous documents of the Soviet Writers' Congress of 1934, with its twin dogmas of 'socialist realism' and 'revolutionary romanticism', one can see where the travesty of Lenin's cultural politics would lead. Lenin had objected to Mayakovski's excesses, but did not stand in the way of the poet reaching his readers; he merely recommended a trimming of the print run from 5,000 to 1,500. If one looks at the trials and tribulations of the leading artists and theorists of the 1930s and 40s – Bakhtin, Bulgakov, Eisenstein, Mandelstam, Pasternak and many others – one can see the consequences of 'one party, one leader, one doctrine' in grisly exemplars. Lenin's vision of universal cultural freedom remained as much a dream as his notion of moving from a vanguard party to a mass party. 'Democratic centralism' – that theoretically void oxymoron much in fashion even today – took no time to turn into 'bureaucratic centralism', which can be a killing process, literally and figuratively.

But the fervid experimental work of the pre-revolutionary years, continued in the beginning of the revolution, even if it lasted only a couple of decades, remains a model of modernism under socialist auspices. The theatre of Meyerhold and Stanislavski; the cinema of Eisenstein, Pudovkin and Yutkevich; the poetry of Blok, Akhmatova, Mayakovski, Mandelstam and Pasternak; the novels of Bulgakov, Sholokov and Ehrenburg; the theories of Bakhtin, Voloshinov, Propp, Tynianov, Eikhenbaum and Shklovsky; the music of Stravinsky and Shostakovich – one can go on listing the many flowers which bloomed in a new ambience. This is the first obvious sign of the reinvention of culture. The second thing is probably not so evident, but more lasting. This is the expansion of the base of culture, which had always been Lenin's major concern. If one takes the customary notion of culture in Chekhov's day, as indeed in our own day, one realizes that the mandatory equation of 'culture' with high culture, that is, poetry and fiction and painting and drama and music, and the discursive apparatus proper to these, is yet another device to ensure hegemony and perpetuate class rule. This is not to say that there is anything wrong with Kalidasa and Dante and Shakespeare, or indeed with Darwin and Marx and Freud; these geniuses extended the possibilities of human endeavour and left behind them 'monuments of unaging intellect' which constitute a legacy for all human beings. The second point about revolutionary culture is a radical understanding of the *differential* access to these common assets of humankind. A class society will allocate the natural resources, land and water for instance, unequally among the people, the lion's share going to a few; the most telling inequity relates of course to human labour power itself, which is, in Marx's sense, a special kind of natural resource. Similarly, the access to Pushkin and Tagore, to Cezanne and Picasso, to Shaw and Brecht, to Joyce and Sartre, to Beethoven and Amir Khan, to Bunuel and Ghatak and innumerable others, is controlled not only by the financial and technical resources needed for their production and distribution, but also, more importantly, by the possession of cultural and intellectual capital without which you cannot make sense of these texts. Lenin tried intervening in this area. There has never been a state that made available to its citizens, first, universal literacy and cultural competence, and second, universal access to the classics as well as the experimental and the heterodox.

Unfortunately, that legacy of an open and free culture, of untrammelled speech and unhindered listening, did not last very long. The party was originally an organization of all working people. And it was doubly unfortunate that the repressive apparatus of the subsequent Stalin era became something of a model for communist parties elsewhere. The party apparatus was viewed as the repository of all knowledge and understanding. The party speaks and does not listen. It issues dictats, much in the manner of repressive religious organizations all over the world. We have to take stock of what the party and the movement miss out.

The Artist and the Bad New Times

The usual thesis is that artists learn politics, and produce political texts and performances, after being trained and motivated by the party and the movement. This view is universal inside the communist parties of the world, the subcontinent included, and paradoxically but logically, accepted by the enemies of promise unquestionably, both dyed-in-the-wool reactionaries and the god-that-failed brigade. There are many stories about individual artists and authors who had toddled along pretty much the feudal or bourgeois way, with variable public and artistic success, but come the moment of ideological illumination, and the author changes his ways drastically and starts producing revolutionary texts. Saul is transformed into Paul. Usually the content of whatever the artist is producing gets pride of place in such conversion narratives; the novels come to have proletarian protagonists, the pictures depict ravages of imperialism, the drama unmasks bourgeois illusions, the cinema turns to protest. (Gorky, Brecht, Bunuel, Manik.) Technical or epistemic breaks are ignored. Some narratives are not about conversions at all, because the artists concerned had started off as insiders of the movement and/or of the party, but in such cases slides and deviations from the received wisdom of the day are keenly looked out for and severely reprimanded. It happened to Mayakovski and Bulgakov and Brecht, for instance, and Manik Bandyopadhyay and Balraj Sahni and Utpal Dutt nearer home. The problems are not doctrinal as such but largely organizational: power and control to the fore, command and discipline being the matter at issue. This is a familiar story of all tightly-knit authoritarian structures in history, in which the exigencies of control attenuate the exalted purposes for which the organization was set up. You can't really perpetuate the initial impetus – prompted by the juncture which urged the best to act up to their conviction – of selfless, devoted, vigilant commitment to the cause of the people. A kind of Gresham's Law starts operating in the interstices of the command structure, driving out the good species with the bad, replacing wisdom with mediocrity, commitment with ambition, ideal with greed, democracy with bureaucracy, movement with stability. That time-dishonoured doctrine of democratic centralism – a vacuous oxymoron if ever there was one – comes to the aid of the intellectually inadequate apparatchik barely in touch with reality. The corruption of a section of the Left leadership by the lure of corporate-driven, media-propagated GDP-fetish is enough evidence of the rot. The leadership stops listening to the people. And since there is no movement without organization, no progress without theory and no democracy without the people, the task of the hour is to start bombarding the headquarters.

The party, however, is indispensable; human efforts at improving and changing our lot will otherwise get lost in the morass of do-gooding or cynicism or adventurism. The prospects appear to be dim, but the radical quest for understanding a bad new world never stops and the urge to turn the world upside down never dies down. If you look around, you will find that the world is really full of goodness and decency and civilization; the vast majority of the working people retain and reproduce this stock of goodness, however subjected they may be to divisive pressures, or lured by easy promises, or dogged by ignorance and superstition. The conditions for the perpetuation of unfreedom persist and worsen, but even then there is so much selfless devotion to causes, so much hospitality and answerability and friendship around, so many quests for knowledge and understanding, so much of 'rage, rage against the dying of the light', that it is really impossible to despair at the present state of injustice, barbarity and violence. If one looks into the basic building blocks of the party and its source of strength, not its present leadership, but the millions of its workers and supporters, one finds that goodness and commitment and answerability shine through tireless work that goes on all the time. Much of this goodness persists in the dark times. A tough fighting position, then, against the chains which imprison mankind seems still possible.

Let me end with a gloss on a favourite poem. Sukanto Bhattacharya, the revolutionary communist poet of Bengal, had declared in a poem written in the early 1940s: 'I'll leave this world liveable for the child' (in 'Chharpatra', 'The Passport', the first poem in a book of the same name in Bangla, published after his death). The poem celebrates the coming of a newborn baby whose first cries are heard by the poet deep into the night, and he goes into a highly charged description of the world in which human beings face ruin and misery and into which the child has been brought. Sukanto would die fairly soon of galloping TB after this poem was written, fulfilling the second part of his prophecy of being history very much before his time was due, and the first part, making the world liveable for the child – he knew as much as anyone else – was a pretty long haul. The poet therefore promises to remove the accumulated litter of a failed civilization and declares, confident of his mission being fulfilled: 'And then I'll be history.'

The positive goal, by a tacit compact with the presumptive reader, was a rhetorical foreshortening of history, the unknowable gestation time of the unforeseeable revolution brought to the doorstep. The long story is cropped and the ending imagined to fit a favoured trajectory, emblematic of particular lives after the world is turned upside down. What needed stating was the resolve. This particular promise is what revolutionary consciousness declares as one of those vital objectives crying out for the necessity of the revolution. The human mind does not remain idle while the good fight is fought and the process of transformation in relations of production goes on; it is constantly engaged in the social and ideological rebuilding of lives. But the resolve, as stated, is prior to action; it is linked to revolutionary theory, which transforms ordinarily acquired thoughts and feelings – all part of the ideological baggage of bourgeois or feudal hegemony – into a different state of mind. Love for a child is almost universal, but a threshold is crossed when that love is inserted into the schema of universal well-being. There is also a temporal sequence in the practical consequences of this mental transformation. Working up to the revolution demands all the resolve and all the energy of the working class, engaged in the praxis of trying out possibilities and strategies and tactics. So, matters of the mind have a priority after all. In the process of achieving its goal, the revolutionary vanguard turns to the task of reconstructing the hitherto existing class society into a brave new world where the child would fulfil the possibilities of her species-being. Speech and thought and grace and beauty, among other things, will flourish unhindered for her in the process.

References

Bakhtin, Mikhail (1984), *Rabelais and His World*, translated by Helene Iswolsky, Bloomington: Indiana University Press.

Bakhtin, Mikhail (1986), *Speech-Genres and Other Late Essays*, translated by Vern W. McGee, Austin, Texas: University of Texas Press.

Barker, Chris (1999), *Television, Globalization and Cultural Identities*, 1999, McGraw Hill Education.

Benjamin, Walter (1973), 'Conversations with Brecht', in *Understanding Brecht*, translated by Anna Bostock, London: New Left Books.

Gramsci, Antonio (1971), *Selections from the Prison Notebooks of Antonio Gramsci*, edited and translated by Quintin Hoare and Geoffrey Nowell Smith, London: Lawrence and Wishart.

Gramsci, Antonio (1985), 'Culture and Class Struggle' (*Il Grido del Popolo*, 25 May 1918), in *Selections from Cultural Writings*, translated by William Boelhower, edited by David Forgacs and Geoffrey Nowell-Smith, London: Lawrence and Wishart.

Habermas, Jurgen (1976), *Legitimation Crisis*, translated by Thomas McCarthy, London: Heinemann.

Hall, Stuart (1997), 'The Work of Representation', in Stuart Hall, ed., *Representation*, London: Sage.

Marx, Karl (1975), *Economic and Philosophical Manuscripts, Third Manuscript, 1844–45*, in Karl Marx and Frederick Engels, *Collected Works*, Vol. 3, Moscow: Progress Publishers: 297–306.

Patnaik, Prabhat (2003), *The Retreat to Unfreedom*, New Delhi: Tulika Books.

Contributors

ASHOK MITRA is an economist and columnist, and former Finance Minister of West Bengal.

RAJENDRA PRASAD is Managing Editor of *Social Scientist* and a member of the editorial committee of *People's Democracy*.

IRFAN HABIB is Professor Emeritus of History, Aligarh Muslim University, Aligarh.

AKEEL BILGRAMI is Sidney Morgenbesser Professor of Philosophy, Columbia University, New York.

SITARAM YECHURY is the General Secretary of the Communist Party of India (Marxist).

C.P. CHANDRASEKHAR is Dean, School of Social Sciences and Professor, Centre for Economic Studies and Planning, School of Social Sciences, Jawaharlal Nehru University, New Delhi.

AIJAZ AHMAD is Chancellor's Professor of Comparative Literature and Critical Theory, University of California, Irvine.

JAYATI GHOSH is Professor, Centre for Economic Studies and Planning, School of Social Sciences, Jawaharlal Nehru University, New Delhi.

BISWAJIT DHAR is Professor, Centre for Economic Studies and Planning, School of Social Sciences, Jawaharlal Nehru University, New Delhi.

PRAKASH KARAT is a Polit Bureau member of the Communist Party of India (Marxist).

TEESTA SETALVAD is a civil rights activist and journalist, and the secretary of Citizens for Justice and Peace, Mumbai.

ZOYA HASAN is Professor Emerita, Centre for Political Studies, School of Social Sciences, Jawaharlal Nehru University, New Delhi.

AMIYA KUMAR BAGCHI is Founder-Director of the Institute of Development Studies Kolkata, and former Director, Centre for Studies in Social Sciences, Kolkata.

PRAVEEN JHA is Professor, Centre for Economic Studies and Planning, School of Social Sciences, Jawaharlal Nehru University, New Delhi.

SAM MOYO was Professor of Agrarian Studies, founder-member and Executive Director of the African Institute for Agrarian Studies, Zimbabwe.

PARIS YEROS is Professor at the Catholic University of Minas Gerais, Belo Horizonte, Brazil, and Research Associate of the African Institute for Agrarian Studies.

ANIL BHATTI is Professor Emeritus, Centre for German Studies, School of Language, Literature and Culture Studies, Jawaharlal Nehru University, New Delhi.

MIHIR BHATTACHARYA is Professor Emeritus, Department of Film Studies, Jadavpur University, Kolkata.